African Development and Global Engagements

"The book, African Development and Global Engagements is well-researched, and promises to be of great use to anyone wishing to gain more knowledge about the African continent, both past and present. Of particular note is its section on the Decolonization of Knowledge Production in African Societies. It is well-argued, that for Africa to move forward, it is imperative that its citizens should adopt and adapt knowledge bases that worked very well in Pre-colonial African societies, and that modernizing efforts must not "throw out the baby with the bath water", as it were. The authors here have made a very good case."
—Dr. Victoria A., *Metropolitan Community College, Omaha, USA*

"...a most informative guide full of important information for those of us who want to assess the impact of colonization in African education and how to foster agency in the post-colonial era."
—J. R. Severin, *City University of New York, CUNY, New York, USA*

"This collection of articles reviews a wide range of social issues cusped in the broad themes of Africa's development, impact of Covid 19, transnationalism and climate change in the 21st Century. It highlights the challenges facing Africa's development and provides innovative ways to mitigate these. Given its contemporariness, it provides voice for the urgency for Africa to come to grips with its development woes."
—Professor Sultan Khan, *Sociologist, School of Social Sciences, University of KwaZulu-Natal*

"*African development and global engagements* presents a most auspicious detail on how to approach sustainable development in Africa, particularly in the light of emerging challenges of the 21st Century - expanding South-North economic migration, Covid-19 aftermaths, climate change crises and political cum economic recession in Africa. Various chapters of the book offer apt interventions in addressing related incongruence in an efficient manner, putting into perspective the dynamics of global engagements. Being an interdisciplinary compendium of knowledge on contemporary challenges inhibiting sustainable growth and development of Africa, I strongly recommend the book to students, scholars, researchers and practitioners of African development at all levels."
—Prof. Sola Akinrinade, *Professor of History, Obafemi Awolowo University, Ile-Ife, Nigeria*

Adebusuyi Isaac Adeniran
Editor

African Development and Global Engagements

Policy, Climate Change, and COVID-19

Editor
Adebusuyi Isaac Adeniran
Ife, Nigeria

ISBN 978-3-031-21282-6   ISBN 978-3-031-21283-3   (eBook)
https://doi.org/10.1007/978-3-031-21283-3

© The Editor(s) (if applicable) and The Author(s), under exclusive license to Springer Nature Switzerland AG 2023
This work is subject to copyright. All rights are solely and exclusively licensed by the Publisher, whether the whole or part of the material is concerned, specifically the rights of translation, reprinting, reuse of illustrations, recitation, broadcasting, reproduction on microfilms or in any other physical way, and transmission or information storage and retrieval, electronic adaptation, computer software, or by similar or dissimilar methodology now known or hereafter developed.
The use of general descriptive names, registered names, trademarks, service marks, etc. in this publication does not imply, even in the absence of a specific statement, that such names are exempt from the relevant protective laws and regulations and therefore free for general use.
The publisher, the authors, and the editors are safe to assume that the advice and information in this book are believed to be true and accurate at the date of publication. Neither the publisher nor the authors or the editors give a warranty, expressed or implied, with respect to the material contained herein or for any errors or omissions that may have been made. The publisher remains neutral with regard to jurisdictional claims in published maps and institutional affiliations.

This Palgrave Macmillan imprint is published by the registered company Springer Nature Switzerland AG
The registered company address is: Gewerbestrasse 11, 6330 Cham, Switzerland

To Almighty GOD

Acknowledgements

My profound gratitude goes to my wife, Tolu and our children, Othniel, Ehud, Hadassah and Zuriel for being pillars of support to me. I appreciate my brother, Dotun Afolabi and his amiable wife, Atinuke and their children, Dabira and Feranmi for their goodness; also, to my Ivorian brother and research partner, Kabran Aristide Djane, I say thank you. Our mummy, Mrs Eunice Jegede, you are well appreciated. My sisters Kemi, Sade, Sola and Anti Aarin and brother, Seyi, you are highly appreciated. My mentor, Professor Pablo Idahosa, York University, Canada and my Dean of Social Sciences, Obafemi Awolowo University, Professor Philip Olomola, have been great helpers. Thanks to my research secretary, Ms. Olashege and my reliable personal assistant, Taye Akande.

CONTENTS

Introduction: Africa and the World   1
Adebusuyi Isaac Adeniran

Policy and Covid-19 Matters

**The National Development Plan (NDP) in South Africa:
An Inspiration to Shape Communities by 2030**   7
Bongiwe M. Zulu and Shanta B. Singh

**African Demographic Dividend: Case Study of Nigeria's
Age Structure**   31
Abiodun Adewale Adegboye, Ebube Agbanusi,
and Sunday Idowu Oladeji

**Emergency Healthcare Accessibility in the Context
of COVID-19 in Nigeria**   65
Olufemi Mayowa Adetutu, David Aduragbemi Okunlola,
Ayoola Peter Ijisakin, Sukurah Adewumi Hammed,
and Yusuf Segun Ogunsanya

**Self-medication Practices in Covid-19 Era: Insights
from Caregivers to Under-Five Children in Southwestern
Nigeria**   83
Oluseye Ademola Okunola, Mabayoje Anthony Olaniyi Aluko,
and Abdulrahman Azeez Aroke

Research and Development

The Globalisation of Social Environmental Research
and the Practices of University Researchers in Africa: Case
from Côte d'Ivoire   103
Kabran Aristide Djane

Exploring the Experiences and Benefits of Postgraduate
Studies in South Africa: The Research Masters Degree   115
Gerelene Jagganath

Decolonization of Knowledge Production in African
Societies: Contextual Analysis of Language of Instruction   139
Remi Alapo and Doghudje Doghudje

Leadership in the Management of Higher Education
in Nigeria   169
Abdulkareem Amuda-Kannike and Bolanle Waliu Shiyanbade

Transnationalism, Migration and African Integration

The Motivations for Return Migration to Somalia: Beyond
the Voluntary and Forced Binary   197
Jacqueline Owigo

AfCTA and African Integration: Prospects and Challenges   217
Emmanuel Zwanbin

Transnationalism Revisited: Interrogating Structural
Factors Impacting Prospective Migrants' Decision-Making
Process in Nigeria   243
Olufemi Mayowa Adetutu, Oluwaseun Joseph Onaolapo,
Abayomi Folorunso AWOLEYE, and Fumnanya Ofili

China in Africa: Whose Interest?   271
Folasade Abiodun

Strategic Framework of African Union on the Management
of Migration in Africa   293
Serifat Bolanle Asiyanbi and Omolara Victoria Akinyemi

Historicising Urhobo Migration, Settlement and Identity
in Jos, 1940–1970   313
Meshach Ofuafor

CONTENTS xi

Climate Change, Conflicts and Environment

Repowering Local Governance for Sustainability: Climate Change Mitigation of Healthcare Delivery in Nigeria   335
Bolanle Waliu Shiyanbade, Wasiu Abiodun Makinde, and Gbeminiyi Kazeem Ogunbela

Strategies for Mitigating Conflicts, Insecurity and Insurgency in Africa   357
Olasehinde Seun, Issah Moshood, and Noah Yusuf

Air, Land, and Water Pollution in Africa   383
Ayobami Oluwaseun Aluko

Index   409

LIST OF CONTRIBUTORS

Folasade Abiodun Migration and Development in Africa Monitors (MDAM), Ile-Ife, Nigeria

Abiodun Adewale Adegboye Obafemi Awolowo University, Ile-Ife, Nigeria

Adebusuyi Isaac Adeniran Obafemi Awolowo University, Ile-Ife, Nigeria

Olufemi Mayowa Adetutu Department of Demography and Social Statistics, Obafemi Awolowo University, Ile-Ife, Nigeria

Ebube Agbanusi Usman Dan-Fodio University, Sokoto, Nigeria

Omolara Victoria Akinyemi Department of History and International Studies, Federal University, Oye-Ekiti, Nigeria;
Department of International Relations, Obafemi Awolowo University, Ile-Ife, Nigeria

Remi Alapo York College, City University of New York (CUNY), New York, NY, USA

Ayobami Oluwaseun Aluko Department of Jurisprudence and Private Law, Faculty of Law, Obafemi Awolowo University, Ile-Ife, Nigeria

Mabayoje Anthony Olaniyi Aluko Obafemi Awolowo University, Ile-Ife, Nigeria

xiv LIST OF CONTRIBUTORS

Abdulkareem Amuda-Kannike Directorate of Information, Publicity & Protocol, Kwara State College of Education, Ilorin, Nigeria

Abdulrahman Azeez Aroke Obafemi Awolowo University, Ile-Ife, Nigeria

Serifat Bolanle Asiyanbi Department of History and International Studies, Federal University, Oye-Ekiti, Nigeria

Abayomi Folorunso AWOLEYE Obafemi Awolowo University, Ile-Ife, Nigeria

Kabran Aristide Djane Universite Peleforo Gon Coulibaly, Korhogo, Ivory Coast

Doghudje Doghudje American College of Education, Indianapolis, IN, USA

Sukurah Adewumi Hammed Department of Demography and Social Statistics, Obafemi Awolowo University, Ile-Ife, Nigeria

Ayoola Peter Ijisakin Department of Demography and Social Statistics, Obafemi Awolowo University, Ile-Ife, Nigeria

Gerelene Jagganath University of KwaZulu-Natal, Durban, South Africa

Wasiu Abiodun Makinde Obafemi Awolowo University, Ile-Ife, Nigeria

Issah Moshood University of Ilorin, Ilorin, Nigeria

Fumnanya Ofili Obafemi Awolowo University, Ile-Ife, Nigeria

Meshach Ofuafor Obafemi Awolowo University, Ile-Ife, Nigeria

Gbeminiyi Kazeem Ogunbela Obafemi Awolowo University, Ile-Ife, Nigeria

Yusuf Segun Ogunsanya Department of Demography and Social Statistics, Obafemi Awolowo University, Ile-Ife, Nigeria

David Aduragbemi Okunlola Department of Demography and Social Statistics, Obafemi Awolowo University, Ile-Ife, Nigeria

Oluseye Ademola Okunola Obafemi Awolowo University, Ile-Ife, Nigeria

Sunday Idowu Oladeji Obafemi Awolowo University, Ile-Ife, Nigeria

Oluwaseun Joseph Onaolapo Obafemi Awolowo University, Ile-Ife, Nigeria

Jacqueline Owigo United States International University—Africa, Nairobi, Kenya

Olasehinde Seun University of Ilorin, Ilorin, Nigeria

Bolanle Waliu Shiyanbade Department of Public Administration, Faculty of Administration, Obafemi Awolowo University, Ile-Ife, Nigeria

Shanta B. Singh University of KwaZulu-Natal, Durban, South Africa

Noah Yusuf University of Ilorin, Ilorin, Nigeria

Bongiwe M. Zulu University of KwaZulu-Natal, Durban, South Africa

Emmanuel Zwanbin United States International University—Africa, Nairobi, Kenya

LIST OF FIGURES

The National Development Plan (NDP) in South Africa: An Inspiration to Shape Communities by 2030

Fig. 1   Proposed integrated implementation model for safer communities   27

African Demographic Dividend: Case Study of Nigeria's Age Structure

Fig. 1   GDP per capital Nigeria age structure   33
Fig. 2   The interrelationship among age structure, investment in human capital and economic growth   42
Fig. 3   Stability test: CUSUM   50
Fig. 4   Stability test: CUSUM SQUARE   51
Fig. 5   Stability test: CUSUM   54

Decolonization of Knowledge Production in African Societies: Contextual Analysis of Language of Instruction

Fig. 1   Vygotsky's socio-cultural model of cognitive development (Vygotsky, 1978)   155
Fig. 2   Meta-analysis research method   156

xviii   LIST OF FIGURES

Leadership in the Management of Higher Education in Nigeria

Fig. 1   Determinant factors of leadership style in the management of students' affairs in selected colleges (*Source* Field Survey [2021])   185

LIST OF TABLES

The National Development Plan (NDP) in South Africa: An Inspiration to Shape Communities by 2030

Table 1	Timeline for the development of policy framework for community safety	15

African Demographic Dividend: Case Study of Nigeria's Age Structure

Table 1	Trends of Nigeria's population size and growth rate	34
Table 2	Drivers of population growth in Nigeria	35
Table 3	Requirements for demographic dividend	37
Table 4	Measurement of variables	44
Table 5	Correlation matrix	44
Table 6	Descriptive statistics	45
Table 7	Unit root test	46
Table 8	The bounds F-test for cointegration test	46
Table 9	Long-run coefficient efficient dependent variable: growth rate	47
Table 10	Short-run error correction coefficients	48
Table 11	ARDL model diagnostic tests-economic growth model	49
Table 12	Long run estimates	52
Table 13	Estimation of long run coefficients dependent variable: POPGR	52

xix

LIST OF TABLES

| Table 14 | Short-run estimation coefficients dependent variable: ΔPOPGR | 52 |
| Table 15 | ARDL model diagnostic tests-population growth model | 53 |

Emergency Healthcare Accessibility in the Context of COVID-19 in Nigeria

Table 1	Descriptive statistics	71
Table 2	Mcnemar's test	73
Table 3	Multiple logistic regression of access to health facilities before and during COVID-19	74

Self-medication Practices in Covid-19 Era: Insights from Caregivers to Under-Five Children in Southwestern Nigeria

| Table 1 | Distribution of discussants by socio-demographic characteristics | 88 |

The Globalisation of Social Environmental Research and the Practices of University Researchers in Africa: Case from Côte d'Ivoire

| Table 1 | Profile of articles studied by type of research | 107 |
| Table 2 | Research objectives of the articles evaluated | 111 |

Leadership in the Management of Higher Education in Nigeria

| Table 1 | Determinant factors of leadership style in the management of students' affairs in selected colleges | 184 |

The Motivations for Return Migration to Somalia: Beyond the Voluntary and Forced Binary

| Table 1 | Return as a continuum across the forced and voluntary binary | 209 |

Transnationalism Revisited: Interrogating Structural Factors Impacting Prospective Migrants' Decision-Making Process in Nigeria

Table 1	Percentage distribution of respondents by related factors associated with migration decision	251
Table 2	Bivariate analysis of migration decision by social factors	255
Table 3	Multivariate analysis of social factors and migration decision	259

Repowering Local Governance for Sustainability: Climate Change Mitigation of Healthcare Delivery in Nigeria

Table 1	Model summary	347
Table 2	ANOVA	347

Strategies for Mitigating Conflicts, Insecurity and Insurgency in Africa

Table 1	For specific cases of social uprisings in Africa	365
Table 2	African countries with the highest share of global population living below the extreme poverty line in 2022	367

Introduction: Africa and the World

Adebusuyi Isaac Adeniran

1 Contextualizing the Problem in Africa

Being the continent with the most youthful population, Africa appears to still lack in requisite innovative interventions to transmute such demographic dividend into economic opportunities for the benefits of the larger population. Instead, there has been an increasing trend in South-North migrations among both skilled and unskilled Africans across all age groups, for example as it is applicable in the case of 'japa' syndrome in Nigeria, which is indicative of 'no-return migration'. Besides, the impacts of climate change on the continent have also implied unstructured migratory trends within and beyond the bounds of Africa.

While African countries have contributed less than 5% of global carbon dioxide (CO_2) emissions, they have been collectively impacted more than the five countries (China, United States, India, Russia and Japan) that contribute more than half of the total global CO_2 emissions. Yet, Africa

A. I. Adeniran (✉)
Obafemi Awolowo University, Ile-Ife, Nigeria
e-mail: adebusuyi@oauife.edu.ng

© The Author(s), under exclusive license to Springer Nature
Switzerland AG 2023
A. I. Adeniran (ed.), *African Development and Global Engagements*,
https://doi.org/10.1007/978-3-031-21283-3_1

has continued to play a feeble role in various United Nations (UN)-enabled 'Conference of Parties' (COP) negotiations, such as the COP-26 in Glasgow, Scotland in 2021.

The management of the Corona Virus-2019 (i.e., Covid-19) epidemic across the world has presented a clear pointer to Africa that except development is internally driven, no one is ready to exogenously drive sustainable good life for others. Ostensible 'vaccine nationalism' that did dot the production and availability of various Covid-19 vaccine brands, which has ultimately left Africa as the 'begging continent' one more time calls for in-depth interrogation in contextualizing what the place of Africa has been, is and to be within the global interactive mode. Undue internationally induced land-grabbing system across the length and breadth of Africa, recurrent political instability and attendant conflicts across the continent are issues that seem to be placing Africa in a particularly uncomfortable position now and beyond.

As good as the ongoing 'decolonization of knowledge' drive across the continent is, how could one situate such within the realm of sustainable intervention when it is being exogenously driven? Of course, decolonizing the process of knowledge production does not seem to be the area that should be of priority concern in Africa as such has little or no impact on the larger process of enabling good life for the generality of the African citizens. The need for institutionalizing 'good governance' across all existential sectors in Africa should be of great interest at the level of policy.

Lackadaisical disposition of the political leadership in Africa towards investment in education, innovation and research appears to be the single, but the most potent factor that will persist to inhibit creativity and self-reliance as long as it takes to reason correctly. As a case reference, all public universities in Nigeria were under locks and keys for most parts of 2022 due to poor funding by the governments at both state and federal levels. Loss of critical manpower to the developed world in particular from the continent will assuredly continue to deteriorate and the continent will be worse for it. Significantly, economic growth and development will be worse for it.

To be mild, the extent of the discouraging socio-developmental outlook of the African continent has implied that it has persistently occupied the most unenviable position of the least developed of all continents of the world in modern time. In this light, it is believed that a more holistic, endogenous framework for societal transformation has become expedient for Africa in connecting its realities putting into consideration such aspects as socio-philosophical thinking, international relations, medicine and health sciences, law, migration, science and technology, humanities, demography and population studies, agriculture, environment and land management, government and public policy, education, *et cetera*.

Reference

Adebusuyi, A. I. (2020). *Migration crises in 21st century Africa: Patterns, processes and projections*. Palgrave Macmillan.

Policy and Covid-19 Matters

The National Development Plan (NDP) in South Africa: An Inspiration to Shape Communities by 2030

Bongiwe M. Zulu and Shanta B. Singh

1 Introduction

Creating an environment where people can feel safe and live without fear of crime is the priority of the South African government. This is evident in the National Development Plan (NDP) Vision 2030 (Government of South Africa, 2012), where the government prioritises building safer communities. This forms part of planned interventions to enhance the standard of living for all South Africans and create a better, more prosperous, socially just, globally competitive, and fully developed South Africa (Government of South Africa, 2012). Crime eradication through creating a crime-free South Africa is one of the NDP's priority goals. This study explores the South African Police Service (SAPS) implementation of the NDP Vision 2030 for building safer communities. This research is grounded on the SAPS implementation of the NDP Vision 2030 for building safer communities. The researcher has reviewed literature pertaining to the NDP and building safer communities in order

---

B. M. Zulu · S. B. Singh (✉)
University of KwaZulu-Natal, Durban, South Africa
e-mail: Singhsb@ukzn.ac.za

© The Author(s), under exclusive license to Springer Nature Switzerland AG 2023
A. I. Adeniran (ed.), *African Development and Global Engagements,*
https://doi.org/10.1007/978-3-031-21283-3_2

to demonstrate the research problem. The literature review first elucidates concepts related to the study. Secondly, it pays attention to victims of crime. Thirdly, it focuses on the National Crime Prevention Strategy (NCPS), which emphasises the crime prevention approach and crime control. Fourthly, the NDP Vision: 2030 for building safer communities is scanned. Lastly, the literature review dwells on the issue of crime in South Africa.

2 Concept Elucidation

2.1 South African Police Service

According to the Constitution of RSA, 1996, Section, 205 (1) (Act 108 of 1996), the national police service should be designed to function in the national, provincial, and, where appropriate, local spheres of government (Government of South Africa, 1996: 105). The South African Police Service (SAPS) is legislated by the SAPS Act, 1995 (Act 68 of 1995) and operates in four-tier locations of policing, namely, SAPS Head Office, which includes divisions and national components, provincial offices which includes offices at provincial commissioners, cluster stations, and police stations (Government of South Africa, 1996). According to the Constitution of RSA, 1996, Section 205 (3) (Act 108, 1996), "the objectives of the police service are to prevent, combat and investigate crime, maintain public order, protect and secure the inhabitants of the Republic and their property, and uphold and enforce the law".

2.2 Building Safer Communities

The NCPS states that reducing crime cannot be the sole responsibility of the police. Creating safer communities entails the dedicated participation of communities, diverse government departments, local authorities, and the private sector. Combatting crime demands a "multi-pronged approach" which includes law enforcement, and situational prevention (Department of Safety & Security, 1996). The NDP Vision 2030 specifically addresses the concept of building safer communities, connecting it to:

a. the necessity of strengthening the CJS,
b. providing professional police service,
c. demilitarisation of police,
d. integrated approach to community safety, and
e. community participation in creating safer communities (Government of South Africa, 2012).

3 National Development Plan Vision 2030

In 2012, the Cabinet of South Africa adopted the detailed blueprint known as National Development Plan Vision: 2030, which aims at guiding South Africa on how poverty can be eliminated and inequality be reduced by 2030 (Government of South Africa, 2012) and seeks enhancement of the living standard of all South Africans and create a better, more prosperous, socially just, globally competitive, and fully developed South Africa by 2030 through economic growth (Government of South Africa, 2016). A decent standard of living consists of the core elements that include safety and security. A vision for a safe and secure South Africa is enunciated in the NDP and building safer communities is acknowledged as fundamental to realising an integrated and progressive approach to safety and security, which includes all government departments and tiers of government (Civilian Secretariat for Police, 2016). The NDP Vision 2030, Chapter 12: Building Safer Communities sets out South Africa's vision of becoming a safer country.

The study uses the acronym NDP to refer to the National Development Plan. In the words of Trevor Manuel, erstwhile chairperson of the National Planning Commission, the NDP is a "plan for the country to eliminate poverty and reduce inequality" as well as to enhance "the capability of the state and leaders working together to solve complex problems" (Government of South Africa, 2012: 1). Fox and Meyer (1995: 96) define policy as a "guide of action or statement of goals that should be followed in an institution to deal with a particular problem or phenomenon or a set of problems of phenomena". The NDP is described as a "plan or blueprint". Hence, according to Fox and Meyer (1995), the NDP constitutes a policy. Thus, the researcher regards the NDP as a public policy for South Africans.

4 National Crime Prevention Strategy (NCPS)

In May 1996 the National Crime Prevention Strategy (NCPS) was passed by the South African Cabinet which acknowledged "the importance for a 'new paradigm' for addressing crime" (Government of South Africa, 1996: 6). It was seen as representing "a critical point in the fight against crime". The NCPS remained South Africa's initial effort to "take lessons from the developing body of universal work on prevention of crime and implement it to South African setting" (Newham, 2005). The NCPS emanated from the discussions and research conducted by a multi-disciplinary "team of experts from public and private sectors mandated to take care at creating a prolonged strategy to help the government in tackling the roots of crime in South Africa". The NCPS further presents an outline for the creation of nationwide crime prevention plans.

Newham (2005: 5) maintains that "while the NCPS was hailed as a progressive document and opened the government to some of the latest international thinking on the role of the state in preventing crime, there were a number of key challenges to its implementation". Sixteen years after the adoption of the NCPS, the government in 2012 advanced the paradigm and adopted the NDP, which aimed that by 2030 "people living in SA [...] should [...] feel safe and have no fear of crime" (Government of South Africa, 2012: 350). The NDP argues, as does Newham (2005), that "although this strategy [NCPS] incorporated cutting-edge international thinking and was widely recognised as sound, it was never fully institutionalised as holistic and comprehensive strategy that focused on all factors that produce crime and insecurity" (Government of South Africa, 2012: 357).

The NCPS has adopted a four-pillar approach to guide crime prevention plans across the board (Department for Safety and Security, 1996). These pillars focus on (i) enhancing the efficiency of the criminal justice system; (ii) decreasing crime through environmental design; (iii) improving public values and school education; and (iv) tackling transnational crime (NCPS, 1996). Although the basis of NCPS was the Criminal Justice System (CJS) it went beyond the Criminal Justice System. The NDP (2012) argues that while this strategy integrated pioneering global thinking and was broadly acknowledged as comprehensive, it was certainly not completely implemented as a comprehensive strategy that concentrated on addressing issues that contribute to crime and insecurity.

THE NATIONAL DEVELOPMENT PLAN (NDP) IN SOUTH ...   11

Both the NCPS and the NDP have been criticised (Rauch, 2002). Rauch (2002) identifies challenges and criticism regarding NCPS implementation. She claims that the basis of NCPS was the hypothesis that the transecting national programmes would obviously lead to interdepartmental cooperation. Conversely, the fiscal and performance motivations in government acted contrary to cooperation. Rauch (2002) argues that the NCPS could not apportion committed government funding to implementation, however somewhat stimulated departments to downsize and apportion existing resources to the state plans. In addition, she criticises the NCPS that the "connection between the four pillars of NCPS and the seven priority crimes by then was not articulated well" (Rauch, 2002). As a result, there was an extensive emphasis on the pillars, resulting in the processes and structures being far removed from "the content of the crimes that were intended to be addressed".

5   NATIONAL INTEGRATED CRIME AND VIOLENCE PREVENTION STRATEGY (2022)

The Integrated Crime and Violence Prevention Strategy (ICVPS) is the implementation mechanism for the 2016 White Paper on Safety and Security. It ensures that the basics are in place in every aspect of a person's life in order to circumvent the possibility of the occurrence of crime and violence. It advocates for an integrated and developmental approach to the prevention of crime and violence. The ICVPS adopts a developmental life course approach building on the socio-ecological model that recognises that violence results from a combination of multiple factors that put people at risk. It recognises the factors that make individuals, from the time they are conceived, vulnerable to violence and crime. This approach requires interventions at a primary level (for the public), secondary level (for those regarded as being "at risk" of offending or of criminal victimisation), and tertiary level (for those who have already succumbed to criminality or victimisation). The ICVPS also acknowledges the need for interventions to address a multiplicity of socio-economic factors that contribute towards crime and violence including poverty, inequality, and unemployment. It further requires improvements in the social welfare, health, and education sectors.

6 METHODOLOGY

This mixed-method study is significant because of the need to derive qualitative data from different sources through literature review, interviews, focus group discussions, and document analysis and quantitative data through the administration of questionnaires. Participants, using their own power of voices, experiences, expertise, and offered noteworthy viewpoints on the SAPS implementation of the NDP in building safer communities. Hence, this research adds value to the policing body of knowledge (BOK), policy-makers, government, and other departments.

In this study, quantitative and qualitative approaches were together used to answer the aims of this research. The quantitative method was mainly used to analyse how the SAPS had translated the five priority areas of the NDP Chapter 12 to attain safer communities and to determine the SAPS understanding and internalisation of the NDP vision of building safer communities. Qualitative methods were mainly used to analyse how the SAPS business units were aligning themselves with the NDP, the progress that the SAPS had made in achieving the NDP vision of safer communities; and the challenges the SAPS had experienced in implementing the NDP. The mixed-methods research design was employed, among others, to allow triangulation. This included the usage of manifold methods to study the research problem, i.e. methodological triangulations; the use of a variety of data sources, i.e. data triangulation; and the use of multiple perspectives to interpret the results, i.e. theory triangulations (Greene et al., 1989: 259). Purposive sampling was implemented for this research as SAPS members and community members at the chosen provinces and police stations were accepted as the study population to analyse their views and tendencies regarding the SAPS understanding, internalisation, and implementation of the NDP in building safer communities (Leedy & Ormrod, 2010: 236).

7 THEORY OF CHANGE AS THEORETICAL FRAMEWORK

The theory of change (ToC) approach is used in this study. Laing and Todd (2015: 3) describe the ToC as a theory-based approach in the direction of planning, executing, and evaluating change at the community, organisational, or individual levels. Reisman et al. (2007) refer to ToC as an engine of change, a roadmap, a theory of action and a blueprint. The ToC clearly enunciates how an initiative or a project will achieve outcomes. Weiss (1995) describes ToC as "a theory of how and why an initiative works". The ToC is applied in various disciplines which include community development as well as education and public health. In the context of this study, ToC is applicable in implementing change with the purpose of developing communities. The ToC is in line with the aim of the study which seeks to determine how SAPS is implementing the NDP in building safer communities.

Laing and Todd (2015: 4) point out various usage of a ToC in the life-cycle of any initiative or plan, beginning with "planning an idea through to implementation, delivery, and review". The implementation and assessment of plan can be done using ToC. Using a ToC could facilitate an understanding of why a plan does or does not work, when the implementation of the plan is in progress, allows an actor or implementer to identify where the challenges are. The ToC contributes towards planning improvement and identification of gaps in knowledge that are lacking in clarity (Laing & Todd, 2015: 5).

The ToC is utilised as an instrument to conceptualise the NDP implementation in building safer communities and develop the police-based and community-based plans for developing community safety in SA. Such plans are grounded on three themes in the setting of police and communities, viz. (Laing & Todd, 2015): "the starting situation, the steps to change and strands of action".

8 Policy Design Affecting Community Safety

The quality of life of citizens and mobility are highly affected by safety within communities and public spaces. Furthermore, this affects citizens' opportunities to freely engage in developmental processes and public life. Crime and violence caused in South Africa remain multi-layered and complex. Confronting them requires a systemic approach that facilitates active cooperation across disciplines and stakeholders as well as on all levels, from national to local. Since 1994, among other things, SA has partaken in the development of several policies and laws supporting the advancement to a democratic state.

It is the government's commitment that "all people in SA are and feel safe" (Government of South Africa, 2012). The government's strategic priorities commit to addressing safety matters. To address the issue of "feeling safe" government has enacted various policies in an effort to achieve safety in society. This suggests that prevention of crime and violence remained a subject of importance and priority for the SA governments from the time of the 1994 democratic dispensation. A number of comprehensive policies and strategies over years that provide important frameworks for preventing violence and promoting community safety have been developed by the South African government. These include the NDP, National Crime Prevention Strategy (NCPS), the Integrated Urban Development Framework (IUDF), Integrated Social Crime Prevention Strategy (ISCPS) and 2016 White Paper on Safety and Security.

Is South Africa on the right track to achieving NDP Vision 2030 where "people living in South Africa" in 2030 will "feel safe and have no fear of crime"? Table 1 depicts some of the critical pieces of policies and strategies that have been adopted over the years providing important frameworks for preventing crime and violence and promoting community safety. The subsections below review some of the critical pieces of policies and strategies.

Effective NDP implementation and the achievement of NDP goals and objectives are dependent on the active involvement of all government actors. This includes the facilitation, coordination and implementation techniques for the establishment of an enabling environment for the active participation of community and civil society. If socio-economic challenges contribute to a lack of safer communities, the NDP Vision will remain a dream as long as they are not addressed.

Based on the legislative, policy and strategic response trajectory towards building safer communities in SA, it is clear that there is a need for a predominant policy for crime and violence prevention and community safety to coordinate cooperation and configuration of government policy as well as facilitate the establishment of well-resourced, sustainable, coordination and implementation mechanisms in aligning government and non-government actors. Successful NDP implementation in different spheres and departments within the government depends on their cooperation in bringing high-quality, comprehensive and integrated services in partnership with communities and civil society. For effective delivery of interventions and programmes to advocate crime and violence prevention and community safety, requirements of the system levels are imperative to build essential enabling environments and coordinate implementation.

THE NATIONAL DEVELOPMENT PLAN (NDP) IN SOUTH ...   15

Table 1 Timeline for the development of policy framework for community safety

Year	Policies and strategies adopted for preventing crime and violence and promoting community safety
1994	Comprehensive legal and institutional reforms brought transformation of Department of Law and Order to Department of Safety and Security
1996	The enactment of Constitution of the Republic of SA, 1996 (Act 108 of 1996) enacted
1996	The endorsement of National Crime Prevention Strategy aimed at promoting all-inclusive techniques of addressing developmental and social crime generators
1998	The enactment of White Paper on Safety and Security for execution by Department of Safety and Security
1999	New administration
1999	The establishment of Justice, Crime Prevention and Security Cluster to promote cooperation between law enforcement and security departments in the execution of programmes to enhance functioning of the Criminal Justice System (CJS)
2004	The endorsement of Service Charter for Victims of Violence and Crime to promote unwaveringly extraordinary service levels to victims through commitment of entire criminal justice organisations in SA
2007	CJS revamp was the review of the CJS and Cabinet adoption of a seven-point plan to transform the CJS
2009	New administration
2011	The endorsement of Integrated Social Crime Prevention Strategy (ISCPS) for promotion of "integral approach" in the direction of "a Safer Community of Opportunity" by the Department for Social Development addressing community safety in a bottom-up-approach
2011	The promulgation of Community Safety Forums Policy aimed at promoting CSFs to "serve as platform for coordination, integration and monitoring of the implementation of multisectoral crime prevention and community safety initiatives"
2012	The enactment of the National Development Plan—Vision for 2030 for promotion of broader and holistic reflection on crime and violence, multisectoral collaboration among governmental actors and non-governmental actors to deal with crime and violence generators
2014	New administration
2016	The promulgation of White Paper on Policing endorsing "a community-oriented police service and professionalisation of SAPS"
2016	The endorsement of revised White Paper on Safety and Security underlining the significance of "a holistic approach" as well as "the role of local government in building safer communities"
2018	The consultation on the draft implementation plan of White Paper on Safety and Security underscoring the importance of "a holistic approach" as well as "the role of local government in building safer communities"

(continued)

16   B. M. ZULU AND S. B. SINGH

Table 1   (continued)

Year	Policies and strategies adopted for preventing crime and violence and promoting community safety
2019	New administration

Source Adapted from Spohr, H. & Erkens, C. (2016). *Building safer communities through systemic approaches to violence prevention*

9   CRIME PREVENTION AND COMMUNITY SAFETY

In building safer communities there are various crime prevention strategies and approaches for a decrease of real levels of anti-social behaviour and crime that cause distress as well as anxiety regarding communities' quality of life. According to Shaftoe and Read (2007: 248–249), using "Crime Prevention through Environmental Design (CPTED)" stays among the approaches that "focuses on the design of the physical environment and situational crime prevention" as a method to prevent crime and reduce opportunities for crime to occur. This includes developing social and economic strategies s to produce sustainable communities.

Kruger et al. (2016: 5) describe a strategy for community crime prevention as "an action plan or strategy to prevent crime and violence and reduce public fear of crime [...] A tool to bring together different role-players involved in crime prevention [...] A means of developing local crime prevention partnerships [...] A method to ensure co-ordination and management of crime prevention initiatives [...] A way to identify priority areas and tasks". According to Brown (2013: 163), crime prevention, in contrast to community policing, is a set of programmes designed by the police to involve the community in the process of preventing crime. Crime prevention is an educational programme the police provide to teach the public how best to protect themselves from becoming victims of crime. Community policing, however, incorporates the concepts of crime prevention into its philosophy.

Understanding aims and objectives in building safer communities

Kruger et al. (2016: 49) maintain that "it is not always easy to get a common understanding of the meaning of aims and objectives, and it could be a challenge to define these for a project (plan, strategy"). The authors explain that the aims of the plan clarify "what the desired end results or intentions of the plan are". In the case of the NDP, its aims are "what it would like to accomplish and not how it will be done" and "how the aims will be achieved" (Kruger et al., 2016: 49).

Understanding of outputs and outcomes in building safer communities

Kruger et al. (2016: 50) define outputs as the "tangible or intangible deliverables that are produced as part of certain tasks in the process of meeting the objectives or ultimate aim of the project (plan, strategy)". Therefore, visibly describing the NDP Chapter 12's outputs carries value for those responsible for the implementation of it, especially for understanding the expectations and the level of accountability. Kruger et al. (2016: 50) explain outcomes as the result of implemented activities and outputs. In this case, effective implementation of the NDP Chapter 12 could result in safer communities as the outcome. For successful NDP implementation, it is also required that the NDP's tangible and intangible deliverables tackle actual problems and challenges, bear objectives that are clearly defined, grounded on precisely crafted and clearly assessed plans, closely implemented and managed through a skilled knowledgeable, inspired and dedicated team, who receives the vital stakeholders' support, sufficiently capacitated and resourced, possessing strong leadership skills; and their evaluation founded on effective delivery of service (Kruger et al., 2016: 50).

Understanding monitoring in building safer communities

Successful NDP implementation also requires monitoring and evaluation. Monitoring is described by Kruger et al. (2016: 53) as an "ongoing process that measures progress of an initiative by tracking activities, milestones and outputs to establish if planned results are being achieved.... normally a management function that improves decision-making and helps identify the need for remedial action". Kruger et al. (2016: 53) mention involvement of "continuous, systematic collection of data and information and the documenting of processes and results to guide decisions regarding the future of the initiative". From monitoring the NDP Chapter 12 implementation, the SAPS and other stakeholders could learn from experience which can enhance future implementation as well as advantage further interventions aimed at improving the safety of communities.

Understanding of evaluation in building safer communities

Evaluating policing successes and effectiveness is essential (Brown, 2013: 171). According to Kruger et al. (2016: 53) "evaluations are conducted to find out if an initiative has achieved the desired results as a consequence of the activities being implemented and the outputs being delivered". During evaluation, achievements, results of the initiatives of the plan, as well as priorities, objectives and aims are assessed. Therefore, the evaluation of NDP implementation is the cornerstone for realising safer communities in SA. Kruger et al. (2016: 53) argue that evaluation involves a "systematic assessment of aspects such as efficiency, impact, effectiveness, relevance, quality, and sustainability". They further argue that preferably and regularly "the responsibility for an evaluation should be given to an external, independent agency in an effort to ensure impartiality". The initiatives are usually evaluated after the work is done or in phases during implementation. Evaluation of NDP Chapter 12 evaluation should not just be a compliance issue but should also add value: the information gathered should inform "strategic decisions as well as offer learning that could be applied to other initiatives that support the realisation of safer communities" (Kruger et al., 2016: 53).

10 Selection of SMART Indicators in Building Safer Communities

The SMART indicators refer to goals that are Specific, Measurable, Achievable, Realistic, and Timely (SMART). Kruger et al. (2016: 57) argue that carefully selected indicators help with the monitoring and evaluation function, to "ensure that they provide reliable information when needed and without undue effort". Therefore, the identification and selection of indicators to measure the execution of the NDP and associated strategies are of paramount importance. It is important that indicators must assist with the facilitation of the SAPS' assessment of progress achieved in implementing NDP Chapter 12 concentrating on and aligning with inputs, outputs, results, objectives, and aims. In a nutshell, these indicators are generally selected to aid in tracking progress in reaching certain milestones and delivering planned outputs.

As the NDP is executed, associated strategies, plans, programmes, and projects should use "various types of indicators to measure performance, including input, process, output, outcome, and impact indicators" (Kruger et al., 2016: 57). Usually, straight monitoring is linked with the first three types (input, process, and output) while the last two (outcome and impact) is linked more with straight evaluations. Kruger et al. (2016) further emphasise the importance of selecting smart and good indicators that are specific, measurable, achievable, relevant, and time-related.

Establishing indicators related to monitoring NDP implementation and developing specific indicators for Chapter 12 and each of the individual strategies, plans, programmes, and projects should be a priority for the SAPS. Through monitoring, stakeholders' commitment levels in implementing the NDP could be measured. Implementation of effective local crime prevention plays a key role in realising the vision of safer communities. Kruger et al. (2016: 63) argue that "institutionalising the local crime prevention process means changing structures and/or attitudes".

11 Community Policing in Building Safer Communities

The concept of community policing did not emerge overnight and it has been evolutionary process and among others, its main goal is to enhance "the quality of life in a community" (Brown, 2013: 172). Therefore, safer communities remain the sign of "the quality of life in communities". Community policing's objectives include crime, victimisation, and crime fear reduction, as well as crime prevention, arrest of criminals, and promotion of security of the community (Brown, 2013; Farrell, 2007). Community policing seeks to directly reduce the frequency of victimisation in a number of ways.

Tilley (2007: 758) describes "community policing" as a "decentralised form of policing with a particular focus on local neighbourhoods where local priority issues are identified and addressed, often through problem-solving involving residents and businesses". According to Brown (2013: 152), the overall philosophy of community policing acknowledges police's accountability not only "to the law" but also to law-abiding people. To ensure effective policing and have police actions accepted and supported by the community, people should authorise police actions that deal with crime and disorder, and should approve of the strategies used.

Accountability is critical in policing. Accountability strengthens partnership, collaboration, and trust. The community policing philosophy, according to Brown (2013: 152), provides a mechanism for police accountability to communities, recognises the need for community legitimacy, and creates a framework within which the police can work in collaboration with residents to solve community problems that are related to crime, fear, violence, and quality of life. The basic principles of community policing are community collaboration and problem-solving. Based on analyses of communities' crime and disorder problems, prioritised in collaboration with citizens, officers seek to identify police government, business, and citizen resources that could be mobilised to eliminate the conditions that give rise to community unrest (Brown, 2013: 152).

Under community policing, the police no longer simply incident responders, nor do they position themselves as the sole experts dealing with criminal problems. The community policing collaboration is described by Brown (2013: 153) as an intense and active affair, providing a true sharing of responsibility for the achievement of the desired police and community goal of safe and secure communities. In the manifestation of community policing, when a crime or quality-of-life problem is identified as a pattern, a solution is developed through collaborative discussion between the community and the police. Therefore, according to Brown (2013: 153), community policing is regarded as "a philosophy that governs how citizens' expectations and demands for police services are integrated into police actions to identify and address those conditions that have an adverse effect on the safety and welfare of neighbourhood life".

Community policing rather than being a technique, is a style for delivering police services (Brown, 2013: 164). Community policing's concentration is also on the reduction of "opportunities for crime" to be committed and preventing crime through problem-solving. Crime does not occur in a vacuum; it results from conditions that create environments that are conducive to illegal activities. According to Brown (2013: 115), in poorer communities, where there is substantial unemployment, poor education, and limited opportunities to participate in the economic system, opportunities for crime flourish. The level of neighbourhood cohesiveness contributes to the social and economic settings that create environments in which crime flourishes. Highly organised communities, areas in which there is full participation of residents and business people in the life of the neighbourhoods, have far less fear of crime than disorganised communities that are more susceptible to crime (Brown, 2013: 115).

According to Brown (2013: 156), the primary focus of community policing is solving chronic problems by means of intervening in an actual or potential pattern of incidents of concern to a community so that the underlying conditions which created the problem are eliminated. Community policing problem-solving orientation recognises that community problems rarely just arise. Community policing tries to find the problems' nature and take action that impacts the fundamental causes.

Furthermore, Brown (2013: 157) states that developing a community's capacity to existing in a peaceful and orderly state is essential in reducing levels of crime. The degree to which a community is organised will impact its level of fear. The degree of organisation will also impact the community's ability to control its environment since it is primarily in disorganised communities where crime and disorder flourish. The police alone cannot guarantee safe streets and order. According to Brown (2013: 157), when communities depend on police—"who cannot be omnipresent – for maintenance of order, residents often keep their doors locked, and are unwilling to use their streets for recreation, seldom venturing outside of their four walls for fear of criminals who may roam the streets of the areas in which they live".

Community policing recognises the role citizens should play in upholding safe and orderly surroundings. Usually, the police attempt to take total responsibility for community safety and order by asking the communities to inform them whenever they observe the criminal activity. This type of system is usually not sustainable. Community policing recognises that the police can only be co-producers of order in a community. It recognises the residents should commit themselves to maintaining an orderly environment. Community policing seeks to maintain neighbourhood order and stability through community involvement, with police aiding as needed and requested by residents (Brown, 2013: 157). It is in this context that community policing fosters "a sense of trust", not only among the police and residents but also among residents. Brown (2013: 158) maintains that properly implemented community policing serves as "the catalyst that facilitates the engagement, voluntarism and trust that enables the cooperation and coordination of all available resources to the benefit of the community".

According to Brown (2013: 157), this interpersonal trust "creates an atmosphere of reciprocity which brings to bear resources of individuals and their organisations to collaborate with police and other agencies to address the issues of crime and quality of life in communities". He further argues that this idea remains "consistent with the concept of social capital", which describes the accessibility of resources through the organisations in which they are members. In short, social capital refers to societal relations features—like "interpersonal trust, norms of reciprocity and membership in civic organisations– that function as resources for individuals to facilitate collective action for mutual benefit" (Putnam, 1993). Brown (2013: 58) states that "in addition to encouraging communities to mobilise against violence through 'self-help' strategies of informal and social control, perhaps reinforced by partnerships with agencies of formal control (community policing), strategies to address the social and ecological changes that beset many inner-city communities need to be considered". Appropriately executed community policing can enhance collaboration between communities and police and promote community trust in the police. This could contribute to building safer communities.

Economic and social conditions influence community safety. The working partnership between the public–private sector and the community provides a foundation for strong and highly organised communities. This, in return, influences the safety feeling in the community. The police should also focus on the conditions that generate criminal behaviour and work in partnership with other agencies, governments, and all other sectors of the community. There should be a legitimate collaboration among the criminal justice system and community as well as private agencies. The interaction, communication, and collaboration among the police, the criminal justice system and private agencies to solve problems is another attribute of community policing and building safer communities.

12   WAY FORWARD

The RSA Public Service Charter commits to "create an enabling environment within the provisions of available resources for public servants to perform their duties". It further commits public servants "to accept the responsibility to undergo ongoing training and self-development". The SAPS Code of Conduct commits police officers to "utilise all available resources responsibly, efficiently and cost-effectively and develop their skills and participate in the development of fellow colleagues to ensure equal opportunities for all". Although the SAPS implement various policies, strategies, and programmes to capacitate police officers, according to a significant number of police participants, police still lacked certain resources to do the job. However, from this research, a considerable number of community members were not convinced that police did not have adequate resources to do the job. They believed those police officers used state resources inappropriately for their private benefit and not to solve crimes. More participants viewed police as well-informed of the policing role and that they understood and performed their functions and duties accordingly than those who viewed police as well-trained and having required skills. This study confirms that there was still a need for ongoing training of police officers for them to acquire various skills.

The Community participants (CPs) did not rate police officers highly—they viewed them as not being trustworthy, not honest, not displaying exemplary conduct, not providing progress on complaints, and using powers responsibly, and not being accountable, reliable, doing what was right in performing duties and treating community members with respect.

The NDP endorses the "professionalisation of the police by enforcing a professional police Code of Ethics". In the views of Community participants (CPs) and Police Participants (PPs), to a certain extent police unbiasedly attended to complaints, and respected the right of children, people with disabilities, all faiths, religious, spiritual groups and diverse cultures. Much as both police and community participants had less confidence in police helping people in sign languages and respecting the LGBTQI+ community, police participants themselves did have confidence that police respected diversity overall. However, community participants had less confidence that police (from lowest to highest confidence score) treated all with dignity, respected males and females equally and did not unlawfully discriminate against anyone.

The SAPS Code of Conduct obligates police to "cooperate with the community, government at every level and all other related role-players". The RSA Public Service Charter, "motivated by the proven value of collaboration in service delivery improvement", suggests that government, public servants and other stakeholders collaborate in building South Africa. Both PPs and CPs had little confidence that there was a good relationship between communities and police and that communities were providing much information related to criminal activities to the police.

The VOC surveys show a steady decline in the feeling of safety (Statistics SA, 2018). The SAPS vision and "Code of Conduct commit to create a safe and secure environment for all the people in South Africa". The NCPS affirms the establishment of a comprehensive police framework to empower the government to tackle crime in a coordinated and focused way. It requires all government agencies and civil society to draw on all their resources to prevent crime. The Community Safety Forum Policy promotes "integrated and coordinated multi-agency collaboration among organs of state and various communities towards safer communities". The White Paper on Safety and Security has "an integrated approach to crime and violence prevention" as well as acknowledges that "building safer communities is not only the work of the police". The White Paper on Policing recognises that building a safer community through crime prevention is a shared responsibility. Both PPs and CPs agreed, and some strongly agreed that all role-players should take responsibility for communities feeling safe, whether at home or on the street. The lack of role players taking responsibility for communities feeling safe ranks them from lowest to highest—the lowest being political leaders, government departments, communities, various community leaders, and the highest being Community Policing Forums and police.

13   Conclusion

The findings of this study confirm the importance of police demonstrating professionalism, competency and excellence in the performance of their obligatory duties for them to earn community respect and support. Even though the NDP endorses "the professionalisation of the police by appointing highly trained and skilled personnel, and establishing a body to set and regulate standards of training", both police and community participants had little confidence that the police had the required skills. While the SAPS values emphasise the importance of "ensuring effective, efficient and economic use of resources and developing the skills of all members through equal opportunities", the public participants indicated less confidence in the police, specifically on how effectively and efficiently they use various resources and whether they had the necessary skills and resources to do their mandatory work.

The CPs also indicated that they lacked confidence that police were committed to their mandate of policing (from lowest to highest confidence score) participating in addressing root causes of crime, ensuring offenders are brought to justice, investigating crime without bias, protecting human rights when human rights were violated, creating a safe environment and preventing and combating crime. Such a lack of commitment to the policing mandate would have a negative impact on the police's role towards building safer communities.

Furthermore, while the NDP endorses "the professionalisation of the police by enforcing the Code of Conduct and a police Code of Ethics", adherence to ethical standards still remains a challenge. While the SAPS Code of Ethics endorses the integrity of SAPS employees and directs that "they should continually strive to uphold the mission, values, ethical principles and ethical standards of the SAPS" by acting honestly and responsibly in all situations and setting an example in the communities they serve, devotion to the Code remains a challenge. Although the values of the SAPS underscore the "using of powers given to police in a responsible way and providing a responsible, effective and high-quality service with honesty and integrity", community participants had little confidence in police on the constructs of ethical standards.

Although SAPS values emphasise the protection of everyone's rights and impartiality, respectfulness, openness and accountability to the community, community participants to a certain extent has little confidence in the police regarding certain constructs of respect for diversity. The CPs were not convinced that police were committed to service excellence, even though the SAPS Code of Ethics states that SAPS employees will undertake to work towards service excellence; SAPS employees' conduct will bring professionalism and commitment to service excellence; and the NDP directs the SAPS to recruit and select professional police for excellence and professionalism.

The values of the SAPS promote "cooperation with all communities, spheres of government and other relevant role-players" in creating safe and secure environments. The SAPS Code of Ethics encourages police to work with the public for the SAPS to gain public approval. It places emphasis on SAPS employees serving the best interests of the community and seek the approval of the broad community. The NDP underscores an integrated approach and coordinated efforts in building sustainable community safety. Though the PPs have comparatively high confidence that there is cooperation in policing, the CPs remain uncertain about this.

Together PPs and CPs were certain that there were high levels of crime in the community, a high incidence of becoming victims of crime in communities and of residents fearing crime. This feeling of unsafety nullifies the hypothesis of "the NDP Vision 2030 of people living in SA feeling safe and having no fear of crime". The study revealed that there are very few people who were investing in their safety by installing burglar alarm systems/guards in their houses. This indicated that people were still putting their safety in the hands of police and law enforcement. The role of media in community safety awareness still remained insignificant.

Police and community participants stated there was a lack of role-players taking responsibility for communities feeling safe. This validated the arguments of the researchers, scholars and actors and implementers of policies that policy implementation had become unsuccessful *inter alia* owing to a lack of public–private partnerships to assist the government in doing so. According to NDP, for communities feeling to feel safe, state and non-state capabilities should be mobilised and this necessitated "shifting to an integrated approach of active citizen involvement and co-responsibility". Further, for communities to feel safe, there should be interventions and plans to capacitate police, professionalise the police service, institutionalise and internalise accountability of management and leadership at all levels, eradicate illegal firearms in communities, address root causes and the impact of substance abuse, provide support programmes to empower parents and family structures, create a safe and supportive environment for women and children, institutionalise accountability of political leaders at all levels, advance economic development, collaborate with and mobilise communities, strengthen the CJS, institute an integrated approach to build safer communities, intensify police visibility, and provide access to suitable basic living conditions.

Based on the findings of this study, the research proposed a Safer Community Model for South Africa as depicted below.

13.1 Proposed Safer Community Model for South Africa

Chapter 12 of the NDP emphasises the significance of ensuring that by 2030 people must be and feel safe in the country and this includes while at home, work, school, and everywhere where they might be able to live freely without fear of some sort. The subsequent Safer Community Model for South Africa is recommended.

At the core of the model is an investment in the democratic principles as enshrined in the 1996 Constitution of RSA (Fig. 1).

In realising the objective of safer communities, the model proposes the four elements:

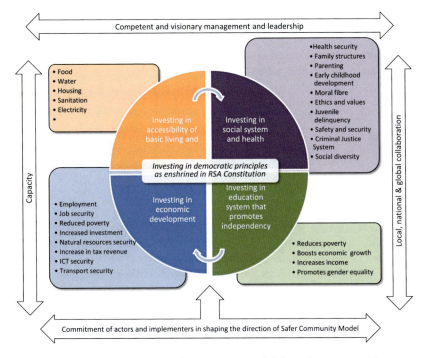

Fig. 1 Proposed integrated implementation model for safer communities

- Investing in the **accessibility of basic living and human needs** that encompasses food, water, housing, sanitation, electricity and clothing.
- Investing in **social and health system**s that address the following: health security, family structures, parenting, early childhood development, moral fibre, ethics and values, juvenile delinquency, safety and security, the criminal justice system, and social diversity.
- Investing in **an education system** that promotes independency for growth to address the reduction in poverty, boosts economic growth, increases income and promotes gender equality.
- Investing in **economic development**, addressing employment, job security, reduced poverty, increased investment, natural resources security, increase in tax revenue, ICT security and transport security.

The four **enablers** to realise the objective of safer communities are:

- Competent and visionary management and leadership
- Local, national and global collaboration
- Commitment of actors and implementers in establishing the direction of safer communities
- Building capable and sufficient capacity.

REFERENCES

Brown, L. P. (2013). *Policing in the 21st century: Community policing.* Author House.

Civilian Secretariat for Police. (2016). *White Paper on safety and security.* CSPS.

Department of Safety and Security. (1996). *The national crime prevention strategy.* Government of South Africa.

Farrell, G. (2007). Progress and prospects bin the prevention of repeat victimisation. In N. Tilley (Ed.), *Handbook of crime prevention and community safety.* William Publishing.

Fox, W., & Meyer, I. H. (1995). *Public administration dictionary.* Juta.

Government of South Africa. (1996). *The constitution of the Republic of South Africa Act (Act 108 of 1996).* Government Printers.

Government of South Africa. (2012). *National development plan vision 2030: Our future—Make it work.* National Planning Commission, Republic of South Africa; Government Printers.

Government of South Africa. (2016). *National crime prevention strategy summary.* https://www.gov.za/documents/national-CRIME-prevention-strategy-summary (Accessed 2 April 2018).

Greene, J. C., Caracelli, V. J., & Graham, W. F. (1989). Toward a conceptual framework for mixed-method evaluation designs. *Educational Evaluation and Policy Analysis, 11*(3), 255–274.

Kruger, T., Lancaster, L., Landman, K., Liebermann, S., Louw, A., & Rory Robertshaw, R. (2016). *Making South Africa safe: A manual for community-based crime prevention.* The Council for Scientific and Industrial Research (CSIR).

Laing, K., & Todd, L. (2015). *Theory-based methodology: Using theories of change for development, research and evaluation.* Newcastle University.

Leedy, P. D., & Ormrod, J. E. (2010). *Practical research planning and design* (9th ed.). Pearson Education.

Newham, G. (2005). *A decade of crime prevention in South Africa: From a national strategy to a local challenge.* Research report, Johannesburg: The Centre for the Study of Violence and Reconciliation.

Putnam, R. (1993). The prosperous community: Social capital and social life. *The American Prospect, 13*, 35–42.

Rauch, J. (2002). *Thinking big: The national urban renewal programme and crime prevention in South Africa's Metropolitan cities.* Research report, Johannesburg: Centre for the Study of Violence and Reconciliation.

Reisman, J., Gienapp, A., & Stachowiak, S. (2007). *A guide to measuring advocacy and policy.* Organizational Research Services for the Annie E. Casey Foundation.

South African Police Service. (1995). *South African Police Service Act, 1995 (Act 68 of 1995).* South African Police Service.

Shaftoe, H., & Read, T. (2007). Planning out crime: The appliance of science or act of faith? In N. Tilley (Ed.), *Handbook of crime prevention and community safety.* William Publishing.

Spohr, H., & Erkens, C. (2016). *Building safer communities through systemic approaches to violence prevention.* Deutsche Gesellschaft für Internationale Zusammenarbeit (GIZ) GmbH.

Statistics South Africa. (2018). *Victims of Crime Survey 2017/2018.* STATS SA.

Tilley, N. (Ed.). (2007). *Handbook of crime prevention and community safety.* William Publishing.

Weiss, C. H. (1995). *Nothing as practical as good theory: Exploring theory-based evaluation for comprehensive community initiatives for children and families.* New Directions for Evaluation.

African Demographic Dividend: Case Study of Nigeria's Age Structure

Abiodun Adewale Adegboye, Ebube Agbanusi, and Sunday Idowu Oladeji

1 INTRODUCTION

One of the major and pertinent factor that affect government and organisations as well as economic development around the globe is population age structure. It is the different share of individuals of the population at different life stages. Due to the distinct effects each age group has on economic growth, age structure has become of utmost importance globally, especially in developing nations like Nigeria. There are three age groups that make up a population: the young, the working/youthful, and the old. These variations in population composition are caused by changes in fertility or mortality rates (demographic transition). Changes in demographic composition can result in either a higher percentage of the elderly population, as is the case in the majority of developed countries, or a higher percentage of the young population, as is the case in developing countries.

A. A. Adegboye (✉) · S. I. Oladeji
Obafemi Awolowo University, Ile-Ife, Nigeria
e-mail: aadegboye@oauife.edu.ng

E. Agbanusi
Usman Dan-Fodio University, Sokoto, Nigeria

© The Author(s), under exclusive license to Springer Nature Switzerland AG 2023
A. I. Adeniran (ed.), *African Development and Global Engagements*,
https://doi.org/10.1007/978-3-031-21283-3_3

Currently, the world has been facing a decline in both the rate of fertility and mortality, however, in Nigeria, the rate of fertility and mortality have been slow in reduction (Nyamongo & Shilabukha, 2017). Nigeria's population has grown dramatically over the past few decades, going from 88 million people to over 201 million people. Similarly, the youthful population almost tripled and accounted for about 70% of the total population (Efuntade & Efuntade, 2020). This has made the country experience a rising increase in the youthful population which is currently an issue in population studies and literature in Nigeria.

However, given the rapid increase in both the total population and the youthful population, it was recorded that as of 2020, Nigeria had a GDP per capita of only USD 2083. This has made Nigeria the 135th in the world when compared to some of the developed countries that are currently experiencing an ageing population but recorded a higher GDP per capita. For instance, according to World Development Indicators (2020), Japan and United States have an ageing population but recorded GDP per capita of 28th and 13th positions respectively in the world. Also, even within the sub-Saharan region, South Africa recorded the 92nd position in the world. As the current growth rate has been decreasing over time, it suggests that Nigeria is experiencing a significant expansion in the total and youthful population without a corresponding increase in GDP per capita (Ogunleye & Owolabi, 2018). This has also affected both human and social development as postulated by the demographic dividend hypothesis.

The United National Population Prospect (2012) reported that more than half of Nigeria's population is less than the median age of 30 years. The youthful group has been projected to continually increase in the next 10–20 years. This increase should trigger the growth of an economy. However, in the context of the Nigeria, the graph below indicated that the larger youthful population has failed to impact economic development as expected, but rather it has contributed to an increasing crime rate, unemployment rate, and other social and political hazards (Fig. 1).

In Nigeria, various policies by the government and policymakers at different levels have been implemented to manage population growth and its effects. However, the investment in human capital stands out to be one of the major determinants for maximizing the output growth effect of youthful populations, as argued by a number of scholars including Barro (2001). This is because an increasingly youthful population with effective skills and knowledge may multiply and create a surplus of resources

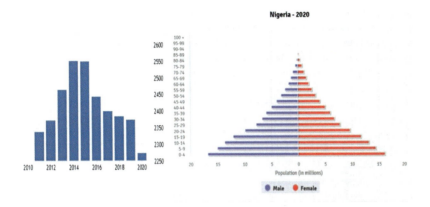

Fig. 1 GDP per capital Nigeria age structure

through their productivity that can improve economic growth and create sustainable development rather than hampering growth (Ahmad & Alikhan, 2018). This paper, therefore, attempts to examine the effect of age structure on economic growth in Nigeria by accounting for the role of human capital investment. This is to provide an enriched understanding and better prediction of the contributions of the interactions between age structure and human capital investment. Recent studies have shown that the emergence of an increase in the youthful population can introduce a window of opportunities that the country can benefit from and improve economic growth. Over the years, Nigeria has constantly witnessed significant growth in the total population. This made the country the most densely populated country in Africa and further tagged as the "Giant of Africa". From Table 1, it was shown that the average rate of Nigeria's population grew from 105.03 million to 180 million from 1991 to 2019. Also, in 2021, the total population increased to above 201 million populaces (Mariam, Tunde and Oluwakemi, 2016; and National Population Commission, 2021).

Table 1 indicates that the average growth rate of the population has been increasing in Nigeria. This has led to various debates on whether population growth can either contribute to rapid growth or negate growth and the need to identify the channel that an increasing population can contribute to growth. In the mid-1990s, the government of Nigeria promoted various policy measures to reduce fertility and mortality

34 A. A. ADEGBOYE ET AL.

Table 1 Trends of Nigeria's population size and growth rate

Population age structure and its growth in Nigeria: an overview

Year	Mean population size (million)	Mean annual growth (%)
1991–1994	105.03	2.53
1995–1999	113.60	2.49
2000–2004	128.77	2.53
2005–2009	146.54	2.63
2010–2015	176.65	2.65
2015–2020	193.07	2.73
1991–2020	143.94	2.59

Source Computed by the Author from World Development Indicator, 2020

rates as well as to increase the life expectancy rate of the population. These measures include the introduction of the use of contraceptives, the improvement of health services, nutrition and medical services for the population (Lee, 2003; Weil, 1999). This shifted the country from high fertility and mortality rate to a slightly decreasing level of fertility and mortality rates. Nigeria moved from the first phase of demographic transition to the second phase of demographic transition. In 1990, Nigeria experienced a decrease in the fertility rate from 6.49 births per woman to 5.28 in 2020. The number of children relative to the working population has been narrowing down, thus, increasing the number of the working population. Similarly, the mortality rate reduced to 24.95 deaths per 100 populations from 34.25; and the life expectancy rate increased from 45.92 to 54.81 at birth from 1990 to 2020 respectively.

In contrast to the global transition due to slow decline in both fertility and mortality rates, Nigeria stands as an outlier. Nigeria has only experienced a slight reduction in the dependency ratio. In 2020, the dependency ratio reduced to 87.32 dependent per 100 working-age adults from 92.76 dependents per 100 working-age adults as of the early 1990s. This contributed to approximately 12.2 million youthful populaces from approximately 32 million in 1990. This rapid increase affected the labour market as unemployment and under-employment rates in Nigeria have been exceptionally high. This has frustrated and discouraged some

Table 2 Drivers of population growth in Nigeria

Years	Fertility rate (births per woman)	Mortality rate (death per 1000)	Life expectancy at birth (years)	Dependency ratio (%)	Working-age population (%)
1991–1994	6.40	18.50	45.86	89.08	56.09
1995–1999	6.19	18.26	45.95	88.26	55.35
2000–2004	6.06	17.34	46.91	86.73	54.90
2005–2009	5.93	15.43	49.34	87.31	54.78
2010–2014	5.75	13.63	51.70	88.31	55.04
2015–2020	5.35	11.80	54.49	86.90	56.93
1991–2020	5.95	16.29	49.68	88.86	57.00

Source Computed by the author from World Development Indicator, 2020

of the youth from searching for jobs, making them economically inactive (World Trade Organisation, 2017). For example, out of the over 122 million youth in the country, it was recorded that those who are economically active and employed are approximately 47 million youth, those under-employed are more than 18 million, those who are unemployed are 23 million, and approximately 34 million of the working population are not in the labour force. This menace can be a result of low health services and lack of proper investment in education. The level of enrollment in education and investment in the educational sector and health sectors in Nigeria have been decreasing. In 2018, Nigeria was tagged the 157th out of 161 countries with low investment in human capital, while in Africa, it was the 24th country with a low human development rate (Odusola & Obadan, 2018) (Table 2).

2 THE DEMOGRAPHIC DIVIDEND HYPOTHESIS

Changes in population age structure have a significant effect on economic growth as each of the age groups can either hinder or promote the per capita income of a nation. As the proportion of children and the elderly increases, a nation tends to devote a higher ratio of its resources to cater to this group. This hampers economic growth. However, as the proportion of the working population increases due to the demographic transition from high fertility and mortality rate to low ones, thus, output per capita increases. The resulting output growth is referred to as a "demographic dividend".

A demographic dividend occurs when the dependency ratio is less than the working age. This is a result of a fall in fertility and mortality rate from high to low rates (demographic transition). A decline in the fertility rate reduces the proportion of young and dependent age groups and relatively increases the size of the productive labour force (Diogo et al., 2019). This makes the rate of investment and resources in catering to the youngest age group reduce and help to increase welfare of families as well as economic development. When the working population surpasses the non-working population, economic growth is positive and dividend is realized. On the contrary, when the working-age population is less than the non-working-age population, economic growth may be retarded and it hinders demographic dividend.

The demographic dividend is not spontaneous. Several phases and conditions are necessary for demographic dividends in a country to be ascertained. Each condition leads to different phases of demographic dividend. The phases are—*the first and second demographic dividend*. The first dividend can be realized from the fulfilment of the necessary condition in a country, while the second demographic dividend can be achieved from the fulfilment of the sufficient condition. However, among the various conditions, it has been proven that the necessary condition—fertility and mortality decline as well as an increase in the life expectancy of a country—favours the emergence of the first demographic dividend, provides a window of opportunity for a country and it can only occur once during a demographic transition (Mason, 2005). This dividend just lasts for a few decades and the opportunity must be exploited by the government while it lasts if such a nation desires to benefit from the second dividend. However, sufficient conditions—investment in human capital, working-age population, savings, financial market and job creation are prominent for the second demographic dividend to emerge and for it to become factual rather than potential. The first demographic dividend is significant and the benefit comes early, does not yield many benefits as it cannot last long. However, the second demographic dividend takes time to be realized, but when the various appropriate policy is fully fulfilled, the benefits are huge and remain longer in boosting economic growth (Mason, 2005). Table 3 shows the various conditions and phases of demographic dividend.

Nigeria as a nation has the potential in reaping the benefits of a demographic dividend, as its determinants in Nigeria are no different from the rest of the world (Topinka, 2018). However, fertility and mortality rates

Table 3 Requirements for demographic dividend

Necessary conditions (First phase of dividend)	Sufficient conditions (Second phase of dividend)
Declining fertility rate	Job creation/employment
Declining mortality rate	Financial market development
Increasing life expectancy	Human capital investment
	Female labour force participation
	Working-age population
	Saving

Source Adapted from Bloom et al. (2003)

have been slow. This has made the proportion of the youthful population (Bloom et al., 2016). In contrast, without the actualization of the various conditions, especially sufficient conditions, a country tends to miss the benefit attached to the opportunity. The working population must be well-matched with an increase in employment, proper investment in health and education (human capital investment) and an opportunity to open trade, there may be prevention of an increase in the rate of crime, political instability and retarded economic growth. These conditions are elucidated further in the next presentation.

2.1 First Demographic Dividend

The first demographic dividend opens the window of opportunity that can lead to a lasting dividend (second dividend). It has been argued that the first dividend which can last for 20 years could be influenced by factors such as a decline in fertility and mortality rates, and an increase in life expectancy.

Fertility rate/Mortality Rate: In global context, the fertility and child mortality rates have reduced the level of dependency ratio and increased the level of the working-age group over the last 30 years (Chaurasia, 2017). This increase in the working-age population has led to an increase in output per capita/demographic dividend. However, the fertility rate and mortality rate in Nigeria are still high. The majority of the population in Nigeria is still below the age of 19 years, according to the

National Population Commission, 2020. This means that the country has the potential in reaping the benefits of her age structure provided the fertility and mortality rate keeps decreasing or remains moderate. On average the fertility rate has only decreased from 6.4 average numbers of children in 1991 to 5.5 in 2021. This shows that there is already a gradual decline in the fertility rate and by 2050 it has the potential in doubling the working population and reducing the dependency ratio (Ahmad & Ali-khan, 2018). This decline in fertility spurs and encourages female participation in the labour market, as well as improve the level of investment in human capital, which is one sufficient condition for a lasting dividend.

Life expectancy: Globally, life expectancy has improved over the last 50 years to close to 60 years (Economic Commission for Africa, 2016). Similarly, the life expectancy rate in Nigeria has shown an increasing trend. In the last 30 years, the life expectancy rate rose from close to 46 years to 54 years. This implies that an increase in life expectancy can usher in the demographic dividend in Nigeria. This is captured in Table 2.

2.2   Final Demographic Dividend

The second and final demographic dividend sustains the window of opportunity and leads to a lasting dividend. It has been argued that the second dividend could be influenced by factors such as job creation or employment, financial market, human capital investment, female labour force participation, working-age population, and saving. From Table 3, it was depicted that to benefit from an increase in the working population, the decline in fertility and mortality rate which are the necessary condition for dividend, job creation/employment, and female participation rate must be encouraged. Also, an environment that encourages human capital investment, saving and financial market is needed to stimulate demographic dividends. Without actual realization of these conditions (policies), it is difficult for the necessary condition to strive in yielding the expected long-lasting demographic dividend. In sum, the gradual increase in the working population enhances Nigeria's potential to attain huge economic growth, but the actualization of sufficient conditions will be critical.

3 Review of Related Literature

From the theoretical viewpoint, population growth affects the level of resources and it tends to grow geometrically (Malthus, 1978) while the resources of a country only grow in arithmetic order. In line with this, there are three different schools of thought to verify the impact of population on resources, the standard of living and economic growth. They are the pessimistic, optimistic and neoclassical schools. However, based on the various controversies between the theories on the population–economic growth nexus, the need to look in-depth at the composition and structure of the population became necessary. Based on this, a theory of demographic transition emerged.

The theory of demographic transition provides more clarity on population, and how the different compositions emerge. It evaluates the effect of the different population age compositions resources and economic growth, emphasizing that an increase in resources and economic growth is majorly dependent on a 65% increase in the working population when compared to the dependent population (Foong, 2015; and Abbani, 2021). However, for the working population to be more effective and productive, there is a need to have technology (Solow, 1956), improve the skills and knowledge; the health of the population through a proper investment in human capital (Becker, 1993); and an increase in labour supply. This was further buttressed by the endogenous growth model, especially the AK model, which argued that an increase in the working population is not a guarantee for higher productivity. The theory concluded that the outcomes in an economy are dependent on the inputs (physical and human capital) as well as the technology invested into the population. In summary, this is justifiable in the context of the Nigerian economy where numerically, the population has been growing at a geometric rate while the GDP of the country grows at an arithmetic rate. Similarly, due to the introduction of demographic transition in the mid-1990s, Nigeria has been experiencing an increase in the youthful population as the majority of the population's median age is less than 20 years (Adeleke, 2019).

Using the empirical standpoints, the study provides an overview of the literature on population and economic growth. Just like the contradiction in the theoretical literature, the empirical findings also produced contradictory claims. Based on the numerous studies that were conducted on the relationship between population growth and economic growth, studies such as Bakan and Gokme (2016), Boztosun et al. (2016), Chen et al. (2015), Chong and Jeon (2006), Savaş (2008), Furuoka (2009), Bloom and Freeman (1988), Bloom and Sacks (1998), Bloom et al. (2011), Nwosu et al. (2014), Tartiyus et al. (2015), Hajamin (2015), Koduru and Tatavarthi (2016), Chaurasia (2017), Menike (2018) as well as Ogunleye and Owolabi (2018) supported the optimist view and concluded that an increase in population drives productivity through innovations and creativity. However, scholars such as Klasen and Lawson (2007), Prettner and Prskawetz (2010a), Song (2013), Jelilov and Musa (2016), Samuel (2016), Jaiyeoba (2015), Aidi et al. (2016), Young (2019) supported the pessimistic school of thought and concluded that an increase in population suppresses resources and further reduced the standard of living of the population, while Atanda et al. (2012) supported the neoclassical scholar and concluded that population growth can either drive or limit economic growth using the developed and developing countries. Their studies claimed that population growth in developed countries was positive to economic growth, while the developing countries' populations have a negative result on economic growth.

Based on the inconclusivity of population growth effects on resources, scholars have extended their exploration to the relationship between age structure and economic growth. For instance, Malmberg (1994), Bloom and Finlay (2009), Bloom and Williamson (1998), Lindh and Malmberg (1999), Brunow and Hirte (2006), Bloom et al. (2007), Lindh and Malmberg (2009), Brunow and Hirte (2009), Wei and Hoa (2010), Rutger and Jeroan (2011), Nagarajan et al. (2013), Young (2013), Drummond et al. (2014), Paulo (2014), Zhang (2015), Abrigo et al. (2016), Sarker et al. (2016), Wongboonsin and Phiromswad (2017), Miri and Maddah (2018), Bengtsson (2018), Ogunjimi and Oladipupo (2018), Wei et al. (2019), Lutz et al. (2019), Frini and Jedidia (2019), Kajimura (2020), Rovný et al. (2021), discovered a positive relationship, while scholars like Prskawetz et al. (2007), Thakur (2012), Nagarajan (2013), Golley and Zheng (2015), Young (2019), Ye et al. (2020) discovered a contradictory result.

Moreover, a few scholars have also hinted that the reason for the discrepancy in findings on the impact of age structure on economic growth is that there might be a relationship between age structure, human capital, and economic growth. For instance, Darrat and Yousef (2004), Peng (2006), Masoud and Marzie (2011), Cuaresma et al (2014), Ayuba (2016), Topinka (2018), Munir and Rana (2018), Kotschy and Sunday

(2018), Ekperiware et al. (2018) and Moroz et al (2021) concluded that the effect age structure has on economic growth is dependent on the level of investment in human capital and the utilization of the labour force.

4 Methodology

4.1 Theoretical Issues and Conceptualisation

The demographic dividend hypothesis forms the basic theoretical foundation for this study. This hypothesis makes claims on the long-term relationship between age structure and economic growth. It also helps in understanding economic growth that can result from an increasing proportion of working-age groups in a population that helps to foster productivity as a result of the level of investments in education and health. This hypothesis posits that an increase in the working-age population (15–64), as a result of the transition, raises the countries per capita productivity and opens a window of opportunity when compared to an increase in the dependency ratio. Thus, the demographic dividend is influenced by the changing population structure determined mainly by the combined forces of life expectancy and fertility rates (Bloom et al., 2013). In another view, the demographic dividend is not spontaneous and guaranteed as there is a need to fulfil certain conditions for this dividend to be actualized. Therefore, to verify this hypothesis in Nigeria, this study will look at the necessary and sufficient conditions that can ascertain demographic dividends. These will serve as a yardstick to determine if this hypothesis holds in Nigeria.

In the conceptual framework, the study established a relationship among population size, age structure, labour force, increase in labour supply, investment in human capital as well as economic growth.

As depicted in Fig. 2, the total population comprises different groups of population namely the younger age group, the labour force or the working-age group, and the elderly age group. Each of these groups has its various roles, significances, needs and levels of investment that affect economic growth. For instance, an increase in dependency ratio (children or older age group) as a result of an increase in fertility or an increase in life expectancy can reduce the standard of living and socioeconomic status of the citizenry. It is generally believed that an increase in the dependency ratio may increase consumption in education and health, reduce production, increase the budget deficit, decrease the income tax base, etc.

However, an increase in the working-age group (labour force) of a nation could increase productivity, the standard of living and economic growth (Uddin & Rezwana Karim, 2016; Zhang et al., 2015).

An increase in the working population, however, may be almost impossible if some enabling mechanisms are not present and/or implemented. These mechanisms include human capital development, and increase in labour supply through better employment opportunities can help the labour force contribute to their quotas, and acquire higher productivity and reap the demographic dividend. The working population or labour force can only give out what they have, and improve the productivity level in the labour market. Also, studies have shown that the size of a country's young population may not be the sole factor in enhancing economic growth.

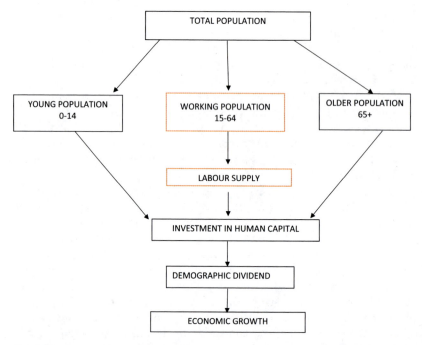

Fig. 2 The interrelationship among age structure, investment in human capital and economic growth

4.2 Model Specification

To capture the relationship between the role of human capital growth rate and population growth rate in explaining economic growth, this study propounded its conceptual framework. Following the empirical literature, this study examines the effect of age structure and human capital investment on economic growth using the employed model by Eigbiremolen and Anaduaka (2014) and Ahmad and Ali-khan (2018). Another variable such as gross fixed capital formation as used by Bloom et al. (2003) also seems to affect the productivity level of the population and impact economic growth. Integrating this variable into equations. The model specified in a functional form for both the growth and population rates are:

4.3 The Growth Rate Model

$$GDPGR_{t2} = \alpha_2 + \beta_2 POPGR_t + \phi_2 GFCGR_t$$
$$+ \delta_2 HCI_t + \gamma_2 CON\_C_t + \mu_{t1} \qquad (1)$$

where *GDPGR* denotes economic growth, *GCFGR* is gross capital formation growth rate, *CON_C is* control of corruption and *HCIGR* denotes human capital investment growth rate at time t. Control of corruption was also later identified as an important factor that can affect the transition of population growth to economic growth, especially in developing countries.

4.4 The Population Growth Rate Model

$$POPGR_{t3} = \alpha_3 + \beta_3 GDPGR_t + \phi_3 GFCGR_t + \delta_3 HCIGR_t + \mu_{t3} \qquad (2)$$

Meanwhile, all the variables are as already defined before while α_i is the intercept, β_i, ϕ_i, δ_i and γ_i are the coefficients of the defined variables and μ_{ti} is the error term (Table 4).

5 Results and Discussion

See Tables 5 and 6.

44   A. A. ADEGBOYE ET AL.

Table 4   Measurement of variables

Data descriptions

Label	Variable	Description	Source
GDPGR	Gross domestic product growth rate	Services, value added (constant LCU)	WDI (2020)
GCFGR	Gross capital formation (Annual % growth)	General government final consumption expenditure (current LCU)	WDI (2020
HCIGR	Annual human capital investment gross rate	This is the annual growth rate of the expenditure on Education and Health	WDI (2020)
POPGR	Annual population growth rate	Annual growth rate of the population ages 15–64	WDI (2020)
CON_C	Control of corruption	Measuring perceptions of the extent to which public power is exercised for private gain, including both petty and grand forms of corruption, as well as capture ¨ of¨ the state by elites and private interests	WGI (2020)

Table 5   Correlation matrix

	GDPGR	GCFGR	HCIGR	POPGR	CON_C
GDPGR	1.000				
GCFGR	0.159	1.000			
HCIGR	0.342	−0.092	1.000		
POPGR	−0.615	−0.129	−0.350	1.000	
CON_C	−0.659	−0.197	−0.260	0.569	1.000

GDPGR: Gross Domestic Products Growth Rate; GCFGR: Gross capital formation (Annual % growth). HCIGR: Annual Human Capital Investment Gross Rate; POPGR: Annual Population Growth Rate; CON_C: Control of Corruption
The correlation matrix shows the correlation between the variables of analysis to ensure that all the variables of interest are free from the problem of multicollinearity in the analysis.

Table 7 shows the results of the unit root test performed to know whether or not the data conform to the stationarity criteria of the ARDL model that is all the variables must be integrated either at a level I(0) or in the first difference I(1) or a combination but not of a higher order than one. The Augmented Dickey–Fuller (ADF) and Phillips–Perron (PP)

Table 6 Descriptive statistics

	GDPGR	GCFGR	HCIGR	POPGR	CON_C
Mean	2.572	0.024	0.142	0.026	2.295
Median	3.514	0.033	0.114	0.026	2.339
Maximum	12.458	0.342	0.703	0.029	2.437
Minimum	−4.260	−0.243	−0.218	0.024	2.005
Std. Dev.	3.925	0.133	0.244	0.002	0.117
Skewness	0.277	0.093	0.905	0.306	−1.150
Kurtosis	3.643	3.719	3.621	2.354	3.466
Jarque–Bera	0.570	0.436	2.897	0.627	4.362
Probability	0.752	0.804	0.235	0.731	0.113
Sum	48.864	0.464	2.700	0.501	43.605
Sum Sq. Dev	277.342	0.317	1.068	0.000	0.245
Observations	19	19	19	19	19

unit root test results shown in Table 7 show that all the variables are stationary at level I(0) or in first difference I(1). The length in ADF was automatically selected by Akaike Info Criteria (AIC) while that of Phillips–Perron (PP) truncation lag was based on the Newey–West bandwidth.

The ARDL bounds testing test developed by Pesaran (2001) for the cointegration of the dependent variable (GDP growth rate) and the independent variables to the established long-run relationship between GDP growth rate and all the independent variables (population growth rate, gross capital formation growth rate, human capital formation growth rate and control of corruption) in the first and second model. Table 8 shows the ARDL cointegration bounds test for Models 1 and 2. Both Models are statistically significant at 1%. Since the cointegration has been established for both models, we then proceed to the estimation of the long-run and short-run coefficients of each ARDL model. The Error Correction Model captures the short-run dynamics by the first differenced variables. The subsequent tables show the coefficients of the estimation of both the long run and short run respectively.

Table 9 (Model 1) indicates that the population growth rate has a significant negative effect on the GDP growth rate's present value at a 5% level of significance. Contrarily, the population growth rate doesn't have a significant effect on the growth rate of GDP at the 5% significant level in Model 2. The human capital investment growth rate coefficient for model 2 is statistically significant at a 1% significant level in the long

46   A. A. ADEGBOYE ET AL.

Table 7   Unit root test

| Variables | Augmented Dickey–Fuller (ADF) unit root test | | | | Status |
| | Levels | | First difference | | |
	Constant	Constant + trend	Constant	Constant + trend	
GDPGR	0.040**	0.328	0.000***	0.000***	I(0)
GCFGR	0.000***	0.000***	0.001***	0.006**	I(0)
HCIGR	0.013**	0.028**	0.007**	0.038**	I(0)
POPGR	0.732	0.304	0.002***	0.010**	I(1)
CON_C	0.057	0.219	0.001***	0.009**	I(1)

| Variables | Phillips–Perron (PP) unit root test | | | | Status |
| | Levels | | First difference | | |
	Constant	Constant + trend	Constant	Constant + trend	
GDPGR	0.132	0.017**	0.000***	0.000***	I(0)
GCFGR	0.000***	0.000***	0.000***	0.000***	I(1)
HCIGR	0.000***	0.001***	0.000***	0.000***	I(1)
POPGR	0.794	0.396	0.000***	0.000***	I(1)
CON_C	0.009**	0.252	0.001***	0.000***	I(0)

*** Significant at 1% and ** Significant at 5%

Table 8   The bounds F-test for cointegration test

| Models | F-statistic | Significance level (%) | Bound critical values** | |
			I(0)	I(0)
Model 1	5.886***	1	4.29	5.61
	3	5	3.23	4.35
		10	2.72	3.77
Model 2	11.535***	1	3.74	5.06
	4	5	2.86	4.01
		10	2.45	3.52

*** Significant at 1% and ** Significant at 5%

run. For model 1 in Table 8, unlike Model 2, the growth rate of human capital investment is not statistically significant at the 1% level in determining the growth rate in GDP in long run in Nigeria. While population growth rate maintains the same effect on the GDP growth but differs in the magnitude of the effect it produces. The result for Model 1 has the position that an increase in the population growth rate has a significant negative effect on the growth rate of GDP. Furthermore, the control of the corruption coefficient in Model 2 and the growth rate of gross capital formation is not significant in determining the growth rate in GDP in Nigeria in the models.

Table 10 shows short-run GDP growth rate dynamics. In model 1 the GDP growth rate for one period lagged has a retard immediate effect on the presents of GDP growth rate by 0.25 in Nigeria. Both one period lagged population growth rate and population growth rate have an immediate increase on the growth rate of GDP showing a temporary dividend from the increases in population growth rate to GDP growth rate while it varies in magnitude 1078.85 and 1222.12 in models 1 and 2 respectively at 5% level of significance in both of the models.

The gross capital formation growth rate coefficient of 4.768 and −1.062 for models 1 and 2 respectively, although the coefficients of GCFGR in each model contradict each other, only model 1 is statistically significant at a 1% significant level. One period lagged in the gross capital formation growth rate is statistically significant for both models at the same level of significance. While a 1% increase in a period lagged by gross capital formation growth will increase the GDP growth rate by 4.96 and 8.14% in models 1 and 2 respectively. This shows how crucial gross capital formation is in achieving growth in GDP in Nigeria. The ECM (−1) coefficients are −0.39 and −0.60 for models 1 and 2 respectively both are statistically significant at a 1% level. This indicates a quick rate of adjustment to the equilibrium point at 39 and 60% per annum for models 1 and 2 respectively, whenever there is a shock to the GDP growth rate in

Table 9 Long-run coefficient efficient dependent variable: growth rate

Variables	Model 1	Model 2
C	31.181 (0.019)**	52.510 (0.004)***
POPGR	−3117.061 (0.007)**	−10.522 (0.495)
GCFGR	4.670 (0.856)	9.428 (0.046)
HCIGR	12.899 (0.160)	2197.959 (0.002)***
CON_C		−13.417 (0.126)

*** Significant at 1%, ** Significant at 5%. The ARDL models were estimated based on Akaike Info Criterion (AIC)

48 A. A. ADEGBOYE ET AL.

Table 10 Short-run error correction coefficients

Variable	Model 1 (2, 2, 2, 0)	Model 2 (1, 2, 1, 2, 2)
C	31.181 (0.001)***	52.510 (0.001)***
ΔGDPGR$_{-1}$	−0.255 (0.034)**	
ΔPOPGR	1374.639 (0.001)***	1204.308 (0.001)***
ΔPOPGR$_{-1}$	1078.852 (0.010)**	1222.118 (0.006)**
ΔGCFGR	4.768 (0.008)**	−1.062 (0.341)
ΔGCFGR$_{-1}$	4.965 (0.004)***	8.136 (0.000)***
ΔHCIGR		4.677 (0.001)***
ΔCON_C		−5.701 (0.065)*
Δ(CON_C)$_{-1}$		11.810 (0.007)**
ECM$_{-1}$	−0.392 (0.001)***	−0.596 (0.000)***
Diagnostic		
R-squared	0.890	0.977
S.E. of regression	0.901	0.460
Equation Log likelihood	−17.839	−4.517
R-bar-squared	0.824	0.954
F-statistic	13.490 (0.000)***	42.591 (0.000)***
AIC	2.922	1.590
DW-statistic	1.676	2.379

*** Significant at 10%, ** Significant at 5%, * Significant at 10% and Δ is the Difference Operator

the previous period in Nigeria. It is negative as expected and statistically significant.

Table 11 showed for gross domestic product (GDP) growth rate models certified all the necessary diagnostic tests which are serial correlation, functional form, normality and heteroscedasticity. The cumulative sum of recursive residuals (CUSUM) and the cumulative sum of squares of recursive residuals (CUSUMQ) plots which show the stability tests of all the models showed that all the models are stable (Figs. 3 and 4).

6 Population Growth Rate

The population growth rate of a country can be economically induced as economic fortune can bring about an increase in the population of a country. This increase can be either from the natural growth rate of a country or from net emigrants. High income tends to population growth as people migrate to such a country coupled with the advancement in the healthcare system which has kept the death rate as low as possible. Given

Table 11 ARDL model diagnostic tests-economic growth model

LM test statistics	Model 1	Model 2
Serial correlation: CHSQ (1)	0.145 (0.868)	0.280 (0.782)
Functional form: CHSQ (1)	1.234 (0.309)	1.153 (0.362)
Normality: CHSQ (2)	6.391 (0.049)	1.044 (0.593)
Heteroscedasticity: CHSQ (1)	0.489 (0.843)	0.644 (0.750)

the above assertions, we proceed to make the population growth rate (POPGR) the dependent variable as a function of GDPGR, GCFGR, and HCIGR for Model 1, and analysis was carried out starting from bounds test cointegration to know whether or not a long-run relationship exists among the variables of interest. A model was also run to see the effect of the institution on population growth rate control in Nigeria. It results are present in the appendix.

Table 12 presents the results of the ARDL bound test for cointegration of the population growth rate and all the independents' variables for model 1. The result for model 1 in Table 12 established the existence of a long-run relationship among the variables of interest. Since the long-run cointegration has been established, we then proceed to the estimation of the long-run coefficients and the Error Correction Model (ECM) coefficients to obtain the coefficient of adjustment of the ECM (Table 13).

The long-run coefficient of GCFGR shows a negative impact of gross capital formation growth rate on the population growth rate but is not statistically significant at the 5% level, a 1% increase in the gross capital formation growth rate will lead to 0.108 decreases in Nigeria population growth rate in model 1 above. Similarly, the growth rate of human capital has a retard effect on the Nigeria population growth rate as a 1% increase in the growth rate of human capital will cause 0.065% decrease in population growth rate as people spend more years in schooling which elongate their settlement for family affairs and reduces their propensity for large family size. In Table 13, none of the coefficients of the variables in model 1 above is statistically significant at a 5% level of significance in the long run (Table 14).

In Table 13 while the GDP growth rate has no effect on the Nigeria population growth rate in the short run, it has an immediate effect on

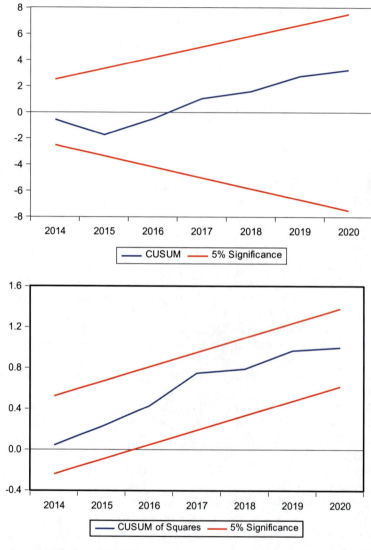

Fig. 3 Stability test: CUSUM

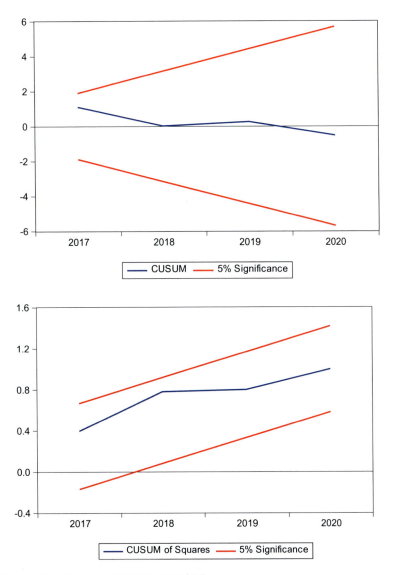

Fig. 4 Stability test: CUSUM SQUARE

52   A. A. ADEGBOYE ET AL.

Table 12   Long run estimates

Models	F-statistic	Significance level (%)	Bounds critical values**	
			I(0)	I(0)
Model 1	8.0128***	10	2.37	3.20
k = 3		5	2.79	3.67
		1	3.65	4.66

*** Significance at 10% and ** at 5%   k=lag length

Table 13   Estimation of long run coefficients dependent variable: POPGR

Variables	Model 1
C	0.050 (0.576)
GDPGR	−0.108 (0.799)
GCFGR	−0.108 (0.799)
HCIGR	−0.065 (0.796)

Table 14   Short-run estimation coefficients dependent variable: ΔPOPGR

Variables	Model 1 (1, 2, 0, 0)
ΔGDPGR	0.001 (0.001)***
ΔGDPGR$_{-1}$	0.001 (0.002)***
ECM$_{-1}$	−0.045 (0.000)***
Diagnostic	
R-squared	0.824
S.E. of regression	0.001
Equation Log likelihood	106.880
R-bar-squared	0.799
AIC	−12.221
DW-statistic	2.772

*** and ** depicts significance at 1% and 5%, and Δ is the Difference Operator

the population growth rate in model 1 at a 1% level of significance. In the same vein, a period-lagged of GDP growth rate has an immediate positive effect on Nigeria's population growth rate in both models while it differs in the magnitude of effect and level of significance respectively. This implies that a 1% increase in the growth rate of GDP will accelerate

Table 15 ARDL model diagnostic tests-population growth model

	Model 1
Serial Correlation: CHSQ (1)	1.175 (0.145)
Functional Form: CHSQ (1)	0.328 (0.581)
Normality: CHSQ (2)	0.219 (0.897)
Heteroscedasticity: CHSQ (1)	2.600 (0.088)

the growth rate population of Nigeria by 0.001% in the model. The ECM (-1) coefficient for the model is negative and statistically significant as expected. Has a coefficient of -0.045 which indicates a slow speed of adjustment to the equilibrium at 4.45% per annum whenever there is a sudden shock to the population growth rate in the previous period.

The results displayed for population growth models certified all the necessary diagnostic tests on serial correlation, functional form, normality and heteroscedasticity (as shown in Table 15). Also, the population growth rate model passed the stability tests as shown by the cumulative sum of recursive residuals (CUSUM) and the cumulative sum of the squares of recursive residuals (CUSUMQ) graph (Fig. 5).

7 Discussion of Findings

The findings from this study showed that the working population increases steadily as fertility and mortality rate decreases, while human capital investment measured by government investment in education and health fluctuates in some periods. Also, in verifying the demographic dividend hypothesis in Nigeria through some vital conditions that can propel the demographic dividend. The study found that the apriori expectations for the necessary conditions that contribute to the demographic dividend were fulfilled. This includes a large working population relative to the non-working population, low fertility and a decline in the child mortality rate. However, in Table 5.10b, Nigeria as a country did not meet all the sufficient conditions. This implies that Nigeria as a nation has experienced some level of demographic dividend (first stage) by fulfilling all the necessary conditions, however, for a long-time dividend in the country, the sufficient conditions such as an increase and positive impact of human capital investment must be fulfilled which in Nigeria are yet to be fully achieved and fulfilled. Furthermore, the demographic dividend is feasible

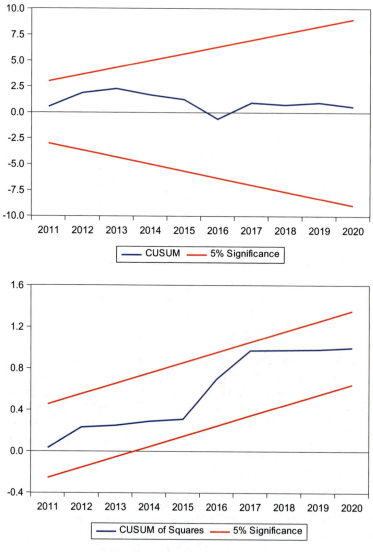

Fig. 5 Stability test: CUSUM

in the country, but may not last long if policies that should promote the fulfilment of the sufficient conditions are not fulfilled. Amparo (2017).

The fulfilment of the necessary condition alone without the commensurate fulfilment of the sufficient condition may limit a country from maximally benefiting from the window opportunity of dividend (Bloom et al., 2016). Similarly, the result shows that all the necessary conditions variables were in line with the expected outcomes by the previous scholars, except for the fulfilment of the sufficient condition such as the human capital investment that revealed a negative impact on economic growth. Therefore, for Nigeria to fully benefit from the demographic dividend there is a need to ensure effective human capital investment and provide employment opportunities for its populace; ensure proper accountability and transparent spending, and if ignored, this will lead to demographic tragedy rather than a dividend.

Unit root test was carried out using the Augmented Dickey–Fuller test. The results showed that some variables were stationary at levels I(0), while others were stationary at first difference I(1) for Nigeria. For the Johansen cointegration test, the null hypothesis of no co-integration was rejected at 5% level of significance, indicating that there was a long-run relationship among the explanatory variables in Nigeria. To evaluate the linkage between age structure and economic growth, the Vector autoregression (VECM) estimation was used, and while verifying demographic dividend in Nigeria, ARDL estimate was used.

It was observed that the average population size increased during the study period. During the period from 1991 to 1994, the population size was 105 million and by 2019, the average population grew to 180 million. Similarly, the average annual growth rate of the population from 1991 to 2019 was 2.78% Throughout the period 1991 to 2019, it was observed that the fertility rate in Nigeria slightly decreased from 6.40 to 5.96. On the issue of life expectancy in the country, the female average life expectancy at birth tends to be higher than the male counterpart. Between the periods of the study, the average male life expectancy rate at birth in years increased from 44.61 to 53.42. Similarly, the average female life expectancy rate at birth in years increased from 47.12 to 54.60. However, for the average rate, the female life expectancy was 49.88 years, while the male counterpart was 47.83 years.

This increase may be accounted for by the improvement in health care services. On the issues of population structure by age distribution, Nigeria had a large working population or youthful population.

Throughout the study period, the median age of the population was 17.83. Similarly, 44.05% of the total population was within the 0–14 age bracket, while approximately 53.19% of the total population comprised the working population, and 2.84% of the total population are above 64+. The study also found a declining share of the dependency population from 44.77 in 1991–1994 to 43.69 in 2015–2019, and an increasing share of the working population from 52.34% in 1991–1994 to 53.50% in 2015–2019.

It was also observed that the percentage of males in the labour force was higher than the female labour force. The male labour during the study period was 56.27% while the female labour force was 43.73%. Also, within the study period, the male labour force decreased from 57.64% from 1991 to 1994 to 54.37% from 2013 to 2019, while the female labour force increased from 42.36% from 1991 to 1994 to 45.63% from 2013 to 2019.

In order to examine the linkage between age structure and economic growth in Nigeria, VECM model is adopted. Based on this empirical analysis, the following findings were identified. The coefficient of the interaction of age structure on economic growth in Nigeria was positive and statistically significant in Nigeria. A one percent increase in age structure is associated with a 0.71% increase in economic growth. The coefficient of the interaction of human capital investment on economic growth in Nigeria was negative. A one percent increase in human capital investment is associated with a 0.20% decrease in economic growth. Also, a one percent increase in gross fixed capital formation is associated with a 0.08% increase in economic growth.

It is also observed that Human capital investment and economic growth shocks on average explain 0.05% and 0.19% of economic growth respectively. It is observed that a one standard deviation shock in gross fixed capital formation (GFCF) generates a negative impact on economic growth. This implies that gross fixed capital formation shocks explain the average −0.15% variance on economic growth. At a rate of about 47% every year, the system corrects its previous period. From the variance decomposition table, it is observed that the working-age population and gross fixed capital formation explained 79.61% and 50.73% variances in the 10th period. Also, human capital investment and gross fixed capital formation account for 68.82% and 32.22% variation % in the long run respectively. The issues of the demographic factors that influenced the age structure of a country were examined graphically as well as with regression estimation. The coefficient of age structure for both the short run and long run was positive and statistically significant in Nigeria ($t = 2.08$, $p < 0.05$; $t = 2.21$, $p < 0.05$) respectively.

The coefficient of fertility rate was positive and statistically significant in Nigeria ($t = -3.01$, $p < 0.05$). The coefficient of the mortality rate was negative and statistically significant in Nigeria ($t = 2.08$, $p < 0.05$). Human capital investment was not sufficient to influence economic growth as it was negative and not statistically significant ($t = -1.11$, $p > 0.05$). Nigeria met the necessary conditions, namely a decrease in fertility rate and mortality rate, an increase in the working population, and an increase in life expectancy rate. However, Nigeria did not meet sufficient conditions, namely an increase in labour force participation, declining dependency ratio, increase in population-employment rate and increase in human capital investment that can lead to a realization of demographic dividend. This signifies that Nigeria has a prospect for dividends, however, to maximally benefit from the window of opportunity both the necessary and the sufficient conditions must be fulfilled (Bloom et al., 2016).

Based on the above findings, the study arrived at the following conclusions. The study found that the working population in Nigeria has been increasing at a steady rate during the study period. Also, the life expectancy rate trended upward, while mortality rate and fertility rate decreased during the study period. This implies that Nigeria currently has a unique chance of attaining and benefiting maximally from a demographic dividend, however, for this to be more realistic and feasible the need to ascertain the sufficient conditions must be considered and realized in the country. This sufficient condition includes government investment in education and health; an increase in labour force participation rate and a reduction in the dependency ratio.

Additionally, based on the findings from the long-run analysis of VECM and ARDL to determine the link between age structure on human capital investment and economic growth, the study concluded that a shock in age structure would increase economic growth, while human capital indicated a negative response to economic growth. Policy such as government investment in education and health should be adopted so that it will not have an adverse effect on economic growth. It is only a healthier and educated workforce that can maximally influence economic growth. Government should ensure transparency and accountability in fund spending so as to yield a more befitting outcome.

Government should adopt a policy that will help reduce the level of fertility rate of the populace such as contraceptives to encourage the female population to participate in the labour market and promote economic growth. Government should provide more employment opportunities for the working age group so as to ensure full utilization of the population. This will enhance dividend and economic growth, reduce the rate of crime and reduce youth unemployment in the nation. A critical look at the economic growth reveals that the input of the working population has been lessened and this has implications in the long run. Therefore, it is suggested that the government encourages the labour force to work by creating a more flexible and favourable labour market that will enable a high labour participation rate in the Nigerian economy.

Earlier studies in this area in Nigeria focused mostly on the impact of population on economic growth. Hence, little attempt was made to the impact of population age structure on human capital investment and economic growth. This research adds to the body of knowledge by examining and providing information on the effect of Nigeria's age structure, human capital investment and economic growth. It further broadens the existing knowledge by adopting impulse response and variance decomposition to examine the linkage between age structure and economic growth by verifying demographic dividend in Nigeria. This study provides a useful guide to the policymakers in making decisions that can help the increasing working-age population. This will help to avert the potential negative effect an increasing working population can have on an economy. The strength of the study is that the effect of age structure on human capital and economic growth was established. A limiting factor of the study is that it did not consider the age structure dependency population such as the young population (0–14) and the ageing population (64 and above). This hindered the study from considering the effect of the dependency ratio on human capital investment and economic growth.

References

Abbani, A. Y. (2021). Nigeria's demographic transition and implications on the attainment of sustainable development goals. *Global Journal of Social Sciences*, *20*, 1–10.

Abrigo, R. M., Racelis, R. H., Salas, J. M., & Herrin, A. N. (2016). Decomposing economic gains from population age structure transition in the

Philippines. *The Journal of the Economics of Ageing, 2,* 2212–8280. https://doi.org/10.1016/j.jeoa.2016.09.00

Ahmad, M., & Ali-khan, R. E. (2018). Age structure, human capital and economic growth in developing economies: A disaggregated analysis. *Pakistan Journal of Commerce and Social Sciences, 12*(1), 229–252.

Aidi, H. O., Emecheta, C., & Ngwudiobu, I. M. (2016). Population and economic growth in Nigeria: Is there empirical evidence of causality? *International Journal of Advances in Social Science and Humanities, 4*(2), 59–66.

Amparo, C. C. (2017). The age structure of human capital and economic growth. *Institute for International Economics, 4*(6).

Atanda, A. A., Aminu, S. B., & Alimi, O. Y. (2012). *The role of population on economic growth and development: Evidence from developing countries* (Online at MPRA Paper No. 37966).

Ayuba, T. (2016). *A comparative study of the effect of age structure on economic growth in Nigeria and South Africa.* MSc Thesis of the Department of Economics OAU.

Bakan, S., & Gökme, S. (2016). A driving force of economic growth in Turkey: Human capital. *Athens Journal of Mediterranean Studies, 2*(1), 7–20.

Barro, R. J. (2001). Human capital and growth. *American Economic Review, 91*(2), 12–17.

Becker, G. S. (1993). *Human capital: A theoretical and empirical analysis with special reference to education.* University of Chicago Press.

Bloom, D.E., Canning, D., & Sevilla, J. (2003). *The demographic dividend: A new perspective on the economic consequences of population change.* RAND Population Matters Monograph Series. RAND Corporation.

Bloom, D. E., Canning, D., & Rosenberg, L. (2011). *Demographic change and economic growth in South Asia: Program on the global demography of aging* (PGDA Working-Paper, No. 67).

Bloom, D. E., Canning, D., Fink, G., & Finlay, J. E. (2007). *Fertility, female labor force participation, and the demographic dividend.* Program on the global demography of aging (PGDA Working Paper No. 2507).

Bloom, D. E., & Finlay, J. E. (2009). Demographic change and economic growth in Asia. *Asian Economic Policy Review, 4*(1), 45–64.

Bloom, D. E., & Freeman, R. B. (1988). Economic development and the timing and components of population growth. *Journal of Policy Modeling, 10*(1), 57–81.

Bloom, D. E., Humair, H., Rosenberg, L., Sevilla, J., & Trussel, J. (2013). *A demographic dividend for Sub-Saharan Africa: Source, magnitude, and realization* (IZA Germany Discussion Paper No. 7855).

Bloom, D. E., Kuhn, M., & Prettner, K. (2016). *Africa's prospects for enjoying a demographic dividend* (Discussion Paper Series IZA DP, No. 10161).

Bloom, D. E., & Sachs, J. D. (1998). Geography, demography, and economic growth in Africa. *Brookings Papers on Economic Activity, 2*, 207–295.

Bloom, D. E., & Williamson, J. G. (1998). Demographic transitions and economic miracles in emerging Asia. *World Bank Economic Review, 12*(3), 419–456.

Boztosun, D., Aksoylu, S., & Ulucak, Z. S. (2016). The role of human capital in economic growth. *Economics World, 4*(3), 101–110.

Chaurasia, R. A. (2017). Fertility, mortality and age composition effects of population transition in China and India. *Federal Institute for Population Research, Comparative Population Studies, 42*, 149–186.

Cuaresma, J. C., Lutz, W., & Sanderson, W. (2014). Is the demographic dividend an education dividend? *Journal Demography, 51*(1), 299–315.

Chen, J., Wang, H., Wen, P. M., Fang, F. L., & Song, M. (2015). Chinese Gini coefficient from 2005 to 2012 based on 20 grouped income data sets of urban and rural residents. *Journal of Applied Mathematics*, 1e17.

Darrat, A. F., & Yousef, D. A. (2004). Fertility, human capital, and macroeconomic performance: Long-term interactions and short-run dynamics. *Applied Financial Economics, 14*(8), 537–554.

Drummond, P., Thakoor, V., & Yu, S. (2014). *Africa rising: Harnessing the demographic dividend* (International Monetary Fund, IMF Working Paper, African Department, WP/14/143).

Economic Report on Africa (2016). United Nations Economic Commission of Africa, Addis Ababa, Ethiopia.

Eigbiremolen, G. O., & Anaduaka, U. S. (2014). Human capital development and economic growth: The Nigeria experience. *International Journal of Academic Research in Business and Social Sciences, 4*(4), 25–35.

Ekperiware, M., Olatayo, T., & Mayor, A. (2018). Forecasting the effect of dominating working age population in the Nigeria economy. *Journal of Scientific and Engineering Research, 5*(3), 23–34. ISSN: 2394-2630

Foong, W. M. (2015). Human capital and economic growth in developing countries. *International Journal of Recent Advances in Organizational Behaviour and Decision Sciences (IJRAOB), 1*(4), 632–642.

Frini, O., & Jedidia, B. K. (2019). The age structure change of population and labour productivity impact. *Economics Bulletin, 38*(4), 1831–1844.

Furuoka, F. (2009). Looking for a J-shaped development-fertility relationship: Do advances in development reverse fertility declines? *Economics Bulletin, 29*(4), 3067–3074.

Hajamini, M. (2015). The non-linear effect of population growth and linear effect of age structure on per capita income: A threshold dynamic panel structural model. *Economic Analysis and Policy*. https://doi.org/10.1016/j.eap.2015.04.002

Jaiyeoba, S. V. (2015). Human capital investment and economic growth in Nigeria. *African Research Review, 9*(1), 30–46.

Jelilov, G., & Musa, M. (2016). The impact of government expenditure on economic growth in Nigeria. *Sacha Journal of Policy and Strategic Studies, 5*(1), 15–23.

Kotschy, R., & Sundez, U. (2018). Can education compensate the effect of population aging on macroeconomic performance? Evidence from panel data. 67th Economic Policy Panel Meeting.

Lee, R. D. (2003). The demographic transition: three centuries of fundamental change. *Journal of Economic Perspectives, 17*(4), 167–190.

Lutz, W., Cuaresma, J. C., Kebede, E., Prskawetz, A., Sanderson, W. C., & Striessnig, E. (2019). Education rather than age structure brings demographic dividend. *Proceedings of the National Academy of Sciences, 116*(26), 12798–12803.

Malthus T. R. (1978). *An essay on the principle of population.* J. Johnson, London.

Mason, A. (2005). Demographic dividends: The past, the present, and the future. *Awaji Yumebutai International Conference Center near Kobe,* Japan, 17–18.

Masoud, A. M., & Marzie, E. (2011). Impact of human capital on economic growth in Iran. *European Journal of Economics, Finance and Administrative Sciences,* (41), ISSN 1450-2275.

Mariam, G. S., Tunde, E., & Oluwakemi, O. (2011). The challenges of human resource management practices in the informal sector in Nigeria. *Chinese Business Review, 10*(5), 340–351.

Menike, H. R. (2018). A literature review on population growth and economic development. *International Journal of Humanities Social Sciences and Education (IJHSSE), 5*(5), 67–74.

Miri, N., & Maddah, M. (2018). The effect of the age structure of the population on economic growth in Iran. In *American Institute of Physics, AIP Conference Proceedings* 1978, 200004. https://doi.org/10.1063/1.5043839

Moroz, S., Palkovič, J., & Horská, E. (2021). Impact of demographic structure on economic development of Ukrainian coastal regions. *Sustainability, 13,* 1798. https://doi.org/10.3390/su13041798

National Population Commission (2021). The National Policy on Population for Sustainable Development. Federal Government of Nigeira. File retrived online: https://drive.google.com/file/d/1_LqDbc249sq_bo_Cmp a8VSZBmk8fHJSj/view

Nyamongo, I. K., & Shilabukha, D. K. (2017). *Youth, health and development: Overcoming the challenges towards harnessing the demographic dividend.* A paper delivered at the African Union second session of the specialised technical committee on health, population and drug control (STC-HPDC-2), Addis Ababa, Ethiopia.

62   A. A. ADEGBOYE ET AL.

Odusola, A. F., & Obadan, M. I. (2018). Productivity and unemployment in Nigeria. *Research in Agriculture and Applied Economics.*

Ogunjimi, J., & Oladipupo, D. (2018). *Dynamics of demographic structure and economic growth in Nigeria.* Department of Economics, University of Ibadan, Nigeria. MPRA Paper No. 94988.

Ogunleye, O. O., & Owolabi, O. A. (2018). Population Growth and Economic Growth in Nigeria: An appraisal. *International Journal of Management, Accounting and Economics, 5*(5).

Peng, X. (2006). Macroeconomic consequences of population ageing in china—A computable general equilibrium analysis. *Journal of Population Research, 30*(4), 12–22.

Pesaran, M. H., Shin, Y., & Smith, R. J. (2001). Bounds testing approaches to the analysis of level relationships. *Journal of Applied Econometrics, 16,* 289–326.

Prettner, K., & Prskawetz, A. (2010a). Demographic change in models of endogenous economic growth. *Institute of Mathematical Methods in Economics, Vienna University of Technology, 18,* 593–608. https://doi.org/10.1007/s10100-010-0179-y

Prettner, K., & Prskawetz, A. (2010b). Demographic change in models of endogenous economic growth: A survey. *Central European Journal of Operations Research, 18,* 593–608.

Prskawetz, A., Kögel, T., Sanderson, W. C., & Scherbov, S. (2007). The effects of age structure on economic growth: An application of probabilistic forecasting in India. *International Journal of Forecasting, 23,* 587–602.

Solow, R. M. (1956). A contribution to the theory of economic growth. *The Quarterly Journal of Economics, 70*(1), 65–94.

Song, S. (2013). *Demographic changes and economic growth: Empirical evidence from Asia* (Paper No. 121, Honors projects Illinois Wesleyan University).

Tartiyus, E. H., Mohammed, I. D., & Amade, P. (2015). Impact of population growth on economic growth in Nigeria. *IOSR Journal of Humanities and Social Science (IOSRJHSS), 20*(4), 115–123. e-ISSN: 2279-0837, p-ISSN: 2279-0845

Thakur, V. (2012). *The demographic dividend in India: Gift or curse? A state-level analysis on differing age structure and its implications for India's economic growth prospects* (Working Paper Series, No. 12–128).

Topinka, M. (2018). The impact of human capital and population age structure on economic growth. Charles University, Faculty of Social Sciences, *Institute of Economic Studies, 61.*

Uddin, M. J., & RezwanaKarim, M. (2016). Harnessing the demographic dividend: opportunities and challenges for bangladesh. *IOSR Journal of Humanities and Social Science (IOSR-JHSS), 21*(8), 8–13.

United National Population Prospect. (2012). http://esa.un.org/unpp

The World Bank, World Development Indicators (WDI), (2020). Population Growth Rate in Nigeria.

World Trade Organisation. (2017). Annual Report. Geneva, Switzerland.

Young, A. O. (2019). Economic growth and demographic dividend nexus in Nigeria: A vector autoregressive (VAR) approach. *Asian Social Science, 15*(2), 37–59.

Zhang, H., Zhang, H., & Zhang, J. (2015). Demographic age structure and economic development: Evidence from Chinese provinces. *Journal of Comparative Economics, 43*(1), 170–185.

Emergency Healthcare Accessibility in the Context of COVID-19 in Nigeria

Olufemi Mayowa Adetutu, David Aduragbemi Okunlola, Ayoola Peter Ijisakin, Sukurah Adewumi Hammed, and Yusuf Segun Ogunsanya

1 BACKGROUND

Published evidence has shown that 82 million persons were forcibly displaced in 2020 across the globe, which comprised 48 million internally displaced persons (IDPs) (UNHCR, 2021). Low- and middle-income countries share the largest burden of internally displaced persons and refugees all over the world (Schneiderheinze & Lücke, 2020; Verme & Schuettler, 2021). In 2022, 235 million people are in dire need of humanitarian assistance, with a surge in internally displaced persons (84 million forcefully displaced in the world), and more than half are below 18 years (UNHCR, 2021). The population of internally displaced persons increased to 51 million and Africa accounts for one-third of this number (Africa Report on Internal Displacement, 2019).

O. M. Adetutu (✉) · D. A. Okunlola · A. P. Ijisakin · S. A. Hammed · Y. S. Ogunsanya
Department of Demography and Social Statistics, Obafemi Awolowo University, Ile-Ife, Nigeria
e-mail: oadetutu@cartafrica.org

© The Author(s), under exclusive license to Springer Nature Switzerland AG 2023
A. I. Adeniran (ed.), *African Development and Global Engagements*,
https://doi.org/10.1007/978-3-031-21283-3_4

Vulnerable populations, including refugees, asylum seekers and internally displaced persons have experienced lack of access to basic needs, such as the high cost of food items, the inability to access basic medical health care and maintain personal hygiene (UNHCR, 2020). Although these vulnerable groups are resilient having survived political persecution and displacement by insurgency, their capacity to sustain their means of livelihood in the context of additional burden tend to be overstretched. Also, the vulnerable groups stay in war-torn contexts where public infrastructure and social services have diminished in quality and quantity to meet the needs of the displaced populations. Meanwhile, people of concern face both supply and demand-driven challenges in accessing health care, including the high cost of medical bills, transport costs, distance to medical facilities and lack of competent personnel (WHO, 2020).

In Nigeria, about 2.3 million persons are displaced in the Northern part of the country owing to terror attacks, banditry and insurgency (UNHCR, 2020). UNHCR (2021)'s report showed that 1.6 million women need humanitarian assistance in Northeastern Nigeria (UNHCR Annual Report, 2020). Many displaced persons fled violence and settled in IDP camps in the region. Women and children in these IDP contexts are disproportionately impacted and vulnerable to socio-cultural, economic and sexual and reproductive health (SRH) challenges. Political instability, insurgency and terror attacks are implicated in this population disruption. Meanwhile, the sudden surge in the number of displaced persons (DPs) creates serious humanitarian needs. Their well-being is negatively affected due to terror attacks which have been a recurring decimal.

In their camps, displaced people's living conditions are squalid, accompanied by a substantial demand for increased financial, material and healthcare needs. Besides, the presence of the vulnerable people in the host community has a profound influence on employment, food supplies, among other public goods such as housing, education and access to sexual and reproductive health within host communities (Verme & Schuettler, 2021). The aggregate welfare of these vulnerable populations depends on support from the government and international development agencies. However, the dwindling financial resources of the international partners owing to economic recession and lack of political will from African countries make their basic needs unmet and well-being deplorable (Becker &

Ferrara, 2020; Maystadt et al., 2019; Verme & Schuettler, 2021). Similarly, previous studies demonstrate that displaced women of reproductive ages require the urgent need of sexual and reproductive health care because, in humanitarian contexts, women are exposed to unwanted pregnancies, unsafe abortion, gender-based violence, forced marriage and exchanged sex. There is growing evidence in scholarly literature that displaced persons are in a volatile context, which is a fertile ground for sexual violence, unsafe abortion and increased early and forced marriage (Okezie-Okeh, 2020).

The social and economic impacts of the COVID-19 pandemic have plunged people displaced by security and environmental challenges also referred to as persons of concern (POC) deeper into hitherto disadvantaged socio-economic conditions. Other deplorable qualities of life attributable to the pandemic include lack of access to quality healthcare services, restricted mobility and loss of means of livelihood, among others (United Nations High Commissioner for Refugee, 2020). Restriction of movement, closure of socio-economic institutions and infrastructure across the country and enforcement of physical and social distancing aimed at preventing and flattening the curve of COVID-19 have negatively impacted many vulnerable groups in Nigeria.

The resources of the government are lean because of the impact of the pandemic. Available evidence suggests that the gross domestic product (GDP) of many African countries has dropped owing to the socio-economic impacts of the pandemic and the fall in the global prices of oil. On account of this, the Nigerian government changed the budget benchmark from $57 per barrel to $30 per barrel (World Bank, 2020). Hence, it has been difficult for the Nigerian government to provide finance to individuals and corporate bodies supporting vulnerable populations, especially those in the informal sector, and displaced population, among others.

Most displaced people are already in need of assistance owing to their vulnerable conditions as a result of displacement, either in refuge settlements, internally displaced population (IDP) camps or camp-like settings or within the host communities with many relying on humanitarian assistance (World Health Organisation, 2020). Their poor sexual and reproductive health, including unwanted pregnancies, sexually transmitted infections and gender-based violence are influenced by lack of food and money, parents' encouragement of exchanged sex and coercive marriage, precipitated by the vulnerable situations of internally displaced persons and/or refugees (Casey, 2015; UNFPA, 2016). This situation may be exacerbated by the COVID-19 pandemic as the health system in Nigeria worsened during the pandemic and affected access to healthcare facility.

There is growing concern about how vulnerable populations access health and medical needs amid the pandemic and limited support from the national government and development partners. However, there is a systematic absence of studies that investigate access to healthcare services for refugees, IDPs and asylum seekers in Nigeria. Hence, this study aims to generate insights into the influence of the pandemic on access to healthcare services among the displaced population in Nigeria.

2 Methods

2.1 Data Source and Sampling Method

The data analysed in this study was collected by United High Commissioner for Refugees (UNHCR) in collaboration with development partners in Nigeria. This survey was conducted during the first wave of the COVID-19 pandemic in Nigeria (between the 1st of June 2020 and to 17th of July 2020). The survey was done to examine the impact of the COVID-19 pandemic on the socio-economic lives of the refugees, internally displaced persons (IDPs), returnees, asylum seekers, stateless persons and communities hosting displaced people (i.e. host communities). The thematic areas covered in the survey were health and nutrition, protection, food security, livelihood and social cohesion and basic needs.

A disproportionate stratified random sampling method was utilized to select households for the interview in Adamawa, Benue, Borno, Cross River, FCT Abuja, Lagos, Ogun state and Yobe state. Survey weighting factors are included in the final data to ensure accurate estimations. Thus, 5134 displaced households were interviewed across the states; the weighted size is 375,090 households. In this study, households with special needs such as having pregnant or lactating women, older persons or children at risk, disabled members, or separated children were considered as the target population. This is because they relatively have a higher need for health and medical care. They constitute 368,685 (i.e. weighted size) in this study.

2.2 Measures

The outcome variable was "access to health facility". Households were asked if they had access to health facilities (a) before the COVID-19 and

(b) during the pandemic. This was a dichotomous variable that indicated access (1) or no access (0). Questions were also asked about barriers to health facilities that the respondents faced before and during the pandemic. There was a multiple-response question in which respondents were to select as many possible barriers they experienced in accessing health facilities. The barriers were proximity to health facilities, quality of care at the facilities, lack of medicines at the facilities, lack of competent personnel, fear of COVID-19 (only applies to the COVID-19 period) and transportation cost. Each response option was treated as a dichotomous variable [1 (picked the option) or 0 (didn't pick the option)] and summed up to arrive at the number (or magnitude) of barriers to a health facility.

Household' income before and during pandemic (less than 21,000 naira (1), 21,000 naira to 40,000 naira, 41,000 naira to 60,000 naira, 61,000 naira to 80,000 naira and above 80,000 naira) were considered. Others are population group (host community member, IDPs/IDPs returnee, Asylum seeker/refugee/refugee returnee), site type (camp (informal/formal) or Collective Settlement/Centre, Host Community and Registration Site), receipt of assistance from humanitarian organization or government due to COVID-19, effect on COVID-19 on means of livelihood, gender of household head (male or female). Also, region of residence was categorized to reflect the geopolitical zones in Nigeria: North East (Adamawa, Yobe, Borno and Taraba), North Central (Benue, Taraba state and FCT Abuja), South West (Ogun state and Lagos) and South South (Cross River state).

Given the threat of insurgency and other forms of crisis in the country especially in the northern region and its threat to health care (Adamu et al., 2019; Solanke, 2018), we included the number of violent events per region from the 1st of January 2020 to 31st of July 2022. This information about violent events was extracted from the website of the Armed Conflict Location and Event Dataset (ACLED, 2022).

2.3 Data Analysis

All variables were described using frequency and percentage distributions. This was followed by a McNemar test which was performed to examine the difference in access to a health facility before and during the COVID-19 pandemic. Multiple logistic regression models were fitted to examine the determinants of access to health facilities before and during

70   O. M. ADETUTU ET AL.

the pandemic respectively. The major differences between the two models fitted under the two timelines were the inclusion of explanatory variables that apply only to the period of COVID-19. The variables include restriction to movement in the area due to COVID-19, the COVID-19 pandemic effect on means of livelihood and receipt of assistance from government and humanitarian organizations during the pandemic. The significance of the odds ratio from the multiple logistic regression models was tested against a 5% level of significance, while their corresponding 95% confidence intervals were also computed.

3   RESULTS

3.1   Descriptive Analyses

Based on Table 1, the vast majority of the households had access to health facilities before (94.5%) and during the COVID-19 pandemic (89.6%). Most households faced less than three barriers to health facilities before the COVID-19 pandemic (88.9%) while less than one-fifth faced less than three barriers during the COVID-19 pandemic (18.6%). Most households earned below 21,000 naira before (77.3%) and during the pandemic (80.1%) respectively. Most of the households were employed (90.2%). More than half of the households were male (56.5%). Majority of the households were host community members (70.9%) while most of the households resided in camps (informal/formal) or collective settlement/centres (80.5%). Most of the households were located in the North East region (95.4%). More than three-quarters of states had experienced a total of 623 crises and violent events (86.7%). More than half of the households (56.6%) experienced movement restrictions due to COVID-19. About 51% of the households experienced income or job loss or reduced income due to the COVID-19 pandemic.

3.2   McNemar Test and Determinants of Access to Health Facilities Before and During the COVID-19 Pandemic

The result from the McNemar test showed a significant difference in access to health facility before and during the COVID-19 pandemic ($p < 0.001$). Based on the results, of women who were able to access health facilities before COVID-19, a considerable number of them (25,354) were not able to access health facilities during the pandemic (Table 2).

Table 1 Descriptive statistics

Variables	%	Frequency
Access to health facilities before COVID-19		
No	5.5	19,757
Yes	94.5	339,611
Number of barriers before COVID-19		
0	36.1	133,033
1	31.0	114,119
2	21.8	80,506
3	8.9	32,800
4	1.6	5883
5	0.3	1231
6	0.3	1112
Current monthly income in naira before the COVID-19		
Less than 21,000	77.3	285,171
21,000–40,000	16.9	62,311
41,000–60,000	3.2	11,963
61,000–80,000	1.1	4016
Greater than 80,000	1.4	5224
Employment status		
Unemployed	9.8	35,966
Employed	90.2	332,719
Age group of the head of household		
<19	0.8	2843
19–59	86.4	317,355
>59	12.8	47,108
Gender of the head of household		
Female	43.5	158,179
Male	56.5	205,473
Population group		
Host community member	70.9	261,359
IDPs/IDPs returnees	10.8	39,761
Asylum seeker/Refugee/Refugee returnee	18.3	67,254
Site type		
Camp (informal/formal) or Collective Settlement/Centre	80.5	293,052
Host Community	19.0	69,097
Registration Site	0.5	1931
Region		
North East	95.4	351,576 ara>
North Central	0.5	2000
South South	3.9	14,210
South West	0.2	900

(continued)

72 O. M. ADETUTU ET AL.

Table 1 (continued)

Variables	%	Frequency
Number of violent crises		
29	0.0	129
35	0.1	288
38	2.4	8789
41	3.9	14,210
51	0.2	612
79	5.0	18,380
111	1.3	4940
113	0.5	1870
623	86.7	319,466
Access to health facilities during COVID-19		
No	10.4	36,873
Yes	89.6	316,848
Number of barriers during COVID-19		
1	0.3	1253
2	18.3	67,650
3	34.9	128,566
4	21.8	80,469
5	16	59,021
6	5.6	20,613
7	2.2	7939
8	0.5	1976
9	0.3	1197
Current monthly income in naira (during the COVID-19 (Ref = Less than 21,000)		
Less than 21,000	80.1	295,407
21,000–40,000	16.5	60,922
41,000–60,000	2.7	10,073
61,000–80,000	0.5	1845
Greater than 80,000	0.1	438
Restriction to movement in area due to COVID-19		
No	43.4	160,145
Yes	56.6	208,541
Impact of COVID-19 pandemic on means of livelihood		
Loss of income/Job/Reduced income	51.9	191,297
Not affected	14.0	51,537
Restrictions to income source	32.4	119,290
Others (including those not affected)	1.8	6561
Any assistance received during the COVID-19		
No	47.2	174,115
Yes	52.8	194,570

Table 2 Mcnemar's test

	Before COVID-19	During COVID-19		Total
		No access	Access	
No access		11,039	7405	18,444
Access		25,354	306,366	331,720
Total		36,923	313,771	350,163

McNemar's $chi^2(1) = 9834.45$, Prob $> chi^2 = 0.0000$.

According to the results from the multivariable analysis (Table 3), female household heads were 40% less likely to gain access to health facilities before the COVID-19 pandemic (OR = 0.60; CI = 0.37–0.98). The likelihood of having access to health facilities was 67% higher among households in the IDPs/IDPs returnees (OR = 1.67; CI = 0.95–2.93), In terms of region, households in the North East, North Central and South South were 82% (OR = 0.18; CI = 0.07–0.44), 87% (OR = 0.17; CI = 0.07–0.41) and 51% less (OR = 0.49; CI = 0.22–1.08) likely to access health facilities respectively than their counterparts in the South West. An increase in the number of violent events was associated with a 0.2% increase in the likelihood of accessing health facilities before the pandemic (OR = 1.002; CI = 1.001–1.004). With respect to income, households earning between 61,000 naira and 80,000 naira were three times more likely to access health facilities than those earning less than 21,000 naira (OR = 3.93; CI = 1.42–10.91).

During the pandemic, factors associated with access to health facilities were movement restriction, receipt of assistance during the pandemic, site type and region. Based on the results, households that experienced movement restriction were 43% more likely to access health facilities (OR = 1.43; CI = 0.99–2.06) than those who did not experience restriction. Households that received any form of assistance were two times more likely to access health facilities than those who did not receive assistance (OR = 2.59; CI = 1.74–3.87). Households in registration sites were 55% less likely to access health facilities (OR = 0.45; CI = 0.24–0.85) than those in host communities. Relative to households in the South West region, those in North East, North Central and South South were 97% and 4 times more likely to access health facilities respectively (OR = 4.91; CI = 2.34–10.3, OR = 1.97; CI = 1.03–3.80 and (OR = 4.37; CI = 2.45–7.77 respectively).

Table 3   Multiple logistic regression of access to health facilities before and during COVID-19

Variables	Before COVID-19 Odds ratio (95% Confidence Interval)	During COVID-19
Number of barriers during COVID-19		1.068 (0.942 − 1.209)
Current monthly income in naira (during the COVID-19 (Ref = Less than 21,000)		
21,000–40,000	0.965 (0.514 − 1.812)	
41,000–60,000	1.390 (0.469 − 4.122)	
61,000–80,000	3.929*** (1.416 − 10.91)	
Greater than 80,000	0.362 (0.0951 − 1.379)	
Employment status (Ref = Unemployed)		
Employed	1.561 (0.842 − 2.892)	1.483 (0.846 − 2.597)
Restriction to movement in area due to COVID-19 (Ref = No)		
Yes		1.430* (0.993 − 2.060)
Impact of COVID-19 pandemic on means of livelihood (Ref = Not affected)		
Loss of income/Job/Reduced income		0.465** (0.227 − 0.955)
Restrictions to income source		0.615 (0.289 − 1.310)
Others (including those not affected)		2.580* (0.935 − 7.118)
Any assistance received during the COVID-19 (Ref = No)		
Yes		2.595*** (1.739 − 3.872)
Age group of the head of household (Ref = 19–59 years)		
Less than 19 years	0.556 (0.0922 − 3.353)	2.032 (0.802 − 5.148)
Greater than 59 years	1.337 (0.659 − 2.716)	1.299 (0.734 − 2.300)
Gender of the head of household (Ref = Male)		
Female	0.601** (0.367 − 0.985)	0.861 (0.602 − 1.233)
Population group (Ref = Host community member)		
IDPs/IDPs returnees	1.671* (0.951 − 2.934)	0.853 (0.489 − 1.487)

Variables	Before COVID-19 Odds ratio (95% Confidence Interval)	During COVID-19
Asylum seeker/Refugee/refugee returnee	0.709 (0.369 − 1.363)	0.943 (0.557 − 1.596)
Site type (Ref = Host Community)		
Camp (informal/formal) or Collective Settlement/Centre	1.288 (0.684 − 2.425)	1.438 (0.919 − 2.250)
Registration Site	0.987 (0.520 − 1.874)	0.452** (0.241 − 0.846)
Region (Ref = South West)		
North East	0.180*** (0.0737 − 0.440)	4.906*** (2.339 − 10.29)
North Central	0.168*** (0.0684 − 0.415)	1.976** (1.027 − 3.801)
South South	0.486* (0.218 − 1.085)	4.367*** (2.453 − 7.772)
Number of violent crises	1.002*** (1.001 − 1.004)	1.001 (1.000 − 1.002)
Number of barriers before COVID-19	0.952 (0.779 − 1.162)	
Current monthly income in naira during COVID-19 (Ref = Less than 21,000)		
21,000–40,000		0.948 (0.594 − 1.513)
41,000–60,000		1.096 (0.425 − 2.826)
61,000–80,000		0.524 (0.0922 − 2.981)
Greater than 80,000		1.570 (0.294 − 8.394)

Confidence intervals (CI) in parentheses
***$p < 0.01$, **$p < 0.05$, *$p < 0.1$

4 Discussion

Vulnerable populations, especially those displaced forcibly are often neglected and humanitarian support from development partners may not be sufficient to address health challenges and other sexual and reproductive health needs of displaced persons because of limited access to essential services (UNCHR & REACH, 2020). Against this background, we examined the factors associated with access to health facilities before the pandemic; we went further to examine the extent to which these factors and other pandemic-period-related factors determine access to health facilities. This is with a view to generating empirical insights that policymakers and humanitarian agencies can leverage in addressing the health challenges among displaced persons amid the pandemic.

The study revealed that the likelihood of accessing health facility before COVID-19 pandemic was associated with some socio-demographic and economic factors such as being a female-headed household (than a male-headed household). This study teased out issues that revolve around gender inequality and access to health care which may account for the difference in access to health care before and during the pandemic. The result revealed that female head of households were less likely to have access to healthcare facilities before the pandemic. Available evidence has documented gender inequality in access to basic needs for vulnerable women (IDMC, 2021). In a context where patriarchal values are predominant such as Nigeria, the socio-economic status of displaced persons accounts for their access to health care. The observable explanation for this is that vulnerable men can eke out a living outside of their camps and source for healthcare services. For example, displaced men were able to do menial jobs in a study to access health care despite the lack of medical supplies in the camps (UNHCR, 2021). In Nigeria, the employment rate is 90% higher for displaced women, and 36% of displaced men are employed compared with 15% of displaced women (IDMC, 2021). Therefore, a gender gap exists in the livelihood, social protection, health and education of displaced people which speaks to the need to address these challenges.

Displaced people under humanitarian support most often lack access to sexual and reproductive health services (Kwankye et al., 2021). In this study, other socio-demographic characteristics of displaced persons to a very large extent feed into access to health care, considering that, from this study, IDP/IDP returnees (a population group) were more likely to access health facility before the COVID-19 pandemic than households in host communities. However, amid the pandemic, our results showed that there was no significant relationship between population group and access to health facilities after controlling for other factors most especially COVID-19-related challenges. This implies that there are other factors determining access to health facilities during the pandemic. Among these factors is site type because, in this study, households in the registration site (rather than the host community) was negatively associated with access to health facilities.

Households residing in the North East, North Central and South South regions respectively (relative to the South West region) were less likely to access health facilities before the COVID-19 pandemic. These findings underscore the predominance of population displacement in the Northern part of the country where access to health care is challenging. Also, the incessant crisis plaguing the South South region (unlike in the South West) may cause disruptions in the health system in such regions, leading to limited access to health facilities. Surprisingly, during the pandemic, while controlling for other factors among which were COVID-19-related challenges, we found out that households in North East, North Central and South South regions respectively were more likely to access health facility during the COVID-19 pandemic. This may be due to a low number of COVID-19 cases (as of 17th July 2020) in the northern and South South region than in the South West region which comprises Lagos and Ogun States. This may have combined with rigorous enforcement of movement restrictions and lockdowns especially in Lagos and Ogun State (World Health Organisation, 2020) than in the northern states. This may account for a reduction in access to health facilities (during the first wave of the pandemic) in the South West region.

In terms of income, earning 61,000–80,000 naira (compared to earning less than 21,000 naira) were negatively associated with access to health facility pre-COVID-19. The plausible reason is that displaced people who earn more money can foot medical bills. This is consistent with the claim that access to more income and financial resources can increase health care affordability and accessibility (Tirado et al., 2020). Despite this income-health access nexus, income was not associated with access to health facilities during the pandemic after controlling for factors induced by the COVID-19, which include number of barriers during the pandemic, assistance during the pandemic and impact of COVID-19 on means of livelihood.

A striking finding which is counterfactual is that movement restriction owing to the pandemic was positively associated with access to health facilities during the pandemic. Prior studies have established that displaced persons are disproportionately affected by the COVID-19 pandemic which deprived them of access to healthcare services (UNHCR, 2021). This is because the risks of COVID-19 infection are amplified for displaced persons, in part because of the crowded environment in which they stay. The finding of this study regarding higher access to health care in the context of COVID-19 restrictions is a departure from previous studies because of the availability of medical supplies and other health needs which may be available in the displaced camps. The policy implication of this is that health care should be provided constantly, without stock-out in the camps of displaced persons.

The study further revealed that loss of income, job or reduced income during the pandemic reduced the likelihood of accessing health facilities than those that were not affected. Considering that some out-of-pocket expenses are expected from the vulnerable persons in the context of little health assistance by development partners, welfare interventions should be implemented to cushion the effects of the COVID-19 pandemic on the socio-economic status of displaced households in order to enhance their access to facility-based health services.

The study also revealed that recipients of financial and material support (from humanitarian services of government and development partners) is associated with higher access to health facilities. This stance is echoed by many studies which showed that displaced persons who had access to humanitarian assistance have access to healthcare services (Clingain et al., 2021; Kwankye et al., 2021). Policymakers should not relent in providing humanitarian assistance to displaced households. This study finally established that displaced persons who stayed in IDPs camps had lower access to healthcare services while those in the northern regions had better access to healthcare services during the pandemic. The plausible explanations for these include.

5 Strengths and Limitations

This study used nationally representative secondary data which was developed by international partners and developed countries and this allows for external validity of the study. This is unique in its own right because it compared access to healthcare services in the period before and during

COVID-19 pandemic which is a departure from previous studies. Yet, there are some limitations. The issue of recall bias and social desirability should be considered as regards the implications of the results of the study. Due to the cross-sectional and concurrent nature of the data collected on the outcome and explanatory factors, no causal relationship was established. We cannot rule out the effect of social desirability on the findings, especially with respect to self-reported income levels and impacts of COVID-19.

Although the number of violent events per state was included, this is aggregate-level information instead of cluster-level information on the number of events because there may be cluster/community disparities in the level of violence which may in turn lead to between-cluster disparity in access to health facilities. Besides, the survey data analysed was collected during the first wave of the pandemic, thus limiting the generalizability of our findings beyond the first wave. Nevertheless, this study provided a starting point and preliminary findings among displaced households in Nigeria which future studies can explore further. Besides, in this study, a first of its kind in Nigeria, we analysed nationally representative secondary data which improved the external validity of inferences of our findings. This study is also unique because it compared access to health facilities before and during the COVID-19 pandemic to assist policymakers and humanitarian organizations in addressing emerging challenges of access to health care—induced by the pandemic—among the displaced households in Nigeria.

6 CONCLUSION

This study revealed that access to health facilities among displaced households reduced between the period before and during the pandemic. Specifically, the study established that gender inequality shaped access to health facilities before the advent of the pandemic. Displaced persons with higher income and IDPs returnees had higher access to health care. Displaced persons in the northern parts of the country and households with higher income had better access to health care before the advent of COVID-19. On the other hand, displaced persons whose movements were restricted and had access to humanitarian support had better access to healthcare services. Displaced persons who stayed in IDPs camps and in northern regions had better access to health care.

References

Adamu, P. I., Okagbue, H. I., Akinwumi, I., & Idowu, C. (2019). Trends of non-communicable diseases and public health concerns of the people of north-eastern Nigeria amidst the Boko Haram insurgency. *Journal of Public Health, 29*, 553–561. https://doi.org/10.1007/s10389-01901157-2

Becker, S. O., & Ferrara, A. (2020). Consequences of forced migration: A survey of recent findings, *Labour Economics, 59*, (2019), 1–16, ISSN 0927-5371, https://doi.org/10.1016/j.labeco.2019.02.007.

Casey, S. E. (2015). Evaluations of reproductive health programs in humanitarian settings: A systematic review. *Conflict and Health, 9*, 1–14.

Clingain, C., Jayasinghe, D., Hunt A., & Gray Meral, A. (2021). *Women's economic empowerment in the face of Covid-19 and displacement: Restoring resilient futures* (HPG commissioned report). ODI. https://odi.org/en/pub lications/womenseconomicempowerment-in-the-face-of-covid-19-and-displa cement-restoring-resilient-futures.

IDMC. (2019). *Africa report on internal displacement.* IDMC.

IDMC. (2021). *Global report on internal displacement 2021.* IDMC. https://www.internaldisplacenment.org/global-report/grid2021/

IOM. (2020). *Displacement tracking matrix (DTM) Northeast Nigeria.* IOM.

Kwankye, S. O., Richter, S., Okeke-Ihejirika, P., Gomma, H., Obegu, P., & Salami, B. (2021). A review of the literature on sexual and reproductive health of African migrant and refugee children. *Reproductive Health, 18*, 1–13. https://doi.org/10.1186/s12978-021-01138-3

Maystadt, J. F., Hirvonen, K., Mabiso, A., & Vandercasteelen, J. (2019). Impacts of hosting forced migrants in poor countries. *Annual Review of Resource Economics, 11*(1), 439–459.

Okezie-Okeh, C. (2020, 4 July). 'Baby Factory in the Church' Saturday Sun.

Schneiderheinze, C., & Lücke, M. (2020). *Socio-economic impacts of refugees on host communities in developing countries* (PEGNet Policy Studies, No. 3). Kiel Institute for the World Economy (IfW), Poverty Reduction, Equity and Growth Network (PEGNet).

Solanke, B. L. (2018). Factors associated with use of maternal healthcare services during the Boko Haram insurgency in North-East Nigeria. *Medicine, Conflict and Survival, 34*, 158–184. https://doi.org/10.1080/13623699.2018.151 1358

The Armed Conflict Location & Event Data Project (ACLED) (2022). *ACLED is a disaggregated data collection, analysis, and crisis mapping project.* ACLED.

Tirado, V., Chu, J., Hanson, C., Ekström, A. M., & Kågesten, A. (2020). Barriers and facilitators for the sexual and reproductive health and rights of young people in refugee contexts globally: A scoping review. *PLoS ONE, 15*, e0236316. https://doi.org/10.1371/journal.pone.0236316

UNFPA. (2016). *Adolescent girls in disaster and conflict: Interventions for improving access to sexual and reproductive health services.* UNFPA.

UNHCR. (2020). *Annual report. Sexual and gender-based violence Northeast Nigeria. UNHCR's contribution to prevention, risk mitigation and multi-sectoral response. Internally displaced persons and returnees in Borno, Yobe, Adamawa states Northeast Nigeria.* UNHCR.

UNHCR. (2021a). *Figures at a glance.* https://www.unhcr.org/en-us/figures-at-a-glance.html. (Accessed 10 Sep 2021).

UNHCR. (2021b). *Global trends: Forced displacement in 2020* (Technical report). UNHCR.

UNHCR. (2021c). *Nigeria emergency.* https://www.unhcr.org/en-us/nigeria-emergency.html (Accessed 10 Sep 2021).

Verme, P., & Schuettler, K. (2021). The impact of forced displacement on host communities a review of the empirical literature in economics. *Journal of Development Economics, 150,* 102606.

World Bank. (2020). *COVID-19 (Coronavirus) drives sub-Saharan Africa toward first recession in 25 years.* https://www.worldbank.org/en/news/press-release/2020/04/09/covid-19coronavirus-drives-sub-saharan- africa-toward-first-recession-in-25-years (Accessed 17 Apr 2020).

World Health Organisation. (2020). *State of the world's nursing.* https://apps.who.int/iris/bitstream/handle/10665/331673/9789240003293-eng.pdf

Self-medication Practices in Covid-19 Era: Insights from Caregivers to Under-Five Children in Southwestern Nigeria

Oluseye Ademola Okunola, Mabayoje Anthony Olaniyi Aluko, and Abdulrahman Azeez Aroke

1 INTRODUCTION

The perception of self-medication practice by caregivers to their under-five children needs to be assessed. Nworie et al. (2018), reported different ways in which mothers understand what self-medication meant to them. These include, consulting a doctor if symptoms of an illness are not relieved, using leftover drugs for future illness, and also perceived it that only doctors should give the right to use drugs. These showed that the mothers were knowledgeable of the practice but in different contexts. However, in a descriptive cross-sectional study performed to understand the perceptions and practices about self-medication among college medical students in Pakistan located in Multan by Noor et al. (2017), various perceptions were noted. About 24.2% of them acknowledged it as a good practice, 42.1% of them identified with it as an acceptable practice and 33.7% of the students reported it to be unacceptable practice.

O. A. Okunola (✉) · M. A. O. Aluko · A. A. Aroke
Obafemi Awolowo University, Ile-Ife, Nigeria
e-mail: ookunola@cartafrica.org

© The Author(s), under exclusive license to Springer Nature
Switzerland AG 2023
A. I. Adeniran (ed.), *African Development and Global Engagements*,
https://doi.org/10.1007/978-3-031-21283-3_5

The various challenges observed during the pandemic period were mostly heralded around the healthcare system and healthcare delivery. Among them was the reduced accessibility and limited affordability of healthcare services to the people (Ahmed et al., 2020). The scenario inadvertently influenced the practice of self-medication by individuals. The anxiety caused by the emergence of the novel coronavirus disease (COVID-19) globally has made many Nigerians resort to self-medication for purported protection against the disease, amid fear of contracting it from health workers and hospital environments (Wegbom et al., 2020).

Social distancing phenomenon, a strategy introduced by various countries to mitigate the spread of COVID-19 contributed to self-medication practice (WHO, 2020). This strategy, though well implemented, was met with resistance in some communities. The fear of contracting the virus as the social distancing phenomenon was widely exhibited to curb the spread of COVID-19 culminated into self-medication practices (Wegbom et al., 2020). This was due to variations in the social norms and values in those settings. The attitude and perception of the health workers to the pandemic aggravated the practice. Due to the barrier created by the social distancing in form of inaccessibility to health workers by the patients, hence patients resolved to self-care in the form of self-medication practice whenever they took ill.

Another strategy introduced was the lockdown phenomenon which means closure and non-availability of various social services including healthcare facilities enhanced the practice of self-medication. The COVID-19 pandemic has triggered a general lockdown in most of the world, leaving the general sense that the only resource that people has is to self-help, self-care, and self-medicate (Matias et al., 2020). Also, inappropriate self-medication, recognized as one of the indirect health effects of the COVID-19 pandemic, is especially worrisome because of reported toxicity and unproven efficacy of various drug combinations touted as cures for the disease (Osaigbovo et al., 2020). This evidence has demonstrated the impact of COVID-19 pandemic era on the practice of self-medication.

Suja et al. (2019) highlighted that most (73.3%) residents in an urban slum in India were highly knowledgeable that self-medication means the use of medication without doctor's consent. This was a cross-sectional observational study with the aim to assess the knowledge and attitude of self-medication practices among the residents of an urban community. Though the participants were not specifically the caregivers of under-five children but constituted individuals engaged with the practice. Hence, they demonstrated a considerable understanding of what self-medication practice could be.

Among pregnant women in Northern Nigeria by Attahiru et al. (2018), it was reported that almost all of them (98.4%) were aware of self-medication to be the use of drug without prescription from a qualified doctor and less than half perceived it as a serious threat to their health and the health of their unborn baby. This signified that most pregnant women had a moderate understanding of what the practice is and its attendance complication.

Muoneke et al. (2018) in his assessment of caregivers' perception of self-medication practice to their under-five children during febrile illness revealed divergent views on the practice. It was reported that as much as 92.0% of the parental figures attested that self-medication for febrile conditions in kids who were underneath 5 years was vital. Thirty-two percent additionally said that the administration of fever drugs never recommended by a specialist was inescapable and vital. While, 71.0% of guardians announced that they don't typically counsel specialists for the solution of medication for the feverish condition of kids beneath 5 years old consistently, as much as (85.5%) parental referenced that they utilized medications recently endorsed for fever in dealing with the kids. Medicines and herbs utilization were simply the commonest prescription practices among the caregivers as 91.0%, enjoy such separately. One hundred and eight (48.9%) parental figures avowed that self-prescription for fever kept going as long as the patent medication/customary healer suggested. Evidently, the study pointed out that the majority of the caregivers vividly understand what the practice is, though in different dimensions.

2   Aim of Study

To assess caregivers' knowledge of self-medication practices to under-five children in Southwestern Nigeria.

Brief Literature Review (about 2 pages should be included here as a separate section of the paper).

3 RESEARCH DESIGN

3.1 Study Design and Locations

Qualitative exploratory design was used to explore the self-medication practices by the caregivers to their under-five children in the study area.

Considering the nature of this research study design and the research questions, for the study to have a general representation of the states in southwestern Nigeria, two states were selected for the study based on the cosmopolitanism and non-cosmopolitanism nature of the states. The southwestern (SW) Nigeria comprises of six states which are predominantly of the Yoruba tribe (Ajala, 2009). The language generally speaking in this region is major, Yoruba language. Culturally these states are homogenous. However, there are some features which differentiate the states such as the level of commercialization, population density, religion, land mass, and different cultural practices (Ajala, 2009). The six states in this region are Lagos, Ogun, Oyo, Osun, Ekiti, and Ondo states. Among them, Lagos and Osun states were selected for the study.

4 STUDY POPULATION

This study engaged the caregivers to under-five children within the household. The caregivers in this study refer to any individual that is directly involved in the treatment of the under-five children during illness or diseased period in the house. This may be mothers, fathers, siblings, housemaid, grandparents, neighbors, foster parents, relatives, or as it exists during the study.

5 SAMPLING TECHNIQUE

For the qualitative design, a purposively snowballing technique was used to select the respondents in the study area with the aid of people of influence in the community for the FGDs. The 12 FGDs were stratified into younger caregivers and older caregivers. Each FGD consisted of 6–8 caregivers, and the sessions were conducted until the level of saturation was attained.

6 Data Collection

In the study of this nature, the qualitative data were collected using the FGD with the aid of FGD guide for the caregivers of U-5 children and with the assistance of audio-tape receiver to obtain relevant information from those involved in the practice of self-medicating to the caregivers of the U-5 children.

7 Data Analysis

The data was analyzed based using a thematic analysis. This was developed by the use of codes based on the identified variables from the fieldwork. FGD and the interview were transcribed verbatim and classified into different themes. The data or information from the qualitative design was analyzed with the aid of Nvivo 11.0, a software designed for the analysis of qualitative data.

Table 1 revealed thus: The socio-demographic features of the respondents indicated that the mean age of the 86 respondents was 35.63 ± 7.55 years (range of 19–52 years). The respondents between ages 19–29 were 25.6%, 51.2% were between ages 30–39, 16.3% were between ages 40–49 and 7.0% were between ages 50–59 years of age. There were more female (69.8%) than male (30.2%) and all the respondents were married. The majority of the respondents (74.4%) had two to four children. More so, 11.6% and 14.0% had less than two and above five children, respectively. Regarding ages of children, forty-three of the respondents identified that they had at least one child that was less than one, aged one-two, aged three-four, and aged five and above years. Also, the highest ages of children (67.4%) were between the ages of three-four years. Besides, the majority of the respondents (74.4%) had a family size of four-six.

Furthermore, 53.5% were Christians, and 46.5% were Islam. About their educational qualification obtained and occupation, the majority of the respondents (44.2%) had a senior high school qualification, and 69.8% were self-employed. About 48.8% of the respondents lived in the urban center, and 51.2% of the respondents lived in the rural center. Regarding family monthly income, 32.6% and 32.6% had an income of ₦10,000–₦30,999 and ₦31,000–₦60,999 monthly respectively. Majority of the respondents (93.0%) had no medical insurance. As regard to distance from residence to clinic and existence of the chronic disease, 34.9% noted that

Table 1 Distribution of discussants by socio-demographic characteristics

Socio- demographic characteristics	Freq. (%)		Freq. (%)			Freq. (%)
Age (years)		Gender			Marital Status	
19–29	22(25.6)	Male	26(30.2)		Married	86(100.0)
30–39	44(51.2)	Female	60(69.8)		Ages of Children	
40–49	14(16.3)	Number of Children			Age(years)	Freq. (%)	% of Cases
50–59	6(7.0)	<2	10(11.6)	<1 years	30(16.3)	34.9
Total	86(100.0)	2–4	64(74.4)	1–2 years	42(22.8)	48.8
Family Size		5 and above	12(14.0)	3–4 years	58(31.5)	67.4
3	10(11.6)	Total	86(100.0)	>5 years	54(29.3)	62.8
4–6	66(76.7)	Educational Level		Total	184(100.0)	214.0
7 and above	10(11.6)	No formal Education	4(4.7)	Religion		
Total	86 (100.0)	Primary school	12(14.0)	Christian		46(53.5)
Occupation		Junior high school	6(7.0)	Islam		40(46.5)
Official	10(11.6)	Senior high school	38(44.2)	Total		86(100.0)
Self-employed	60(69.8)	University	26(30.2)	Place of Residence		
Housewife	8(9.3)	Total	86(100.0)	Urban		42(48.8)
Unemployed	8(9.3)	Family Monthly Income		Rural		44(51.2)
Total	86(100.0)	<₦10,000	10(11.6)	Total		86 (100.0)
Distance to Clinic (minutes)		₦10,000-₦30,999	28(32.6)	Medical Insurance		
<10	24(27.9)	₦31,000- ₦60,999	28(32.6)	Yes		6(7.0)
10	30(34.9)	₦61,000- ₦90,999	10(11.6)	No		80(93.0)
20	16(18.6)	₦91,000- ₦120,999	4(4.7)	Total		86(100.0)
30	12(14.0)	₦121,000 and above	6(7.0)	Existence of Chronic Diseases		
40–1 h	2(2.3)	Total	86(100.0)	Yes		2(2.3)
Do not go to the hospital	2(2.3)			No		84(97.7)
Total	86(100.0)			Total		86(100.0)

the distance from house to clinic was 10 minutes and 97.7% stated that there was no existence of chronic diseases in the family.

This objective assessed the knowledge of self-medication practice to under-five children among the caregivers by asking questions based on their understanding of the phenomenon, and their perception of under-five children. These questions are needed to really make a good assessment of their knowledge of self-medication practices.

8 Understanding of Self-Medication

8.1 Re-use of Medicines Based on Someone Else Previous Illness

The study explored the respondents understanding of self-medication. From the literature, self-medication is when the patient did not go to the hospital to find out the cause or getting a doctor's prescriptions before using any drug. Some respondents described self-medication as the re-use of medicines based on someone else previous illness, (they also subscribed to have different medicines at home in case the child falls in) as revealed in these excerpts:

> If for example, someone has an issue, he can say her aunty too used the same drug and she decided to use the drugs as well. (Rural Female, Lagos 2)
> With the way I looked at self-medication at times, too-know can make someone to do self-medication may be we have known about one leaf or drug that we have use or someone use it and talked about it and we also know how the drug was effective so we too will copy the same. (Urban male, Osun State, Ref Civil Servant).

9 The Use of Familiar Drugs

Some argued self-medication to be the use of familiar drugs whenever their children took ill, as seen in these excerpts:

> It means using drugs we are familiar with from the beginning, like paracetamol and other drugs. Most times we buy them and keep them at home in case any sickness or body pain arises, we will just pick it up to use it. Even for the children, we use them. (Rural Female, Lagos 2)
> My view is if the drug has been giving in the hospital before one can go for it. (Rural Female, Osun 2)

10 Use of Medication Without Laboratory Test

It was meant to be using the medication without laboratory test to ascertain the cause of illness, as affirmed by some caregivers. The respondents attached the use of medication to sequel to a confirmatory test for a definitive ailment. These can be deduced from these excerpts:

> But some people if anything happens to them now, they will take paracetamol, another small thing, they will take paracetamol. So, those ones are self-medication. When the headache is becoming common, the person should go and see the doctors and undergo a test to really know the cause of the headache especially if it is occurring like three times. It could be due to malaria or typhoid or anything else, this will determine the prescription of the doctors. (Rural Female, Lagos 1)

> Self-medication is not good they might need to run the test in the laboratory to confirm the illness before giving anything. (Rural Female, Osun 2)

11 Taking Drugs Without Doctor's Consent

Also, other participants were of the opinion or understanding that self-medication equals to taking drugs without doctor's consent. This statement signifies the WHO definition or meaning of self-medication. The real meaning was however indicated in their excerpts:

> ..... if anything happens to a child one needs to see the doctor for instant now if you want to sow a cloth you will take it to the tailor or if it is to build house you will call building so thing like that leads to life we should take it there. (Rural Male, Osun)
> My understanding is that self-medication is the drug that we do not get the prescription from the doctors and it do affect the children. It is better we take the case to the hospital and whatever drug given is what we should use and we must follow the description. (Urban Female, Lagos State 1)
> My first born, maybe he is having high temperature or something, I will go and buy malaria drug for him not just from anyhow chemist but in a good pharmacy. (Urban Female, Lagos 3)

12 Use of Medicine for Minor Ailment

Among other respondents, their understanding of the phenomenon includes the use of Medicine for Minor Ailment:

......if it is a minor thing, not the kind of sickness that grips the child seriously, if it is something that you don't have an understanding of, you may not want to use self-medication but if it is a minor thing that you can handle or you have been handling such before and the drug you have been using is working, then you use self-medication. (Rural Female, Lagos 1)

In general, from the respondents, they have good understanding of what self-medication means, however, it was expressed in different contexts but still attributing it to the concept of self- medication. It could be seen that this practice is very rampant among the participants as it conveyed different categories of practicability in the community. This will contribute immensely to the caregivers' body of knowledge of self-medication practice, because the meaning attributed to a practice will determine to a great extent how it will be practiced whether good or bad.

13 Perception of Under-Five Children by Caregiver

In assessing caregiver's knowledge of self-medication practice to the under-five children, a little digression was done to examine how the caregivers perceived the under-five children. Respondents were asked how they perceived under-five. Perception in the sense of the way they self-medicate to this category of children. In other to determine the form of healthcare practice to these children, the perception of the under-fives by the caregivers most likely will inform the management of the children during illness. The participants in their own view perceived the children to *be fragile* as they were likened to a mirror or glass, or egg which needs to be handled with extra care or caution.

I think we should look at them like an egg. Egg in the sense that you cannot drop an egg on a harsh place will break. You cannot drop the off in a shaking place it will break. It will fall down and break. You should actually watch what they take, wash them properly and make sure they are well clean; make sure they don't put dirt in their mouth... (Rural Female, Lagos 2)

I see these children we are talking of as fragile children they are like Yoruba will call "dingi". Something that is fragile that we need to take care of it very well, example like some one that is feeling hungry and this person cannot talk, all what they know how to do is to cry. (Urban, Male, Civil Servant, Osun 1)

.... that they are like fragile things if we take care of them very well they are our tomorrow because we too we have pass through that stage before and our parents too take good care of us. (Urban male, Osun 1)

I know that they are fragile children that we should not jeopardise their future I you see a new born baby of today, it is not possible for him to call the mother and say I have headache... (Urban male, Osun State 1)

.... under-five children are fragile, they cannot express themselves that this is what they are passing through. That is the reason why we usually take care of them very well. (Urban Female, Osun 1)

The participants in the FGD narrated that, the under-five children most times *cannot express themselves* as they are helpless and need to be supported. The following narratives reveal:

... the children are very small and they cannot express themselves and even if they will explain, they may not be able to say it deeply the way it affects them. (Rural Female, Lagos 1)

....all know that children normally play so we know that there is no other sickness they will have except to have temperature and they cannot explain if they are having headache or stomach ache, so as at any time they can have temperature it might be in the morning or afternoon. (Urban Female, Osun 2)

Children generally under the parental or caregivers control, *need to be guided and monitored* adequately. Even as this applies to the older children, nothing sorts of or less than this must be meted to the vulnerable under-five groups. This is evident in the discussion of the participants while explaining their own view of the perception of under-five children. This position was articulated in different ways among the FGD participants:

My view is they are still small and anything they do we need to be monitoring them. (Rural Male, Osun)

...they may not be able to say it deeply the way it affects them. That is why we as a parent must be very observant.... (Rural Female, Lagos)

As caregivers, their ultimate responsibility is to care for the under-five children within their household.

This was also the perception of their under-five as enunciated in these excerpts:

Whenever I discover that my child is not feeling well, I always want to act fast to make sure the child returns to the normal state of health. (Urban Female, Lagos 2)

We need to take care of them. They cannot use the drug meant for the elderly because their system cannot absorb it. Medicine good for the adult can harm their own system. We should take good care of them and they should not play with a sharp object. (Rural Female, Lagos 2)

14 DISCUSSION OF FINDINGS

Knowledge, attitude, and practice of health behaviors mostly dictate the success or failure of such practices among its practitioners. This assessment of the practice was based on their own intuition and may perhaps determine the efficacy and the outcome of the practice. Various ideations and concepts were posited by the caregivers that culminated to their knowledge of the practice. Though, their understanding of the practice was saddled with different contextual reasons, nevertheless it still connotes a very good knowledge of self-medication practice. Some participants elicited that the practice of self-medication essentially means the re-use of medicines based on the experience from past illnesses in the children. They expressed this view by attributing the practice to the experiences they garnered while managing or treating their wards during sickness episodes. Subsequent ailment among the children attracted the same pattern of treatment by their caregivers based on the management from the previous illnesses. This was corroborated by Nworie et al. (2018) where caregivers of under-five children interpreted self-care practice to imply the use of some leftover medications from past illnesses. The significance of this idea most likely depends on the individual recall ability to vividly capture what was done when a child of theirs or someone close during a similar sickness episode. The recognition of the disease state in the children were assessed subjectively by the caregivers and treatment were based on the individual translation of the symptoms exhibited by the children. However, using the same line of treatment for the children during illness episode does not guarantee a successful outcome.

Self-medication practice was expressed by some of these participants to be the re-use of medicines based on their past encounter from previous illnesses. This means the use of any medicaments or let overs in the household arising from the past illnesses encountered by the children. The use of such products were based on the premise that the treatment outcome was good considering the use of medicaments. Hence, most caregivers employed the same mechanisms to treat future illnesses in the children. This interpretation was confirmed by Cruz et al. (2014) and Oshikoya et al. (2009) from studies that identified the use of home management in treating child with colic and use of over-the-counter drugs. Also, Allotey et al. (2004) corroborated the re-use of medicine as a form of social medication for control and maintenance of good health of their children. Reason adduced to the re-use of medicine is probably a result of the individual remembrance of those medicines and the process of treating the children which could be likened to an individual factor.

Additional findings from the qualitative component revealed that the practice of self-medication symbolizes the use of familiar drugs or medications to their under-five children whenever they are sick. Familiarity with the medications implies recurrent usage and availability of such products either in the household or neighborhood whenever their children took ill. This school of thought by the caregivers was mainly because of the consistent usage of such medicines for treating various ailments among their children. This result confirmed the submission of Sasaki and Kamiya (2015) which reported that the caregivers' understanding of pediatric medication was based on their familiarity with such medications. Most female participants vividly concur with this conception of self-medication practice. As these drugs are in use due to their familiarity and non-prescription by a qualified physician, hence these duos constitute self-medication practice but in different context. This could be attributed to perceived efficacy, cheap cost, various advertisement of these medicaments in the media, and non-regulatory of such products by government institutions. The understanding of this practice from this finding depicts a considerable good knowledge of the practice as they used such medicines based on easy recognition aside getting a prescription from a physician.

In another parlance, findings from some participants interpreted the practice to the use of medication without laboratory tests. These group of participants fathomed self-medication to constitute not investigating the ailment through laboratory investigations. Therefore, to them using any medication without approaching the various diagnostic centers signifies self-medication. Laboratory investigation is part of the clinical procedures that are undertaken in the search for a probable cause of a disease condition and does not entail the medication to use and the procedures. However, lay people lack the technical knowledge that is required in interpreting laboratory evidence and diagnosis of a disease condition. Interpretation of such evidence depends on a professional physician who possess the knowledge and technical skills to read and the jargons of a laboratory scientist. This finding relates to the possible influence of biomedicine on health behavior and the growing awareness around synthetic drugs. Respondents that are likely to have such understanding are slightly educated and familiar with modern or biomedicine. Such caregivers also appear inclined to have preference for evidence-based rationale before drug consumption or administration to their under-five children.

Furthermore, some discussants attributed their meaning of self-medication to taking drugs without doctor's consent. The act of using medications without the permission of a certified medical expert solely constitutes taking medicines without a prescription. Seeking the attention of a medical expert on illness condition of children could be met with bureaucracies at the health facilities or poor health system structures. This succinctly identifies with the WHO's definition of the self-medication practice. In as much as the caregivers revealed their comprehension of the practice to be this term, then it shows they are knowledgeable on the practice. According to Attahiru et al. (2018) and Suja et al. (2019) self-medication connotes the usage of drugs without doctor's consent or doctor's prescription. But this does not imply the practice is done well or wrongly. This signifies probably the caregivers are aware of the pros and cons of engaging in self- medication practice without doctor's consent based on their experiences in childcare practice or increase in their level of education.

The level or degree of the disease condition in the under-five children was highlighted as part of the interpretation for the practice. Having

96   O. A. OKUNOLA ET AL.

cognizance of the extent of the severity of the disease is a dictum for self-medication in the event of a health challenge for an under-five child. Some participants attributed their understanding of self-medication practice to the degree of the children's disease state. They meant the practice to be the method of treatment only when there is a less severe illness in the children. Any other disease of higher severity was perceived to attract non-self-medication practice. The use of medicine for perceived minor ailment by the caregivers was reflected as the picture for self-medication practice. This builds on the report by Nworie et al. (2018) that posited self-medication to be the practice done according to the degree of severity of the ailments in the under-five children. To this set of participants, illnesses of under-five children that are not severe were given non-prescribed medications, hence conceiving the method of managing the extent of disease state in the children as self-medication practice.

In Overall, the finding generally depicted a good conception of the knowledge of self-medication among the caregivers. This is in contrast to the findings of Auta et al. (2012), Oshikoya et al. (2009), and Pavyde et al. (2015) who reported poor knowledge of self-medication practice among their respondents.

15   Conclusion

The act of childcare through self-medication is a well-established practice among caregivers in the study area. Most caregivers were knowledgeable of the practice though in diverse contexts, thereby provided different social milieu for the practice. In overall, the study revealed the various sociological factors influencing the practice of self-medication to the under-five children. This practice was highly influenced by social, economic, and individual factors.

16   Policy Implications of the Study

This study recognizes that the practice of self-medication to under-five children in the southwestern Nigeria has not been sufficiently studied to date. It further revealed how caregivers valued childcare practice of their under-five children and various societal context that intervenes with the practice. Apart from the national policy that prevents the sales of some medicines over-the-counter, though which is not very effective in Nigeria, there is a need for household-based policy that specifically targets the caregivers to under-five children where they are enlightened on the use of drugs irrationally on their children. This idea was supported by caregivers' revelations rendered as part of the information gathering for this study. The goal is to a safe responsible self-medication practice in order to reduce the cost of care, reduce child mortality rate and improve on the quality of healthcare to the under-five children.

Caregivers are still dominated by social and traditional norms of childcare practices as well as some unhealthy and unsafe methods of administering medicaments to their under-five children. This calls for public orientation and sensitization of caregivers on childcare health education. This could be done in form of public health awareness campaign by various stakeholders in the communities.

Acknowledgements and Funding This research was supported by the Consortium for Advanced Research Training in Africa (CARTA). CARTA is jointly led by the African Population and Health Research Center and the University of the Witwatersrand and funded by the Carnegie Corporation of New York (Grant No: B 8606.R02), Sida (Grant No: 54100113), the DELTAS Africa Initiative (Grant No: 107768/Z/15/Z) and Deutscher Akademischer Austauschdienst (DAAD). The DELTAS Africa Initiative is an independent funding scheme of the African Academy of Sciences (AAS)'s Alliance for Accelerating Excellence in Science in Africa (AESA) and supported by the New Partnership for Africa's Development Planning and Coordinating Agency (NEPAD Agency) with funding from the Wellcome Trust (UK) and the UK government.

Authors' Contributions OOA wrote the main manuscript while AMAO was my Supervisor and conceptualized the research topic and AAA collected the data and analyzed it.

Declarations

Ethical Permission Ethical clearance was gotten from the Health Research Ethics Committee Institute of Public Health, Obafemi Awolowo University, Ile-Ife, Nigeria with the approval number HREC NO: IPHOAU/12/1194. The purpose of the study was explained to the participants prior to obtaining verbal and written consent. Their rights to withdraw at any point was also emphasized. Throughout the study, confidentiality and privacy were maintained. Individual participant's responses were not also linked to ensure anonymity.

All the procedure involving humans in this study was in accordance to guidelines of the Declaration of Helsinki in the manuscript as approved by

98 O. A. OKUNOLA ET AL.

the Health Research Ethics Committee, Institute of Public Health, Obafemi Awolowo University, Ile-Ife, Nigeria.

Consent for Publication Not applicable.

Availability of Data and Materials The data are contained in the manuscript.

Competing Interests The author of this work hereby states that there are no competing interests whatsoever in any form as it regards this study.

REFERENCES

Ahmed, S. A. K. S., Ajisola, M., Azeem, K., Bakibinga, P., Chen, Y.-F., Choudhury, N. N., Fayehun, O., Griffiths, F., Harris, B., Kibe, P., Lilford, R. J., Omigbodun, A., Rizvi, N., Sartori, J., Smith, S., Watson, S. I., Wilson, R., Yeboah, G., Aujla, N., … Yusuf, R. (2020). Impact of the societal response to COVID-19 on access to healthcare for non-COVID-19 health issues in slum communities of Bangladesh, Kenya, Nigeria and Pakistan: Results of pre-COVID and COVID-19 lockdown stakeholder engagements. *BMJ Global Health, 5*(8), e003042. https://doi.org/10.1136/bmjgh-2020-003042

Ajala, A. S. (2009). *Yoruba nationalist movements, ethnic politics and violence: A creation from historical consciousness and socio-political space in south-western Nigeria* (Issue 105).

Allotey, P., Reidpath, D. D., & Elisha, D. (2004). "Social medication" and the control of children: A qualitative study of over-the-counter medication among Australian children. *Pediatrics, 114*(3). https://doi.org/10.1542/peds.2004-0759

Attahiru, A., Awosan, K. J., Hassan, M., & Arisegi, S. A. (2018). Awareness, risk perception and practice of self-medication among pregnant women attending Ante-Natal Clinics in Sokoto, Nigeria. *Journal of Drug Delivery and Therapeutics, 8*(4), 256–262. https://doi.org/10.22270/jddt.v8i4.1782

Auta, A., Shalkur, D., Omale, S., & Abiodun, A. (2012). Medicine knowledge and self-medication practice among students. *African Journal of Pharmaceutical Research & Development, 4*(1), 6–11.

Cruz, M., Dourado, L., Bodevan, E., Andrade, R., & Santos, D. (2014). Medication use among children 0–14 years old: Population baseline study. *Jornal De Pediatria, 90*(6), 608–615. https://doi.org/10.1016/j.jped.2014.03.004

Matias, T., Dominski, F. H., & Marks, D. F. (2020). Human needs in COVID-19 isolation. *Journal of Health Psychology, 25*(7), 871–882. https://doi.org/10.1177/1359105320925149

Muoneke, V. U., Una, A. F., Mbachu, C., Eke, C. B., Ododo, C. I., Nkaleke, D. I., Anasi, V. C., & Nwuzor, C. S. (2018). View of caregivers' perception and practice of self-medication for fevers in under-five children: A cross-sectional study in a rural community, South- East Nigeria.pdf. *Journal of Advances in Medicine and Medical Research*, *27*(12), 1–12.

Noor, A., Sahu, E. H., Abdullah, M. U., & Yousaf, A. (2017). Self-medication practices and perceptions among undergraduate medical students of multan medical & dental college, Multan. *Pakistan Journal of Public Health*, *7*(1), 58–61. https://doi.org/10.32413/pjph.v7i1.26

Nworie, K. M., Aluh, D. O., Ezeh, J., Ezeh, C. C., Opurum, C. A., Ndubuisi, L., Unuavworhuo, D., & Ozoh, G. C. (2018). Assessment of self-medication practices for treatment of illnesses among school-children in southeast, Nigeria. *Matters of Behaviour*, *3*(4), 15–25.

Osaigbovo, L., Ogboghodo, E., Obaseki, D., Akoria, O., Ehinze, E., Obarisi-agbon, O., & Okwara, O. (2020). Pattern of drug sales at community pharmacies in edo state as evidence of self-medication during the Covid-19 pandemic: Implications for policy implementation. *The Nigerian Health Journal*, *20*(4), 150–158.

Oshikoya, K. A., Senbanjo, I. O., & Njokanma, O. F. (2009). Self-medication for infants with colic in Lagos, Nigeria. *BMC Pediatrics*, *9*, 9. https://doi.org/10.1186/1471-2431-9-9

Pavyde, E., Veikutis, V., Maciuliene, A., Maciulis, V., Petrikonis, K., & Stanke-vicius, E. (2015). Public knowledge, beliefs and behavior on antibiotic use and self-medication in Lithuania. *International Journal of Environmental Research and Public Health*, *12*, 7002–7016. https://doi.org/10.3390/ijerph120607002

Sasaki, E., & Kamiya, Y. (2015). Caregivers' understanding of pediatric medica-tion in central Malawi. *Journal of Tropical Pediatrics*, *61*(1), 14–19. https://doi.org/10.1093/tropej/fmu057

Suja, V. S., Dutta, S., & Swaroop, A. M. (2019). Knowledge and perceptions of self- medication practices in an urban community. *Asian Journal of Phar-maceutical and Clinical Research*, *12*(8), 42–45. https://doi.org/10.22159/ajpcr.2019.v12i18.33721

Wegbom, A. I., Kevin, C., Raimi, O., Fagbamigbe, A., & Kiri, V. A. (2020). Self-medication practices and associated factors in the prevention and/or treatment of COVID-19 virus: A population-based survey in Nigeria. *Research Square*. https://doi.org/10.21203/rs.3.rs91101/v1

WHO. (2020). COVID-19 strategy up date. In *Covid-19 strategy update* (Vol. 3). https://www.who.int/docs/default-source/coronaviruse/covid-strategy-update-14april2020.pdf?sfvrsn=29da3ba0_19

Research and Development

The Globalisation of Social Environmental Research and the Practices of University Researchers in Africa: Case from Côte d'Ivoire

Kabran Aristide Djane

1 INTRODUCTION

The issue of globalisation has been constantly raised in scientific discourse and research in Africa and the world. The sources of this discussion have also been engaged in order to grasp its level of implication and transformation on scientific approaches in the South. If it intervenes on the axiology of the object in question, it is the praxeology of the scientific construction that it invites, which militates in the start of a socioconstructed analysis of this analysis of the globalisation of social research. The globalisation of social research becomes even more in need of this questioning insofar as it remains contaminated by the ethnology of the scientist who conjugates it. In this sense, can social research have an identity of its own if the instruments of its negotiation, its reflection, but also its financing emanate from the North, from a framework outside the

---

K. A. Djane (✉)
Universite Peleforo Gon Coulibaly, Korhogo, Ivory Coast
e-mail: aristide.djane@upgc.edu.ci

© The Author(s), under exclusive license to Springer Nature Switzerland AG 2023
A. I. Adeniran (ed.), *African Development and Global Engagements*,
https://doi.org/10.1007/978-3-031-21283-3_6

one that develops it in the field? To what extent does such an articulation have consequences for the subject, its approach and its constant relationship to its production? This form of reflection has already been conducted by Claude Abe, who calls for an epistemic and methodological distancing of the African researcher from globalisation in order to capture the quintessence of African productions in a globalised scientific environment, without ignoring or denying it. To do this, Claude Abe follows Samir Amin's register of *disconnection* by indicating three existential dimensions that the researcher must use as an epistemic compass in order to secure his or her production in the face of contagious globalisation. These dimensions are deconstruction, articulation and reappropriation. They thus participate in the construction of the paradigm of the *Great Divide* that Claude Abe regulates as an instrument of epistemic vigilance for the African researcher in the face of globalisation. Our production, which aims to interrogate the paradigmatic dissidence of social research in Environmental Social Sciences at the University of Korhogo in Côte d'Ivoire, is thus in line with Claude Abe's theoretical posture.

2   The Paradigm of the Great Divide Convened by Claude Abe

According to Claude Abe, the paradigm of the *great divide* invokes resistance. Also, based on a conceptual definition by Schwartz (1979). He states that the paradigm of the great divide constitutes a *'dichotomous approach, with its simple and radical oppositions, hostile to any idea of interpenetration and complementarity'*. Thus, the question of the place of construction of the object of research study in an intermingled space, where the West identifies itself with an ascendant stemming from the colonial tradition, remains compelling. This paradigm thus constitutes an affirmation of the originality of the work of scientists from the South, while at the same time asserting their belonging to a community that requires an ethnological, epistemic and praxeological consideration that deconstructs the other major sociological paradigmatic sets (Herman, 1983) not without socioconstructing their own identity. Indeed, the question of the identity of the African researcher in these scientific writings remains the foundation of the emergence of this paradigm. This identity becomes more complex with an obligation of commitment on their part. Sauvé and Van Steenberghe (2015) explain:

They (identity and commitment) refer to two fundamental psycho- social phenomena, one of a phenomenological nature, and the other concerning the projection of the self in this world. These two realities have both an individual and a collective dimension. They may or may not emerge to consciousness, they may be anchored in reflection or they may be nested elsewhere, on other planes of being-in-the-world. They are closely linked, one being the crucible of the other: identity determines and stimulates the spheres of commitment, just as the experience of commitment confronts or consolidates and forges identity. They are associated with the ontogeny of individuals and social groups. (p. 1)

In this paradigm of the *Great Divide*, we can see several social logics that summon the characteristics of identity. The African researcher thus finds particularly a social aggregate in this identity which takes several forms, namely (Sauvé & Van Steenberghe, 2015, p. 2). The African researcher thus finds a social aggregate in this identity which takes several forms, namely biological, cultural, gender, territorial, national, civil, religious, professional, political and virtual identity, which gives the researcher an idiosyncrasy that refutes the identity imposed by globalisation. It is therefore to a form of reading of *scientific Negritude* or *Black Scientific Nationalism* that we add this paradigm. Thus, to this necessary rupture, Claude Abe (2008). In his production, Claude Abe argues for an analytical grid in order to matrix the level of resistance and structuring critical originality of the African researcher in the face of this scientific globalisation in social science. At the end of his analysis, he exposes a possibility of a bridge with the outside world, which he calls *sociology of the bridge*, which should serve to readjust our view of the interpenetration of the scientific dynamics of the social sciences and more particularly, that of sociology in Africa. To achieve this, he associates in this conceptualisation, three essential dimensions which are: deconstruction, articulation and reappropriation. These three axes, which he articulates, will be the subject of orientation in the analysis of the data of this production.

3   METHODOLOGICAL CONTEXT OF DATA PRODUCTION

As Claude Abe points out, '*it is precisely field experience that makes it possible to reflect on the concept, in particular by putting it to the test of everyday realities*' (2008, p. 585). Our reflection is based on 97 articles on social research in the environment carried out and published by the

106   K. A. DJANE

University of Korhogo in Côte d'Ivoire, using a sample at your convenience (Miles & Huberman, 2003, p. 60) between 2013 and 2017, from the departments of sociology, anthropology and geography. The choice of these articles is based on our desire to question the behaviour of researchers at the University of Korhogo in the face of social research on the environment. For a long time, the universities' view of the environment was the prerogative of the Natural Sciences (Tessier & Vaillancourt, 1996). However, the environment as a space, an object of study, also calls upon the social sciences (Vivien, 1999). This provision forces social science researchers to reframe their scientific articulations by taking into account their territorial particularities and epistemic dispositions (Legay, 1999). In our approach, we identify the research objects and methodologies called for in these articles and the search for a mechanics of socio-identified 'deconstruction' based on Claude Abe's indicators, reinforced in this by those of spacing invited in Derrida's work (Ramond, 2008). Following on from this, the approach of 'articulation' with the research object, as well as the provisions of the sociology of the gateway, clarifies a reflection on the place of research and its renewal in the approach of originality and 're-appropriation' that the researchers of the University of Korhogo have to carry in their discourse and work in a contextualised framework. All of this was dissected using a vertical and horizontal content analysis procedure (Henry & Moscovici, 1968) Vertical, because it allows us to observe the conditions of production of the articles under analysis, by the researchers in question, and horizontal, because it invited us to look for themes that were in line with our production, namely, the object, the place of production of the article, the actors involved in the production, its level of interdisciplinarity, as well as the tools of analysis of the article. In total, a profile of the articles according to their type of research (Sauvé, 1999, p. 25) is described in Table 1.

4   The Mechanics of 'Deconstruction' in Environmental Social Sciences at the University of Korhogo

Deconstruction, far from being a concept of dissidence or emancipation, is above all an approach, a 'mechanism'. Thus, in all the developments used in this production, the vertical analysis, which indicates the conditions of existence of the articles, has revealed a reproduction of the

Table 1 Profile of articles studied by type of research

Type of research	Number	%
Theoretical research	1	1
Descriptive research	13	13
Causal research	21	22
Interpretative research	42	43
Intervention research	16	16
Research and development	0	0
Research evaluation	4	4
Total	97	100

Source Analysis data (2022)

scientific structuring of the articles. They all use the IMReD protocol[1] and thus borrow from the approaches of the natural sciences, the articulation of their presentation. The disciplinary mixture invited by questions related to the social environment is apparent. In order to better understand the deconstruction within the articles, we have called upon two indicators, namely, the mode of construction of research problems in the environmental social sciences and the theories used to interpret the realities studied.

4.1 How Environmental Social Science Research Issues Are Constructed in the Articles

The problematic is an essential dimension of social environmental research. It *"...is the theoretical approach or perspective that one decides to adopt to deal with the problem posed by the original question. It is a way of questioning the phenomena under study. It constitutes a pivotal stage of research, between the rupture and the construction."* (Raymond & Van Campenhoudt, 1995, p. 85). All of the productions indicate a scientific construction based on the search for an antinomy, a social rupture that has been a permanent problem in the Korhogo region for two years. The argument that is used is made up of a reasoned set of social facts that imply a relationship between man and the environment. Also, at this stage of our presentation, we can say that the assembly of issues is

[1] Introduction Method Result and Discussion.

108 K. A. DJANE

not homogeneous. If they are similar in structure, they are fundamentally different in their construction; and this is due to the particularity of the type of research in which they are included. Thus, descriptive, causal and interpretative articles are more involved in Quivy and Campenhoudt's approach (1995). They present a construction of the problematic based on two stages: firstly, a census of the literature on the basis of previous statistical writings, and then a finalisation through a choice of social antinomy, which they say they want to question. Theoretical, intervention and evaluation, on the other hand, start from theoretical writings, research projects or development projects whose shortcomings they expose in order to demonstrate the determinants of these shortcomings. In all cases, these articles give the image of an explanatory demonstration based on a hypothetical-deductive approach whose results are locally compartmentalised. An important aspect remains the expression of local writings on the issues dealt with (man-nature), where the statistics used or the means of justifying the problems remain rooted in local subjects. However, if the effort of dissent required by deconstruction is apparent in the problematic of these articles, it is rather the set of theories convened to interpret the data of their production that gives way to insufficiencies.

4.2 *Theory Used in the Interpretation of Analysed Realities*

The theorisation effort observed in the one theoretical article has a speculative approach based on Derrida's model of deconstruction of spacing (2008). Apart from this particularity, all the articles have no imprint in theorisation rooted in the South. All the paradigms borrowed from sociological or geographical explanation are found in a demonstrative complexification derived from the work of Herman (1983). The model of analysis of conceptualisation calls in its great majority for an integration of approaches encrusting functionalism with comprehensiveness, abandoning any dialectical exposition that interprets more African 'topographical' sociology (Copans, 2000). Even if one observes a negotiation with *globalised sociology*, these articles find their limits in an exercise of juxtaposition which demonstrates the lack of mastery of the mechanics of the connection of interpretations of approaches from elsewhere and explaining local African realities on the Man-Environment relationship; to this, it is an absence of questioning of the paradigms borrowed elsewhere which is objectively lacking in their arguments, which is what Claude Abe describes as 'the *lack of adjustment of the gaze*' (2008, p. 584).

5 'Articulation' and Social Environmental Research at the University of Korhogo

·Articulation, as Claude Abe points out, is identified by two essential indicators, namely the locality of the research and the level of inventiveness of the researcher with regard to the globality.

... the articulation is partly linked to this geographical decompartmentalisation; however, it is coupled with an epistemological dimension that requires a significant capacity for inventiveness on the part of the researcher in the African situation... it is a question of putting his or her ingenuity to good use in order to produce knowledge that reveals the truth of the intimacy of local realities, that at work in the field, while at the same time critically echoing what is being done in other research areas of the world... (2008, p. 589)

For this reason, we focus on these two points in the following.

5.1 The Rationale for the Choice of the Location of the Study in Environmental Social Sciences at the University of Korhogo

The choice of whether or not to work in places not far from one's home or work space are the first aspects that emerge from a horizontal analysis of the articles. In fact, 91% of these articles do not expressly indicate their sources of funding; the authors in their various presentations, in most cases, describe a sociological urgency to investigate their various objects of study either because of the sociological or anthropological proximity of the subjects to be studied. The average distance observed and calculated between the study sites and the site of the University of Korhogo in Côte d'Ivoire is 53 km. This indicates a lack of research funding and production not linked to an overall funded research programme. Overall, we have 73% production in the Korhogo district. The schemas 'city', 'crisis', 'post-crisis', 'poverty', 'sacred wood', 'nature', 'sénoufo' constitute, on the whole, the key words that appear in the justification of the study spaces; in all cases, they remain attached to the locality of Korhogo, with an ethnological space of the sénoufo country in the North of Côte d'Ivoire.

110   K. A. DJANE

5.2   Creativity and Innovation in the Field

64% of the studies use a mixed approach to data collection in the field, combining the use of quantitative and qualitative tools such as the questionnaire, the interview guide and the observation grid. 77% of them say that they make up for the shortcomings caused by one of the instruments due to the complexity of the field and capture the quintessence of the information in a holistic view of the object of study. In 13% of cases, the collection framework was based on the approach of Jean Olivier de Sardan (2008). This is seen in the 9% of articles produced by foreign donors in association with the University of Korhogo. The participation of IRD[2], IDRC and CSRS[3] can be observed. The rest of the scientific productions emanating from a single researcher's will not show any particular originality in data collection. They remain marked by a social observation based on an antinomy to be explained or understood. Actions in the field are therefore directed in this direction.

6   'Reappropriation', a Condition of the Ethnological Perspective of the Environmental Social Scientist at the University of Korhogo

Observing the 'reappropriation' in the production of environmental social sciences at the University of Korhogo requires us to qualify the privileged research objects, the actors called upon, as well as the level of interdisciplinarity.

6.1   Preferred Research Objects

As mentioned above, the research topics developed by researchers in environmental social sciences at the University of Korhogo, according to the articles evaluated, are structured along various lines as presented in Table 2.

These objects constitute the research features of the environmental social sciences as recommended by Tessier and Vaillancourt (1996). They

---

[2] Institut de Recherche et de Developpement.

[3] Centre Suisse de Recherche Scienctifique.

THE GLOBALISATION OF SOCIAL ENVIRONMENTAL ... 111

Table 2 Research objectives of the articles evaluated

Research object	Frequency	%
Attitudes and values	12	12
Social representations	13	13
Communication, Media, Education	2	2
Environmental Foundations, Environmental Ethics	1	1
State of play, Assessment, Diagnosis	47	48
Sustainable Development	22	23
Total	97	100

Source Analysis data (2022)

start from the social representations, beliefs, values and attitudes of the Senoufo towards the preservation of the environment and biodiversity through these sacred sites. Some texts also touch on the social reproduction of environmental behaviour through environmental education. The involvement of indigenous beliefs and the local dialect in the achievement of the Sustainable Development Goals (SDGs) are also mentioned in the articles. In sum, a constant search for a state of the art is strongly prevalent in the articles in question. From this presentation, we can observe the *sociology of the gateway* angle that Claude Abe recommends in his writings. Indeed, the latter recommends that the African researcher should not practice the sociology of Them and Us. Rather, he proposes a globalisation of global concerns such as studies on the levels of resilience to current issues, such as climate change, food security, etc. Through these research objects, we examine how researchers in environmental social science at the University of Korhogo are reappropriating international research topics by embedding them in local realities circumscribed to social spaces in crisis.

6.2 Actors Involved and Level of Interdisciplinarity

In order to achieve this goal of the sociology of the atomised bridge to the realities of the researchers in question. They thus call upon the disciplines of sociology, geography and environmental psychology in their writings. The actors interviewed in these studies are multiple and do not emanate from a single entity. They adopt a holistic approach that questions the Man-Nature phenomenon in its entirety. To this end, an average of four communities or colleges of individuals are consulted in the production of

112   K. A. DJANE

data for the studies in the articles. To this we must add the plural character of the authors on the articles. On average, we have two authors on each of the articles. However, it appears that for sociology articles, 94% of the co-authors are from the same discipline, while the remaining 6% are a collaboration between sociologists, anthropologists and geographers. However, for the productions involving international funding, we observe 100% collaboration between sociologists, engineers and biologists. In all the productions, the interdisciplinarity of the authors in collaboration remains low at 31% of all the articles. Yet the environmental social sciences invite this interdisciplinarity (Tessier & Vaillancourt, 1996). Furthermore, Claude Abe recommends interdisciplinarity in the discussion of scientific exchanges in order to achieve the explanatory effectiveness of universality (Abé, 2008, p. 590). However, there is resistance at this level.

7   CONCLUSION

The aim of this production was to grasp the dimensions of the sociology of the gateway in relation to the paradigm of the Great Divide convened by Claude Abe in the production of articles in the Social Sciences of the Environment at the University of Korhogo. The three dimensions that help in the matrixing of these articles show that the act of 'deconstruction' is difficult to perceive in its mechanics by researchers in environmental social sciences at the University of Korhogo, but also in the choice of theories anchored in the South that can support their production. The result is a weak 'articulation' in the search for innovation within the relationship with the field, even if some methodological innovations and creativity based on the work of Jean Olivier de Sardan are apparent. Finally, the 'reappropriation' is presented with internationalised and locally rooted research topics, were it not for the weak disciplinary collaboration between the authors. These authors come from the disciplines of Social Sciences and Biology. The sociology of the bridge in relation to the Great Divide paradigm is struggling to establish itself as an epistemic and methodological protocol in the environmental social sciences at the University of Korhogo. On the one hand, this is due to a mechanism that is difficult to appreciate by researchers, and on the other hand, due to a lack of documentation to feed the globalised theories of the South. There is thus an urgent need at the University of Korhogo to find a balance in the battle of scientific research strategies with regard to the battle between scientific research strategists on the paradigmatic and methodological sides in which every African researcher is required to take a position (Yahisule, 2018).

REFERENCES

Abé, C. (2008). The globalization of sociology in the African situation: Between resistance and structuring dynamics. *Canadian Journal of Sociology, 33*(3), 575–605.

Copans, J. (2000). Globalization of fields or internationalization of disciplinary traditions? The Utopia of a borderless anthropology. *Anthropology and Societies, 24*(1), 21–42.

Henry, P., & Moscovici, S. (1968). Problems of content analysis. *Langages, 11*, 36–60.

Herman, J. (1983). *Les langages de la sociologie.* Presses universitaires de France.

Legay, J.-M. (1999). Is the scientific evaluation of complex research objects a new epistemological situation? *Natures Sciences Sociétés, 7*(2), 60–64.

Miles, M. B., & Huberman, A. M. (2003). *Analysis of qualitative data.* De Boeck Supérieur.

Olivier de Sardan, J.-P. (2008). *La rigueur du qualitatif. Les contraintes empiriques de l'interprétation socio-anthropologique.* Academia-Bruylant.

Ramond, C. (2008). *Derrida.* Presses universitaires de France.

Raymond, Q., & van Campenhoudt, L. (1995). *Manuel de recherche en sciences sociales.* Dunod.

Sauvé, L. (1999). Un "patrimoine" de recherche en construction. *Education relative à l'environnement: Regards-Recherches-Réflexions, 1*, 13–40.

Sauvé, L., & Van Steenberghe, É. (2015). Identities and commitments: Issues for environmental education. *Environmental Education. Regards—Recherches—Réflexions, 12* [online] http://journals.openedition.org/ere/588 (Accessed 12 Jul 2018).

Schwarz, A. (1979). Sociology in Africa or the real issues of the international development paradigm. *Canadian Journal of African Studies/la Revue Canadienne Des Études Africaines, 13*(1–2), 89–160.

Tessier, R., & Vaillancourt, J.-G. (1996). *La recherche sociale en environnement: nouveaux paradigmes.* Les Presses de l'Université de Montréal.

Vivien, F.-D. (1999). La question de l'environnement dans les sciences sociales—Compte rendu de rapport. *Natures Sciences Sociétés, 7*(2), 72–75.

Yahisule, J. O. M. (2018). *Guerre des méthodes en sciences sociales: Du choix du paradigme épistémologique à l'évaluation des résultats.* Editions L'Harmattan. Google-Books-ID: RsJiDwAAQBAJ.

Exploring the Experiences and Benefits of Postgraduate Studies in South Africa: The Research Masters Degree

Gerelene Jagganath

1 Introduction

In a world where university degrees serve as a benchmark for knowledge and skills in the market place, it has become increasingly beneficial for students and employees to pursue postgraduate qualifications to secure employment and further career interests. The completion of a master's degree is an indication of mastery of specific skills and a passion for the field. Graduates with a master's degree are recognized for having advanced skills and knowledge in their field and employers respect both attributes because new employees may need less training and might remain in the profession for a longer period of time. Students often feel empowered and experience more personal satisfaction after mastering new skills. A master's degree provides students with an in-depth education in their field's latest best practices. Some learners pursue a master's degree to qualify for a doctoral programme while some professionals with a master's degree use their skills and expertise to perform their job well and further

---

G. Jagganath (✉)
University of KwaZulu-Natal, Durban, South Africa
e-mail: JagganathG@ukzn.ac.za

© The Author(s), under exclusive license to Springer Nature Switzerland AG 2023
A. I. Adeniran (ed.), *African Development and Global Engagements*,
https://doi.org/10.1007/978-3-031-21283-3_7

their professional advancement. This value may protect them from layoffs and other negative economic trends. Globally, the benefits of a master's degree are associated with the graduate building on current abilities, gaining specialized knowledge, or transitioning into an entirely new field to advance in the working world. As the workforce evolves, a postgraduate degree becomes synonymous with enhanced expertise, professional credibility, critical thinking and innovation. Focus on a particular field of study brings recognition which makes the graduate more competitive and open to further specialization in one's career, promotion to more senior positions and an increase in earnings. In the South African context, whether in employment or not, postgraduate students pursue furthering their studies to increase their employability and to open doors to new opportunities. However, South African Masters students in KwaZulu-Natal face daunting challenges that have been further compounded by the COVID-19 pandemic and one of the world's highest unemployment rates. They often lack financial, institutional and other forms of support to ease the burden of negotiating studies, work, health and family. The postgraduate journey is a lonely experience and not necessarily a positive experience for all students, particularly if the master's degree is solely research based, as is the case of 12 Masters students in this study. The key objective of the study was to explore students and supervisor perceptions and sentiments of the Masters degree experience and the relevance of such a qualification to the workplace.

This paper comprises two parts. Part one briefly addresses: the background, contextualizing the master's degree in social sciences and the research methodology. Part two focuses on the findings and discussion of the study.

1.1 Part One

In South Africa, the growth of postgraduate students among historically disadvantaged individuals and the successful completion of degrees, are important national goals where higher education is not only considered a key driver of the knowledge economy, but also instrumental in redressing historical racial and gender inequities (National Planning Commission & National Development Plan, 2013). What has become clear both globally and nationally, is that the traditional linear model of knowledge production is no longer sufficient. A circular model that begins and ends with society, where knowledge production starts with a problem and integrates scientific excellence with social responsibility, and through challenge-led research, responds to local and global circumstances (Griesel, 2020). Academics and policy-makers alike, have recognized the need for South Africa to progress from a resource-based economy to a knowledge-based economy, as envisaged by the National Development Plan (National Planning Commission & National Development Plan, 2013: 59). That understanding prompted a shift in emphasis in higher education from producing bachelor's degrees en masse to an increase in the production of graduates with postgraduate qualifications (Thaver et al., 2013: 1138). Transformation at South African universities has to an extent addressed racial, class and gender issues, social justice, poverty, inequality and violence, but continues to be influenced by its own and the sector's combined histories, as well as that of the country. COVID-19 has, however, exposed and exacerbated existing inequalities in South Africa, adding to the burden as institutions simultaneously confront the impact of the past on the present, in anticipating the possible future(s) of universities.

Local studies on the student–supervisor relationship and its concomitant challenges in the South African context are numerous (Cekiso et al., 2019; Nkoane, 2014; Sonn, 2016) but few include the impact on students and supervisors during the recent global calamity of the COVID-19 pandemic. Even less visible, are studies that examine the ways in which postgraduate students and their supervisors perceive the value of a masters degree qualification in the social sciences, against the backdrop of the pandemic and the technologically advanced skills needed in the workplace. As universities are national assets, the value of higher education is linked to its roles in enhancing national economic competitiveness (Lebeau, 2008). The pace of change, however, brought about by several forces, including technological advances, global and local economic forces and demographic shifts—makes it necessary that universities adapt to new circumstances. We now appear to be at a crossroads where the burden of a pandemic, a heightening unemployment rate and the technological developments in the 4IR, place universities in a precarious situation that demands the need to prepare graduates for a rapidly changing world of work. Institutional transformation and innovation—that is meaningful and extensive with a focus on systemic sustainability—is not easily accomplished. It creates uncertainties and places high demands on staff and students alike. The University of KwaZulu-Natal is characterized by a unique and vulnerable student demography that operates in a

118   G. JAGGANATH

region with two economic realms, one of economic wealth and vibrancy; and another of intense poverty and underdevelopment. The university has a total student population of close to 50,000 students and more than 22,000 students are placed in over 200 residences located in the municipalities of eThekwini and uMsunduzi. 78% of the student population comes from households with incomes below R350,000 per annum.[1] It is against this background that the study foregrounds the perceptions and experiences of Masters students and supervisors between 2020 and 2022, during several COVID-19 lockdowns. Imposed lockdown measures CONFINED people to their places of residence, AND strictly limited access to public institutions such as universities. As a result, universities were forced to shut down and students, like all other citizens, had to find innovative ways to continue with their academic tasks and meet their obligations. Notably, "embracing digital technologies that facilitate data acquisition and both one-on-one and group communication – for example, text and video communication applications, such as WhatsApp; cloud-based video conferencing services, such as Zoom; learning platforms or course management systems (CMS), such as Moodle; and online academic research databases" produced a shift in the way in which students were compelled to continue their studies (Sokhulu, 2020: 437).

1.1.1 Contextualizing a Masters Degree in the Social Sciences

Depending on the discipline, a Masters degree in the Social Sciences at South African universities, generally includes the options of a coursework or research masters degree.

A Masters by Coursework is a professional qualification involving the study of a specified set of core units and a selection of eligible elective units. Undertaking a coursework programme will mean that students will attend classes, complete assignments and sit FOR exams where applicable. Some Masters by Coursework also require the completion of a minor thesis as part of the course. This research element forms part of the training in time management and written skills.

A Masters by Research on the other hand, involves the submission of a completed thesis based on an independent research project. Students studying a Masters by Research work independently with the support

---

[1] Daily News Reporter. (6 March 2020). UKZN fundraising drive for poor students falls short. https://www.iol.co.za/dailynews/news/kwazulu-natal/ukzn-fundraising-drive-for-poor-students-falls-short-44243758.

of a supervisor and the School. Students may be required to attend MODULE units to help expand skills in the area of research. Taking on a postgraduate research degree provides you with the unique opportunity to follow your interest in an area of research and contribute to the field with the aim of producing, presenting and submitting a final thesis. This final thesis is the culmination of the students original research and investigation. Such programmes aim to train students in analyzing their thesis topic at an advanced level; research methodology and techniques; and the application of such methodology by conducting a specified programme of research under appropriate supervision. Many research masters students choose to continue with their studies in order to obtain a Ph.D. The research-based Masters thesis should demonstrate the Candidate's knowledge of the research topic and the discipline/s it embraces, as judged by external examiners that apply accepted contemporary institutional standards. A study conducted by Zewotir et al. (2015: 1) on full-time masters students across several faculties who registered in the period 2004–2011 at UKZN indicates that, the higher education institution funding formula is weighted in favour of research-based master's programme throughput rather than structured master's programmes based on structured course modules.

2   RESEARCH METHODOLOGY

The study adopted a primarily qualitative approach to accessing and analyzing data, combining ethnographic techniques such as participant observation, unstructured interviews (in-person as well as via WhatsApp video calls), online group discussions (via Zoom), in-person focus groups, as well as an email questionnaires that were used to generate data about the participants' demographic (such as age and gender) and supplement fieldwork findings. Online video conferencing platforms such as WhatsApp and Zoom have become increasingly popular among social scientists during the pandemic. The data obtained from both the traditional and online methodologies conducted, was used in a threefold way to write this paper. Firstly, it was from a compilation of information derived from the observations, interviews and focus groups that the researcher was able to identify suitable candidates for case studies to present the narratives of masters students in particular. Case studies express the perspectives of the research participant (students) in an in-depth way and was used to illuminate themes or draw inferences. The case study approach usually involves the collection of multiple sources of evidence, using a range of quantitative (including questionnaires) and more commonly qualitative techniques such as interviews, focus groups and observations (Crowe et al., 2011). Case study research is founded on the premise of deriving a close or otherwise in-depth understanding of a single or small number of "cases," set in their real-world contexts (Bromley, 1986). Secondly, online group discussions on Zoom with supervisors whose narratives were presented in the form of excerpts or quoted fragments, gave a voice to their concerns. Zoom is a collaborative, cloud-based videoconferencing service offering features including online meetings, group messaging services, and secure recording of sessions (Zoom Video Communications Inc., 2016). The user-friendly, secure and cost effective functions of this online platform proved an efficient means of real-time communication and the recording option provided an effective means of replaying the session for further observation of non-verbal cues. The research protocols of the pandemic dictated much of the rules and regulations at the time of the study and all University research protocols relating to social distancing, appropriate sanitization and wearing of masks, were observed as per the level of lockdown. The basis of the study was informed by seven key research questions from which themes were developed and articulated.

3 RESEARCH PARTICIPANTS

The participants in this study were purposively selected. Purposive/selective sampling involves identifying and selecting individuals or groups of individuals that are knowledgeable about or are experienced with a particular phenomenon (Cresswell & Plano Clark, 2011). Beyond knowledge and experience, Bernard (2002) and Spradley (1979) note the importance of factors such availability and willingness to participate, and the ability to communicate experiences and opinions in an articulate, expressive, and reflective manner.

Students: Twelve purposively sampled Masters degree students were selected for this study from a pool of currently/previously supervised students of the 4 supervisors who were also participants in the study. The 12 research masters students consisted of 8 female and 4 male students in the School of Social Sciences at the University of KwaZulu-Natal. Their ages ranged from 24 to 36 years. The students represented varying levels of study between 2020 and 2022. Some were second or third year masters students, most had exceeded the required 3 year time frame, and a few had completed their masters degree and were already Ph.D. candidates.

Supervisors: The four supervisors (2 females and 2 males) who participated in the study, were experienced supervisors of both Masters and Ph.D. students whose background as Senior Lecturer and Professorial-level academics, made them suitable for the needs of the study.

The study was based on several key questions that examined the masters student perceptions on the experience and challenges of doing a research masters in the social sciences and the value of pursuing such a postgraduate degree in the context of the workplace. These questions were as follows:

1. How would you rate your masters degree experience? (10 for excellent and 1 for very poor)
2. Why did you choose to pursue a masters degree?
3. Has pursuing/obtaining a masters degree helped you accomplish any goals (personal or otherwise)?
4. How important do you think a masters degree is for entering/remaining in the South African workplace currently?
5. How have you benefited (or not) from pursuing/completing a masters degree?
6. Have you experienced any mental health challenges during the pandemic that impacted your studies?
7. What is the most challenging aspect of doing a research masters vs. a coursework masters?

4 Limitations of the Study

The study focuses on a small sample of research masters degree students in KwaZulu-Natal. The sample size and specific context do not warrant generalizations about other postgraduate students in the country or globally. The students were purposively selected and comprised of a pool of students supervised by the group of supervisor participants in this study. It is not possible to gauge if they answered as objectively as they would have, if interviewed by a researcher they were not familiar with. Perhaps they would have provided different responses if interviewed by someone unknown.

122   G. JAGGANATH

The data collected for this study was used to address the themes outlined in the subsections below. Each question is accompanied by a table that illustrates the numerical values and responses derived and these are further elaborated through the inclusion of related excerpts and case studies.

4.1   Part Two

Part Two of the paper focuses on two aspects, firstly, the key research questions, and secondly, the narratives of supervisors' experiences during the pandemic.

The findings and discussion presented in this section **Are** based on a combination of primarily qualitative ethnographic techniques, supplemented with quantitative research methods. This culminated in the formation of the eight key themes that are presented and discussed below. Ethnography is an open and flexible method that aims to offer a rich narrative account of a specific culture, allowing the researcher to explore many different aspects of the group and setting.[2] The central premise of a mixed methods approach is that the combined use of quantitative and qualitative approaches provides a better understanding of research problems than either approach does on its own.[3]

Theme 1: Student perceptions of the research masters degree experience

QUESTION 1: How would you rate your masters degree experience? (10 for excellent and 1 for very poor)

Between 0 and 5	Exactly 5	Between 5 and 10	Exactly 10
1 (1)	1	2 (6)	1
2 (4)	2	1 (7) + 1 (8)	1
TOTAL = 3 STUDENTS	TOTAL = 3 STUDENTS	TOTAL = 4 STUDENTS	TOTAL = 2 STUDENTS

Author's survey 2020–2022

[2] Caulfield, J. (2020). An introduction to ethnography: What is it and how is it used? https://www.scribbr.com/methodology/ethnography/.

[3] Gunnel, M. (2016). Research methodologies: A comparison of quantitative, qualitative and mixed methods. https://www.linkedin.com/pulse/research-methodologies-comparison-quantitative-mixed-methods-gunnel.

The table represents the way in which the student participants felt about their experiences as master's students in the social sciences. Based on a scale of 1–10, they rated their experiences in an email questionnaire accordingly. Out of the total number of students ($N = 12$), 50% ($N = 6$) of the sample rated their experience as above average to excellent. The other 50% rated their experience as average to below average and poor. The table indicates a clear division between those who enjoyed the experience vs. those who did not find it pleasant. On polar ends, 2 students claimed theirs was an excellent experience, rating it $10/10$, while on the other extreme, 1 student rated the experience as very poor ($1/10$). The following excerpts from interviews with students express their sentiments and further elaborates their experiences:

I worked hard and had the support of a good supervisor and study group so I finished in 2 years. It was a very positive experience because I did not lose my focus, there were challenges like switching to online – but I threw myself in the deep end and did not complain. The writing skills workshops were useful and it was reassuring to hear other students share the same concerns as me...

It was ok but there were so many personal and research challenges. I found it difficult to finance my studies so I could not be regular with my writing. With Covid things changed very fast and it was an overwhelming time with death all around us... I could not go to campus to consult my supervisor and doing these things online is not easy for me, it means more time and money for data and my laptop was not reliable. I could not attend all the School workshops because I had to work. Writing in English was also not easy and it delays the work, there are so many corrections...

It was not good at all. I had to change supervisors, one year after I started my studies. This was an adjustment because they had very different supervision styles. I became sick and there were big gaps in my writing. The only contact I had with my supervisor was on email and WhatsApp because I did not always have access to the online platforms like Zoom. Depending on where I stayed, I sometimes had no connectivity at all. Covid 19 made me feel very isolated from the world and it became more about surviving than being a student. The research proposal and ethical clearance on RIG took a long time to do because I was not working consistently and the revisions took forever because I was not used to working online...

The students experience of the research masters degree during the pandemic indicates that a key challenge was the shift to online platforms and the use of digital technology. Much of the negativity around the masters experience was the alienation felt by those students with no internet access. Hedding et al. (2020: 1) aptly state that in a country where a large percentage of students depend on financial assistance to make ends meet, where data costs are high and even a mobile connection may not be readily available to all, and where devices such as laptop computers are seen as a luxury, it is not surprising that contact universities have faced push-back from students who have argued that universities cannot expect them to continue with online learning without providing the necessary resources. To address the resource issue, universities have negotiated with several cellular networks to make data available to students (at a cost to the university, thereby forcing universities to reshuffle their financial budgets and/or asking the general public to donate to discretionary funds), and various universities are already providing devices to disadvantaged students. Sokhulu (2020) in a recent study on student experiences using digital technologies during the COVID-19 lockdown, further elaborates that students digital skills during the pandemic were acquired more through the personal needs of certain students who used their knowledge to meet their research needs, than a systematic acquiring of digital skills through the institution.

Theme 2: Student motivations for pursuing a research masters degree

QUESTION 2: Why did you choose to pursue a masters degree?

Response	No. of students	Most popular combined responses
1. I could not find employment with an Honours degree	3	
2. I want to pursue an academic career and move towards a Ph.D.	5	√
3. I wanted to improve my chance of a promotion in my current job	4	√
4. OTHER		
	TOTAL = 12	

Author's survey 2020–2022

The table provides some insight into the motivations behind the student sample choosing to study for a masters degree in social science. Most of the students ($N = 5$) claimed it was part of the process towards acquiring a Ph.D., as they wanted to become academics, while some ($N = 4$) wanted to improve their chances of promotion in the workplace. Three students could not find employment and stated they continued with studying so as to use their time in a productive way, while seeking employment. The case study to follow provides an interesting student perspective on the perceived challenges and benefits of choosing a research masters degree in the social sciences:

Case Study 1: Amahle

"I wasn't sure at first if I should do my masters in social science. As a research degree it did not really meet the expectations of what I was trying to achieve, to become an online teacher. But my background in social sciences did not allow me other options and so I went ahead. My research topic focused on youth and I felt as if I was keeping within my interests. I support myself financially and that included paying my fees so I had to complete it within a maximum of two years. However, Covid19 threw a curve ball on all my plans and it took a lot longer. I think being infected with the virus while there was no vaccine available and taking a few months to recover, was one of the greatest challenges and I almost gave up studying. My supervisor encouraged me to complete my work as I had already done a fair amount. I was already working as an online tutor so finishing my masters was not a foremost priority. However, when I applied to teach online overseas and got the job, I wanted to complete my studies so that I had the additional recognition in an Asian country where employment was so competitive. I felt that having a masters would distinguish me from other graduates I knew who were also applying and possibly give me more options once I had settled there. The worst experience was waiting for the examiners to mark my thesis. I only received the outcome of my dissertation 7 months after I had submitted it. This was very stressful as I was waiting to graduate and get my certificate before leaving South Africa..."

Theme 3: Perceived goals achieved from pursuing a research masters degree

QUESTION 3: Has a master's degree helped you accomplish any goals (personal or otherwise)?

Response	No. of students	Most popular combined responses
1. Improved writing & research skills	5	√
2. More opportunities in the job market	3	√
3. Securing employment with my masters degree		
4. Job promotion due to my masters degree	2	
5. Change in job at the same workplace because of my masters degree	2	

Authors survey 2020 to 2022

The table illustrates the perceived goals students accomplished while studying or having completed their masters degree. Most students ($N = 5$) stated that they had acquired better writing and research skills while some ($N = 3$) claimed they had more opportunities in the job market with a masters degree, which they gauged through the increased number of job interviews obtained after submitting their CV's. Fewer students ($N = 2$) said their goal for a promotion at work was achieved and the same number ($N = 2$) said they were able to change to better employment positions, as masters students. Improved writing/research skills and more employment opportunities were the most achieved goals in the sample. These two categories seemed more popular than job promotion or the changing of jobs. These responses were largely influenced by the low number of masters students in employment at the time of the study.

The excerpts to follow represent some of the student narratives on this question:

> My goal was to improve my researching, analyzing, and writing skills and I'm able to solve problems in a scientific manner. It has helped me gain specialized knowledge in the research topic that I was conducting.

> It has helped me to connect with various organizations and people. It has also helped me to advise and assist those who still want to pursue research masters degree

> My goal was to get a higher paying job. This did not happen but I did get a job with better benefits at the same workplace, so it was a positive change...

The aforementioned responses and excerpts indicate that most of the participants were aiming towards a Ph.D. degree in the future, to pursue a career in academia. This is reflected in the high number of students in the sample who wished to improve their writing and research skills.

Theme 4: The importance of a research masters degree for the current workplace in South Africa

QUESTION 4: How important do you think a research masters degree is for the workplace in South Africa?

Response	No. of students	Most popular combined responses
1. VERY IMPORTANT—it makes finding ANY employment possible and is necessary to be recognized		
2. IMPORTANT—It makes finding employment easier	4	√
3. IMPORTANT—it is necessary to be promoted & re-numerated accordingly in employment	4	√
4. NOT SO IMPORTANT—you don't need a Masters degree to find a job, nor for promotions purposes	2	
5. NOT IMPORTANT—it is not really necessary and doesn't make much difference in the South African context	2	

Author's survey 2020 to 2022

The table shows that most participants ($N = 8$) believed the masters degree qualification to be important in accessing employment and for upward mobility in the workplace in terms of promotion and re-numeration. These 2 categories were mentioned together during discussions. However, 4 of the 12 students (**33%**) did not think it was important to find a job nor be promoted, and that a masters degree did not make much difference in the South African context. These students appeared to adopt a survivalist perspective towards postgraduate education, claiming that the high unemployment rate of graduates in the country, made no

128   G. JAGGANATH

difference to their opportunities versus that of a graduate or an honours level student.

Case Study 2: Khanyi

"Completing my masters made a difference to my career and my job at the municipality. I was given more recognition and did get a slight increase in salary. I think it will be easier for me to apply for higher level positions now. I feel that postgraduate degrees in the social sciences should be more balanced and consider the working environment. What we learn and write about is important but our skills must include technical knowledge as well so we can use these for the systems and technology used in the working world. There should be training for postgraduate students to prepare them and there must be exposure to certain computer skills and programmes - instead of learning it only when you get employed. The covid19 pandemic brought us into remote working and it was so problematic for our municipal staff because of lacking resources and know-how. But we were forced to adapt and learn as much as we could and it made me realize how important technology will be in the future. If our degrees stay the same then we won't have anything to offer employers who are looking for experience and technical skills to solve problems. There has to be more than the qualification based on academic writing and research skills. Students feel the aim of getting a masters degree is to find full-time employment but this is not always true and there is no guarantee."

The case study of Khanyi resonates with a media report in which Rodny-Gumede (2019)[4] highlights that South Africa's education system has not fostered innovative and creative thinkers, upon which the success of education in the future is dependent. Encouraging innovation and fostering creative talent are directly linked to the success and growth of Research & Development (R&D). Moreover, in order to obtain the best results from new technological advancements, governments, together with higher education institutions, must invest heavily in research and new university curricula. Kayembe and Nel (2019) state that the fourth industrial revolution (4IR) will need a new set of skills for the future and that such technologies and their applications will require specialized skills, beyond basic digital literacy.

---

[4] Rodny-Gumede, Y. (2019). South Africa needs to think differently and embrace 4IR. *Mail & Guardian*, 09/03/2019.

EXPLORING THE EXPERIENCES AND BENEFITS ... 129

Theme 5: The benefit of pursuing or obtaining a masters degree
QUESTION 5: How have you benefited (or not) from pursuing/obtaining a research masters degree? Please write your response in the space below:

- **I have not benefited yet—it has not changed my life in any visible way.**
- **Having a Masters' Degree has not benefited me in terms of employment. I face greater challenges in seeking employment as I am often told that I am 'over qualified'. There are several instances when I have applied for employment and yet individuals with no qualification or a lower qualification than me, get shortlisted and I am not considered.**
- **A Masters' Degree is amazing to have obtained, for me personally, I feel more accomplished and I know that I am heading towards being an academic but it has also significantly limited my ability to obtain financial independence through employment.**
- **I personally think that having a Masters' Degree is advantageous but our current economic and social situation in South Africa does not permit those with Masters' Degrees to progress with ease. Also your choice of research topic does not influence the kind of employment you get even though it is said we become experts in that field...**
- **It has not benefited me and employment is very difficult to find. It is sad when a postgraduate student has to work as a part-time waitress to support herself and family...**
- **I feel like I have matured through this experience. I was able to be employed as a tutor and gain teaching experience as my goal in the future is to become an academic**
- **Good jobs now require more online and communication skills which you do not get from doing a masters degree. Writing skills are important but more important are computer skills such as familiarity with Excel and other programs. Not everyone wants to become an academic...**

Theme 6: Mental health challenges during the pandemic

QUESTION 6: Did you experience any mental health challenges during the pandemic that impacted your studies? (RESPONSES: $N = 6$)

Responses based on gender	Problems experienced	Duration	Impact on your studies
FEMALE (4)	Anxiety, depression, panic attacks, forgetfulness due to covid mind fog	Erratic attacks; 6–12 months; continuous but managed with medical treatment	Writing goals not fulfilled; inconsistent working schedule; prolonged absence
MALE (2)	Physical and mental exhaustion due to financial stress, depression, burnout	At irregular intervals; ongoing for 2 years	Gap in timetable due to health; impact on studies and work life; unpaid leave

Author's survey 2020 to 2022

Based on the table, where only half the sample responded, stress and anxiety manifested in various forms (depression, panic attacks, forgetfulness, fatigue and burnout) and with varying duration (lasting for periods of up to 2 years and longer). The impact of mental health conditions on studying, resulted in prolonged absences from submitting draft chapters, inconsistency with writing and taking a leave of absence from work to recover.

According to the World Health Organization, mental health is related to mental and psychological well-being. It is more than the absence of a mental disorder and also includes the ability to think, learn and understand one's emotions and the reactions of others.[5] The COVID-19 pandemic changed and challenged the lives of students in multiple ways, including displacement from their homes and campuses, financial struggles, loss of family members and employment opportunities, and the need to learn new technologies. Chen and Lucock (2022) state that the stresses and restrictions associated with the pandemic have put university students at greater risk of developing mental health issues, which may significantly

---

[5] World Health Organization. Promoting mental health: Concepts, emerging evidence, practices [homepage on the Internet]. World Health Organization; 2004. Available from: https://www.who.intl/mental_health/evidence/en/promoting_mhh.pdf.

impair their academic success, social interactions and their future career and personal opportunities. A survey conducted by the O'Regan (2021) found that over 65% of South African students experienced mild to severe psychological distress as a result of the pandemic. The data also showed that psychological distress was more prevalent among female than male students.[6]

Theme 7: Research Masters vs. Coursework Masters

QUESTION 7: What do you think is the most challenging aspect of doing a research masters vs a coursework masters degree?

The students responses are articulated in the excerpts below:

- **It is a lonely experience to work on your own with occasional support only from the supervisor. For coursework, there is more student and staff interaction because of the structured modules.**
- **It is difficult to become disciplined and have a routine when you are on your own. Peer support is helpful but does not take away the fact that you have to do everything by yourself**
- **Trying to work in a structured way and juggle everything else during the pandemic...**
- **There is no structure and you have to be strict with yourself to get your work done on time**
- **As older students, we have more personal and work related issues to cope with. A course work masters is easier than the research masters which is very demanding. If I had a choice, I would choose the coursework...**
- **Even after doing a research masters it is a challenge to find stable employment. I feel a research masters is good training but doesn't seem to make much difference in the real world if its research or coursework...**
- **I found it hard to work independently but then I realized if I want to do my Ph.D. it provides the foundation to taking that step**

---

[6] Special Report. (2021). 'It is okay not to be okay'—Mental health issues and coping skills among the youth amidst the Covid-19 pandemic—Webinar. https://mg.co.za/special-reports/2021-08-12-it-is-okay-not-to-be-okay-mental-health-issues-and-coping-skills-among-the-youth-amidst-the-covid-19-pandemic-webinar/.

- By doing a research masters I could finally apply to do tutoring and get some teaching experience and this is part of my journey to getting my Ph.D. and becoming a lecturer or researcher
- Full research is not for everyone, we should have a choice between coursework and research at master's level. Coursework would be better for me...
- It is better if there is a smaller thesis with modules that teach you skills for employment (like how to approach the job interview) and technical skills (where you get a certificate).

The supervision of postgraduate students is considered a form of guidance and mentoring that facilitates student mastery of disciplinary research knowledge, over a set period of time. This journey is intellectually and emotionally challenging for both supervisor and student alike. The final theme, on the supervisors' experience and perception of supervision conducted during the pandemic, is presented below.

Theme 8: Supervisor's Narratives ($N = 4$) on their perceptions of the main challenges facing supervisors of Master's students during COVID-19

- Email, Learn (Discussion Forum) and Zoom have become the new tools of communication which has it's restrictions for those students who prefer written feedback that they can refer to at a later stage. Even with Zoom recordings, they had to make their own notes and a few felt this to be tedious. On the other hand, most students expressed a preference for the online interaction with the supervisor—which email does not provide. I combined these online technologies to suit the student during the pandemic...
- One of my students brought to my attention that during the pandemic most of her time was spent at home with family. This meant that she was not speaking in English at all. This led to the deterioration of her writing academically in English. This was also visible among other students as well for whom English was not a first language—there was a decline in the quality of their writing.
- Depending on the level of lockdown, most masters students were no longer residing at the student residences and had to visit the

campus to access the Lans and continue their work. This was an added expense and for some, not possible because of work and family demands. This led to large gaps of time elapsing between sending written work to me. It took a lot of effort to remain focused on their study and this reflected in the draft chapters submitted. It also became disillusioning to struggling students to receive feedback that not favourable.

- The main problem for me, was the diminished amount of time my students spend on reading and writing during the pandemic, due to financial and personal constraints (such as unemployment and illness). The work presented was often irregular and of poor quality and lacked the depth needed for masters level. Receiving feedback that was considered negative was also taken personally by students who were already so vulnerable by their circumstances.

- In adapting to the context of the pandemic, I tried new approaches to supervision. I found that allocating more time to simple chatting on social media enquiring about their well being, was highly appreciated. However, the setting of timelines and goals each month was not well received (actually it was ignored) and we ended up reverting to the old way (of working within their own time frames). This prolonged the research process...

- I combine Whatsapp, Zoom and a coffee shop meeting in person (every 3 months) for masters and Ph.D. students. It works well and I have found they are more motivated to do the work. Illness (Covid19 infections and mostly depression) were my main concerns, it takes away so much time in the process and delays completion.

- There was no enthusiasm for peer review of work produced. I set up WhatsApp groups for master's students I was supervising simultaneously. These proved successful as support systems and information networks but students did not want to share and review each others work...

- Supervision of master's students must be supported by cohort supervision administered by the school or college—online. It is very important for students to expose themselves to the perspectives of other supervisors and the challenges of other postgraduate students. Further, their writing and research skills need to be renewed and refined throughout their studies. The challenge during the pandemic was maintaining consistency...

- Regular workshops, exposes them to work alongside different academic staff and a range of masters level students. This removes them from the comfort zone and monotony of working with a single supervisor. This experience should also expedite the number of years they take to complete the degree so that supervising Masters students does not become a wasteful exercise for the university. Most of my students had exceeded the required time for completion...

In the above excerpts, several issues emerged among the perceived supervisor concerns. The most prominent were: adapting to the online context for supervising students; the deteriorating quality of writing in English; consistency and focus from students; institutional support for students and supervisors; the mental health of students during the pandemic; and the prolonged time taken for completion of studies. A report on the graduation and throughput of masters by research students at South African universities during the period 2005 to 2017, indicates that those who graduated in regulation time increased from 36 to 39% while those students who graduated after 6 years increased from 54 to 59% (Essop, 2020: 31).[7] The percentage for master's students graduating after the required time frame since the pandemic, must surely have increased.

5 Conclusion

Postgraduate students in South Africa, such as the sample in this study indicate, face a myriad of social, financial and academic constraints, which influence their ability to complete their degrees, as well as their mental health. The high graduate unemployment rate makes their circumstances all the more complex and challenging. According to StatSA, South Africa's unemployment rate reached 32.6% in the first three months of 2021. Of the 7.2 million unemployed persons in the first quarter of 2021, more than half (52.4%) had education levels below matric, followed

---

[7] Essop, A. (2020). The changing size and shape of the higher education system in South Africa, 2005–2017. Ali Mazrui Centre for Higher Education Studies—University of Johannesburg (uj.ac.za).

by those with matric at 37.7%. Only 2.1% of unemployed persons were graduates, while 7.5% had other tertiary qualifications as their highest level of education.[8] Despite these challenges, the student narratives in this study indicate a recognition that the structure and purpose of the research masters degree need to change.

Universities will not only have to develop the skills needed for today, but also those that will leverage the technological advances of tomorrow. Allowing graduates to obtain postgraduate qualifications is considered a way of creating a link between the value of knowledge and national economic growth (Sonn, 2016). Critical thinking, creativity, cognitive flexibility and emotional intelligence, as opposed to rote learning, to match the way people will increasingly work and collaborate in the 4IR, will have to be nurtured. Modalities of learning including where and how we learn require the integration of university curricula with the online world. Tensions inevitably arise in these conversations because universities continue to develop curricula in line with traditional organizing principles around knowledge (Menon & Castrillon, 2019). Research that interfaces and converges with social, human and technological sciences will support the production of goods and services in Africa in the new digital age (Xing & Marwala, 2017). Universities could help to prepare students for a digital future by offering multidisciplinary education, where students in human and social sciences include technological subjects and students in technological subjects include human and social sciences in their training.

References

Bernard, H. R. (2002). *Research methods in anthropology: Qualitative and quantitative approaches* (3rd ed.). Alta Mira Press.

Bromley, D. (1986). *The case study method in psychology and related disciplines.* Cambridge University Press.

Cekiso, M. Tshotso, B., Masha, R., & Saziwe, T. (2019). Supervision experiences of postgraduate research students at one South African Higher Education institution. *South African Journal of Higher Education, 33*(3), 8–25. http://dx.doi.org/https://doi.org/10.20853/33-3-2913

---

[8] Author Unknown. (2021). The chances of employment in South Africa based on your level of education. https://businesstech.co.za/news/business/495113/the-chances-of-employment-in-south-africa-based-on-your-level-of-education/.

Chen, T., & Lucock, M. (2022). The mental health of university students during the COVID-19 pandemic: An online survey in the UK. *PLoS ONE, 17*(1), 1–17.

Cresswell, J. W., & Plano Clark, V. L. (2011). *Designing and conducting mixed method research* (2nd ed.). Sage.

Crowe, S., Cresswell, K., Robertson, A., et al. (2011). The case study approach. *BMC Medical Research Methodology, 11,* 100. https://doi.org/10.1186/1471-2288-11-100

Essop, A. (2020). *The changing size and shape of the higher education system in South Africa, 2005–2017.* University of Johannesburg. https://heltasa.org.za/wp-content/uploads/2020/08/Size-and-Shape-of-the-HE-System-2005-2017.pdf

Griesel, H. (2020). *Reinventing South Africa's universities for the future: A synthesis report on the National Higher Education Conference 2019.* Universities South Africa | USAf.

Hedding, D. W., Greve, M., Breetzke, G. D., Nel, W., & van Vuuren, B. J. (2020). COVID-19 and the academe in South Africa: Not business as usual. *COVID-19 and the academe in South Africa, 116*(7–8), 1–3.

Kayembe, C., & Nel, D. (2019). Challenges and opportunities in the fourth industrial revolution. *African Journal of Public Affairs, 11*(3), 79–94.

Lebeau, Y. (2008). Universities and social transformation in sub-Saharan Africa: Global rhetoric and local contradictions. *Compare, 38*(2), 139–153.

Menon, K., & Castrillon, G. (2019). *Universities have a pivotal role to play in the Fourth Industrial Revolution.* https://www.dailymaverick.co.za/article/2019-04-15-universities-have-pivotal-role-to-play-in-fourth-industrial-revolution/

National Planning Commission & National Development Plan. (2013). *Our future, our plan.* NPC. http://www.gov.za/issues/national_development_plan_2030

Nkoane, M. N. (2014). Revisiting pedagogic practices: A case for sustainable learning environments for postgraduate supervision studies: Part 1: Exploration of the critical relationship between higher education and the development of democracy in South Africa. *South African Journal of Higher Education, 28*(3), 697–706. https://hdl.handle.net/10520/EJC159158

O'Regan. (2021, June 14). Covid-19: Survey finds 65% of students reported psychological distress in 2020. https://www.dailymaverick.co.za/article/2021-06-14-covid-19-survey-finds-65-of-students-reported-psychological-distress-in-2020/

Rodny-Gumede, Y. (2019). The fourth industrial revolution, the changing world of work and imperatives of internationalisation in higher education. *The Thinker, 82*(4), 56–60.

Sokhulu, L. H. (2020). Students' experiences of using digital technologies to address their personal research needs during the COVID-19 lockdown. *African Identities, 19*(4), 436–452. https://doi.org/10.1080/14725843.2020.1801384

Sonn, R. (2016). The challenge for a historically disadvantaged South African university to produce more postgraduate students. *South African Journal of Higher Education, 30*(2), 226–241.

Spradley, J. P. (1979). *The ethnographic interview.* Holt, Rinehart & Winston.

Thaver, B., Holtman, L., & Julie, C. (2013). Inducting BEd Hons students into a research culture and the world of research. *South African Journal of Higher Education, 27*(5), 1135–1148.

Xing, B., & Marwala, T. (2017). Implications of the fourth industrial age for higher education. *The Thinker, 73,* 10–15.

Zewotir, T., North, D., & Murray, M. (2015). The time to degree or dropout amongst full-time master's students at University of KwaZulu-Natal. *South African Journal of Science, 111*(9–10), 1–6.

Zoom Video Communications Inc. (2016). *Security guide.* Zoom Video Communications Inc. https://d24cgw3uvb9a9h.cloudfront.net/static/81625/doc/Zoom-Security-White-Paper.pdf

Decolonization of Knowledge Production in African Societies: Contextual Analysis of Language of Instruction

Remi Alapo and Doghudje Doghudje

1 Background

Post-Colonial African societies continue to function with the cultural and educational framework inherited from colonialists more than fifty years ago. There has been a break in this continuity since the early 2000s or the beginning of the twenty-first century, when Nigerian Federal Universities introduced, as a universal prerequisite, courses that relate to pre-colonial African history. The goal of this curriculum innovation, as explained at the time by the scholarly authorities, was to foster a more African identity in graduates which will support them in creating and using the knowledge that is more African in essence (Maina, 2003). Decades since this began, it turns out that curriculum innovation is just one aspect of knowledge-creation decolonization. This cultural trend in education has expanded toward other factors such as the language of instruction (Adebisi, 2016).

R. Alapo (✉)
York College, City University of New York (CUNY), New York, NY, USA
e-mail: oalapo1@york.cuny.edu

D. Doghudje
American College of Education, Indianapolis, IN, USA

© The Author(s), under exclusive license to Springer Nature Switzerland AG 2023
A. I. Adeniran (ed.), *African Development and Global Engagements*,
https://doi.org/10.1007/978-3-031-21283-3_8

We now have educational pilot projects across Africa (in Kenya, Piper et al., 2016; and in Cameroon, Ramachandran et al., 2018) that are using local or mother tongue as the language of instruction in educational systems instead of the public European or foreign languages that have been used until now. The randomized control trial by Piper et al. (2016) is evaluated in this paper.

In this paper, we examined this cultural trend in African education from the perspective of language of instruction and the corresponding results it has for knowledge creation in Africa. We looked at the questions behind these pilot projects and checked if they are addressed in the literature. The Research Questions that guided our study included the following:

RQ1: Is there a relationship between the language of instruction and the ease of learning for students?

RQ2: Does literacy improve for students when the mother tongue or local language is used for instruction instead of a foreign public language?

RQ3: Does an epistemological or indigenous knowledge base exist from which schools in Africa can draw their cultural framework?

RQ4: Does using the mother tongue as instructional language in schools support knowledge decolonization in African societies?

Further in this paper, we outline the work and findings of researchers who have looked at one or some of our research questions. Following is an outline of the major contributors to the background of this study.

Cummins (1979) is one of the earliest researchers on this topic in the literature. The major thesis of his work is that children find it easier to learn a second language only after mastering their own first language or mother tongue. This is relevant because most African children, at the age when they begin formal education, are still struggling to gain mastery of their own first language or mother tongue. According to Cummins, this will result in poor educational outcomes for African children, who will end up average in the mastery of both languages.

Present in the literature is a body of work on this subject by the United Nations Educational Scientific and Cultural Organization (UNESCO), who term the dominance of foreign languages in African education and society as *'linguistic imperialism'*. Benson (2004), in a background paper published by a UNESCO initiative, argued for formal biliteracy for minority children who have to experience education in a language other than their mother tongue. She observed the ease with which students who are literally bilingual can learn and transfer concepts from one language to the other. Benson (2004) insisted this is more effective than memorization or rote learning.

Oluwole (2016) in a set of video interviews titled 'Oro Isiti' laid emphasis on the mother tongue as the preferred language of instruction. She argued that certain localized experiences and concepts have no equivalent translation into English for example. She also argued that learning, when done in a foreign language, will therefore be incomplete, foreign to learners, and not useful for knowledge creation. We examined ideas by Chumbow (2009) and Adebisi (2016) and evaluated a randomized control pilot project in Kenya carried out by Piper et al. (2016), who sought to provide qualitative evidence found in the medium-scale implementation of Mother Tongue Education in Kenya. Piper recommends that similar experimental programs should be conducted on a larger scale; and that corresponding policy challenges to implementation be addressed by the relevant government agencies in Kenya.

2 Colonization, Post-Colonial Theory, and Decolonization

Colonialism is a defining event in the history of what is today known as Africa. While some have traced the genesis of this event to pre-European occupation of Africa, other authors pinpoint the Berlin Conference of 1884 as the moment real colonization of Africa began (Adebisi, 2016). The result and after-effect of colonialism have been profound and linger on to date. The nature of this result is best described by Sertima (1984) who compared the colonization of Africa to a disaster of unequaled proportion which tore into shreds the threads of cultural and historical continuity in Africa such that Africa before and after colonization are two very different entities. Sithole (2014) commented on Achille Mbembe's work and stated that the consequence of colonization in Africa was to silence African History, knowledge, and autonomy, which is where post-colonial theory comes in. It (Post-Colonial Theory) is the analysis of the effects of colonialism or colonization on the Colonized, in this case, African societies. Post-Colonial Theory also shows a passageway to a healing process such as Decolonization. Syrontiski (2007) reflected on the dominant ideology in post-colonial theory, where Africa is perceived as uncivilized, and the colonizing powers are seen as civilized. This dominant idea continues till today, controlling power structures, politics, language, and knowledge.

In this paper, we are concerned with the decolonization of Africa using the post-colonial theory. In *Decolonizing Methodologies: Research and Indigenous Peoples*, by Cain (2013), Linda Tuhiwai Smith defines decolonization as 'a social and political process aimed at undoing the multifaceted impacts of the colonial project and re-establishing strong contemporary indigenous nations and institutions based on traditional values, philosophies and knowledge'. This has been an ongoing process since African nations attained political independence in the second half of the last century. It is a multifaceted process that includes the political, religious, art, and education in and of Africa. Here, we restrict our interest in decolonization to African Education.

3   DECOLONIZING AFRICAN EDUCATION

Wisker (2007) in describing the impact of colonialism on Africa, referred to it as 'epistemic violence' which has silenced the 'colonial subjects' of Africa by appropriating and replacing their Education systems with Eurocentric ones. Rodney (1972) further noted the introduction and the use of written texts and non-lyrical European languages in colonial education. These had the result of splitting the African Character into two; one, that is indigenous and at home with inherited genetics, epistemology, and practices, and two, another that is imposed and calculated, inorganic and assimilated into, with very little interaction between both. In this type of colonial education, Rodney identified a focus on English, French, and Portuguese as languages of instruction and communication with a parallel erasure of African Languages and practices. Decolonizing African education will mean a reversal of this process, a form of 'epistemic restoration' if we look at it from Spivak's point of view.

Wright et al. (2007) concluded that the main objective of decolonizing African education should be to critically engage with and include African Knowledge (both pre-colonial and post-colonial) in formal schooling while refusing to affix the label of inferiority to 'other' systems of knowledge as has been the case until now. Decolonization of education, knowledge, and thought implies that there are several and different ways of knowing and that these ways, including indigenous ones, are valid.

4 Education as Knowledge Creation

The main goal of education is to examine, critique, create, and use new Knowledge to meet the needs of people and the host-Society. Oluwole (2016) defined education as the comprehensive process in which traditions, customs, and indigenous knowledge of a people are systematically transmitted from one generation to another. There are other definitions of education in literature. However, for the intent and purpose of this paper, we will defer to Oluwole's definition of education. In addition, we will consider education and knowledge creation to be the same thing in practice. So that, hereon, both terms will be used interchangeably.

It can be argued that much of the knowledge creation that occurs in the schooling system does take place at the postgraduate or Ph.D. level. Such an argument will mean to restrict the focus of our paper to the decolonization of language in education at that stage of learning. Nonetheless, for our study, we assumed that knowledge creation, just like literacy, occurs at all stages of education; and that the learning process is innately creative and innovative.

5 Language and Decolonizing African Education

Brock-Utne (2000) discovered that the failure of African countries to achieve development targets can be traced to the colonial era as most of these States continue to use English, French, and Portuguese as the language of instruction in Schools. Arnove (2005) insists that African intellectuals need to rethink the use of English, a language introduced by colonization, as the medium of instruction in African schools. Further, Geo-Jaja and Azaiki (2010) have shed more light on the persistent danger of not recognizing indigenous languages in schools in the Niger-Delta region of Nigeria. This is contrary to a previous finding by Geo-Jaja (2006) that education and its curriculum, if they are to be effective, should be grounded in the indigenous knowledge and language of the people whom it serves. This also explains why Fafunwa (1990) condemned colonization for allowing 'linguistic domination' to take place in Africa, creating various 'linguistic blocks' such as Francophone, Anglophone, and Lusophone Africa. He noted very clearly that except for Kenya, Somalia, and Tanzania, African countries are yet to realize that literacy does not mean being fluent in writing or oral in a Western language.

The subject of foreign languages in African education in relation to decolonization continues to be investigated. Several African scholars define a reformed African education that includes rather than excludes indigenous knowledge. Indeed, they imagine local African languages being used as the medium of instruction in schools, just as you have it in Western Europe and Asia, for example. In this sense, Prah (2001) reminded us that no society in the world has developed on the strength of a borrowed or colonial language. In the form of a rhetorical question, Mazrui (1986) inquired to know if any country achieved first-rank economic development with the overwhelming use of foreign languages for its discourse on growth and development.

The common underlying thread in literature is that decolonization of African education is also the decolonization of the language of instruction, a replacement of the colonial language with an Indigenous one. Throughout this paper, we will explore this relationship using similar research that has examined changes in the result of education or literacy by switching the language or medium of instruction.

6 Literacy and Language, Cummins (1979)

James Cummins is one of the earliest researchers whose work focuses on the relationship between the knowledge-creation process (or literacy) and language, in particular the home language or L1. He conducted his research with bilingual children who are often minority children immersed in a school experience and society that uses a language of instruction other than their own home language. We highlight the overview, approach, findings, and suggestions from his study.

Cummins set out to investigate the reasons why a home-school language switch resulted in proficiency in learning outcomes for majority-language students and a deficiency in the same outcomes for minority-language students. In his work, the mother tongue or home language is referred to as L1 while the school language is L2. He identified three major factors affecting his research problem namely, (1) linguistic factors, (2) socio-cultural factors, and (3) school program factors. Under linguistic factors, he referred to a 'linguistic-mismatch' hypothesis which was used in a 1953 UNESCO report to conclude that 'the best language to instruct a child in his or her own mother tongue'. This report was prepared by Skutnabb-Kangas and Toukomaa (1976). They provided evidence, on page 48 of the report, from a minority-language learning situation which was consistent with the developmental interdependence hypothesis.

The original purpose of the UNESCO report was to determine the linguistic level and development in both the mother tongue and Swedish language of Finnish migrant children attending Swedish comprehensive schools. It was observed that attention was paid to the interdependence between skills in the mother tongue and Swedish. For example, the hypothesis that was tested proved that learners who have best preserved their mother tongue are also best in Swedish. This hypothesis was strongly supported by the findings cited by Cummins who also discovered that Finnish migrant children had average levels of nonverbal intellectual ability and that their skills in both Finnish and Swedish were considerably below that of Finnish and Swedish expectations. Prior to this discovery, it was observed there was an extent to which mother tongue was developed in each learner before their contact with Swedish students and was strongly related to how well Swedish was learned by the Finnish migrant students.

This UNESCO finding is consistent with the 'developmental interdependence hypothesis' proposed by Cummins (1979), as one of two hypotheses that can be used to understand the relationship between linguistic development and cognition in bilingual children. The developmental interdependence hypothesis is the central thesis of Cummins' work, and it states that bilingual children attain a level of competence in L2 based on the level of competence they already achieved in L1 prior to exposure to L2. It has also been referred to as the 'vernacular advantage' by some authors, one of them being Modiano (1968). She, Modiano, found that Mexican-Indian children who were taught to read firstly in their home or vernacular language and then in Spanish scored higher on Spanish reading after three years than those children who learned to read only in Spanish.

Further, Toukomaa and Skutnabb-Kangas, have conducted previous research on bilingual education and mother tongue instruction for bilingual children in the US. They, both authors, defined three levels or types of bilingual education and categorized the cognitive effect linked to each level or type of bilingualism. 'Additive bilingualism'—which has a positive cognitive effect on learners, 'dominant'—which has neither a negative nor positive effect on learners but provides a higher level or threshold of

146   R. ALAPO AND D. DOGHUDJE

bilingual competencies and finally 'semilingualism'—which has a negative effect on learners and also has a lower level or threshold of bilingual competence.

According to Cummins, previous research is done on linguistic development and bilingual education has generated inconclusive or ambiguous results because of an incomplete theoretical framework that failed to include certain variables. He, therefore, came up with a framework that includes child input and educational treatment as variables and adopted a model for his research that uses these variables. Based on this model and framework, he concluded that if the cognitive and academic success of a bilingual child is a goal, then the school program must operate an additive form of bilingualism that involves literacy in both L1 and L2. For further research, Cummins suggested another look at motivational and linguistic variables and how they interacted with educational treatment using the same hypotheses and framework that he developed.

7   LANGUAGE OF INSTRUCTION AND EDUCATIONAL QUALITY, BENSON (2004)

Decolonizing education in African societies has to do with removing all the colonial nature, properties, and intent of education as it was inherited from colonial powers. We are interested in how this decolonization (of education or knowledge creation) relates to the language used for instruction in the schooling system in West and East African schools. Benson studied a similar problem, and we include here a review of her work and findings. Benson established that language and communication are vital to educational quality. She wanted to see what changes occur in educational quality when the language of instruction is L1, the mother tongue rather than a full submersion in L2, a school language that differs completely from students' mother tongue and home language. Her work drew extensively from our previously cited researcher, Cummins (1979), *the interdependency theory*, and the concept of *common underlying proficiency* whereby literacy skills and cognition in one language can be used to achieve literacy and cognition more quickly in another language.

Benson explained that many developing societies are characterized by individual as well as societal multilingualism but most follow a single foreign language as the language of instruction and not their mother tongue. In contrast, mother tongue-based bilingual programs use the learner's first language, known as the L1, to teach early reading and writing skills along with academic content. She insisted that the second or foreign language, known as the L2, should be taught systematically so that learners can gradually transfer skills from the familiar language to the unfamiliar one. Advantages that result from this system of instruction (competence in L1 before L2) include an understanding of sound-symbol or meaning-symbol correspondence. Students are able to learn L2 through communication rather than memorization. They are able to transfer linguistic and cognitive skills from L1 to L2 in this type of bilingual program or schooling, which is what she recommended.

In terms of educational quality, Benson referred to 'the affective domain' which is the emotional experience of education on the part of the student. Whereas submersion bilingual programs and schools are more likely to generate alienation, disconnection, frustration, and a possibility of dropout, mother tongue-based learning improves student confidence, self-esteem, and sense of identity which leads to increase in motivation, creativity, and initiative. This is because, according to her, students in mother tongue-based learning are allowed to be themselves, to develop their personalities and intellect.

These benefits to educational quality, she asserts, are based on two assumptions: one, that basic human needs have been met and two, that mother tongue-based bilingual schooling can be properly implemented. She cites as example an implementation of a pilot project in Nigeria where Yoruba language was used as mother tongue or L1 from primary 1 to 6 and gradually replaced with the English language as L2 from primary 5 onward. The project reported an easier transition into L2 for the students involved with better transfer of skills in literacy, comprehension, reading, speaking, and the ability of students to grasp instruction content faster. Benson suggested that mother tongue-based learning be implemented from small scale to large scale through experimentation.

8 Language and National Development, Chumbow (2009)

In his paper titled *Linguistic Diversity, Pluralism and National Development in Africa*, Chumbow (2009) connected the failure of several development programs in Africa including the Structural Adjustment Program (SAP), and the New Partnership for African Development (NEPAD) to the neglect of language as a factor. Drawing upon Bamgbose (1991, 2005), Chumbow stated that social and economic development in Africa depended crucially on the development and use of African languages in education, commerce, and society. As a background to his study, Chumbow reminded us of the origin of this problem (the neglect of African languages in public life) in colonialism. His effort, to highlight the necessity for and to bring African languages back into popular and public use, therefore falls under decolonization. He agreed with Benson that the language of education and development in post-colonial Africa has remained foreign languages introduced by colonial power and influence. This has economically and politically marginalized up to 50% of such countries' population, especially rural populations who are often not literate in foreign languages and do not use them in their daily lives.

He noted that intervention efforts, in response to previous studies in the literature, have been forthcoming from various organizations, chief among whom is the UNESCO and the African Union who in 2006 proclaimed the need to adopt and use African languages in education, governance, and other areas of development in partnership with English, French, and other colonial languages. According to Chumbow, both organizations agreed that, for the national development enterprise to be effective, African languages need to be developed, revitalized, revalorized, and instrumentalized so that they can assume development-related functions as the language of education and language of communication in the economic sphere.

Implementation programs and initiatives have closely followed this declaration with average success. Chumbow attributed this lack of implementation success to the linguistic diversity and pluralism of most African societies. He claimed that most societies in Africa are multi-ethnic or multi-cultural, displaying both majority and minority constituents with majority and minority languages, respectively. This, however, may lead some people to decry multiple languages as a bad phenomenon or problem in Africa. To Chumbow, this is not the case. He asserted that both multilingualism and multiculturalism are a plus and not a negative, correlating the same to the biodiversity of nature which preserves life on our planet. At the same time, he admitted that there is a 'survival of the fittest' conflict among languages in a linguistically diverse society, this conflict being sponsored more by political and economic factors than by the languages themselves. As a result of this conflict, some languages are bound to be assimilated into the majority languages or lost over time.

Extinction of languages, according to Chumbow, is not really a good thing because language is a historical heritage, and consequently a repository of the history of humanity. Language is the means of accessing knowledge, ideas and beliefs of the past". This means that we should strive to preserve as many languages as possible, even in a linguistically diverse society where some languages are spoken by fewer peoples and have minority status. He even goes so far as to assign human rights to languages, saying that 'language is a right; a human right of the same level of importance as all other inalienable human rights'. Citing Skutnabb-Kangas and Phillipson (1995), Chumbow declared that all forms of linguistic discrimination should be fought against and countered.

Toward this end, to facilitate the use of African languages given the linguistic diversity of African societies, Chumbow proposes a theoretical framework which assigns place and value to both minority and majority languages which can then be preserved and used in partnership with foreign languages in the public sphere. This framework is his chief contribution and what he believed is missing in the implementation of previous such programs. In Chumbow's framework, all languages fall under the public or private realm, where public realm languages are those used in larger society outside of the home and local districts while private realm languages are those used at home and in local districts. Mother tongue and the home language are L1 or 'private realm', and official languages including foreign languages are L2 or 'public realm'. In a multilingual society, there will be a couple of public realm languages denoted L2, and L3. It is a tier-based stratification model that aims to create a place and relevance for all languages spoken in Society and considered as private realm languages. In addition, a few of these languages are then chosen to be used in the public sphere (for education, government, and commerce) in collaboration with a colonial or foreign language.

Chumbow cited Nigeria and Tanzania as good examples of countries where this model has been implemented, where both differ in the number of languages adopted for use in the public sphere. Tanzania uses one language, Kiswahili, as a public language in partnership with English, whereas Nigeria uses three major languages (Hausa, Yoruba, and Ibo) as public language in partnership with English. These two different tier-systems are labeled by Chumbow as 'One National-Language Stratification' and 'Two-or-More National Language Stratification'. Practically, Chumbow addressed the problems that may result from implementing such a model. These problems are mainly two: one, dominance and tension among the languages; two, negative attitude toward what is considered 'weaker languages' or, reversely, positive attitude toward the official foreign language. Under this topic of model implementation, he quoted a relevant thought by the famous Kenyan writer Ngugi wa Thiong'O (1986), who asked, 'how can one transform the climate of opinion so that we can shift the colonial minds from the groundless belief that only knowledge which is packaged in the languages of the colonial conquerors is worthwhile language?'.

It is thought that forms part of the conclusion of Chumbow's study and which is related to our concern in this paper: decolonizing knowledge creation in African societies. Chumbow has proposed a model that associates language with national development in a way that leads to partial decolonization. Among areas under national development is education which is where most knowledge creation happens in today's world. Lastly, Chumbow suggested more research needed to be done on how to build and transform the attitudes of people toward the use and successful implementation of the language tier-stratification model.

9   Mother Tongue Education, Oluwole (2016)

Oluwole, in her video series on YouTube titled 'Oro Isiti', has remarked on 'the importance of the mother tongue in education'. In her remarks, she associated the high-value African societies place on foreign languages with the impact of colonialism. This impact has created, according to Oluwole, an educational system that ignores or even penalizes the use of mother tongues and local languages for instruction in the classroom. She argued that this has a direct connection to a weak sense of identity in African students and also to little original creation of knowledge at the university or postgraduate level. As evidence for her claim that education in the mother tongue leads to knowledge creation and invention, she cited the examples of Germany and Japan, two nations with big economies driven by knowledge creation and invention. She emphasized that education in both countries is done in German and Japanese, respectively, which are local languages or mother tongues. In contrast, she pointed to Nigeria as representative of African societies where education is not done in the mother tongue, and which demonstrate little or no knowledge creation.

Education in Africa, Oluwole asserted, is misdefined by policymakers who assume that education means the ability to read and write in English, a colonial language. This misdefinition has skewed the focus of education from literacy and knowledge creation to mastery of the English language. She explained that one can be educated without being fluent in the English language, as is the case in some parts of Europe and Asia. In other words, African educationists and African educational policymakers need to re-examine their understanding of education, what it means, how it can be achieved, and what it is meant to be used for. This wrong focus of education in Africa, according to her, has made education and its products or graduates of less relevance in society. They, the graduates, are fluent in spoken and written English, but demonstrate no quality skills or ability to create and use local knowledge. As a result, they are not fit to be good employees or entrepreneurs.

Oluwole did not think that the implementation of mother tongue education will be without problems. For example, in her remarks, Nigeria with 253 languages will face certain struggles in operating mother tongue education. Some of these challenges have been covered by Chumbow in his study on language and national development. A more practical study by Piper et al. (2016) documents, in a medium-scale randomized controlled trial, some of the challenges faced in implementing mother tongue education in Kenya.

10   Mother Tongue Literacy, Piper et al. (2016)

In 2013 and 2014, a team of researchers led by Benjamin Piper conducted a trial study of Mother Tongue (MT) instruction as part of the Primary Math and Reading (PRIMR) initiative in Kenya. Their findings and conclusion were published in the *Comparative and International Education* journal in 2016. At the time, it was the first medium-scale randomized controlled trial to address the question and the practical reality of implementing a mother tongue (MT) literacy program in a multilingual Sub-Saharan African country. Among other things, they found that a MT program can improve early grade reading skills even in the face of resistance by Stakeholders. They discovered evidence for the interdependence hypothesis which is that literacy and cognitive skills in the Mother Tongue (MT) were transferred to similar skills in the school language which were Kiswahili and English.

Their suggestions for further research included: carrying out the same study using a larger sample that is more representative of the population, and extending the investigation of MT education beyond reading skills or literacy skills to other subjects such as Math and Science. This was a practical trial, and they therefore had recommendations for policymakers in Kenya. These recommendations were that: (1) policymakers in Kenya need to decide on whether or not MT education is right for a multilingual society like Kenya. A firm decision in this wise will lay the grounds for a more even implementation as opposed to the uneven implementation of research recommendations in MT education that exists today; (2) upgrading Teacher Education with professional development in mother tongue learning; (3) that policymakers in Kenya need to determine whether to implement mother tongue literacy or mother tongue as the language of instruction.

As a background to their study, Piper et al. cited a UNESCO (2014) report on Kenya that showed evidence that one in five Kenyan youth aged 15–24 cannot read. To explain this, they identified a mismatch between the home language of learners and the language of instruction in Kenyan schools, which is usually English, a foreign language. They hypothesized that a switch to mother tongue instruction will produce different reading outcomes in learners. Previous research has obviously been done on this topic which led the Kenyan Institute of Education (1992) to declare that children in grades 1–3, have the right to be taught in the language of their educational zone or district. A more recent white paper (Republic of Kenya, 2012) affirmed this, and so did a new Kenya Education Sector plan (Ministry of Education, Science and Technology, MoEST, 2014).

The problem however lies in the lack of implementation. Few pilot studies on implementation exist, and this is the gap that introduced their research. Piper et al. (2016) used data obtained from the Primary Reading Initiative (PRIMR), a project funded by both the United States Agency For International Development (USAID) and the UK Department for International Development (DFID). As stated earlier, the purpose of their study was to investigate the causal effect of PRIMR-MT intervention on reading skills of Kenyan learners using a medium to large-scale implementation. They achieved this by using a randomized control trial group, PRIMR, whose causal effect they evaluated against PRIMR-MT, a version of PRIMR.

We have included Piper et al. to showcase the practical implementation of mother tongue-based learning in an African society. Their research focus came close to ours which is 'Decolonization of education in African societies in the context of language of instruction'. We hoped that highlighting some of the difficulties they went through in implementing mother tongue-based learning could shed light on potential questions that our research will attract. One of these difficulties was parents' resistance to mother tongue (MT) education. Piper et al. noted, in agreement with Begi that parents are unhappy if mother tongue education became the norm instead of the exception.

This may explain why, as found by Spernes (2012), the use of mother tongue in schools by both teachers and students is not allowed. In addition to parents' resistance, resource constraints remain a challenge in implementing MT education. Jones and Barkhuizen (2011) stated, for example, that while other texts in a particular school were printed in color, MT-Texts were only printed in black and white, leading students to surmise that MT education is not as important as education in a foreign or colonial tongue. Finally, there remains the political question of what language to pick as the mother tongue for instruction. Skutnabb-Kangas (2001) and Gacheche (2010) have found that stakeholders fear that promoting one local language over another may lead to ethnic tension or violence despite evidence that one-language policies do not imply ethnic cohesion.

11   DECOLONIZING AFRICAN EDUCATION AND IHRL, ADEBISI (2016)

At Independence, leadership of African societies was placed in African hands. Adebisi noted that these were not just normal hands, but actually the hands of African elites who had been educated in colonial schools, and whose thoughts had been colored by colonial Education. In this colonial or Eurocentric education which continued to be the currency in post-colonial Africa, indigenous African knowledge was seen as pre-critical, pre-logical, and by nature inferior. Later efforts in decolonization will spread to remove these vestiges of colonial influence. She cited, in this regard, the 'Rhodes Must Fall' decolonization movement in South Africa in 2016; and that the decades-long drive by African intellectuals to make African education stand on an Afrocentric curriculum. However, there are limitations to this effort. One of them is the international investment in African education which is more concerned with the 'right to education' or access to the neglect of the right of Africans to their own education. According to Adebisi (2016), this complex international education relationship between Africa and the world needed revisiting, with consideration given to African culture and indigeneity.

Citing Sertima (1984) to illustrate the roots of Africa's education crisis in colonialism, Adebisi pointed to the solution to this crisis in post-colonial theory which can be used to deconstruct colonialism. She agreed with Syrotinski (2007) that post-colonialism can heal the trauma of colonialism and create new narratives that contain more freedom and opportunity for all. This, however, is only possible if the decolonization of education is done in the context of International Human Rights Law (IHRL), and as suggested by wa Mutua (1994). In this sense, the subject of decolonizing African education is resolved by giving voice and value to African indigenous thought and knowledge. One manifestation of context would be the language of instruction in African education, which reasonably changes from the colonial languages to local tongues possessive of more depth, warmth, and character.

Spivak's (1994) position that colonialism is epistemic violence which stripped learners of voice and language is addressed by this contextual relationship. It means that in the properly decolonized African education (which post-colonial theory and deconstruction lead us to), all indigenous knowledge is restored; and not only this, but the international understanding of indigenous thought is also transformed as well. Instead of assigning inferiority to African values, the new web of relationships in knowledge will allow various systems of knowledge to co-exist, admitting that value is inherent in all of them.

12 Research Method

The two major theories underlying our research are post-colonial theory and Lev Vygotsky's theory of socio-cultural development. We were concerned with isolating the relationship between knowledge creation decolonization and language of instruction in Africa (West and East). The geographical context of Africa brings post-colonial theory into relevance. While Adebisi (2016) has defined post-colonial theory as the search for the truth about Africa by way of analyzing the consequences of colonialism on the colonized, and proposing ways to correct negative influences and structures, Ahluwalia (2012) states that post-colonial theory is helpful in the total examination of a society from the moment it is ruptured by colonialism until the present post-colonial period. Birgit Brock-Utne and Babaci-Wilhite are examples of prominent authors who have used the post-colonial theory as a lens to investigate problems in twenty-first-century Africa.

The second theory that underpins our research is Lev Vygotsky's sociocultural theory of cognitive development. In a sense, Vygotsky attributes cognitive development to the learner's culture. He states that social interaction plays an important role in cognitive development (Vygotsky, 1978). This social interaction is between the Teacher and the Student, and is influenced by variables such as local culture and language. Infact, he places language front and center among factors that impact cognition which in later stages of school becomes knowledge creation. Elliot (1994: 41) cited Vygotsky's idea that 'thought development is determined by language, for instance, by the linguistic tools of thought and by the sociocultural experience of the child'. This implies that a child is more likely to learn better or have better cognitive development if the language of instruction is as close to the mother tongue as possible. His theory indicates that a relationship exists between the language of instruction and knowledge creation. It also could mean that we can decolonize knowledge creation or education by decolonizing the language of instruction from a foreign one to the mother tongue. The figure depicts Vygotsky's model of learning, showing the factors that contribute to cognition in the child-learner (Fig. 1).

For our research method, we used the Meta-Synthesis of findings in the examined Literature. This is a form of 'qualitative secondary analysis of primary data' that has been used by Paterson et al. (2001), and Evans and Popova (2016), the primary data in this case being the findings by

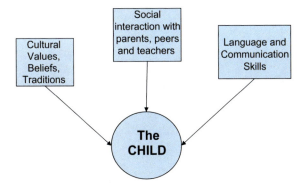

Fig. 1 Vygotsky's socio-cultural model of cognitive development (Vygotsky, 1978)

previous researchers. We collated these findings, meta-analyzed them for thematic similarities, differences, and uniqueness, paying careful attention to our research questions in the process. As a Meta-Study, we wanted to be able to synthesize these observed outcomes and themes to create new knowledge in the matter under inspection. For this study, our aim was to see how introducing the mother tongue or indigenous language as the language of instruction in African schools contributed to decolonizing knowledge creation or education. In the next section, findings by authors in the literature will be outlined and discussed. These authors are; Cummins (1979), Benson (2004), Chumbow (2009), Oluwole (2016), Piper et al. (2016), and Adebisi (2016).

13 Research Design

The figure shows the research method (Meta-Analysis) and design for our study. In short, we systematically reviewed a collection of studies and a randomized controlled trial related to our problem. Then, we meta-analyzed their findings and overlapping recommendations, which we synthesized into our insights and recommendations. Systematic review, as used in our study, has been defined by The Campbell Collaboration (2015) as one where transparent procedures are used in evaluating and synthesizing the findings of relevant research. The procedures are clearly identified and outlined to enable understanding and replication of similar future research (Fig. 2).

Fig. 2 Meta-analysis research method

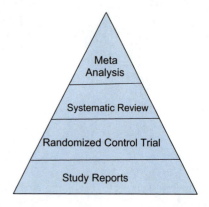

14   Search Strategy

We included in our search those authors who had conducted research in 'knowledge creation', 'african education', 'decolonization', 'decolonization of african education', 'linguistic development of children', 'bilingual education', 'language of instruction', 'mother tongue', and 'mother tongue education'. In this way, the keywords that made up our research problem and which are duplicated in our research questions overlapped with those of the authors that we reviewed. One of these authors, Piper et al., was a pilot study: we wanted to make sure that the ideas and theories underlying research in this area had been tested in practice, yielding practical recommendations instead of just laboratory ideas.

15   Data Analysis

What we did in our study was a secondary analysis of existing research or primary data. This is a form of data analysis that can, as stated by Glaser (1963), contribute new ideas to the body of social knowledge. Hinds et al. (1997), and Heaton (1998), noted that authors who have used secondary analysis have done so when they wanted to pursue related interests to the original one; carry out further analysis of the original dataset or apply a new orientation to the same research problem. In our study, we used Meta-Analysis (a form of secondary data analysis) for the following reasons: time constraints, fewer problems with data collection, availability of research materials, and to offer insights on research in existence.

16   Limitations of the Study

Our research was limited to the primary data collected and analyzed by the authors we reviewed and examined. We do not have access to this data in its original form and cannot validate its quality. Hence, our conclusions reflect this data skeleton and architecture that we have no influence over. In other words, we are subject to similar errors that must have been made in the reviewed literature, especially errors in data collection and analysis. Also, only one study, Piper et al. is a practical trial. It means that most of our conclusion is still a theory and will need further practical study to validate them in use and operation. Even though our focus was on African education, one author we cited, Cummins, concerned himself with Finnish migrant children struggling with bilingual education in Sweden. His conclusions, which we have synthesized into ours, will have to be tested in African society for more cultural relevance.

17 FINDINGS AND DISCUSSION OF FINDINGS

17.1 Review Statistics

As our research was focused on Africa and African education, 75% of the review (four out of the six studies selected) had been done by Africans or conducted in Africa. Also, one out of six of the studies reviewed was a randomized controlled study done in Kenya to practically evaluate theoretical findings in this area. Both genders were equally represented (50% of each) in the literature that we reviewed. In addition, half had been carried out in the last decade with the most recent being Piper et al. (2016) and Adebisi (2016). Cummins (1979) and Chumbow (2009) developed and used a theoretical framework and model, close to an empirical study, to achieve results, while Oluwole was more of a position paper. Except for Oluwole which was cited from a YouTube video of the author, all were published by Journals, one of which was by UNESCO (Benson) and another (Piper et al.) by DFID and the USAID.

17.2 Findings in the Literature

Cummins discovered that the extent to which a learner was proficient in a mother tongue or home language before their introduction to their school language strongly determined their proficiency in learning. This can also be referred to as the 'vernacular advantage', where mastery of a home language equips the learner with cognitive skills, he or she can use to transfer meaning and literacy when learning a new language. It is a reaffirmation of the developmental interdependence hypothesis. In addition, he contributed, to the literature, a new theoretical framework that included child input and educational treatment. His conclusion was that the best form of bilingualism for early childhood and elementary education is additive bilingualism, which ensures literacy in the home language, L1, and the school language L2 with careful attention being paid to initial mastery of the home language.

Benson agreed with Cummins that learners can transfer literacy and cognitive skills from the mother tongue, which they have mastered, to a new language used in school. She found, using a review of several studies, that mother tongue education impacts educational quality in the affective or emotional domain of learning. Instead of alienation, disconnection, and frustration, we have increased student confidence, self-esteem, and sense of self. This leads to an increase in creativity and innovation as well.

Chumbow created a theoretical framework and model that makes it possible for mother tongue or local languages to be organized in partnership with foreign and public languages, in a way that ensures national development. This language pyramid model or tier-stratification system he created has a mother tongue or local African languages as the ground or foundation language used in the homes and local districts. Above this is one or two majority languages used in partnership with foreign languages such as English or French for commerce and government at the national level. He claimed that this model maintains the value and place of most African languages while advancing national goals and development at the same time.

Piper et al. found that instruction in the mother tongue at the primary level of education in Kenya led to increased reading outcomes (which makes a case for mother tongue education in African schools). They pointed out that the problem with such education is not just the language problem, but rather an implementation one. The practical implementation issues they found, include the negative perception of parents and teachers to mother tongue education, and the fear of stakeholders that they may elicit ethnic tensions or violence if one ethnic language is picked over another. These are issues of consideration in implementing mother tongue education.

Finally, Adebisi extended the issues in African education from just right to education or basic literacy (which is at an all-time high) to rights in education. From her analysis, the solution to the issues in African education lie in using the post-colonial theory to deconstruct African education, restoring its indigenous roots and proper foundation. The problem of African education is under International Human Rights Law (IHRL) which means we need to assign and accept value and place to African indigenous knowledge, and not just to Western value in knowledge creation. This leads to decolonization of African education, producing changes in curriculum, philosophy, pedagogy, and purpose. The following are discussions of findings of knowledge creation in African societies.

17.3 Discussion of Findings

In this section, we discuss our research questions using a meta-analysis and meta-synthesis of findings in literature. The research questions and findings are as follows:

RQ1: Is there a relationship between the language of instruction and ease of learning for students?

Benson directly showed that a relationship existed between the language of instruction used in school and the ease of learning of students. A local language or mother tongue was more likely to put students at ease, increasing student confidence, and participation in classroom activities. Oluwole agreed with this in her position remarks. While Cummins does not directly address this, he showed that students in submersion bilingual programs that ignored the home language of learners are more likely to experience frustration and difficulty with learning the concepts taught in schools.

RQ2: Does literacy improve for students when the mother tongue or local language is used for instruction instead of a foreign public language?

Benson showed that literacy and cognitive skills improved when the mother tongue is used for instruction instead of a public language. She cited a Nigerian example of a pilot project where the Yoruba language was used as L1 from primary 1 to 6, and English language introduced in primary 5. The result was better skills in literacy, comprehension, reading, speaking, and ability of students to grasp instructional content faster. Piper et al. particularly found that reading outcomes of children in primary level is improved when they received instruction in their own mother tongue.

RQ3: Does an epistemological or indigenous knowledge base exist from which schools in Africa can draw their cultural framework?

Oluwole, in her position remarks, made it clear that pre-colonial African societies, such as the Yorubas in Nigeria, had a wealth of indigenous knowledge embedded in their language and oral tradition. This formed the epistemological base and cultural bedrock of their pre-modern education and should serve the same purpose in the decolonized education of Africa where more place and relevance is given to the mother tongue as the medium of instruction and Africa's indigenous knowledge. Cummins, Benson, and Modiano confirmed that mother tongues contain a rich base of knowledge that children later use to process learning and literacy in a foreign or school language. Piper et al. showed proof that there is enough cultural framework or epistemic base in African languages (for example in Kenya) that can sustain literacy and education at the primary level.

RQ4: Does using the mother tongue as instructional language in schools support knowledge creation and decolonization in African societies?

Chumbow established a direct link between using the mother tongue in the home and local districts (for education, commerce, and governance), and national development. Education at the local district level can be understood as knowledge-creation decolonization while national development can be switched with decolonization. However, more research is needed to show that national development according to Chumbow includes the decolonization of education. Fafunwa as cited by Benson showed clearly that mother tongue education leads to literacy, reproduction, and the creation of new knowledge in that tongue. Further, Adebisi argued that mother tongue education decolonized African education and societies. Fafunwa, Benson, and Adebisi are all in agreement with Oluwole, who stated that mother tongue education will revive indigenous knowledge and decolonize African educational systems in the process.

17.4   Recommendations

Firstly, this has been a meta-analysis of the examined literature. For this reason, we clearly pointed out under 'the limitations of this study that we were limited to the errors made in creating, collating, and processing the primary data'. We, therefore, recommended that this study be carried out in the future as an empirical study with direct access to primary, real-time data. That should offer more original insights into this problem. Secondly, the theoretical framework and model of Chumbow, can and should be further investigated. It has research potential, especially with respect to this relationship between indigenous languages and decolonization in Africa. We want to encourage more researchers to further evaluate the model in the context of mother tongue education (at the private realm and local district) and decolonization (at the public realm level). Our analysis of the findings led us to offer the following recommendations.

One, is that mother tongue education be implemented at the early childhood and primary level of education in Kenya and Nigeria. This is not as formidable a task as it might seem. The challenges faced in such a project are already addressed by Benson in her citation of Fafunwa, as well as by Piper et al. We are suggesting these two countries because both already have theoretical research and trial projects in this area. Other countries that have not been represented adequately in the literature need to first focus on sponsoring academic research and trial projects on this topic. This should give a clear picture of not just the nature of the relationship but also the cultural, policy, and political factors that influence implementation.

Two, we do not recommend completely removing English or French (or another colonial language) as languages of instruction. Instead, we support the additive bilingualism of Cummins, as demonstrated by Fafunwa, where the children (at the primary level) firstly master their own mother tongue or local language from inception until primary 5, where English or French is then introduced to them. Our findings show that this is best for their cognitive development and also, in this cultural context, to achieve indigeneity or decolonization in Africa. It will also remove the fears of parents that their children will be linguistically irrelevant in a global economy conducted largely in English, French, Chinese, and Russian instead of in African languages.

Three, when we conducted our study on the obstacles to mother tongue education, we realized that they were more policy-oriented than research-oriented. On this note, we want to suggest a more formal and developed awareness campaign aimed at educating stakeholders of implementation. This will include relevant government agencies, school boards and districts, parents, and teachers in society. Teacher education, in particular, needs a lot of investment to this end. We recognize that until recently, teacher training was done in foreign or public languages and with educational philosophies that ignore indigenous knowledge. A related reinvention of teacher training is therefore needed. This will make it easier to educate parents and the new generation of learners in such a way that enables knowledge creation and decolonization.

Four, similar to the immediate last point made, we have discovered research-opportunity in the area of training teachers in mother tongue education. There is very little work that has been done on this. We therefore encourage aspiring Ph.Ds., peer-reviewed journals, and research institutes to seize this opportunity to add to existing knowledge in the area of education.

Five, we realize that there is almost no literature on mother tongue education at the secondary and tertiary levels of education. What exists is the study of a few African languages at the tertiary level. We also have, usually in Universities in Europe or America, African Studies departments. What we want to finally recommend is new and further research on mother tongue education at the secondary and tertiary levels. We also think it will be reasonable to mandate the learning of one African language in the African Studies program. Not only this but also most of the coursework of African Studies should be taught in at least one prerequisite African language as part of the curriculum. This will fall under the International Human Rights Law (IHRL) in education that Adebisi referred to, where value and place are assigned to African indigenous knowledge anywhere, inside, or outside of Africa.

18 Conclusion

We set out to investigate the relationship between instruction in a mother tongue or local language and knowledge-creation decolonization in African societies. This is against the background of calls for decolonization of Africa, which extends to education and educational systems, the major places where knowledge creation takes place on the continent. Not that this trend in education research is a bandwagon, but it has achieved some level of popularity in the last two to three decades. Writers such as Benjamin Piper and Adebisi have recently drawn more international attention to this area of research. We wanted to explore what post-colonial theory will reveal in a post-colonial Africa as far as education was concerned.

Our meta-analysis reveals that more work needs to be done in African countries to uncover more theoretical relationships (in mother tongue education in Africa, policy development, and implementation) that can be tested in practice. Beyond recommending areas of further research, we found that African societies possess an epistemological base in their own cultural framework and language. This was preserved in pre-colonial times using oral tradition, which relied extensively on communication by speaking and language. Post-colonial Africa has committed 'epistemic violence' by replacing this indigenous knowledge base with a Western base that does not have the same framework. The result is an education system that has high literacy or availability, but which is not effective or of much use to African people because it is designed by and for others outside of their culture.

164 R. ALAPO AND D. DOGHUDJE

Therefore, the reform of education in Africa must consist of restoring indigeneity. One way to do this is to make the mother tongue or local languages the medium of instruction in schools, particularly in the early childhood and primary level of education. When this process expands to include secondary and tertiary levels of education, decolonization of knowledge creation in African societies is likely to show results in postgraduate research, industry, the economy, government, and a transformed international relations.

REFERENCES

Adebisi, F. (2016). Decolonizing education in Africa: Implementing the right to education by re-appropriating culture and indigeneity. *Northern Ireland Legal Quarterly, 67*(4), 433–451.

Ahluwalia, P. (2012). *Politics and post-colonial theory: African inflections* (p. 14). Routledge.

Akbar, H., & Tzokas, N. (2013). Charting the organizational knowledge-creation process: An innovation-process perspective. *Journal of Marketing Management, 29*(13–14), 1592–1608. https://doi.org/10.1080/0267257X. 2013.800895

Albuquerque, M. B. (2018). Ayahusca's pedagogy: For an epistemic decolonization of knowledge. *Education Policy Analysis Archives, 26.* https://doi.org/10.14507/epaa.26.3519

Arnove, R. F. (2005). To what ends: Educational reform around the world. *Indiana Journal of Global Legal Studies, 12*(1), 79–95. https://doi.org/10.1353/gls.2005.0002

Babaci-Wilhite, Z., Geo-JaJa, M., & Lou, S. (2012). Education and language: A human right for sustainable development in Africa. *International Review of Education, 58.* https://doi.org/10.1007/s11159-012-9311-7

Bamgbose, A. (2005). Mission and vision of the African Academy of Languages. In N. Alexander (Ed.), *The intellectualisation of African languages: The African Academy of Languages and the implementation of the language plan of action for Africa* (pp. 15–20). PRAESA.

Bamgbose, A. (1991). *Language and the nation: The language question in Sub-Saharan Africa.* Edinburgh University Press.

Begi, N. (2014). Use of mother tongue in early years of school to preserve the Kenyan culture. *Journal of Education and Practice, 5*(3), 37–39.

Benson, C. (2004). *The importance of mother tongue-based schooling for educational quality.* UNESCO Electronic Publication.

Brock-Utne, B. (2000). *Whose education for all?: The recolonization of the African mind* (1st ed.). Routledge. https://doi.org/10.4324/9780203903650

Brock-Utne, B. (2009). *Language, democracy and education in Africa.* (Discussion paper 15. Nordiska Afrikainstitutet, Uppsala printed in 2002 and uploaded on December 19, 2014). DiVA, id: diva2:242109 URN: urn:nbn:se:nai:diva-191.

Cain, T. (2013). *Decolonizing methodologies: Research and indigenous peoples, by Linda Tuhiwai Smith* (2nd ed., 240 pp.). Zed Books (2012). Book Reviews. *Anthropology & Education Quarterly, 44*(4), 443–445. https://doi.org/10.1111/aeq.12032

Chivallon, C. (2019). Research on (post) colonial worlds of meaning—A reflexive essay on the decolonization of knowledge. *Nuevo mundo, mundos nuevas.* http://journals.openedition.org/nuevomundo/78425; *os.* https://doi.org/10.4000/nuevomundo.78425

Chumbow, S. (2009). Linguistic diversity, pluralism, and national development in Africa. *Africa Development, 34.* https://doi.org/10.4314/ad.v34i2.57364

Cummins, J. (1979). Linguistic interdependence and the educational development of bilingual children. *Review of Educational Research, 24,* 273–282. https://doi.org/10.2307/1169960

Elliot, A. J. (1994). *Child language.* Cambridge University Press.

Evans, D. K., & Popova, A. (2016). What really works to improve learning in developing countries?: An analysis of divergent findings in systematic reviews. *The World Bank Research Observer, 31*(2), 242–270. https://doi.org/10.1093/wbro/lkw004

Fafunwa, B. A. (1990, November 27–30). Using national languages in education: A challenge to African educators. In UNESCO-UNICEF, *African thoughts on the prospects of education for all* (pp. 97–110). Selections from papers commissioned for the Regional Consultation on Education for All, Dakar.

Gacheche, K. (2010). Challenges in implementing a mother tongue based language-in-education policy: Policy and Practice in Kenya. *POLIS Journal, 4,* 1–45.

Geo-JaJa, M. A. (2006). Educational decentralization, public spending, and social justice in Nigeria. *International Review of Education, 52*(1/2), 125–148. https://doi.org/10.1007/s11159-005-5605-3

Geo-JaJa, M. A., & Azaiki, S. (2010). Economic growth without human security and quality education in the Niger Delta: The question of inadequacy of policy. In M. A. Geo-JaJa & S. Majhanovich (Eds.), *Policy, politics and economics in comparative education.* Sense Publishers.

Glaser, B. G. (1963). Retreading research materials: The use of secondary analysis by the independent researcher. *American Behavioral Scientist, 6*(10), 11–14. https://doi.org/10.1177/000276426300601003

Heaton, J. (1998). Secondary analysis of qualitative data. *Social Research Update, 22*(4), 88–93. http://www.mendeley.com/research/secondary-analysis-qualitative-data-17

Hinds, P. S., Vogel, R. J., & Clarke-Steffen, L. (1997). The possibilities and pitfalls of doing a secondary analysis of a qualitative data set. *Qualitative Health Research, 7*(3), 408–424. https://doi.org/10.1177/104973239700 700306

Hisnanick, J. J. (2002). Knowledge emergence: Social, technical, and evolutionary dimensions of knowledge creation [Review of *Knowledge emergence: Social, technical, and evolutionary dimensions of knowledge creation*]. *Journal of Economic Issues, 36*(3), 819–821. Routledge. https://doi.org/10.1080/00213624.2002.11506518

Ivekovic, D. (2012). Terms of denationalization and decolonization of knowledge. *Mouvements (Paris, France: 1998), 72*, 35–41. https://doi.org/10.3917/mouv.072.0035

Jones, J. M., & Barkhuizen, G. (2011). 'It is two-way traffic': Teachers' tensions in the implementation of the Kenyan language-in-education policy. *International Journal of Bilingual Education and Bilingualism, 14*, 513–530. https://doi.org/10.1080/13670050.2010.532540

Kao, S. C., & Wu, C. (2016). The role of creation mode and social networking mode in knowledge creation performance: Mediation effect of creation process. *Information & Management, 53*(6), 803–816. https://doi.org/10.1016/j.im.2016.03.002

Kogut, B. (2009). Knowledge, information, rules, and structures. In *Dynamics of knowledge, corporate systems and innovation* (pp. 77–94). Springer Berlin Heidelberg. https://doi.org/10.1007/978-3-642-04480-9_4

Kenya Institute of Education (KIE). (1992). *Primary education syllabus* (Vol. 1). Kenya Institute of Education.

Loflin, C. (1995). Ngugi wa Thiong'o's visions of Africa: Document view. *Research in African Literatures, 26*(4), 76.

Maina, F. (2003). *Integrating cultural values into the curriculum for Kenyan schools*. State University of New York.

Mazrui, A. A. (1986). *The Africans a triple heritage* (1st ed.). BBC Publications.

McClure, J. (2020). Connected global intellectual history and the decolonization of the curriculum. *History Compass, 19*(1). https://doi.org/10.1111/hic3.12645

Melber, H. (2018). Knowledge production and decolonization—Not only African challenges. *Strategic Review for Southern Africa: Strategiese Oorsig Vir Suider-Africa, 40*(1), 4–15. https://doi.org/10.35293/srsa.v40i1.266

Ministry of Education, Science, and Technology (MoEST), Republic of Kenya. (2014). *National education sector plan. Basic education approach, 2013/2014–2017/2018* (Vol. 1). Nairobi (MoEST). http://globalpartnership.org/content/education-sector-plan-2013-2018-kenya

Modiano, N. (1968). National or mother language in beginning reading: A comparative study. *Research in the Teaching of English, 2*(1), 32–43.

Nonaka, N. T., & Hisnanick, J. J. (2002). Knowledge emergence: Social, technical, and evolutionary dimensions of knowledge creation [Review of *Knowledge emergence: Social, technical, and evolutionary dimensions of knowledge creation*]. *Journal of Economic Issues, XXXVI*(3), 819–821.

Oluwole, S. (2016, January 14). *The importance of mother tongue—'Oro Isiti' with Prof. Sophie Oluwole. Youtube video by Tunde Kelani.* https://www.you tube.com/watch?v=KYZyDrx0Rh8

Paterson, B. L., Thorne, S. E., Canam, C., et al. (2001). *Meta-study of qualitative research: A practical guide to meta-analysis and meta-synthesis.* Sage.

Peeren, E. (2009). [Review of the book *Deconstruction and the postcolonial: At the limits of theory*]. *French Studies: A Quarterly Review, 63*(1), 123–124. https://www.muse.jhu.edu/article/257566

Phillipson, R. (2016). Native speakers in linguistic imperialism. *Journal for Critical Education Policy Studies, 14*(3), 80–96. http://www.jceps.com/wp-con tent/uploads/2016/12/14-3-4.pdf

Piper, B., Zuilkowski, S. S., & Ong'ele, S. (2016). Implementing Mother Tongue instruction in the real world: Results from a medium-scale randomized controlled trial in Kenya. *Comparative Education Review, 60*(4), 776–807. https://doi.org/10.1086/688493

Prah, K. (2001). Culture, the missing link in development planning in Africa. *Présence Africaine, 163/164*, 90–102.

Ramachandran, R., Laitin, D., & Walter, S. (2018). The legacy of colonial language policies and their impact on student learning: Evidence from an experimental program in Cameroon. *Economic Development and Cultural Change, 68*, 239–272. https://doi.org/10.1086/700617

Republic of Kenya. (2012). *Sessional Paper no. 14: A policy framework for education and training.* Nairobi: Government Printer.

Rodney, W. (1972). *How Europe underdeveloped Africa* (p. 247). Bogle-L'Ouverture Publications.

Seats, M. R. (2022). The voice(s) of reason: Conceptual challenges for the decolonization of knowledge in global higher education. *Teaching in Higher Education, 27*(5), 678–694. https://doi.org/10.1080/13562517.2020.172 9725

Sertima, I. V. (1984, January 1). *Journal of African Civilizations, 6*(1). *Black women in antiquity.* Transaction Books.

Sithole, T. (2014). *Achille Mbembe: Subject, subjection, and subjectivity.* University of South Africa, Pretoria. http://hdl.handle.net/10500/14323

Skutnabb-Kangas, T., & Phillipson, R. (Eds.). (1995). *Linguistic human rights. Overcoming linguistic discrimination.* Berlin: Mouton De Gruyter.

Skutnabb-Kangas, T., & Phillipson, R. (2001). Discrimination and minority languages. In M. Raj (Ed.), *Concise Encyclopedia of sociolinguistics* (pp. 545–550). Oxford: Elsevier Science.

Skutnabb-Kangas, T., & Toukomaa, P. (1976). *Teaching migrant children's mother tongue and learning the language of the host country in the context of the socio-cultural situation of the migrant family.* Helsinki: The Finnish National Commission for UNESCO.

Spernes, K. (2012). I use MY mother tongue at home and with friends—not in school! Multilingualism and identity in rural Kenya. *Language, Culture and Curriculum, 25*(2), 189–203. https://doi.org/10.1080/079 08318.2012.683531

Spivak, G. C. (1994). Responsibility. *Boundary 2, 21*(3), 19–64. https://doi.org/10.2307/303600

Syrontiski, M. (2007). Deconstruction and the postcolonial: At the limits of theory. *Liverpool University Press, 67*, 83.

The Campbell Collaboration. (2015). *What is a systematic review?* http://www.campbellcollaboration.org/what_is_a_systematic_review/index.php

Thiong'o, N. (1986). *Decolonising the mind: The politics of language in African literature.* Nairobi/Portsmouth: Heinemann.

Tsotetsi, C. T., & Omodan, B. I. (2020). Decolonization of knowledge-construction in university classrooms: The place of social constructivism. *African Journal of Gender, Society and Development, 9*(2), 183–204. https://doi.org/10.31920/2634-3622/2020/9n2a10

United Nations Educational, Scientific, and Cultural Organization (UNESCO). (2014). *Teaching and learning: Achieving quality for all; education for all global monitoring report.* Paris: UNESCO. http://unesdoc.unesco.org/images/0022/002256/225660e.pdf

Vygotsky, L. (1978). *Mind in society: The development of higher psychological processes.* Harvard University Press.

Wa Mutua, M. (1994). Human rights and state despotism in Kenya: Institutional problems. *Africa Today, 41*(4), 50–56.

Wright, H. K., et al. (2007). Guest editorial: Rethinking the place of African worldviews and ways of knowing in education. *Diaspora Indigenous and Minority Education, 1*(4), 243–244.

Leadership in the Management of Higher Education in Nigeria

Abdulkareem Amuda-Kannike
and Bolanle Waliu Shiyanbade⊙

1 BACKGROUND

Across the globe, leadership in higher institution is seen as a mechanism to provide effective and efficient students' affairs management in colleges of education is not only important, but it is necessary and imperative for the accomplishment of instituting the right type of values, morals and skills in the students. The extent to which members of the college staff contribute to the performance of the institution hinge on how well the provost understand and adopt appropriate leadership style in the discharge of his/her responsibilities. This position is corroborated

---

A. Amuda-Kannike
Directorate of Information, Publicity & Protocol, Kwara State College of Education, Ilorin, Nigeria
e-mail: abbahkannike@gmail.com

B. W. Shiyanbade (✉)
Department of Public Administration, Faculty of Administration, Obafemi Awolowo University, Ile-Ife, Nigeria
e-mail: bwshiyanbade@oauife.edu.ng

© The Author(s), under exclusive license to Springer Nature Switzerland AG 2023
A. I. Adeniran (ed.), *African Development and Global Engagements*,
https://doi.org/10.1007/978-3-031-21283-3_9

by Akpala (1998) view that attitude to work, leadership style and motivation are part of the major factors that can prevent negative effect on organisation performance in Nigeria.

Leadership, as viewed by Kouzes and Posner (1987) cited by Agboola et al., is an ongoing method to build and maintain a connection between those who aspire to lead and those who are prepared to follow. An interesting thing about their version of the conception of the term is that it is accommodatingly broad, as it considers every member at the centre of the governance of the institution, with ingenuity, inventiveness, audacity, and inspiration, as well as the ability to exploit engaging possibilities, promote cooperation and empower others, qualities accessible to everyone, no matter where they are in the hierarchy. They add that these qualities allow groups of normal people to achieve exceptional things.

Consequently, it is obvious that scholars generally perceive the term, leadership, as the skilful means of directing and influencing people, in such a way that they willingly obey, respect and enthusiastically and earnestly co-operate towards achieving a purposeful goal/objective. The essential quality of leaders is that if they are convinced that something must be done, they persuade others and equip them in every way possible to work and get it done (Nigro & Nigro, 2014). However, since people should not be forced to do things, there must be something at the core of leadership, which makes people to willingly and continually work towards achieving a goal.

Robson (2009) opined that a leader is one that understands him/herself, his/her followers, tasks and responsibility enough to convince his/her followers to believe in him/her. Followers occupy a very important place in leadership. This is because they decide the success or otherwise of any organisation. It need to be said that aside inducing, persuading and teaching people, building relationships are crucial to effective leadership (Sundi, 2013). From whichever angle one chooses to consider the concept, what is indisputable is that leadership does not operate in isolation; people are at the centre of every decision-making and implementation, engaging in various roles, developing multiple relationships, espousing individuals and institutional ethics, stimulating others to work with zeal, empowering them to achieve challenging tasks and above all, demonstrating other unbelievable qualities of leadership (Agboola et al., 2017; Anyamele, 2004). Leadership cannot be achieved where there is a lack of cooperation on the parts of followers.

As a result, a good leader should take a good hold of his/her followers. It is also stated that a good leader should treat the followers in terms of their needs, emotion, and motivation. The third factor is communication. Communication can be verbal or non-verbal. Whatever method or line of communication a leader chooses, he/she must ensure there is effectiveness and mutual understanding between the receiver and the sender. Fourthly, the situation is very important to leadership. The reason is that leader's decisions and actions should be influenced by the situation at any point of time.

It is safe to add that good leadership is essential for societal growth, even in higher institutions communities as it provides major solution to any societal or organisational problem (Gummerson, 2015). Leadership determines the strength of an institution as well as the morale, motivation and ideology of its subordinates. Leadership requires some mind-sets, namely: to lead by example, to interact positively and efficiently, to be brave and truthful, and to take ownership and responsibility over others.

Instances of students' demonstrations against untoward conditions actually abound in Nigeria. Such increasing outburst has often led to the closure of some tertiary institutions in the country with its attendant and negative consequences on the academic calendar, sometimes loss of life, destruction of properties and expulsion or rustications of students. It should be mentioned here that, Nigerian colleges of education often face challenges of not only sustainability, but also of achieving the required degree of sustainable development that will meet the goals for which they have been founded. Achieving the goal depends on the efficiency of both academic and non-teaching staff in the discharge and execution of their responsibilities to the college and the students. However, achievement of students' growth and development strongly depends on the availability of adequate and effective student affairs services.

Students' affairs include all the programmes and resources provided for college students to meet educational goals and priorities. It includes non-instructional roles given to students in order to improve their academic performance or learning outcome. The roles are thus very important for the efficient and effective functioning of higher institutions. The term students' affairs grew from educational development in United States. The history of the students' affairs dates perceived to be emotionally immature at that time and needed strict adult supervision (Dallas, 2012; Nuss, 2003).

Precisely, reaction to poor student affairs management while Omotoso (2013), relates the institution's problems to a lack of good governance, accountability, and mismanagement of funds meant for institutional developments. Faced with such problems, the students may lose concentration on their studies, be psychologically demoralised and possibly possessed little or no sense of individual value. They may equally become tense and under such conditions not behave civilly, and as such indulged in behaviours that are contrary to the etiquette defined by the college, such as respect for constituted authorities, compliance and adherence to the rules and regulations of the colleges.

1.1 Leadership in the Nigerian Education Sector

This section reviewed existing literatures that are relevant to leadership styles and management of students' affairs. This includes conceptual review of related concepts such as leadership, leadership styles, management, students' affairs and higher education. It also covers empirical review of various studies related to leadership styles in higher educational institutions. It reviewed relevant theory which provides a theoretical framework that explains and establishes the relationship between leadership styles and management of students' affairs. This is with a view to identifying the gap in knowledge.

1.2 Leadership

The meaning of leadership has been conceptualised over the years, yet no acceptable meaning is universally accepted. It need to also be added that this concept is widely studied in management subjects; various management research or academic studies have beam searchlights on issues related to leadership. Various conclusions on the meaning of the term indicate that it has no distinct definition (Agboola et al., 2017; Bass, 1991, 1996, 2008) because the qualities of successful leadership vary among individuals. Burns (2010) in one of his book, *Leadership*, states that leadership encompasses intellectual tasks, and as a concept, has different meanings. Thus, Agboola et al. (2017) reveal that there are about 221 various definitions of leadership. He stated that some of the definitions were narrow while others were broad in explanations.

Leadership has simply been conceptualised as the art or ability to motivate a set of given people in order to make them perform certain roles so as to achieve a desired result (Jaramilloa, 2015). Putting it in a simpler way, leadership is the inspiration and the direction behind any action or set of actions towards the attainment of a set objective. Leadership may also be defined as the derivative of authority which emphasises charisma and outstanding personal qualities of an individual to induce and influence followership in the ardent pursuit of a vision or ideology, even against all odds. In other words, leadership is the ability to influence people (disciples) to buy into a person's vision towards accomplishing the set goals of an organisation or social movement. Generally, people believe that leadership is an attribute of personality, status, title, position or role recognised in a formal organisational chart. However, a leader can be said to be a person that indirectly serves.

In a scholarly perspective, Jim (2014) describes leadership as a quality of exceptional individuals. For the organisation to be run successfully, there is the need for a leader, to be able to facilitate the followers in performing their tasks. The leader is ethical, raising the level of human conduct and moral aspiration, a leader is somebody who administers influence over subordinates and a leaders promote excellence in the development of members of the organisation.

1.3 Leadership Styles

Basically every leader possesses diverse behaviour in leading their followers but the attitude or behaviour is addressed as a leadership style. Leader is expected to possess his own leadership style, display good leadership skills, respect followers, take good decisions whenever the need arises and assign tasks appropriately to followers (Avasthi, 2006) and leadership style is thus central in any organisation for effective personnel management.

Tyagi (2004) cited in Agboola et al. (2017), provides a conceptual clarification that incorporates insightful leadership attributes: "an act of identifying, promoting, cultivating and persuading those with the invaluable gift of inspiring and guiding others, those who know how to persuade others to collaborate with them and participate in achieving the organisation's goals and purposes". Memon (2013) further stated that leadership style as the method a leader adapts to provide direction, motivation and implement plans. To Landis (2011), every leader creates and develops his/her own style in unique way for proper usage and it can deduce the approach a leader uses in leading organisation, department or group of people.

It is pertinent to add that, leadership style includes leadership skills, expertise knowledge and abilities. Leadership needs some mind-sets, namely: to lead by example; to interact positively and efficiently; to be brave and truthful; and to take ownership and responsibility over others. A skilful leader also wins subordinates' heart through admiration, trust and dedication. Leadership style can influence organisational obligation as well as work contentment in a positive way, in terms of performance. It could also determine and affect employees trust, behaviour and commitment to the organisation. Chukwu and Eluka (2013) includes that for any result-oriented institution, the members of staff need to be motivated greatly with a choice of a good and dependable leadership style. However, this should importantly include the full involvement of the staff in the designing and implementation of plans, provision of adequate service and infrastructure. A good leadership style should be distinct; it should have a specific manner through which affairs of any organisation is being directed by the leader. The leader of the organisation is a source and symbol of authority and power. A good leader utilises controls, allocates resources, exercises authority and power, influences and motivates the followers, coordinates and directs the organisation. Nevertheless, effective leadership style includes decision-making, interaction, self-consciousness, the ability to motivate others, and charismatic leadership principles.

However, it is pertinent to note that the degree of success of any institution is a direct function of the leadership style operated by the provost of the college. But the right leadership style will produce the greatest unimaginable success, while just like a wrong leadership approach will also produce the worst possible outcome (Amuda-Kannike, 2021). Thus, leadership style should be selected and adopted to fit the college, situations or possibly individuals. In the last decade, scholars (Muhammad et al., 2015; Mung-Ling et al., 2015; Nakpodia, 2012) have revolutionise the classification of leadership styles and how these styles affect the organisation.

The categorisation moved from being autocratic, democratic, laissez-faire and bureaucratic styles, to creative transformational and transactional leadership styles, among others. However, no style is absolutely perfect, and every leader needs to understand how to use a specific style when the need arises. There is a time and place for all the leadership styles. Choosing a meticulous style in a situation by the leader is based on

LEADERSHIP IN THE MANAGEMENT OF HIGHER ...   175

attributes, the frame of mind, objectives or ambitions, the relative power between the leader and subordinate, the importance of time in the action, the type of effort needed to complete the action, rules, regulations and or authority.

1.4   Students' Affairs

Bees and Dees (2008) posited that the term students' affairs mean "the department or division of services and support for students at institutions of higher education, to enhance students' growth and development". Students' affairs are aimed at satisfying the students' needs and want. The proper and effective management, including adequate provision of the services, makes students to exhibit behaviour desirable for academic performance. Student learning activities take place in a classroom, but the college or university environment itself is a classroom (Dallas, 2012). The interpretation of this position is that the classroom is not the only source of student learning. It includes the experiences students acquire throughout their stay in the college from the day they move into the dormitory to the day they bag degrees. They are also shaped by leadership skills acquired as member or leader of students' organisation; by critical thinking honed through challenging academic work; as well as through a sense of identity they have developed in making meaning out of their experiences, in their several endeavours.

Moreover, Dallas's (2012) view is that there are many management experts regarding students' affairs in every college. These experts have different duties: some are academic personnel or non-teaching personnel who assist students in choosing course majors and planning their class schedules. Some are residential staff supervising residential students. Another set are admissions officers helping students determine if the college is the right place to be, while among the list is a career counsellor who helps students find the right internships and jobs to match their talents and goals. As a result, the discipline of students weakened as the most crucial role in student affairs shifted to educating students about making appropriate choices and decisions (Dallas, 2012; Hirt, 2006).

In Nigerian context, Division of Students' Affairs is one of the divisions in the Registry under the supervision of the Registrar. The division in most universities is headed by Dean of Students (and in Colleges, Director) who is an academic staff and directly responsible to the Vice-Chancellor/The Provost/Rector). He is assisted by a top administrator officer nomenclature, the Students' Affairs Officer (SAO) and the function of the student affairs unit is to render educational support services to all learners (Sandeen, 1988 cited in Amuda-Kannike, 2021).

Student affairs are an important organisational task area that is vital to the progressive functioning of any higher institution of learning. It should be noted that the activities of the student affairs unit support the academic programme in realising the students' comprehensive and healthy learning. Although, academic and capacity growth of students can be achieved by preparing a curriculum and executing it (Dallas, 2012 cited by Amuda-Kannike, 2021), the goal of cultivating their positive behaviour and values can only be achieved by ensuring effective handling of students' affairs.

1.5 Leadership Style and Students Affairs: The Relationship

As stated earlier, students' affairs remain the onus of higher institutions of learning. Each institution is expected to provide several arrays of student affairs programmes that will encourage the students to learn while at the same time providing conducive environment to support academic activities. The provision of effective and efficient students' affairs lies on the leadership of any institution. Today several institutions around the world have problem of ineffective management of students' affairs, and the resultant effects are outburst from students (Nakpodia, 2012).

Consequently, leadership attitudes and behaviour affected the effective management of students' affairs in colleges of education. The attitude or behaviour of leaders towards the operation of students' affairs in any institution affects its effectiveness (Bateson, 2008; Muhammad et al., 2015 cited by Amuda-Kannike, 2021). The interpretation is that enviable level of effectiveness cannot be achieved in the management of students' affairs service without a proper leadership style founded and operated. Absence of effective leadership style in the management of students' affairs may be a link towards students' crisis and staff's low productivity, poor students' growth and development.

Perhaps, one can state that it is not possible to achieve effective and efficient management of students' affairs without establishing and operating proper leadership style. Amuda-Kannike (2021) stated that the way a leader makes decisions, assigns responsibility and communicates with subordinates may have a positive or negative impact on the organisation. Leadership style in students' affairs management can be related to how the leader thinks, conducts, manages, prepares and implements students' affairs policies, and particularly how the leader is related to the rest of his/her team (staff and students).

In line with the above, any leader who has the vision of effective and efficient students' affairs in his institution would learn and display good leadership style. By lording it over his subordinates, he/she does not automatically achieve efficiency; he should rather guide them through the lane of effective students' affairs management, painting the picture to his subordinates through the appropriate use of preferred leadership styles.

1.6 Management of Students Affairs in Colleges of Education in Nigeria

Most managers and administrators will affirm to the fact that the success of any organisation depends upon sound management of the organisation among other variables. Management in students' affairs involves the use of sound and approved techniques, skills and styles to achieve effective students' affairs services, with minimum resources to achieve maximum outcomes. Also, the effectiveness of any students' affairs services in any higher institution could as well be said to hinge upon a sound student affairs organisation and strategies.

Institutions of higher learning utilised various methods and ways to effectively manage students' affairs services on daily basis. Although, there is no universal standard to students' affairs services provision, but Rose et al. (2015) cited by Amuda-Kannike (2021) observed that, it depends on the interest of the individual local needs and wants. The implication is that, each college possessed its own distinct culture and tradition, needs, and wants. Also, the organisation structure of students' affairs in each college differs. However, it is imperative that the directorate of students' affairs in the colleges operates within the administrative policies and procedures using sound managerial practices. These include proper use of fiscal, human, and facilities resources to accomplish the college mission. Others may include students' affair's policy formulation, effective students' affairs planning, administrative arrangement, evaluation, staff/students working relationship and relations with outside stakeholders.

It is pertinent to note that, students come across three most important transitions correlated to their education experience: first is the experience when admitted into the college; the second is the experience through their collegiate life, and lastly, the experience acquired from higher education expected to be carried forward into the outside world. It is expected that considerable assistant must be provided and when necessary. This assistant must be provided for the students during these transitions. This assistant may include provision of timely and accurate information, broad range of students' support services, including activities that enhance learning process within and outside the classroom. Creditable citizenship and community service are imperative values expected to be encouraged during the college education experience.

It is however important that the directorate of students' affairs of the college must provide conducive environment for students learning. The students' affairs unit must advocate for the students and create opportunities for the students to display inherent talent as an individual or as a leader. The college management must examine new ways to manage students' affairs in the institution.

1.7   Theoretical Framework (Trait Theory)

The earliest and the oldest theoretical concepts of leadership, identify the leader's lineage or personal trait as the primary factors influencing effective leadership. The trait theory arose from the great-man theory as a way of identifying the key quality of successful leaders. This was the first major formal move towards the study of leadership (Naidu, 2014). Bass (1990) argued that researchers such as Kohs and Irle (1920), Bernard (1926), Bingham (1927), Tead (1929), Smith and Krueger (1933), Page (1935), Kilbourne (1935), Bird (1940), and Jenkins (1947), all examined leadership in terms of traits of personality and characteristics.

Under this theory, leadership was traditionally analysed in terms of the traits that the leaders possessed and how they influenced the achievements of organisational goals. According to this theory, leaders are conceived of as person blessed with certain personal attributes that are responsible for their success (Bass, 1990). For centuries, according to Naidu (2014), researchers examined the lineage of great leaders in order to identify a set of traits that are universal to many of the great leaders. These include: intelligence, originality, popularity, honesty, cooperativeness, desire to excel, humour and physical energy.

The trait theory was well known in the military and is still used as a set of criteria for the recruitment of commission applicants (Peretomode, 2012). The theory by interpretation subjects organisational success to the traits of effective leadership. It therefore suggests that people without leadership qualities cannot be made leaders even by training (Rose et al., 2015). This also implies that leadership training is helpful only to those who have innate leadership traits. In other words, one can have a trait of leadership and become one or one does not possess the traits of a leader and do not become one. Therefore, leadership, according to this school of thought, cannot be taught nor learned.

The most frequently mentioned traits and characteristics as being correlated with leaders include:

(a) intelligence
(b) physical size (relatively tall or short)
(c) self-confidence/self esteem
(d) dependability
(e) industriousness
(f) extroversion
(g) persuasiveness
(h) responsibility
(i) ambition (for instance: a high requirement for achievement and power)
(j) adaptability (Naidu, 2014).

However, this position has received criticism from different scholars who believe that none of the above-stated characteristics seems to have contributed totally to either leadership success or effectiveness. This theory is found not to give full explanation of leadership because not all leaders possess all the mentioned qualities and traits. Equally, even those who are not leaders may possess most of all these stated qualities and characteristics.

The modern behavioural school listed three significant variables that could have an impact upon leadership success/effectiveness or productivity:

(a) Situation-environment
(b) The leader himself, and
(c) Behavioural assumptions (Naidu, 2014).

The above signified that if emphasis is misplaced on either of the variables even with or without the traits, it could make a lot of difference in leadership effectiveness. It could also be assumed that it is a truism that the possession of incredible intelligence may contribute to a leader's ability to find solution to complex administrative problems more easily. On the other hand, his expression of intellectual superiority can alienate him from the subordinates. More so, the theory lack uniformity of identifying the traits which was taken up by the behavioural theory.

2 Methodology

The study adopted a descriptive survey research design and utilised primary and secondary sources of data. Primary data were collected from questionnaire administration. The population consisted administrative staff of Directorates of Student's Affairs of the study area. The study involved a 116 staff who were involved in leadership position across the selected college of education in Southwestern part of Nigeria. Multistage sampling procedure was employed for the study. At the first stage, Colleges of Education were stratified into Federal and State governments owned, and two Federal Colleges of Education at Abeokuta and Oyo were randomly selected out of the four Federal Colleges of Education in the Southwestern, while the three State-owned Colleges of Education were randomly selected out of the seven in the region. At the second stage, the whole 116 (100%) staff working in the Directorate of Students Affairs selected for questionnaire administration due to their small size. At the third stage, Taro Yemane sample formula ($N/1-N$ (e) 2) was used to select the respondents. Secondary data were sourced from relevant textbooks, journals articles, official documents, government publications and some internet resources. Data were edited, coded and analysed using simple regression analysis, relative impact index and content analysis methods.

3 Data Analysis and Interpretation

This section investigated factors that determined the leadership style adopted in the management of students' affairs. To achieve this, respondents were asked to rate responsible factors that could possibly determine leadership styles on the management of students' affairs. The assertions' values/responses were organised using Likert scale of measurements, such as: Very little extent (5), Little extent (4), Some extent (3), Great extent (2) and Very great extent (1). In addition, the mean value ($\overline{x}$) summarises the strength of the respondents for each of the statements, using a decision rule as thus: where ($\overline{x} < 3.0$), more respondents tended towards disagreement; and where ($\overline{x} > 3.0$), more respondents tended towards agreement.

As prescribed in Table 1 in Chapter 'Emergency Healthcare Accessibility in the Context of COVID-19 in Nigeria', leader's human relation was the first assertion subjected to interrogative opinions of respondents as one of the factors that determined the leadership style to be adopted in the college. In their responses, 70 representing 60.9% of the respondents and 36 (31.3%) of the respondent agreed to a very great extent and great extent respectively; 6 (5.2%) concur to some extent, while 2 representing 1.7% of the respondents and 1 (0.9%) of the respondents agreed to a little extent and very little extent. The mean value and standard deviation ($x = 4.50$, $SD = 0.754$) confirm this frequency distribution.

On the second assertion, respondents were asked if the attitude of staff members could be a factor that determines the choice of leadership style. The assertion was rated 33 (28.7%) a very great extent, 26 (22.6%) of the respondent perceived it to be a great extent. However, 25 (21.7%) of the respondents believed to some extent and 29 (25.2%) of the respondents believed it as a little extent, as well as 2 (1.7%) of the respondents believed very little extent, the mean value and standard deviation ($\overline{x} = 3.51$, $SD = 1.202$).

On the other hand, it was reported that 34 (29.6%) of the respondents believed to a great extent that the size or type of the college determined the leadership style adopted, while 37 (32.2%) of the respondents agreed to a great extent. However, 22 (19.1%) of the respondents, to some extent agreed that the size or type of the college determine the leadership style adopted, while 19 (16.5%) of the respondents' believed that to a little extent the assertion determine the leadership style. While 03 representing 2.6% of the respondents agreed to a very little extent with the assertion. The mean value and standard deviation ($\overline{x} = 3.70$, $SD = 1.141$) confirmed this frequency distribution.

The experience of the staff determined the type of leadership style adopted in the college, respondents were investigated; 30 representing 26.1% of the respondents agreed to a great extent with the assertion that often time, experience of the staff determined the type of leadership style adopted in the college; while 24 (20.9%) of the respondents believed to a great extent. However, 20 (17.4%) of the respondents agreed to some extent; 40 (34.8%) of the respondents and 01 (0.9%) of the respondents perceived it to a little extent and very little extent respectively that experience of the staff determine the type of leadership style adopted in the college. This underlines the fact that often time, the experience of the staff determined the type of leadership style adopted in the college. This submission tally with the submission of Ibara (2010) whose work posited that the prevailing environment, culture and experience of staff greatly influence the choice of leadership styles adopted by leaders. The mean and standard deviation confirm this frequency ($\overline{\chi} = 3.37$, $SD = 1.231$).

In addition, respondents were asked to assess the assertion that the population of students was a factor that determines the choice of leadership style in the college. In their reactions, 31 (27.0%) of the respondents submitted to a very great extent with the assertion, 30 (26.1%) of the respondents opined that it is to great extent. However, 18 (15.7%) of the respondents graded it to some extent and 32 (27.8%) graded the assertion to a little extent. Also, 4 (3.5%) of the respondents graded it to a very little extent that the population of students determined the leadership style adopted, as shown by the mean value and standard deviation ($\overline{\chi}$ = 3.45, SD = 1.251).

Also, it was reported that 73 (63.5%) of the respondents subscribed to a very great extent that government interference in the appointment of college leadership is one of the factors that determined the style of leadership adopted in the institutions, while 25 (21.7%) of the respondents rated it to great extent, 09 (7.8%) of the respondents maintained it to some extent, while 03 (2.6%) of the respondents rated it to little extent and 04 (3.5%) of the respondents acclaimed to a very little consistency. 01 representing 0.9% of the respondents gave no reaction to this assertion. This implies that government interference in the appointment of college leadership is a factor that determined the leadership style adopted, since the mean value (4.37) is beyond the mid-point of 3.0. The mean value and standard deviation ($\overline{\chi}$ = 4.37, SD = 1.071) confirmed this frequency distribution.

The respondents were asked to assess the assertion, that gender (sex) of the leader determined the choice of leadership style adopted, 60 representing 52.2% of the respondents rated it to a very great extent and 26 (22.3%) of the respondents agreed to a great extent. However, 05 (4.3%) graded to some extent; while 12 (10.4%) of the respondents and 11 (9.6%) of the respondents rated it to a little extent and very little extent respectively. 01 representing 0.9% of the respondents gave no response to this assertion. This implies that gender (sex) influences leadership style adopted as shown by the mean value and standard deviation ($\overline{\chi}$ = 3.95, SD = 1.413). This submission, however, corroborated with Okoriji and Anyanwu (2014). They observed that gender determines the leadership style which secondary teachers adopt in teaching.

Also, respondents were asked to examine the availability of fund as a factor that determined the choice of leadership style in the selected colleges, 85 (73.9%) of the respondents affirmed to very a great extent, 11 (9.6%) of the respondents submitted to a great extent while, 6 (5.2%) of the respondents believed to some extent, and 2 (1.7%) rated the assertion to a little extent; with 11 representing 9.6% of the respondents supporting the assertion to a very little extent. The mean value and standard deviation ($\overline{\chi}$ = 4.37, SD = 1.266) confirmed this frequency distribution.

Furthermore, inquire were made on the culture and traditions of the college as determinant to the leadership style adopted, in their reactions 57 representing 49.6% of the respondents strongly agreed and 27 (23.5%) of the respondents agreed with this position. However, 16 (13.9%) of the respondents maintained a neutral position with the culture and traditions of the college determining the leadership style adopted, while 8 representing 7.0% of the respondents strongly disagreed; and 06 (5.2%). Unlike the other respondents, 1 representing 0.9% of the respondents took no position on this assertion. This implies that the culture and traditions of the college determine the leadership style adopted, as verified by the mean value and standard deviation ($\overline{\chi}$ = 4.03, SD = 1.239).

In addition, 32 (27.8%) of the respondents opined to a very great extent that the availability of basic and other infrastructures determined the leadership style adopted, while 14 representing 12.2% of the respondents submitted to a great extent. However, 18 (15.7%) of the respondents pegged the assertion to some extent and 38 (33.0%) of the respondents believed to a little extent. Moreover, a sizeable amount of the respondents 13 (11.3%) of the respondents submitted to a very little extent. The mean value and standard deviation ($\overline{\chi}$ = 3.12, SD = 1.421; Table 1, Fig. 1).

A diagrammatic illustration above seeks to further showcase the strength of each of the factors that could possibly determine the leadership styles with specific reference to the management of students' affairs. However, It was clearly denoted through this graphical illustration that leader's human relation (4.50), government interference in the college

Table 1 Determinant factors of leadership style in the management of students' affairs in selected colleges

	Very little extent	Little extent	Some extent	Great extent	Very great extent	No response	Descriptive statistics	
	f (%)	f (%)	f (%)	f (%)	F (%)	F (%)	Mean value	Standard deviation
Leader's human relation	1 (0.9)	2 (1.7)	6 (5.2)	36 (31.3)	70 (60.9)	– (–)	4.50	0.754
The attitudes of staff of the college	2 (1.7)	29 (25.2)	25 (21.7)	26 (22.6)	33 (28.7)	– (–)	3.51	1.202
The size or type of the college	3 (2.6)	19 (16.5)	22 (19.1)	37 (32.2)	34 (29.6)	– (–)	3.70	1.141
The experience of staff	1 (0.9)	40 (34.8)	20 (17.4)	24 (20.9)	30 (26.1)	– (–)	3.37	1.231
Population of students	4 (3.5)	32 (27.8)	18 (15.7)	30 (26.1)	31 (27.0)	– (–)	3.45	1.251
Government interference in the appointment of college leadership	4 (3.5)	3 (2.6)	9 (7.8)	25 (21.7)	73 (63.5)	1 (0.9)	4.37	1.071
Gender (sex) of the leader	11 (9.6)	12 (10.4)	5 (4.3)	26 (22.3)	60 (52.2)	1 (0.9)	3.95	1.413
Availability of fund	11 (9.6)	2 (1.7)	6 (5.2)	11 (9.6)	85 (73.9)	– (–)	4.37	1.266
The culture and traditions of the college	6 (5.2)	8 (7.0)	16 (13.9)	27 (23.5)	57 (49.6)	1 (0.9)	4.03	1.239
Availability of basic and other infrastructures	13 (11.3)	38 (33.0)	18 (15.7)	14 (12.2)	32 (27.8)	– (–)	3.12	1.421

Source Field Survey (2021)
NB: f = Frequency; % = Percentage

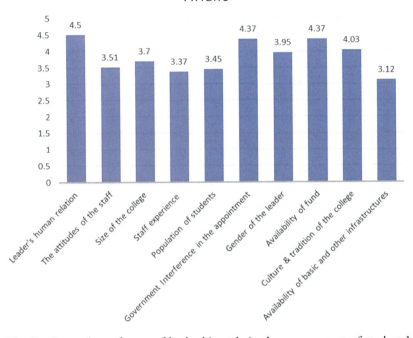

Fig. 1 Determinant factors of leadership style in the management of students' affairs in selected colleges (*Source* Field Survey [2021])

appointment (4.37) and fund availability (4.37) were the key determining factors of leadership styles in the management of students' affairs in the study area.

4 Discussion of Findings

As revealed, the study indicated several factors that determine the leadership style adopted by the leaders in the selected colleges of education Southwestern Nigeria. The qualitative data analysis results revealed that the human relation (personal traits) (RII = 91.12) was documented as the leading factors that determine the leadership style adopted in the selected colleges. This submission is in line with the outcome of Mensah (2015), that personality of the Provost is one important factor that cannot be ignored. The human relation of the Provost is the key factor to effective management of student's personnel service. The interpretation is that the Provost individual basic nature and disposition to issues as it affects students' affairs is most important to the provision, maintenance and operations of students' affairs services. Thus, Manoj and Shilpa (2013) observed that if the leadership traits is transforming and has charisma to motivate and influence staff to be more diligent, staff will be dedicated, efficient and effective in their duties.

The result also indicates that government interference (RII = 85.2) was admitted as one of the factors that determine the leadership style adopted in the selected colleges. Igbaekemen and Odivwri (2015) agreed with the findings that political connections, appointment of institutions leadership by the government without recourse to competency. The findings also corroborate Ololube et al. (2012) submission that the political freedom of institutions protects them from government and political officials' interruption especially in the day-to-day running of the college activities.

Several literatures have also identified the availability of fund; gender (sex); culture and tradition, and size of the college as factors that determine leadership style (Garland, 1986). Amuda-Kannike (2021) affirmed that the major challenge facing higher education institution in Nigeria is inadequate funding. Also Ajayi and Ayodele (2009) opined that Nigerian government in the recent years has not met the stipulated 26% of the total budget as recommended by the United Nation Educational Scientific and Cultural Organization (UNESCO). More so, Jim (2014) observed that insufficient funding dampens the morale of leaders in the development of tertiary institutions since the college management will be rendered ineffective when it lacks adequate funds. Therefore, effective students' affairs services can be said to depend on the availability of fund and concluded that large enrolment without corresponding improve funding can worsen the situation of the institutions.

The result also indicated that Gender (RII = 74.5) is a factor that determine leadership style adopted in the selected colleges. The findings of Okoriji and Anyanwu (2014) established that gender determines the leadership style adopted by secondary school teachers. Another significant finding of this study revealed culture (RII = 73.1) as a factor that determine leadership style adopted in the selected colleges of education in

Southwestern Nigeria. Each college possess its own culture and tradition. The culture and tradition of a college are combinations of the founders, past and current leadership ideas, crises, events, history and size. Thus, this can be sum as the "rites" or ways or how things are done in the college. The finding is in agreement with the finding of Agboola et al. (2017), that, individual leader cannot create or change the culture of the organisation, rather the culture of the organisation influences the characteristics of the leader.

The findings reveal that size of the college, student's population and attitudes of the college staff determine to a great extent the leadership style adopted in the selected colleges. As colleges grow in size, problems may arise which may become more difficult to solve especially at the management level. The attitude of the staff of the college (RII = 50.13) is sacrosanct to the leadership adopted leadership style. The interpretation is that the attitudes and qualities of the staff including their peculiarities influence the leadership style of the provost. This aligned with the submission of the United State Army (1983) which stated that the characteristics of the followers apart from other three factors, is a major determinant of the leadership style that the leader adopt. In another related study, Ibara (2010) opined that effective leader relates with subordinates with deep understanding especially with consideration to their peculiarities to avoid slain relationship.

They further revealed that staff experience and availability of basic infrastructure are the least determinant to the leadership style adopted in the management of students' affairs in Southwestern Nigeria. However, contrary to these findings from the subordinates, the management in their interview submission rated this factor high. They submitted that although much has been done to address the menace of infrastructural development through TETFUND in Nigerian colleges of education, availability of basic infrastructures still remains a factor that affect most operations of the colleges and therefore affect the disposition of the leaders towards certain decision especially towards student's affairs services. The Registrar of one of the colleges maintained that due to the problem of funding to provide basic infrastructures and necessary amenities for the students and the staff, students affairs services are not only inadequate, some of those provided are not satisfactory but equally not sufficient to cater for the present population of students.

5 Concluding Remarks

From the findings of the study, the study concludes that leadership styles adopted in the colleges significantly influence the management of students' affairs. Students' affairs services will function effectively when management adopts a proper leadership styled. The Provost as the chief executive officer of the college plays a significant role towards the organisation, formulation and implementation including the provision of students' affairs services in the institutions. The study is of the opinion that leadership disposition to student's affairs services is sacrosanct to an effective and efficient student's affairs management in colleges of education. Equally, leaders should possess skills necessary for making the right decision which can be beneficial to both staff and school at large.

Policy Recommendation Since leadership in higher institution is primarily associated with the goal of improving students' learning and aiding their growth, leaders are required to promote the success of all students by promoting their progress, articulation, retention and moral development. For the purpose of improving the management of students' affairs, the following recommendations are essential in assisting leaders in their effort to effectively manage the students' affairs.

(a) Accountability and resource management, including good leadership, should be reviewed in the Institutions;

(b) Government interference in the appointment of the Institutions' leadership should be limited, curtailed and if possible eradicated. The proprietors of the public Institutions should curtail their excessive interference, especially in the appointment of the college leadership.

(c) The politicisation of the appointment of leadership personnel in higher institutions has relegated competency to the background and encouraged excessive use of authoritarian leadership style in the Institutions. The Institutions should be allowed to democratically appoint their leaders and this will create a competing ground for qualified and competent candidates to emerge as leaders.

(d) From the data gathered for this study, it is observed that operation of students' affairs in the selected colleges is poorly operated, instituted and coordinated. Although students' affairs are available in the colleges, they are inadequate and of low quality.

LEADERSHIP IN THE MANAGEMENT OF HIGHER ...   189

(e) The leaders of colleges should ensure that the college environment is conducive to learning activities.

(f) Since motivation induces staff to give their best, the leadership of the college should understand that their attitude/behaviours or actions affect the provision of effective students' affairs services.

Acknowledgements We would like to thank and appreciate all the staff in the College of Education selected for this study.

Funding The authors received no financial support for the research, authorship, and/or publication of the article.

Disclosure Statement No potential conflict of interest was reported by the authors.

Declarations The authors of this manuscript have read the journal's policy and have the following competing interests: **AMUDA-KANNIKE Abdulkareem** is employed by the Kwara State Government and deployed to Directorate of Information, Publicity & Protocol, Kwara State College of Education, Kwara State. **SHIYANBADE Bolanle Waliu** is employed by the Federal Government of Nigeria into the Department of Public Administration, Faculty of Administration, Obafemi Awolowo University, Ile-Ife, Nigeria. There are no patents, products in development, or marketed products to declare. This does not alter the authors' adherence to the Author Guidelines on sharing data and materials used in this study.

Informed Consent and Ethical Approval The participants selected in the study gave informed consent and voluntary participated in the study. There was no harm to the participants and also the College of Education selected in the Southwestern part of Nigeria were given fictional names in order to ensure confidentiality and anonymous of the participants in the study.

Conflict of Interest The paper is co-authorship, the authors state that there is no conflict of interest in any form, the participants selected within the study areas participated voluntarily, the College of Education selected were given fictional names for ethical reason, and there are data availability for this study.

References

Agboola, T. O., Lamidi, K. O., & Shiyanbade, B. W. (2017). *Global Journal of Interdisciplinary Social Sciences (GJISS)*, 6(4), 10–19. University of Mauritius.

Global Institute for Research & Education. https://doi.org/10.24105/gjiss. 6.4.1702

Ajayi, I. A. & Ayodele, J. B. (2009). Introduction to Educational System, Administration and Supervision. Abdol-Yommy Publishing Services

Ajayi, I. A., & Ekundayo, H. T. (2009). Towards effective management of university in Nigeria. *International NGO Journal, 4*(8), 342–347.

Akpala, A. (1998). Igbo cultural factors that may bear on management of organisational performance in Nigeria. In E. U. C. Imaga & U. J. F. Ewururu (Eds.), *Business management topics* (Vol. 1).

Amuda-Kannike, A. (2021). *Leadership styles and management of students affairs in selected colleges of education in Southwestern Nigeria.* An unpublished Ph.D. dissertation, submitted to Department of Public Administration, Obafemi Awolowo University, Ile-Ife, Nigeria.

Anyamele, S. C. (2004). *Institutional management in higher education: A study of leadership approaches to quality improvement in University Management— Nigerian and Finnish cases.* Unpublished Ph.D. thesis, University of Helsinki, Finland.

Avasthi, M. (2006). *Public administration.* Lakhmi Narain Agarwal Educational Publisher.

Bass, B. M. (1990). The Transactional Leadership Style and Effective Delivery of Service. *The International Journal of Leadership in Organization, 12,* 120–129.

Bass, B. M. (1991). From transactional to transformational leadership: Learning to share the vision. *Organisational Dynamics, 18*(3), 19–31.

Bass, B. M. (1996). *A new paradigm of leadership: An inquiry into transformational leadership.* U.S. Army Research Institute for the Behavioural and Social Sciences.

Bass, B. M. (2008). *The Bass handbook of leadership: Theory, research, & managerial applications* (4th ed.). Free Press.

Bateson, R. (2008). *The role of students services in enhancing the students experience: Cases of transformation in central and eastern Europe.* Unpublished Ph.D thesis, University of Southampton, School of Management. A Mini— Dissertation submitted in partial fulfilment of the requirement for the degree of Bachelors of Social Work.

Bees, J. L., & Dees, J. R. (2008). *Understanding college and University Organisation: Theories for effective policy and practice* (1st ed.). Stylus.

Bernard, L. L. (1926). The Qualities of Leaders. *An Introduction to Social Psychology. Henry Holt and Co,* 528–540.

Bingham, W. (1927). *The psychological foundations of management.* Shaw.

Bird, P. E. (1940). Examining teamwork and leadership in the fields of public administration and management. *Team Performance, Leadership and Management, 1* (31/32): 19–26.

Burns, J. M. (2010). *Leadership*. Harper Perennial.

Chukwu, B. I., & Eluka, J. (2013). Applications of leadership theories in Nigerian Business Organisations. *European Journal of Business and Management, 59170*, 166–171.

Dallas, L. (2012). The foundations of student affairs: A guild to the profession. In I. J. Hinchliffe & M. A. Wong (Eds.), *Environment for student growth & development* (pp. 1–39). Librarians & Students Affairs in Collaboration. Chicago Association of College & Research Libraries.

Garland, H. C. (1986). Emergent leadership Style and Productive time: The functional value of positive motivation. *International Journal of Personality, Psychology and Social Sciences. 62*(6): 191–203.

Gummerson, W. M. (2015). Augmenting sustainable leadership practices with complexity theory. *Literacy Information and Computer Education Journal (LICEJ), 6*(1), 1247–1255.

Hirt, J. B. (2006). *Where you work matters*. M.D. University Press.

Ibara, E. C. (2010). *Perspective in educational administration*. Rodi Printing and Publishing.

Igbaekemen, G. O., & Odivwri, J. E. (2015). Impact of leadership style on organization performance: A critical literature review. *Arabian Journal of Business Management Review, 5*, 142. https://doi.org/10.4172/2223-5833.1000142

Jaramilloa, R. C. (2015). Examining teamwork and leadership in the fields of public administration, leadership, and management. *Team Performance Management: An International Journal, 21*(3/4), 199–216.

Jenkins, W. O. (1947). A review of leadership studies with particular reference to military problems. *Psychological Bulletin, 44*(1), 54–79.

Jim, A. M. (2014). Situational, tranformational & transactional leadership & leadership development. *Journal of Business Studies Querterly*, ISSN 2152-1034.

Keeling, R. P. (2006). *Learning reconsidered 2: Implementing a campus-wide focus on the student experience*. ACPA.

Kilbourne, C. (1935). The elements of leadership. *Journal of Coast Artillery, 78*, 437–439.

Kohs, S.C., & Irle, K.W. (1920). Prophesying army promotion. *Journal of Applied Psychology, 4*(1), 73–87.

Kouzes, J. M., & Posner, B. Z. (2002). *Leadership challenge*. Jossey-Bass.

Landis, E. A. (2011). 21st century leadership issues as they pertain to a small private liberal Arts University. *Journal of Management Policy and Practice, 12*(3), 108–111.

Manoj, K. S., & Shilpa, J. (2013). Leadership management: Principles, models and theories. *Global Journal of Management and Business Studies, 3*(3), ISSN 2248-9878.

Memon, B. Y. (2013). The influence study of transformational leadership in university on teachers' organisational commitment: The construction and verification of a theoretical model. *Canadian Social Science, 9*(4), 126–137.

Mensah, J. (2015). Service quality in Higher Education: A comparative study in Higher Education: A comparative study in tertiary institutions in Sub-Saharan Africa. *Global Journal of Educational Studies,* http://www.researchgate.net/publicatio1282730418

Muhammad, S. K., Irfanullah, K., Qamar, A. O., Hafiz, I., Hamid, R., Abdul, L., & Muhammad, T. (2015). The styles of leadership: A critical review. *Public Policy and Administration Research, 3*(3), 2015.

Mung-Ling, V., May-Chiun, L., Kwang-Sing, N., & Sungan, P. (2015). Leadership styles in context of institution of Higher Education in Malaysia, downloaded from the Internet, 3 November 2019.

Naidu, S. P. (2014). *Public administration: Concept and theories.* New Age.

Nakpodia, E. D. (2012). Leadership development skills: A Nigeria education institutions review. *Global Business and Economics Research Journal, 1*(2), 93–110, ISSN 2302-4593.

NASPA-Student Affairs Administrators in Higher Education. (2012). Considering a career in student affairs? *Journal of Education and Practice, 2*(4), 15–23. Retrieved November 30, 2018, from http://www.naspa.org/career/default.cfm. Nigeria.

Nigro, F. A., & Nigro, L. G. (2014). *Modern Public Administration.* Horper Collings.

Northouse, G. P. (2013). *Leadership: Theory and practice* (6th ed.). Sage.

Nuss, M. E. (2003). The development of student affairs. In S. R. Komives, D. B. Woodard Jr., & Associates (Eds.), *Student services: A handbook for the profession* (4th ed., pp. 65–88). Jossey Bass.

Okoriji, I. I., & Anyanwu, O. J. (2014). Impact of leadership styles on teaching and learning process in Imo State. *Mediterranean Journal of Social Sciences, 5*(4). MCSER Publishing, Rome-Italy.

Ololube, N. P. (2013). *Educational management, planning and supervision: Model for effective implementation.* SpringField Publishers.

Ololube, N. P., Egbezor, D. E., Kpolovie, P. J., & Amaele, S. (2012). Theoretical debates on school effectiveness research: Lessons for Third World education development agendas. In N. P. Ololube & P. J. Kpolovie (Eds.), *Educational management in developing economies: Cases 'n' school effectiveness and quality improvement* (pp. 1–18). Lambert Academic Publishers.

Omotoso, F. (2013, November). Re-inventing governance and public accountability for improved productivity in Nigeria Higher Education. *Academic of Interdisciplinary Studies, 2*(2), ISSN 2281-3993.

Page, D. (1935). Measurement and prediction of leadership. *American Journal of Sociology, 41*, 21–33.

Peretomode, V. F. (2012). *Theories of management: Implications for educational administration*. Justice Jeco Printing & Publishing Global.

Robson, A. (2009). *Leadership in Universities and Research Organisation, Lecture at the Melborne School of Leadership and Environment (pdf)*. Retrieved September 26, 2017, from http://www.handford.unimelb.edu

Rose, N. A., Gloria, J. S., & Nwachukwu, P. O. (2015). Review of leadership theories, principles, and styles and their relevance to Education Organisations. *Management, 5*(1), 6–14. 10.5923jmn20150501.02

Sandeen, A. (1988). Student affairs: Issues, problems and trends. *Eric/CAPS* 48109-1259.

Smith, H. & Krueger, L. (1933). *A brief summary of literature on leadership*. Bloomington: Indiana University, School of Education Bulletin.

Sundi, K. (2013). Effect of transformational leadership and transactional leadership on employee performance of Konawe Education Department at Southeast Sulawesi Province.

Tead, O. (1929). The technique of creative leadership. *Human Nature and Management*. McGraw-Hill.

Tyagi, P. (2004). *Public Administration: Principles and practice*. Atmaram & Sons.

Transnationalism, Migration and African Integration

The Motivations for Return Migration to Somalia: Beyond the Voluntary and Forced Binary

Jacqueline Owigo

1 INTRODUCTION

Given the increased level and complexity of international migration and refugees, returning refugees and migrants to countries of origin is one of the main topics of research and policy. Acceptance and integration of migrants and refugees in destination countries have been hampered by numerous obstacles, including discrimination and human rights abuses. In this case, the repatriation or return to the country of origin remains the main and important policy for the host and home countries (Mohammadi et al., 2018).

The politicisation of return has far-reaching consequences for returnees after their return. Chimni (1993) alludes to self-interested motivations behind the promotion of return and has questioned the voluntary nature of many repatriation programmes (Hathaway, 2007). Drawing from migration literature and semi-structured interviews with Somali returnees and deportees, the study aims to advance discussions on the

---

J. Owigo (✉)
United States International University—Africa, Nairobi, Kenya
e-mail: jowigo@usiu.ac.ke

© The Author(s), under exclusive license to Springer Nature Switzerland AG 2023
A. I. Adeniran (ed.), *African Development and Global Engagements*,
https://Doi.org/10.1007/978-3-031-21283-3_10

forced–voluntary dichotomy in analysing returnees' decision-making and return experiences and builds on Erdal and Oeppen's (2018) work on theoretical understanding of voluntariness in return migration.

The first section presents literature on return and reintegration on how the concept of volition has been addressed in the return migration literature. This is followed by a brief overview of the return situation in Somalia. The following section then outlines the data collection strategy, sampling and methodology adopted for the analysis. This is followed by the findings drawing from the qualitative interviews with returnees to examine how they experience voluntariness, choice and alternatives in their return migration decisions and how it is labelled by immigration authorities. Lastly, the study findings and implications on return migration management in the Somalia context will be discussed.

2   Context of Migration and Return in Somalia

In recent years, there has been an increase in the return migration of Somalis to their home country, both from the East and Horn of Africa, Yemen, and the Arabian Peninsula. According to UNHCR, 133,166 Somali returnees have been recorded and assisted as of August 2021 (UNCHR, 2021c). The majority of the returnees come from Kenya through the 2013 Tripartite Agreement between UNHCR and the Governments of Kenya and Somalia (UNHCR, 2021b), while Somali refugees to whom Yemen offered prima facie refugee status over the decades are having to return as a result of the fighting in Yemen (Maimuna, 2016). Moreover, migrants are being deported from western countries such as the United States (Van Lehman & Mckee, 2019) and the kingdom of Saudi Arabia (Owigo, 2021). Instability and environmental disasters have also caused the internal displacement of 2.9 million Somalis as of Jan 2021 (UNHCR, 2021a).

According to the Failed State Index (FSI), which is regarded as one of the most reliable indicators of states' performance by development researchers across the world (Sekhar, 2010), Somalia is considered a fragile state, a position it has remained in for the last decade. While it would be too simplistic to assert that refugees are the result of decades of conflict, it is the case that food insecurity, drought, environmental degradation, climate change and weak governance constitute significant drivers of forced migration (Zetter, 2011). This assertation brings to fore the multi-causality that underpins the displacement of most refugees. In this context, Somalia offers a good case study where there have been repeated displacements over several decades due to overlapping episodes of conflict, drought, food insecurity, bad governance and state fragility.

Efforts to address the refugee issues in Somalia are closely linked to the challenges of responding to internal displacement. Given the reality that large-scale returns to many parts of Somalia may not be possible due to the challenging context as explained above, it follows that the processes of return and reintegration for the returning refugees present significant policy challenges for the government of Somalia and the international community. Covid-19 has also had an impact on the mobility trends in Somalia, with many migrants being stranded or deported from the Gulf countries like Saudi Arabia. In recent months, several cases worldwide have highlighted the challenges surrounding repatriation processes. Many migrants see returning home as a viable survival strategy, which was not an option in the pre-Covid-19 period (Jones, 2020).

Growing literature emphasises an alarming trend advocating for return, even forced or involuntary, while very little regard is paid to the reintegration processes that Somali returnees experience when relocating to their country of origin. For example, Garre (2017) documents the experiences of the returning refugees from Kenya, who reported that even though they were not physically forced to leave, their return to Somalia was involuntary due to factors such as reduced food rations and mistreatment by Kenya's armed forces.

Schuster and Majidi (2015) and Arowolo (2000), for example, show that most of those who are forcibly removed from the country to which they have migrated will have challenges reintegrating and consequently will leave again. Deportees and returned asylum seekers whose claims have been refused to face additional challenges. They not only return to the material and social conditions from which they fled, but they also bear the stigma of failure. They may be rejected, even by their own families, who expected them to succeed and support them abroad. In recent literature, Majidi and Schuster (2019) have highlighted how unsustainable return practices often heighten the vulnerability of migrants to precarious re-migration, putting them at risk of trafficking, exploitation and abuse. Yet little attention has been directed to the experiences of return migrants themselves or the structural factors shaping returnees' experiences, particularly those from countries still in conflict. It is also important to consider the extent to which voluntariness in migration can be assessed in voluntary repatriation programmes, such as those usually overseen by UNHCR, in collaboration with other humanitarian agencies and governments of host countries and countries of origin. The Somalia case study provides a unique case study to illuminate these issues both at macro and micro levels.

The gap in the literature indicates that there is still little understanding of these processes linked to return migration in the global south, despite mounting evidence of the interconnectedness of African migrants' migration to high-income countries like Europe. At the same time, various countries in global south and the Middle East are emerging as hot spots for regional migration and return patterns. For example, countries like Kenya, Yemen and Saudi Arabia which have been traditional destination countries for most Somali migrants (Al-Sharmani, 2010; Shaffer et al., 2017).

Moreover, return is often used as a substitute for deportation and other forms of forced return, even when state officials, international organisations and civil society organisations refer to it as "voluntary" (Kalir, 2017). These various meanings are significant because the conceptualisation of return has implications for the assistance provided to migrants experiencing relocation to their country of origin via various means, such as removal, deportation, UNHCR tripartite repatriations or assisted voluntary return.

To begin with, the United Nations High Commissioner for Refugees (UNHCR) defines voluntary return as stemming from a freely made decision return, based on "full knowledge of the facts" and occurring in "conditions of safety and dignity" (UNHCR, 2004). Therefore, individual agency to make an informed decision is prioritised, while at the same time, conditions in the country of return are considered crucial for a "voluntary return" to be successful. Schuster and Majidi (2013), on the other hand, describe deportation as involuntary return that is "the physical removal of someone against their will from the territory of one state to that of another" (p. 222). While these well-defined terms represent opposite ends of the spectrum, the findings reveal experiences of return occurring between the two.

3   Conceptualising Return Migration

On return migration literature, studies of return of "refugees" are mainly referred to as repatriation, and the return of rejected asylum seekers is mainly referred to as "return migration" (Lietaert & Gorp, 2019, p. 2).

Scholars have emphasised the need to incorporate them into one group for the following reasons.

First, the strict distinction between the two groups has been questioned for its delineation based on policy and concerns (Bakewell, 2008). For instance, the term refugee is mainly used in its political sense, referring to a person outside their country of origin and recognised as a refugee by governments of host countries, the United Nations High Commissioner for Refugees (UNHCR) and other aid actors. On the other hand, an asylum seeker is a term that refers to people whose claim to receive asylum in another county is still in process. If the asylum claim is unsuccessful, people are expected to return to their county of origin and referred to as rejected asylum seekers. Despite the formal recognition of a refugee or not, the two groups possess similar migration trajectories and experiences (Bakewell, 2008), and therefore, their return process might also have many resemblances. Moreover, in the field of return, this blurring of categories is reinforced by the fact that the support for the programmes for refugee return formed the basis for the programmes aimed at returning rejected asylum seekers (Black & Gent, 2006) which further adds to the literature that the distinction between the two groups is artificial and risks omitting the need to support those compelled to return. Focussing on the returnees who have been in touch with the formal aid system allows the study to shed light on how the outcomes of return and reintegration are defined from the perspectives of host countries and international organisations (Zetter, 2007).

The concepts of "sustainable return" and "reintegration" are employed to conceptualise successful return for refugees and failed asylum seekers (Lietaert & Gorp, 2019). Although the concepts are widely used in literature, they have been criticised for their vagueness and political nature (Hammond, 1999). According to Black and Gent (2006), a distinction can be made between the narrow and broad definitions of sustainability in government discourses (p. 29). Within a narrow conceptualisation focussing on individual returnees, sustainable return refers to returnees' physical return and stay in their country of origin and thus not re-migrating. The absence of re-migration is considered by policymakers as removing the international dimension of displacement and thus ending host states' obligations towards a particular group of refugees (Long, 2011). Alternatively, the broader conceptualisation of successful return and reintegration is considered a long-term and multidimensional process involving the reintegration of the individual returnee and the development of the country of origin (Lietaert & Gorp, 2019).

In general, five domains of reintegration are embedded in various studies of reintegration processes—political, economic, legal, social and cultural (Koser & Kuschminder, 2015; UNHCR, 2004). The UNHCR definition of reintegration is "equated with the achievement of a sustainable return – in other words, the ability of returning refugees to secure the political, economic, [legal] and social conditions needed to maintain life, livelihood and dignity" (UNHCR, 2004, p. 4).

4 Voluntariness in the Management of Returns

To understand whether the return decision-making of Somali returnees can be conceptualised against the frameworks developed within the migration scholarship, there is a need to study the key categories of forced and voluntary migration. In both migration and forced migration scholarship, the analysis of the implications of volition on migration processes is somewhat limited despite the forced–voluntary being a key dichotomy in typologies of migration. The traditional approach to these categories is based on the distinction between forced displacement and its normative understanding in accordance with the legal definitions of a refugee and an asylum seeker, on the one hand, and a free or voluntary migrant, most often associated with economic motivations, on the other.

In forced migration studies, much of the debate has centred on the implications of expanding "refugee studies," which focusses on those who have fled their home country due to a well-founded fear of persecution (as defined by the 1951 Refugee Convention). James Hathaway (2007), in emphasising the legal category, argues against the trend of viewing refugees as just one type of forced migrant. He emphasises that refugees are unique in that they are exempt "from the usual right of governments to impose immigration or other penalties for illegal arrival or presence] which makes clear that the refugee protection system is a self-operationalising, fundamentally autonomous mechanism of human rights protection" (Hathaway, 2007, p. 354).

Scholars have convincingly argued that the insistence of states on forced and voluntary distinction is a political tool that enables them to deny refugee protection to great numbers of people who might otherwise qualify for it (Gibney, 2004). Indeed, Chimni points out the coincidence that attention forced migration coincided with the emergence of the non-entrée asylum regime and redoubled efforts to quarantine displaced people in the Third World (Chimni, 2009).

In mainstream migration studies, theorising on why individuals migrate has been centred on migrants assumed to be travelling voluntarily, as opposed to analysing the complete continuum of forced–voluntary migration. In recent literature recognising the migration complexities, Crawley and Skleparis (2018) emphasise that the term "voluntary migration" is deeply flawed because the reasons for migration cannot be neatly tucked into black and white boxes and frequently change over time. The definitions do not take into account "the shifting significance for individuals over time" (Crawley & Skleparis, 2018, p. 48) regarding their movement. Erdal and Oeppen (2018) critically examine the forced–voluntary dichotomy focussing on the migration cycle: leaving, journeying, arriving, settling and returning. Drawing from qualitative research with people from Afghanistan and Pakistan coming to Europe, they posit three distinct depictions of migration: migrants' own experiences, qualitative scholarly observations and immigration authorities' labelling. They find that the role of agency is important, as virtually no migration occurs without a great deal of it in place (Erdal & Oeppen, 2018).

In line with previous research, there is also an emerging limited body of work bringing to attention the counterpart to forced migration. For example, Bartram (2015) advances the notion of unacceptable alternatives and posits that migration can be "forced" because of one's rejection of local subsistence options that amount to violations of human rights (e.g. being forced to convert religion or accept certain beliefs) which are considered as unacceptable alternatives to fleeing, while others (such as great poverty) are not. Thus, in migration decisions, voluntariness is closely informed by the available acceptable alternatives and the agency to act on those options.

It has been argued that migration decision-making and experiences cannot be simplistically labelled either forced or voluntary since it is problematic to characterise migration either as "whimsical preferences" or by "coercive circumstances": instead, Ottonelli and Torresi describe migration as a voluntary choice guided by "important values and goals in people's lives" (Ottonelli & Torresi, 2013, p. 793). In sum, understanding migration decisions is critical for the broader society and policymakers, as well as migrants and potential migrants. Migration decisions are made at important crossroads in people's lives, shape and are shaped by long-term life trajectories, and have long-term consequences for the decision-maker and the people affected by the decisions.

Based on Erdal and Oeppen's (2018) work, which forms the main theoretical framework for this paper, the study explores the role that the notion of voluntariness plays in return migration decisions.

5 RESEARCH DESIGN

The data were collected between 2019 and 2021 as part of doctoral research conducted in Mogadishu, Somalia and Nairobi, Kenya. Relying on snowball sampling methods, through professional and personal networks, the researcher conducted semi-structured, qualitative interviews with 41 returnees from Kenya, Yemen and Saudi Arabia living in Mogadishu, Somalia. Expert interviews were held with government officials, international organisations (IOM and UNHCR), NGOs and other researchers. The study involved collecting data in the Somali language to allow the returnees to freely express themselves in a language they could understand (Resch & Enzenhofer, 2018). The open-ended questionnaire covered different migration phases: experience before migration, experience in the host country and post-return experience focussing on return decision in addition to data on demographic and contextual factors. To overcome the language barrier and take into consideration the power relations around the lines of gender and ethnicity, the researcher recruited two community researchers—one male and one female to facilitate access to and trust. All of the participants were informed about the research verbally. They were made aware that their answers would be confidential, that their participation in the research was voluntary, and that they had the right to stop the interview at any time. The transcripts of interviews with returnees were analysed through a combination of inductive and deductive analysis. To ensure confidentiality and anonymity, the researcher used pseudo names to represent the interviewees and no quotations that could reveal any participants' identities have been used in the paper.

6 FINDINGS FROM THE STUDY

This section draws from interviews with returnees and deportees and explores the motivation impacting their return decisions and the labelling by the authorities.

6.1 Motivations Impacting Return Decisions

The findings illuminate that there are no clear-cut boundaries between voluntary and involuntary return decisions: almost no decision to return was entirely free, as there were legal constraints, structural constraints, personal circumstances, family pressure, economic needs or socio-cultural difficulties at the basis of this decision. Therefore, the results highlight a continuum of return categories: almost no decision was taken out of volition.

6.2 "Voluntary Returns"

Returnees from Kenya highlighted the role of UNHCR and the host government in contributing to their decision to return. Respondents reported that even though they were not physically forced to leave, their return to Somalia was involuntary due to factors such as reduction of food rations and mistreatment by Kenya's armed forces. Mohamed a returnee gave his story as follows "*The UNHCR provides refugees with scant information. Kenyan officials are spreading the message that individuals who do not willingly register would be forced out later, forfeiting the package provided to refugees who voluntarily registered for repatriation.*" Cabdi 50-year-old returnee from Kenya, regretted his decision to return to Somalia. According to him, his expectations and the reality on the ground were different. After receiving a 600 USD grant from UNHCR to return with his children, he expected to find a good life in Somalia as per the advisory from UNHCR. However, upon return, he encountered a challenging condition with a lack of livelihood opportunities and no access to social protection from the government.

Even though some respondents returned through voluntary repatriation or on their own initiative, their reasons for returning were frequently motivated by their inability to build a life in country of origin; disability; incentives from the UNHCR grants; situations of exploitation; violence; abuse; or psychosocial factors such as discrimination and psychological problems.

I was involved in an accident by motorbike; therefore, I couldn't work and make a living for my family. I also heard the situation in my country was becoming better. That was why I decided to return to my home country.
[Shariiif, 51-year-old male returnee]

I decided to come back because my leg was amputated due to a shooting incident. Due to that disability, I cannot work there, so I decided to return home. [Luul, 46 uear old female returnee]

The narratives about the decision-making processes also show the difficulties that different returnees encountered before returning to Somalia, which contributed to their motivation to return. For example, discrimination, insecurity and economic difficulties in countries of asylum were among the primary reasons for refugees' return. The latter theme was strong among those returning from Yemen, where some refugees also indicated feeling increasingly unsafe. Farhiya, a 28 female returnee, narrated her experience "*I decided to return because there in Yemen, there are no basic needs such as water, cooking gas, shortage of food. Life is extremely difficult.*"

For some of the respondents, the experience of discrimination in the host country and lack of security contributed to their decision to leave.

The area where we were staying was dangerous, and there were many rape cases and people being killed. I am better off in my country Somalia. [Sahra 33-year-old female returnee]
there was war there[Yemen] and most Somalis were returning to Somalia, so I decided to come back with them. [Ali, 54-year-old male returnee]

This confirms that harsh living conditions due to the Yemen conflict are starting to push Somali refugees to return back to Somalia. The ongoing fighting has hampered the ability to offer refugees with necessary aid and protection.

6.3   Compelled Return Due to Family Pressures and Personal Circumstances

For some of the respondents, their return was a result of the sickness of their close family member and therefore they had to leave the host country and return back to Somalia. As explained by Hibaaq 39-year-old female returnee: "*yes, I came back once in 2015 because I wanted to see my father, who was ailing. I had to remain behind and take care of him.*" As for Halima, her return decision to Somalia was informed by her husband, whom she had left behind in Somalia.

My husband, who was living in Somalia insisted I should return to Somalia.
[Halima 30 female returnee]

The findings also reveal the role of family networks and clans in returnees' decision-making. Mohammed a Somali youth migrated to Kenya with his aunty, who had since returned to Somalia. Given that he had no family support system in the host country, he decided to return and live with the aunty.

No, I was not happy to return, but circumstance forced me since I was alone and my Aunty went back to Somalia, and I left with no choice but to follow her. [Mohammed 29 male returnee]

6.4 Involuntary (Forced) Returns

This study interviewed eleven returnees recently deported to Mogadishu. Most deportees interviewed for this study in Mogadishu entered Saudi Arabia illegally crossing the border from Yemen. Furthermore, some participants became undocumented after fleeing abusive employment and seeking alternative employment in the informal sector.

It was not my decision to return, but I was deported. I was working and hoping more beautiful life to come, but things went bad, and I was deported and returned to Somalia without my personal consent. [_Nimco 30-year-old female returnee]

Sahro a 46-year-old woman from Mogadishu, recalled her harrowing experience of detention at a deportation centre in Jeddah. "*the police beat me and threw me from the stairs. I was hurt, and they had to take me to a nearby hospital, and after a week they came and took me back to the cell and later deported me*" [Sahro 46 female returnee].

A similar experience is described by Hodan a 33-year-old Somali. According to her account, Saudi authorities kept her for nine days along with her two children, ages seven and nine, and her sister's three children before expelling them. Hodan narrated her ordeal in tears. "*The room we shared with 120 other women and children was hot and lacked air conditioning. The children fell ill. My son was vomiting and had a bloated stomach. There were no mattresses, so everyone slept directly on the floor*" [Hodan 33-year-old female returnee].

208   J. OWIGO

The majority of the participants returned to Somalia empty-handed and were unable to purchase food or pay for transportation to their homes due to Saudi Arabia's arbitrary confiscation of their personal property, which authorities refused to allow them to take.

> *No!! It is not my decision to come back to my homeland, but unfortunately, they have deported me from Saudia.* [_Aisha, 37-year-old female returnee]

Respondents who were deported reported that they could not acquire new skills or experiences while in the host country, which increased their vulnerability upon their return. Returnees who had returned involuntarily lacked access to social networks as their return was unexpected, leaving them with no time to prepare or mobilise their social networks prior to return. Those deported, particularly those who spent significant periods overseas and from minor clans, frequently lacked the social networks necessary to find employment.

The finding also highlights mixed return perceptions among the deportees. The terrible living conditions, violence and abuse and frequent feeling of being a burden on host countries cause many migrants to lose hope. Because of this, some believe they are better off returning to Somalia, as explained by Sahro, who had mixed feelings upon return to Somalia following her deportation from Saudi Arabia recounted below:

> *Yes, I was happy to return because I had no other option left... And I know it's my country and there is no better place than home. I felt at home when I reached Mogadishu and was happy to see my family and friends.* [Sahro 46-year-old female returnee]

Despite the challenges faced in Saudi Arabia, Sahro had a positive outlook on their return situation. A dynamic sense of agency was transparent in their resilience to their reintegration experience work for them even though they had undergone a traumatic deportation experience.

As the reasons mentioned were diverse, they have been grouped and organised into several categories depending on the apparent degree of the agency involved in each circumstance. The "voluntary" and forced categories at each end of the volition spectrum and, in the blurry middle, are compelled to return due to structural constraints and compelled to return due to personal and gendered life course constraints (Table 1).

THE MOTIVATIONS FOR RETURN MIGRATION ...   209

Table 1 Return as a continuum across the forced and voluntary binary

Codes
Involuntary (forced) Return
Compelled return due to structural constraints
Compelled return due to family pressures and personal circumstances
"Voluntary return"

Source Interviews with returnees in Mogadishu

6.5   Re-Migration Plans

The lack of livelihood opportunities, access to basic services and the inability to access education are some of the factors that have contributed to returnees' aspirations for a further migration plan. Returnees who reported aspirations for re-migration also tended to be jobless with little access to income and lacked clan protection. They often reported feelings of shame and unworthiness within their communities.

The interviewees expressed the need to find a longer-term solution to their displacement by seeking opportunities in the previous host country—in Kenya or other destinations. For some, re-migration was an aspiration but not a possibility due to financial constraints. Other reasons included policy constraints, such as not being recognised as a refugee if they should return to Kenya, as they had already relinquished their status upon signing up for the repatriation programme. These returnees lamented:

In case the situation worsens, I might go back to Kenya as don't think I am hoping for the best life in my country ... I prefer Kenya because of free education for our children and free distribution of food, free medical services; and Kenya is a peaceful country. (Sacdiyo female returnee; 35 years)

The situation is worse [in Somalia] in terms of getting access to livelihood. I don't want to migrate because my ration card was canceled and I wouldn't get assistance. Depending on the current circumstances, if I could see anyone requesting to return to Kenya or any other country, I would encourage them to go and find a better life since the situation here remains worse. (Cumar, female returnee; 33 years)

Many of the respondents expressed a desire to re-migrate as a fallback plan due to the challenging context. However, due to their financial constraints, they remained unable to realise their migration project resulting to involuntary mobility when there is the aspiration but not the ability to migrate.

> *I want to go back to Kenya as it is better there, but I currently cannot afford it. I don't have money to go back to that country. When you have the money, you can travel wherever you want.* (Cawo, male returnee; 33 years)

On the contrary, respondents who were not interested in re-migration had the support of their families and stronger relationships with their communities. A female returnee explained:

> *I am feeling good since I came back. I am now with my people in Somalia, and I have everything since I returned home to be with my family.* (Mxmud, female returnee, 37 years)

7   Discussion of Findings

This section draws on the themes to reflect on how degrees of voluntariness, agency and coercing operate at different levels of migrants' return decision-making and post-return experiences.

The management of return migration is integral to many aspects of the migration policy regimes, particularly those related to refugees, as well as policies for controlling migration. Based on the study findings, return migration can be said to be managed in two ways in the Somalia context. Firstly, it is the individualised returns based on bilateral agreements between Somalia and other destination countries. The migrant is returned through the assisted voluntary return programme or deported. Secondly, it is the large-scale return movement through the Tripartite Agreement between Kenya, Somalia and UNHCR for the voluntary repatriation of Somali refugees. Lastly, it is the spontaneous returnee movement where migrants return on their own volition, sometimes with no assistance, as it is the case with the migrants from Yemen. The voluntariness of these returns is an essential concept of how they are viewed by society, individuals and organisations (Erdal & Oeppen, 2022).

There are modes of individual returns where non-voluntariness is indisputable because of the way government authorities restrict returnee agency in decision-making, for example, the deportation of returnees from the detention camps in Saudi Arabia. In addition, the voluntariness of the UNHCR-assisted voluntary repatriation programme proved rather complex as the return money given to the returnees offered an incentive for them to return. Despite the name, the extent to which the programme can be said to be voluntary has been challenged earlier by scholars (Garre, 2017) and is consistent with the findings of this study. In some cases, migrants approached the UNHCR and IOM for assistance to benefit from the grants but returned to the camps once they had exhausted their allocation. Thus the study findings resonate with work from previous scholars, for example, Carling et al. (2015), that accepting to return via the programme does not necessarily mean the migrant wants to return. The decision to return was made due to other constraining factors; in this case, the benefit from the grant provided the incentive to return.

The UNCHR makes a formal distinction between facilitating returns that is assisting refugees to return when they choose to do so, whatever the circumstance and promoting returns which are encouraging returns in post-conflict situations, particularly when it is viewed that there is peace (UNCHR, 2004). It also stresses that the returns must be voluntary. Despite this recognition of the challenges of genuinely voluntary return, UNCHR has been criticised for submitting to political pressure and promoting return when the peace is neither durable nor sustainable (Garre, 2017). The UNCHR and other government agencies have overseen the implementation of push factors such as reduced food rations and constant threats, which have contributed to refugees signing up for the repatriation program. This act, although not entirely forced, could be considered a form of coerced return (Hathaway, 2007). While it is obvious that some returnees have a genuine desire to return, the findings also demonstrate how discourse and labels such as voluntary can shape migrants' aspirations (Erdal & Oeppen, 2018). For migration management, the term voluntary can be seen as giving legitimacy to coerced returns (Collyer, 2012). Furthermore, return, or deportation, is not the end of the refugee cycle, particularly when the return is neither voluntary nor sustainable. Instead, it could be the beginning of new migration plans.

When examining forced migration, the state is typically regarded as the main actor of coercion and force. The findings also call attention to types of coercion outside the state. The question of return voluntariness, whether in connection to the decision to return or the post-return experience, can interact with many agents of force that may exert influence on an individual. For instance, life stages such as marriages can be a catalyst for return which wouldn't have taken in the first place. In the case study, migrants' disability was found to contribute to returns. Other factors include the sickness of a family member, which can also compel a migrant to return even if they are not ready to do some. Gender dynamics is also relevant in the Somalia case study as the patriarchal structures will significantly influence and pressure the individuals' decision-making. There is a common movement of young women from Somalia, which is often motivated by the family's decision to protect their women from the dangers of war and sexual violence (Al-Sharmani, 2010). Within the Somalia context, the question of which alternatives are available to the individual is not one that can be agreed upon on a personal level but only at the collective level.

Findings also point to the role of clans in coercing return. The extended kinship networks also exert power through expectations that lock in the migrants' agency based on the shared clan identity. On the flip side, the collective can simultaneously offer a safety net back in Mogadishu. Thus clannism may enable or constrain access to acceptable alternatives. For example, returnees from the minority clans experience challenges reestablishing their lives upon return due to a lack of social networks.

The study highlights a clear state of actors involved, from the individual, clan, community, state immigration authorities, NGOs and international organisations like UNHCR and IOM. All of these actors can facilitate or constrain voluntariness in a practical sense, as well as shape normative discourses on what is and is not deemed an acceptable alternative to return, the presence of which, as previously stated, is a precondition for voluntary return (Erdal & Oeppen, 2022).

Further, Erdal and Oeppen (2017) emphasise that understanding voluntariness in return migration is further complicated by the difficulty of decoupling policymakers' labels and how they use the phrase "voluntary return" from a broader philosophical view of what constitutes a genuinely voluntary action. As demonstrated by the Somalia case study, voluntary returns have been utilised to legitimise returns that would not be deemed voluntary in a theoretical or practical sense.

8 CONCLUSION

The objective of this chapter has been to explore the role that the notion of voluntariness plays in return migration decisions. In doing so, findings have shown that returnees go back to Somalia for various reasons and under a wide variety of circumstances. According to the respondents, they returned for multiple reasons, which have been captured as a continuum between forced returns, policy constraints, personal circumstances, family pressure, economic needs or socio-cultural difficulties at the basis of this decision.

Still, others return because they have been forcibly removed from the country of destination, e.g. Saudi Arabia or Europe, by the state, stripping them of their agency to return to Somalia on their own terms. Conceptualising return migration in the binary of "voluntary" or "forced" obscures the fact that all returnees, including "voluntary" ones, operate in response to various forces and under considerable constraints, whether they are primarily economic, social or political in nature. Similarly, categorising all deportees as "involuntary" returnees overlooks the multiplicity of ways in which deportation can impact the lives of deportees, given their specific social and economic circumstances at the time of deportation and the agency that deportees possess upon return to Somalia to shape the meaning that deportation has for them. Given the intricacies of return migration illustrated by findings, the study argues for a more complex and nuanced understanding of the causes of return migration that recognises that no migration is either free or involuntary but is always both.

The particular configurations of the voluntary and involuntary elements of a migrant's return to their place of origin create a range of reasons for return, demonstrating that return migrants, like everyone else, are actors who exercise their agency within various social situations constrained by several limitations. These findings emphasise the significance of understanding the dynamics of return and reintegration beyond administrative labels. This is consistent with the previously cited publications, for example, Erdal and Oeppen (2018) who emphasise the importance of individualised circumstance rather than a bureaucratic approach to the issue of voluntariness in return.

References

Al-Sharmani, M. (2010). Transnational family networks in the Somali diaspora in Egypt: Women's roles and differentiated experiences. *Gender, Place & Culture, 17*(4), 499–518.

Arowolo, O. O. (2000). Return migration and the problem of reintegration. *International Migration, 38*(5), 59–82.

Bakewell, O. (2008). Keeping them in their place: The ambivalent relationship between development and migration in Africa. *Third World Quarterly, 29*(7), 1341–1358. https://doi.org/10.1080/01436590802386492

Bartram, D. (2015). Forced migration and "Rejected alternatives": A conceptual refinement. *Journal of Immigrant & Refugee Studies, 13*(4), 439–456. https://doi.org/10.1080/15562948.2015.1030489

Black, R., & Gent, S. (2006). Sustainable return in post-conflict contexts. *International Migration, 44*(3), 15–38.

Carling, J., Bolognani, M., Bivand, M., Rojan, E., Ceri, T., Erlend, O., Silje, P., Pettersen, V., & Sagmo, T. (2015). *Possibilities and realities of return migration* [online]. https://files.prio.org/Publication_files/Prio/Carling%20et%20al%20(2015)%20-%20Possibilities%20and%20Realities%20of%20Return%20Migration.pdf. Accessed 25 June 2022.

Chimni, B. S. (1993). *International law and world order a critique of contemporary approaches*. Cambridge University Press.

Chimni, B. S. (2009). The birth of a "discipline": From refugee to forced migration studies. *Journal of Refugee Studies, 22*(1), 11–29. https://doi.org/10.1093/jrs/fen051

Collyer, M. (2012). Migrants as strategic actors in the European Union's global approach to migration and mobility. *Global Networks, 12*(4), 505–524. https://doi.org/10.1111/j.1471-0374.2012.00370.x

Crawley, H., & Skleparis, D. (2018). Refugees, migrants, neither, both: Categorical fetishism and the politics of bounding in Europe's 'migration crisis.' *Journal of Ethnic and Migration Studies, 44*(1), 48–64. https://doi.org/10.1080/1369183X.2017.1348224

Erdal, M. B., & Oeppen, C. (2017). Forced to leave? The discursive and analytical significance of describing migration as forced and voluntary. *Journal of Ethnic and Migration Studies, 44*(6), 981–998. https://doi.org/10.1080/1369183x.2017.1384149

Erdal, M. B., & Oeppen, C. (2018). Forced to leave? The discursive and analytical significance of describing migration as forced and voluntary. *Journal of Ethnic and Migration Studies, 44*(6), 981–998. https://doi.org/10.1080/1369183x.2017.1384149

Erdal, M. B., & Oeppen, C. (2022). Chapter 5: Theorising voluntariness in return. In *Handbook of return migration*. Edward Elgar Publishing. Retrieved May 27, 2022.

Garre, M. Y. (2017). *Durable solutions for Somali refugees a case study of the involuntary repatriation of Daadab refugees.* Heritage Institute for Policy Studies.

Gibney, M. (2004). *The ethics and politics of asylum: Liberal democracy and the response to refugees.* Cambridge University Press.

Hammond, L. (1999). Examining the discourse of repatriation: Towards a more proactive theory of return migration. In R. Black & K. Koser (Eds.), *The end of the refugee cycle?* Berghahn Books.

Hathaway, J. (2007). Forced migration studies: Could we agree just to 'date'? *Journal of Refugees Studies, 20*(3), 349–369.

Jones, R. (2020). *Jobless migrants flee oil-rich countries to the chagrin of their home countries.* https://www.wsj.com/articles/jobless-migrants-flee-oil-rich-countries-to-the-chagrin-of-their-home-countries-11590235200

Kalir, B. (2017). Between 'voluntary' return programs and soft deportation: Sending vulnerable migrants in Spain back 'home.' In Z. Vathi & R. Kings (Eds.), *Return migration and psychosocial wellbeing* (pp. 56–71). Routledge.

Koser, K., & Kuschminder, K. (2015). Comparative research on the assisted voluntary return and reintegration of migrants. In *International organisation for migration.* Geneva.

Long, K. (2011). *Permanent crises? Unlocking the protracted displacement of refugees and internally displaced persons.* Refugee Studies Centre, University of Oxford.

Lietaert, I., & Gorp, L. V. (2019). Talking across borders: Successful re-entry in different strands of re-entry literature. *International Migration, 57*(4), 105–120.

Maimuna, M. (2016). Somalia-Yemen links: Refugees and returnees. *Forced Migration Review, 52*, 55–56.

Majidi, N., & Schuster, L. (2019). Deportation and forced return. In A. Bloch & G. Donà (Eds.), *Forced migration: Current issues and debates* (pp. 88–105). Routledge.

Mohammadi, A., Abbasi-Shavazi, M. J., & Sadeghi, R. (2018). Return to home: Reintegration and sustainability of return to post-conflict contexts. In G. Hugo, M. Abbasi-Shavazi, & E. Kraly (Eds.), Demography of refugee and forced migration. *International studies in population* (Vol. 13). Springer, Cham

Ottonelli, V., & Torresi, T. (2013). When is migration voluntary? *International Migration Review, 47*(4), 783–813. https://doi.org/10.1111/imre.12048

Owigo, J. (2021). Return migration during the Covid-19 crisis: The experiences of Somali female returnees from Saudi Arabia. *Refugee Review.*

Resch, K., & Enzenhofer, E. (2018). Collecting data in other languages—Strategies for cross-language research in multilingual societies. In U. Flick (Ed.), *The*

216   J. OWIGO

sage handbook of qualitative data collection (pp. 131–146). Sage. https://doi.org/10.4135/9781526416070.n9

Schuster, L., & Majidi, N. (2013). What happens post-deportation? The experience of deported Afghans. *Migration Studies, 1*(2), 240–241.

Schuster, L., & Majidi, N. (2015). Deportation stigma and re-migration. *Journal of Ethnic and Migration Studies, 41*(4), 635–652.

Sekhar, C. S. C. (2010). Fragile states. *Developing Societies, 26*(3), 263–293. https://doi.org/10.1177/0169796X1002600301

Shaffer, M., Ferrato, G., & Jinnah, Z. (2017). Routes, locations, and social imaginary: A comparative study of the ongoing production of geographies in Somali forced migration. *African Geographical Review, 37*(2), 159–171.

UNHCR. (2004). *Handbook for repatriation and reintegration activities UNHCR UNHCR handbook for repatriation and reintegration activities* [online]. https://www.unhcr.org/411786694.pdf. Accessed 21 Sep 2021.

UNHCR. (2021a). *Situation horn of Africa Somalia situation* [online]. data2.unhcr.org. https://data2.unhcr.org/en/situations/horn/location/192. Accessed 23 Sep 2021.

UNHCR. (2021b). *UNHCR Somalia monthly refugee returnee report—August 2021* [online]. UNHCR Operational Data Portal (ODP). https://data2.unhcr.org/en/documents/details/88562. Accessed 23 Sep 2021.

UNHCR. (2021c). *UNHCR Yemen 2021 country operational plan.* Retrieved December 26, 2021, from ReliefWeb website: https://reliefweb.int/sites/reliefweb.int/files/resources/UNHCR%20Yemen%202021%20Country%20Operational%20Plan.pdf

Van Lehman, D., & Mckee, E. (2019). *Removals to Somalia in light of the convention against torture: Recent evidence from Somali Bantu Deportees* [online]. https://www.law.georgetown.edu/immigration-law-journal/wp-content/uploads/sites/19/2019/08/GT-GILJ190032.pdf. Accessed 5 July 2022.

Zetter, R. (2007). More labels, fewer refugees: Remaking the refugee label in an era of globalization. *Journal of Refugee Studies, 20*(2), 172–92.

Zetter, R. (2011). *Protecting environmentally displaced people: Developing the capacity legal and normative frameworks.* Report commissioned by UNHCR and Governments of Switzerland and Norway Oxford Refugee Studies Centre. www.rsc.ox.ac.uk/files/publications/other/rr-protecting-environmentally-displaced-people-2011.pdf

AfCTA and African Integration: Prospects and Challenges

Emmanuel Zwanbin

1 Introduction

Post-independence Africa has been preoccupied with efforts to galvanise states for continental development and mutual cooperation. Africa's quest for regionalism is rooted in the desire to solve its numerous social, economic and political challenges, from 1963 when Organisation of African Unity (OAU) to 2002 when it was transformed in the AU. In trying to situate regional integration trajectory in Africa, African scholars are broadly divided into opposing camps: Afro-optimists and Afro-pessimists. Afro-optimists claimed that the opportunities and benefits of pan-African regionalism can exceed the difficulties and constraints. In contrast, the Afro-pessimists (or Afro-sceptics) argued that the difficulties and constraints of African integration can undermine prospects, chances and advantages (Okafor & Aniche, 2017). While Afro-optimism and Afro-pessimism continue to dominate academic discourse and African studies, a third force debate has emerged: the Afro-realist. Afro-realism recognises the prospects and the reality of socio-cultural diversities and

---

E. Zwanbin (✉)
United States International University—Africa, Nairobi, Kenya
e-mail: ezwanbin@usiu.ac.ke

© The Author(s), under exclusive license to Springer Nature Switzerland AG 2023
A. I. Adeniran (ed.), *African Development and Global Engagements*,
https://doi.org/10.1007/978-3-031-21283-3_11

the associated physical and institutional and cultural violence against fellow Africans in Africa.

The consummation of the Organisation of African Unity in 1963 was followed by series of incremental efforts to ensure a fully integrated continent both politically and economically. The late Adedeji Adebayo's leadership in the United Nations Economic Commission for Africa UNECA helped to drive the vision of African integration. Some of the profound steps included the 1980 Lagos Plan of Action, the 1991 Abuja Treaty culminated in the promotion of the African Economic Community. The LPA envisioned the integration of Africa based on developmental regionalism, self-reliance and self-sustenance. Subsequently, the OAU adopted the African Economic Treaty that led to the establishment of the African Economic Community to promote cooperation, regional integration, common market and intra-African trade. Thereafter, the Abuja Treaty provided the framework for the creation of Regional Economic Communities (Bach, 2016). The 2000 Constitutive Act ushered the African Union as a replacement of the defunct Organisation of African Unity (Obeng-Odoom, 2020, p. 168). The AU became the precursor for pan-African trade pact known as the African Continental Free Trade Area (AfCFTA). The AfCFTA created the largest African regional trade agreements (RTAs) with the potential to enhance the economic wellbeing of its about 1.4 billion people (Saleh, 2022) and huge market share. By 2018, the AfCFTA treaty was signed and later 50 states out of 54 ratified the treaty. Thus, AfCFTA was signed in March 2018, ratified by May 2019, and came into effect in January 2021 (Signé, 2022). As part of the expected goals, AfCFTA will enhance free movement of people, goods and services. Regional integration by default increase labour migration and also induced by the rise in political, economic and environmental crises across Africa (Ozel et al., 2017) in search of opportunities and safety. However, the emerging violence against foreigners threaten the aspiration for free movement of persons in the continent. The study explores the complexities of Africa's integration while it theorised Africa as people, geographical metaphor and ideology. The study centralises intra-African people-to-people diplomacy and consciousness as key ontological discourse in Africa's regional integration and as well as the rising tide of Afrophobia.

2 Pan-Africanism, Regionalism Integration in Africa and the OAU

African regional integration is often linked to the African Diaspora which pioneered regionalism and laid the foundation for, and institutionalised the idea integration and decolonisation. The efforts of Pan-African congresses fronted by African diaspora such as Sylvester William, W. E. B. Du Bois, Marcus Garvey, Kwame Nkrumah, and Jomo Kenyatta, among others, pushed the Pan-African ideology. Subsequently, Pan-Africanism spread to African continent, leaders began to advocate for a united African state. This culminated in the formation of the Organisation of African Unity (OAU) in 1963. The OAU suffered several challenges such as the widespread regional conflict and lack of clearcut mechanism for conflict resolution, cold war ideological divides. Also, African unity was fragmented along the colonial affiliations such as Lusophone, Anglophone and Francophone dichotomy. The post-cold war era saw the transformation of the supranational organisation into the African Union (AU) in 2002, which marked the most deliberate attempt to achieve a robust Pan-African political and economic integration (Alexander & Garba, 2021, pp. 92–93).

At the onset of independence, there were divergent perspectives on the approach to regional integration in Africa. Three groups emerged, the Monrovia, Casablanca and the Congo-Brazzaville blocs. The Monrovia Group also known as the gradualist, supported the idea of a supranational organisation that promotes gradual integration. The Casablanca Group had a radical disposition and advocated for a complete integration. While The Brazzaville Group prefer to keep strong affiliation with its former coloniser, France for economic, political and military support (Edo & Olanrewaju, 2012). For instance, Nkrumah and Awolowo argued for a union of African states while Nyerere and Balewa supported gradual and incremental African integration. The gradualist approached was embraced by independence leaders to safeguard the sovereignty and political grip over their respective states (Gumede, 2019, p. 98).

The proponents of strong regionalism argued that the imperialists with vast interests in developing countries will continue to keep a hold on the continent and its resources if a strong unified front is not maintained. The imperialist will use several means to disrupt unity among the population for maximum exploitation such as sowing the seed of disunity. Nkrumah argued that only by a unified front can African states effectively achieve their goals and aspirations (Nkrumah, 1963, p. xvi) to achieve an African integration that will translate the continent into a powerbase. Furthermore, he contended that the formation of a United States of Africa and the abolition of colonial borders will be the only path to Africa's greatness. He postulated that:

> Our essential bulwark against such sinister threats and the other multifarious designs of the neocolonialists is in our political union. If we are to remain free, if we are to enjoy the full benefits of Africa's rich resources, we must unite to plan for out total defence and the full exploitation of our material and human means, in full interests of our peoples. (Nkrumah, 1963, p. xvii)

3   REGIONAL INTEGRATION: THEORETICAL PERSPECTIVES

Regional Integration is viewed as a process where neighbouring states within a projected geographical location pursue political, economic, cultural, social and security relations aim at collective and mutual benefit (Vickers, 2017). Four theories have been advanced to explain regional integration; market integration, open regionalism, geography theory and developmental cooperation (Viner, 1950). First, the market integration theory sees integration in terms of all the efforts geared towards the removal of trade barriers among states to increase trade through policy framework such as common market, free trade area, custom union and monetary union and may culminate into a political union. Second, the open regionalism derives its ideas from the neoliberalists who argue that liberalisation enhances global trade and result in an integrated global economy. Third, the new geography theory proposes that small states can integrate with bigger states to benefit from the collective advantage in international trade. Finally, the developmental cooperation theory states that the protection of local industries, import substitution and industrial development is core to the values of integration (Gumede, 2019). Most integration theories are state-centric and stressed economic cooperation while ignoring other fundamental components of integration such as social and cultural issues. Although economic factors drive integration, social integration is equally sacrosanct for the success of any integration (Oloruntoba, 2018, p. 101).

Theoretical perspective on regional integration is evolving due to the trend of interdependence and globalisation. Since the end of the cold war, the concept of new regionalism has been explained through alternative theories such as neoliberal institutionalism and constructivism. Constructivism provides a departure from the traditional international relations theories which emphasised the state and not the people. Statist theories stressed the structure of supranational organisation and state interaction at the detriment of non-state actors, ideas, culture and social institutions. The traditionalist (state-centric) regionalism gained traction during the cold war era while the wideners regionalism emerged during post-cold war era in Africa. Constructivism is at the centre of wideners regionalism (Ghica, 2013).

Regional interaction in the era of globalisation aligns with the assumptions of constructivism which creates intersectionality between the state, people and transnational issues such as identity and ideas. It stresses the importance of perception and social construction of reality in international politics. Therefore, socialisation is linked to ideas, identity and norms shape the security, political (Haas, 2001, p. 117) and economic governance of states and regional organisations. Essentially, to underscore regionalism as new approach in post-cold war era, material and normative values are key assumptions of the constructivists (Acharya, 2012, p. 9). Constructivism has transformed the framework for the study of regional integration in Africa with motivation to focus on normative issues such as culture, identity and ideas.

4 THE AFRICA CONTINENTAL FREE TRADE AREA

An important milestone was achieved in Africa's integration. In January 2017, at the 28th Ordinary Session of the African Union Heads of State and Government, Issoufou Mahamadou, President of the Republic of Niger, was appointed to facilitate negotiations with member states on the African Continental Free Trade Area (AfCFTA). Subsequently, in March 21, 2018 at Kigali, Rwanda, the African Union (AU) Assembly accepted the treaty establishing the AfCFTA accompanied by three protocols on trade in commodities, trade in services, and dispute settlement. The AU Agenda 2063 and the AfCFTA are the two most notable and historic trajectory in the history of African integration. Other important milestones include the 1979 Monrovia Strategy, the 1980 Lagos Plan of Action (LPA), and the 1991 Abuja Treaty and the African Economic Community (AEC) (Aniche, 2020).

The African Continental Free Trade Area (AfCFTA) is acclaimed to be the largest free trade area in the world. AfCFTA's pan-Africanist ideology envisaged an inclusive and a departure from the restrictive integration. It is expected to help Africa attain it economic, political and social aspiration as well as "greater self-assertion on the international stage" (Obeng-Odoom, 2020, pp. 178–179). AfCFTA's general objectives supports open market, harmonisation of regional economic community membership, industrialisation of the agricultural sector by creating diversification through value chains. Also, to enhance the free movement of goods, services and persons (African Union, 2018). By 30 May 2019 AfCFTA came into force (Lunenborg, 2019, pp. 1–2). The Agreement connects 55 nations and 1.3 billion people across the continent projecting to increase productivity, job creation and poverty reduction targeting 30 million people out of extreme poverty and 68 million out of moderate poverty by 2035 (Apiko et al., 2020, p. 3).

The Agenda 2063 and AfCFTA both supports a united Africa and its people. For instance, Agenda 2063 Aspiration 4 reinforces AfCFTA's objectives to pursue a Pan-African security, economic and political integration. Explicitly, the Aspiration 5 of the Agenda 2063 calls for efforts to create socio-cultural integration which captures one of the objectives of AfCFTA's free movement, labour mobility and people-driven development (Aniche, 2020, pp. 9–10). The protocol on free movement lessens immigration restrictions for entrepreneurs, professionals, workers and consumers under the AfCFTA provision (Apiko et al., 2020, p. 11). Significantly, the framework supports free movement of persons. However, the free movement prescribed in the framework is tied to trade and services. The success of the free movement enshrined in AfCFTA is no doubt an important milestone in Africa's integration, however, the rising cases of Afrophobic attacks across Africa pose threat to its implementation.

Although AfCFTA provides sufficient policy groundings for free movement of people in Africa, however, the consequences may induce socio-cultural difference not envisioned. Therefore, although trade and services are connected to free movement of people, social factors are very important. While Intra-African free movement of persons in Africa may cut the tide of migration to Europe and other parts of the world, open borders could result in tension due to lack of strong social integration. The perceptions of the African people about themselves do not align with

Pan-Africanist aspiration and values. Therefore, AfCFTA seeks political and development regional integration (Gumede, 2019, p. 98) driven by people-oriented approach.

5 Theorising Africa, People and Ideologies

Africa is a metaphoric representation; it means different thing to different people. Depending on which spectrum one stands, Africa can be viewed as a people, an idea or a geographical location. Contentions such as Africanity, Africanness, Global Africa and colourism creates both ontological and epistemic debates. Even at that, it is very difficult to determine who is an African, the values they hold and their locations. Theorising Africa, its peoples and ideologies put to rest the misleading characterisation of Africa as a monolithic entity without underscoring the continent as a people, geographical expression with ideological standpoint and cultural diversity.

Geographically, Eurocentric epistemology believed that Africa got its name from the Greek and Latin words Phrike and Aprica. Phrike connotes cold and horror, while Aprica means sunny (Nanjira, 2010). But African historians such as Diop in his Kemetic History of Afrika believed the original name of what is known today as Africa had several representations such as Af-Rui-ka which was believed to have been missed pronounced by European anthropologists (Ejikeme, 2019, p. 38). The geographical space known as Africa is multi-ethnic with different names used by the peoples. Other names that were well-known in Islamic, Christian and Jewish traditions include Alkebulan, Egypt, Ethiopia, Libya and Sudan (Ochuko, 2020). The controversy about the origin of the name Africa has continued to be debated through the Afrocentric and Eurocentric lenses. Afrocentric perspective alleged that Africa is a precolonial name used by the indigenous people represented in different languages. In the ancient history of the Akan people of Ghana, Abibiman was used to refer to the continent as the land of the Black people. This agrees with the argument, the name is not essentially a Eurocentric imposition but derivation from the material description of the peoples of the continent (Dei, 2018).

Descriptively, the Atlantic Ocean, the Mediterranean Sea, the Red Sea and the Indian Ocean all encircle Africa, the second-largest continent. The Equator divides it approximately evenly in half. Physical geography, environment, and human geography of Africa can all be taken into consideration independently. The Sahara, the Sahel, the Ethiopian Highlands, the savanna, the Swahili Coast, the rainforest, the African Great Lakes and Southern Africa are the continent's eight main geographical regions (National Geographic, n.d.).

6 African People: Africanity and Africanness

Are there people with distinct identity called Africans? Rather, we have a conglomeration of peoples who shared common geographical location, common history of humiliation and subjugation and aspire to forge common destiny. Generally, the conceptualisation of African people as a single race creates an artificial identity based on blackness and geographical location which limits the emerging idea of the global Africa. African identity is a complex construct embedded in the inferiorisation of the people situated within the geographical location called Africa. Dei (2018, pp. 120–122) theorised that blackness is an identity entrenched by shared histories of people in specific geographical locations. Additionally, blackness can be classified as more robust rather than racial identity which conglomerates the culture, politics, social organisation, history and experiences of African peoples. Therefore, blackness is a matter of self-consciousness about one's identity either ascribed and acquired. The African identity can be explained through the concept of Africanness which does not have a fixed racial ideology. But Hountondji contend that blackness cannot be classified as a different racial category (Hountondji, 1983, p. 177). As a global idea, blackness or Africanness cannot be confined to a geographic area or cartographic design but a social construction.

The other controversy about blackness is how black Africans are seen as distinct from other Africans with Arab heritage. This tends to remove Africans whose descent can be linked to Arabs from the Africanity discourse (Dei, 2018). This brings the debate as to whether Africa is a people with multiple heritage or a mere geographical location. Therefore, it is erroneous to situate Africa as a single entity or a place, but as a convergence of complex historical, ideological, socioeconomic and political discourse. An attempt to create a homogenous African culture and identity contradicts the diversity in African history. Therefore, blackness is not same as being African. For instance, people in Africa with Arab descent tends to see themselves more as Arabs living in a geographical location called Africa, while blacks see themselves as more African.

Moore (1999, p. 32) recognised the diversity in the historical peopling of Africa and the impact of the extra-African contact with the rest of the world. Therefore, the peopling of Africa is a global phenomenon rather than a geographical discourse. Thus, Du Bois (1946, p. 7) and Palmié (2007, p. 165) contest that Africa has extraordinary meaning which transcends the continent to its diaspora across the globe. The African culture and people have undergone endless deconstruction and recreation influenced by exchanges culminating in the contemporary black culture (Sansone, 2003, p. 59).

7   African Identity: Africanity and Africanness

African identity has been described using the concepts such as blackness, Africanity and Africanness. Africanness is an evolving phenomenon that is not static but continued to receive innovative contribution from academics, fashion designers, musicians, movie makers, craft makers. Davis sees Africanness as a movement deliberately targeted at crafting a new African identity and culture (Davis, 1999, p. 72). De Witte & Spronk (2014, pp. 167–168) called it the "I am an African" ideology. The African identity is a highly contested phrase due to it ambiguity and evolving nature.

Africanness refers to the geographical representation, culture and a people whose aspiration is philosophically grounded in moral code of humanity, mutuality, friendliness, equity, dignity and respects for humanity while recognising its diversity in unity. Palmié (2007) sees "Africa" and "Africanity" in terms of theorical framework rather than an assigned ontological reality. Paradoxically, Africa is largely an imposed definition where Africa is viewed in terms of theoretical contradiction or an ontological question. The derogatory representation of Africa as dark continent is rooted in racism and the categorisation of its people as an inferior race to justify the motive behind slave trade and the civilisational mission and the eventual colonial subjugation. The stereotype echoes with the current attempt to recreate African identity in the effort to ensure social integration (De Witte & Spronk, 2014, p. 169).

Pre-colonial African societies were well organised based on moral philosophy or ethics. The philosophy, although not written, is held with uttermost respect for the regulation of moral conduct. Human dignity, mutual respect, tolerance, restorative justice, peaceful and dispute resolution are central to most moral philosophy of African societies. Some of the examples of moral philosophy in Africa include the South African's ubuntu (Agyeno, 2019), The Hausa word mutuncI expresses the moral philosophy of humanness in every aspect of life and Kiswahili word nyayo literally meaning footstep or continuity in governance (Amupanda, 2018). They all promote the concept of shared humanity. But colonialism divided the people on the basis of colonising states as well as manipulating and subjugating them into submission. They exploited the linguistic difference among the peoples. This created a web of recognisable ethnic and linguistic social difference, later used by African leaders to politicise public policy. Adeola argued that colonially constructed borders by default conferred national identity and the trajectory of independent African states (Adeola, 2015), thus, the foreign-othering within Africa and among its citizens. This has continued to define access to opportunities and resources in an African state and political and populist rhetoric by the elite in public policy processes (Arthur, 2000).

Africa's quest to forge political, social and economic ideologies is linked to Africanity. Ideology has been defined as "a system of ideas, beliefs, values and symbols of moral, political, economic and social nature that provide communities with an identity, sense and direction to their political action, and it allows the development of ...social order" (Orjuela, 2007, pp. 219–220). Africanity is an all-encompassing African values, aspirations, political thought and ideologies. Africanity is seen as the aspiration to enhance unity and cooperation among Africans and the diaspora to create cohesion. It also means oneness, solidarity, brotherliness, wholeness, and togetherness. This according to proponents of Africanity, Africa and its diaspora can deal with the issues of disjointed aspiration and fragmentation (Akinrinde, 2020, p. 135).

8   Afrophobia: Africa's Social Integration Challenge

The increase in the number of physical, psychological, institutional and cultural violence across Africa against black foreigners brings to question the basic tenets of Pan-Africanism and the laudable goals of African integration.

Xenophobia is believed to have originated from two Greek words, xeno and phobos which entails stranger and fear respectively. When combined, it connotes fear of strangers. Xenophobia is usually expressed through discriminatory attitudes and violence targeted at foreigners, fellow nationals and refugees. According to Harris (2002, p. 170), xenophobia is both an attitude and action against strangers such as migrants and refugees. The attitude is discreetly exhibited through the behaviour of the public, government and the media. Xenophobia is also defined as "a rejection of outsiders" (United Nations General Assembly, 1994, par. 29).

If xenophobia exists in Africa, then, can Africans be strangers in Africa? Afrophobia is a strand xenophobia which is contextualised to explain the peculiarity of violence targeted at Africans by Africans. Afrophobia is concerned with the rejection of Africans by Africa. Ironically, those who perpetuate Afrophobia tend to welcome, be tolerant and eulogies non-Africans even when they are perceived to have constitute competition for resources or opportunities. Therefore, Afrophobia is derived from two words Afro and Phobia which means the fear of Africans by Africans. Afrophobia, and negrophobia have been used interchangeably to describe social, economic and psychological violence against Africans or the blacks (Dube, 2018). Although Afrophobia has been drawn from the rising xenophobia in South Africa (Mngomezulu & Dube, 2019), the concept has since been generally applied to cases of hostility against Africans in Africa.

Like xenophobia, Afrophobia is expressed through physical, institutional and cultural violence. Fear and hatred for fellow black Africans including securitising them as threats. The use of slur and derogatory words are common such as "makwerekwere", "Hottentot", "kaffir" and "coolie" including slurs that stigmatise Africans as criminals (Mbowa, 2020). Violence and physical abuse are intricately connected to xenophobic action and practices targeted at black Africans. Afrophobia is an expression of citizens' frustration, institutional violence, lack of opportunities, corruption, human rights abuses, bad governance and police brutality. These domestic conditions breed radical and populist leaders and political parties. Discourse on populism explains that migration is an important rhetoric for anti-foreigners, in this case Africans. When the people are helpless in demanding change, foreigners become scapegoats and are readily blamed for the economic crisis and crime (Akinrinde, 2020).

9   Cases of Xenophobia in Africa

Cases of violence against Africans in Africa have long history from the 1960s to the 2000s. The menace is challenging the pan-African value held by the founding fathers of Africa to promote the peaceful coexistence of the African peoples. In the 1960s when African states began to attain independence, the disposition of the leaders was to maintain the sovereignty of their respective states. This encouraged economic protectionist policies and restrictive immigration regimes, however, the post-cold war era recorded increased xenophobia across the continent. The cases of Afrophobia are too numerous to mention. For instance, in 1968, the government of Ghana ordered the deportation of aliens from Ghana, largely Africans on the grounds of lack of documentation and work permit (Quarshie, 2021). In 1972, Idi Amin Dada, the military head of state of Uganda expelled Africans from Kenya, Tanzania and Zambia as well as Asians living in the country (Nogel, 2020). Also, in Gabon in 1978, President Bongo expelled Beninese exiles in Gabon (Oni & Okunade, 2018). Nigeria's troubled economy of the late 1970s and the early 1980s saw the expulsion of foreigners largely Africans. For example, in 1983, Nigeria evicted over one million Ghanaians and later in 1985, another 300,000. Afrophobic actions and attitudes were driven by government's institutional violence and speech act under the guise of economic revival. The cycle of Afrophobia between Nigerians and Ghanaians following the 1960s and 1980s has created people-to-people tensions and hatred between the peoples of both countries.

In Cote d'Ivoire, the rhetoric on the idea of "Ivoirite" identity while "othering" other Africans. It was used for national consciousness to blame migrants for the economic crisis in the country. Migrants were humiliated and discriminated against such as from Burkina Faso and other West African countries (Akinola, 2020). Also, at the instance of military coup in Equatorial Guinea, foreigners were blamed. Hence, foreigners were harassed, arrested and deported (Samah, 2021). Stringent conditions were put in place to constrain other Africans from doing business in the country. In 2004, Angola deported over 100,000 Congolese (Awosusi & Fatoyinbo, 2019), while between 2008 and 2009 another 64,000 Congolese were deported on the grounds of illegally exploiting natural resources in the country (Bavier, 2008). Also, in 2012, Burundi, expelled over 1200 African migrants under the guise of curbing criminal activities in the country. Somali migrants in Kenya also suffered anti-Somali rhetoric following the al-Shabaab group attack at the Westgate Mall in Nairobi. Kenyan instituted the "Operation Usalama Watch" a counterterrorism measure (Mwangi, 2019). In 2018, the Government of Kenya cracked down on migrants, mostly African from Democratic Republic of Congo, Ethiopia, Nigeria, Ghana, Cameroon. Four Nigerians were believed to have been killed by the police brutality. Nigerians demonstrated in Nairobi at the Nigeria High Commission calling its government to institute diplomatic action against the abuses and discrimination (Muraya, 2018). In Congo-Brazzaville, 50,000 DRC citizens were deported in 2015. Chad also deported 3000 Cameroonians and 2500 on suspicion of perpetuating terrorism. In Morocco, 37 Africans trying to enter Spain were murdered by the police (Oloko, 2022) and many were also wounded. King alleged that the discrimination targeted blacks called Negrophobia.

In 2012, Nigeria and South Africa were ensued in diplomatic row on the deportation of their citizens over yellow fever vaccination. South Africa deported 125 Nigerians for presenting fake yellow fever certificates while Nigeria reciprocated and deported 84 South Africans. This culminated in public outrage where Nigerians threatened South Africa's investments in Nigeria such as DSTV, MTN and Shoprite (Eboh, 2017). Also, in South Africa nationals of Senegal and Mozambique were murdered in 1994 induced by hatred. In 2015, Afrophobia surged in South Africa. The "Let us pop our head lice" hate comment alleged to have been made by Goodwill Zwelithini, Zulu King, sparked the violence of "foreigners must go" in Durban. Intermittent Afrophobic attacks continued unabated in the country (Oatway & Skuy, 2021). The rise of the Operation Dudula, a Zulu word literally means "force out" has further institutionalised Afrophobia in South Africa. It was a well-coordinated and funded anti-immigration by politicians. The group assumed the power of the state to enforce government immigration rules (Wroughton, 2022). African migrants are expelled for alleged drugs, diseases, theft and taking their jobs (Machinya, 2022). However, what is clear is that it is institutional through government policies and in the large South African polities (UN News, 2022). Afrophobia in South Africa and elsewhere in Africa is influenced by the perception that foreign nationals are responsible for lack of jobs and economic opportunities. Many migrants faced restrictive administrative constraint to secure work permit. Illegible and skill workers who would have contributed to the development of the economy of the host country were denied work permit (Kanayo et al., 2019, pp. 72–73).

10 Afrophobia and Some Contending Issues

While the AU has continued to achieve giant strides in formulating strategic frameworks and instruments for integration to facilitate integrated infrastructure and trade. However, emerging social and cultural issues remained not attended to. The African Union (AU) and its departments have roles to play in dealing with the root causes of Afrophobia in line with the AU Constitutive Act which aspires to promote human rights and peaceful coexistence (Makinda et al., 2016, p. 183). Also, to have AU member states is to commit to eradicating all forms of xenophobia, discrimination, racism and intolerance (Adeola, 2015, p. 260). The AU is dealing with symptoms without proactive approach to forging efforts to induce social integration of its people.

Furthermore, Adebajo (2014, p. 177) quoted Salim Ahmed Salim, former secretary-general of the Organization of African Unity as saying "every African is his brother's keeper". Salim like most Africans laments the divisiveness among African people. The way blacks who are citizens of countries other than Africa are treated is different from those with citizenship from African states. Africans born in Africa and those of the diaspora are inherently connected to the idea of "Global Africa" (De Witte & Spronk, 2014, p. 171). Bob Marley in his "Africa Unite" speaks to the core of Africa's integration problem. Although, xenophobia is a global phenomenon and manifests itself in integration process, the number of killings and displacement caused by xenophobia is enormous. Although xenophobia is a global phenomenon, Africa's is rising due to lack of united effort to deal with it. Populism and domestic politics is fuelling the Afrophobic rhetoric emanating from national policies.

The governments of African states have systematically promoted institutional Afrophobia knowingly and unknowingly through discriminatory policies. For example, intra-Africa tourism should have been promoted to help create social integration, but immigration restrictions, high cost of flight tickets and poor transport, lack of integrated infrastructure, social stereotype and stigma, discriminatory tourism charges at parks, hotels and ferries constitute a huge constraint to social. Cases of inflated rates, mistreatment and discrimination targeted at black tourists in Kenya were reported. These discriminatory actions were perpetuated by black people (Ochami, 2016).

Several policy frameworks have been put in place in recognition of the importance of regional migration in Africa such as the AU Migration Policy Framework for Africa (MPFA). The framework provides policy standards on management of migration. The AU Free Movement of Persons Protocol also provided additional policy guidelines on mobility and labour migration and protection of the fundamental human rights of migrants and their families (pp. 8–9). Additionally, Regional Economic Communities have also adopted free movement of people instrument. There has never been lack of policy framework for the free movement of African people (AU Commission, 2020, pp. 8–9).

While migration and labour mobility frameworks are necessary to enhance social integration, however, discriminatory policies emerging from domestic politics brew social discontent. This calls for urgency to forestall the increased institutional and cultural violence particularly against Africans. For instance, work permits for non-citizens in Africa cost averagely $2000. In South Sudan, work permits cost $4000 (Akwei, 2017), Tanzania charges $1750 with the exception of East Africa Community which has been slashed to $500 (Anami, 2021). The fees are not affordable to most African migrants. African countries tend to recruit non-Africans and sometimes offer them work permit exemptions. Kenya engaged 100 doctors from Cuba yet Nigeria has a lot of doctors. Anti-African sentiment is possibly why Kenya avoided employing doctors from other African countries for public backlash (Ombuor, 2018).

Nigeria imports milk worth $1.5 billion annually from Europe yet Ugandan and Kenyan farmers pour out milk due to low cost (Ewepu & Eromosele, 2021). Kenya has a lot of skilled manpower in agriculture especially dairy sector while Nigeria lacks. Nigeria has huge human capital endowment especially in the academics. For instance, according to Tekedia, 17,000 Ph.D. holders are unemployed apart from those who are fully employed (Iyanda, 2020), while Kenya has only 10,000 Ph.D. holders with an annual rate of 400 graduating from doctoral programmes putting Kenya's higher education under due pressure to meet teaching and supervision needs (Nyaundi & Kimani, 2019). Both countries can leverage on their comparative advantage to promote bilateral agreement on labour mobility and migration on specific sectors.

Ghana in 2019 began the Year of Return programme to attract African diaspora to mark 400 years since the end of the Trans-Atlantic Slave trade. While the initiative is highly praised (Ankomah, 2020), ironically the rate of Afrophobia against Africans in Ghana is alarming. Deportation, harassment, over taxation, closure of shops belonging to other Africans are rampant. Critics believed the programme is laudable but lacks inclusivity to show that Ghana is a welcoming country for people with African descent (Yeboah, 2019). In line with this, Dube tries to provide the distinction between xenophobia and Afrophobia such that "these negative attitudes towards other Africans are in contrast to the more positive attitudes towards white immigrants from Europe and America" (Dube, 2018, p. 1005). While Africans are stigmatised as criminals, non-Africans are called tourists and investors. Additionally, "Africans attack fellow Africans on their own lands; sometimes they prefer the Whiteman in their midst to fellow Africans" (Njoku, 2019, p. 2637).

Julius Malema, a Pan-African activist and South African politician called for the adoption of a single language such as Kiswahili in order to promote social and cultural integration in the continent. Malema's advocacy buttressed the fact that lack of social integration will jeopardise the ambitious AfCFTA's promise for regional integration in Africa. Beyond to the need to forge an African identity, proactive measures will give impetus to the formation of deliberate African socialisation programmes such as mechanism for African citizenship and civic education. Unify costs and charges on services for African people separate from non-Africans in sectors such as health, education and tourism.

The importance of the economic implication of AfCFTA cannot be overemphasised. It will deepen economic integration by eliminating of tariffs and liberalisation of trade, close deficit in infrastructure development, continental and regional comparative advantage and financing of African trade and development. The framers of AfCFTA envisaged that it will reduce poverty significantly as a result of wage growth. Also, it anticipates that 30 million people will be moved out of extreme poverty by 2035. African states will experience shift from the subsistence and import dependence to diversified exports, economic growth, competitive integration into the globalised economy thereby becoming a hub for foreign direct investment. Consequently, this will culminate in increased employment opportunities and incomes, and broadening economic inclusion. Additionally, it will entrench transparency in trade throughout Africa and globally through the notion of "Trade Integrity" (Kende-Robb, 2021). It is also anticipated that the AfCFTA will have a major positive influence on earnings, which will vary by location, skill level especially among women who are largely trapped within the informal and subsistent economic sector since AfCFTA's prospects for success will rely a lot on women's labour force. Therefore, women's wages are expected to increase by 10.5% by 2035 (Madden, 2020). Also, the integrated infrastructure in internet and communication technology, road, power, electricity, railway, maritime, aviation and banking will give huge impetus to trade and ease of doing business across the continent (Lufumpa et al., 2017). Expectedly, this will reduce the tide of migration across Europe and North America thereby enhancing labour input to drive production and industrialisation (Spel, 2020). Despite the economic and political importance of the trade area, a number of challenges are expected to be hampered by weak institutions, accountability, armed conflicts, overlapping membership of regional economic communities, low production, neo-colonial affiliations, poor infrastructure and the big power politics between the West and China in Africa (Wapmuk & Ali, 2022).

11 Discussion of Findings

In contrast to the state-centric approach to regional integration, where institutional framework is emphasised by theoretical standpoints, social issues are not stressed such as free movement and the consequent impact on people-to-people relations. It is pertinent to state that, issues arising from migration will either make or mare the intent of free movement in the continent due to social and political considerations. Also, the study underscores the fact that the political economy of most African states is driven by economic nationalism with underlining domestic politics. Therefore, the coexistence between the state and the market cannot be said to be fully compatible where corruption and political interference are imminent. Although Western literature supports the distinctive role of state and market, erroneous to assume that in African integration, the separation between the state and the market can be achieved. Hence, we should expect some echoes from domestic politics affecting the overall goals of AfCFTA over time as it evolves. The rise in military expenditure in Africa also correlates with the escalation of intrastate conflicts and those caused by transnational actors due to terrorism. Integration is a lengthy process, and maintaining political commitment to the vision of regional and continental integration throughout political shifts will be crucial to its success (Fofack, 2020).

While it is noted that AfCFTA will contribute to a 52% increase in intra-African trade by 2022 (Pasara, 2020), infrastructure deficit will challenge the realisation of the goal. Infrastructure is an important element of regional integration. Therefore, developing effective transportation and logistics infrastructure to provide regional interconnectivity has the potential to enhance intra-Africa regional trade. Without effective and integrated infrastructural capacity, low export and post-harvest losses will impede AfCFTA's promise for industrialisation and economic growth. Regional integration in Africa cannot be achieved where disjointed infrastructure, competing political policies and poorly integrated African people exists. Policy instruments such as open visa regimes are not sufficient to ensure that while economic sector is integrated, the African people will embrace free movement and labour without prejudice and discrimination. Control or regulated migration is expedient to achieve strategic opening of economic sector of the continent. For example, Rwanda and Zimbabwe signed a memorandum of understanding which saw the employment of Zimbabwean teachers to work in Rwanda. Such mutually beneficial migration regimes can help to alleviate human capital deficit across the continent and improve public perceptions about intra-African migration (Nyathi, 2022).

The post-Covid-19 era has left many African states with struggling economy and debt crisis. This will pose a lot of constraints to the success of the AfCFTA. Although prospects for the successful implementation of the AfCFTA are high, concerted efforts at the continental level to ensure Africa's participation in global political economy are very imperative. However, peace and security, good governance, the rise of populism and military coups will shape the narratives about the commitment of African states to an inclusive integration.

Centrally, the discourse of this paper stressed that African people are key to the success of AfCFTA. Without recognising the need to create an African identity, common history and shared values AfCFTA will induce social challenges that have the potential to degenerate into security problem. Furthermore, it argues, upholding an open border, although essential, will not address the social differentiation among African people. An AfCFTA without people who viewed themselves as one with common goal and shared history may result in unforeseen consequences.

12 Conclusion

African integration and the AfCFTA has been hyped as the most proactive effort towards boosting the intra-continent, trade, integrated infrastructure and free movement of African people. Apart from the institutional constraints characterised by proliferation of regional economic communities (RECs), disjointed infrastructure, political rivalry, democratic deficit, colonial affiliation, immigration bottlenecks, terrorism, populism and economic nationalism ensuring free movement and social inclusion is necessary. However, defining and recognising who is an African is at the centre of conceptualisation of Africanness. The impetuous rise in Afrophobic attacks across the continent speaks to the reality of violence and the need to create social bond among the people. AfCFTA is founded on constructivist inclination which emphasises state and non-state actors and the importance of ideas, culture, identity and socialisation to drive regional integration. The study acknowledged that the characterisation of Africa as a monolithic people is misleading and fundamentally why supranational institution like AU is not doing enough to deliberately forge policies and programmes that will enhance social integration,. without underscoring the continent as a people, geographical expression with ideological standpoint and cultural diversity.

African identity is complex construct. Sir Ahmadu Bello, Nigeria's former Northern Premier once said "let us not put our difference aside but try to understand why we are different. Understanding the unique difference among African peoples is key to cross-cultural communication. Afrophobia is an expression of citizens' frustration, institutional violence, lack of opportunities, corruption, human rights abuses, bad governance and police brutality. The paper concludes that the success of African integration and the tenets of free movement of African people will only be achieved through deliberate effort to advance the idea of social integration, African civic education, history and cross-cultural studies.

References

Acharya, A. (2012). Comparative regionalism: A field whose time has come? *The International Spectator, 47*(1), 3–15.

Adebajo, A. (2014). Nigeria and South Africa: On the concept "every African is his brother's keeper." In M. Serrano & T. G. Weiss (Eds.), *The international politics of human rights* (pp. 197–217). Routledge.

236   E. ZWANBIN

Adeola, R. (2015). Preventing Xenophobia in Africa: What must the African Union do? *African Human Mobility Review, 1*(3).

African Union. (2018). *Agreement establishing the African Continental Free Trade Area.* African Union.

Agyeno, O. (2019). Xenophobic violence and the African philosophy of Ubuntu in South Africa. *African Journal of Democracy and Governance, 6*(1), 24–44.

Akinola, A. O. (2020). Xenophobia, the media and the west African integration agenda. In D. Moyo (Ed.), *Mediating xenophobia in Africa* (pp. 147–166). Palgrave Macmillan.

Akinrinde, O. O. (2020). Africanity and the politics of African xenophobia: A study of two parallels. *Annals of Spiru Haret University. Economic Series, 20*(4), 133–151.

Akwei, I. (2017, October 28). *South Sudan to charge foreigners $4,000 for work permit, up from $100.* Retrieved July 2022, from Africanews: https://www.africanews.com/2017/10/28/south-sudan-to-charge-foreigners-4000-for-work-permit-up-from-100/

Alexander, W. A., & Garba, D. (2021). Africa and regional integration: The challenges. *UZU Journal, 8*(2), 91–112.

Amupanda, J. S. (2018). Who is in the '"we"'? Interrogating the African Union's Agenda 2063 and youth political participation. *International Journal of African Renaissance Studies-Multi-, Inter-and Transdisciplinarity, 13*(1), 56–76.

Anami, L. (2021, December 20). *Good news to workers as Tanzania, Kenya slash permit fee.* Retrieved July 2022, from The East Africa: https://www.theeastafrican.co.ke/tea/business/good-news-to-workers-as-tanzania-kenya-slash-permit-fee-3658210

Aniche, E. T. (2020). African Continental Free Trade Area and African Union Agenda 2063: The roads to Addis Ababa and Kigali. *Journal of Contemporary African Studies,* 1–16.

Ankomah, J. (2020, April 17). *How Ghana's "Year of Return" Sparked a Pan-African Phenomenon.* Retrieved July 2022, from Culture Trip: https://theculturetrip.com/africa/ghana/articles/how-ghanas-year-of-return-sparked-a-pan-african-phenomenon/

Apiko, P., Woolfrey, S., & Byiers, B. (2020). The promise of the African Continental Free Trade Area (AfCFTA). *ECDPM Discussion Paper, 287,* 1–16.

Arthur, J. A. (2000). *Invisible Sojourners: African immigrant diaspora in the United States.* Greenwood Publishing Group.

AU Commission. (2020). *Report on labour migration statistics in Africa second edition-2017.* The African Union Commission and JLMP Partners.

Awosusi, O. E., & Fatoyinbo, F. O. (2019). Xenophobic prejudice in Africa: Cultural diplomacy as a panacea to the deteriorating inter-African relations. *International Journal of Research Publications, 40*(1).

Bach, D. C. (2016). *Regionalism in Africa: Genealogies, institutions and trans-state networks*. Routledge.

Bavier, J. (2008, August 22). *Angola expels thousands of Congolese before polls*. Retrieved July 2022, from Reuters: https://www.reuters.com/article/idU SLM706428

Davis, C. (1999). Exchanging the African: Meetings at the crossroads of the diaspora. *South Atlantic Quarterly, 98*(1), 59–83.

De Witte, M., & Spronk, R. (2014). Introduction: 'African': A contested qualifier in global Africa. *African Diaspora, 7*(2), 165–176.

Dei, G. J. (2018). "Black like me": Reframing blackness for decolonial politics. *Educational Studies, 54*(2), 117–142.

Du Bois, W. (1946). *The world and Africa*. Viking Press.

Dube, G. (2018). Afrophobia in Mzansi? Evidence from the 2013 South African social attitudes survey. *Journal of Southern African Studies, 44*(6), 1005–1021.

Eboh, C. (2017, March 7). *Nigeria, South Africa feud over yellow fever jabs*. Retrieved July 2022, from Reuters: https://www.reuters.com/article/us-nig eria-south-africa-feud-over-yellow-idUSTRE8261VV20120307

Edo, V. O., & Olanrewaju, M. A. (2012). An assessment of the transformation of the Organization of African Unity (OAU) to the African Union (AU), 1963–2007. *Journal of the Historical Society of Nigeria*, 41–69.

Ejikeme, P. O. (2019). Africa and terrorism in a world of change. *Journal of African Studies and Sustainable Development, 1*(4), 35–50.

Ewepu, G., & Eromosele, F. (2021, March 31). *Nigeria's dairy product importation stands at $1.5bn*. Retrieved July 2022, from Vangaurd: https://www.vanguardngr.com/2021/03/nigerias-dairy-product-importation-stands-at-1-5bn-nanono/

Fofack, H. (2020, December). *Making the AfCFTA work for 'The Africa we want'*. Retrieved August 2022, from Africa Growth Initiative Working Paper: https://www.brookings.edu/wp-content/uploads/2020/12/20.12. 28-AfCFTA_Fofack.pdf

Ghica, L. A. (2013). Beyond regional integration? Social constructivism, regional cohesiveness and the regionalism puzzle. *Studia Politica Romanian Political Science Review, 13*(4), 733–752.

Gumede, V. (2019). Revisiting regional integration in Africa-towards a Pan-African developmental regional integration. *Africa Insight, 49*(1), 97–111.

Haas, E. B. (2001). Does constructivism subsume neofunctionalism. In T. Christiansen, K. E. Jørgensen, & A. Wiener (Eds.), *The social construction of Europe*. Sage.

Harris, B. (2002). Xenophobia: A new pathology for a new South Africa? In D. Hook & G. Eagle (Eds.), *Psychopathology and social prejudice* (pp. 169–184). University of Cape Town Press.

Hountondji, P. (1983). *African philosophy: Myth and reality.* Indiana University Press.

Iyanda, M. (2020, August 16). *17,000 Nigerian PhD graduates without jobs: Questions of programmes standardisation, career roadmap.* Retrieved July 2022, from Tekedia: https://www.tekedia.com/17000-nigerian-phd-gradua tes-without-jobs-questions-of-programmes-standardisation-career-roadmap/

Kanayo, O., Anjofui, P., & Stiegler, N. (2019). Analysis of ramifications of migration and xenophobia in Africa. *Journal of African Foreign Affairs, 6*(3), 65–85.

Kende-Robb, C. (2021, February 9). *World Economic Forum.* Retrieved August 2022, from 6 Reasons Why Africa's New free Trade Area is a Global Game Changer: https://www.weforum.org/agenda/2021/02/afcfta-africa-free-trade-global-game-changer/

Lufumpa, C. L., Letsara, N., & Saidi, S. (2017). Infrastructure development index. In M. Ncube & C. L. Lufumpa (Eds.), *Infrastructure in Africa: lessons for future development* (pp. 25–88). Policy Press.

Lunenborg, P. (2019). Phase 1B'of the African Continental Free Trade Area (AfCFTA) negotiations. *South Centre, Policy Brief, 63,* 1–15.

Machinya, J. (2022). Migration and politics in South Africa. *African Human Mobility Review, 8*(1), 59–78.

Madden, P. (2020, September 2). *Brookings.* Retrieved August 2022, from Figure of the Week: The AfCFTA's Effects on Trade and Wages in Africa: https://www.brookings.edu/blog/africa-in-focus/2020/09/02/figure-of-the-week-the-afcftas-effects-on-trade-and-wages-in-africa/

Makinda, S. M., Okuma, F. W., & Mickler, D. (2016). *The African Union: Addressing the challenges of peace, security, and governance.* Routledge.

Mbowa, S. (2020). Exploring the use of South African ethnic and racial slurs on social media. *International Journal of Critical Diversity Studies, 3*(1), 53–68.

Mngomezulu, B. R., & Dube, M. (2019). Lost in translation: A critical analysis of xenophobia in Africa. *Journal of African Union Studies, 8*(2), 67–81.

Moore, D. C. (1999). African philosophy vs. philosophy of Africa: Continental identities and travelling names for the self. *Diaspora, 7,* 321–350.

Muraya, J. (2018, October 17). *Dozens of Nigerians protest extra-judicial killing, harassment by Kenya police.* Retrieved from Capital News: https://www. capitalfm.co.ke/news/2018/10/dozens-of-nigerians-protest-extra-judicial-kil ling-harassment-by-kenya-police/

Mwangi, O. G. (2019). The "Somalinisation" of terrorism and counterterrorism in Kenya: The case of refoulement. *Critical Studies on Terrorism, 12*(2), 298–316.

Nanjira, D. D. (2010). *African foreign policy and diplomacy from antiquity to the 21st century* (Vol. 2). Praeger Security International.

National Geographic. (n.d.). *Africa: Physical geography.* Retrieved July 2022, from National Geographic: https://education.nationalgeographic.org/res ource/africa-physical-geography

Njoku, F. O. (2019). Is it African identity or a matter of survival for the African? *Journal of African Studies and Sustainable Development, 2*(3), 2630–7073.

Nkrumah, K. (1963). *Africa must unite.* Heinemann.

Nogel, R. J. (2020). Human rights and Uganda's expulsion of its Asian minority. *Denver Journal of International Law & Policy, 3*(1), 107–115.

Nyathi, K. (2022, August 2). *Rwanda starts hiring teachers from Zimbabwe.* Retrieved August 2022, from Nation: https://nation.africa/africa/news/rwa nda-starts-hiring-teachers-from-zimbabwe-3900160

Nyaundi, L., & Kimani, T. (2019, March 21). *Varsities face staff crises as half of PhD students quit.* Retrieved July 2022, from The Star: https://www.the-star.co.ke/news/2019-03-21-varsities-face-staff-crises-as-half-of-phd-students-quit/

Oatway, J., & Skuy, A. (2021, June 21). *Documenting violence against migrants in South Africa—A photo essay.* Retrieved July 2022, from The Guardian: https://www.theguardian.com/world/2021/jun/21/documenting-vio lence-against-migrants-in-south-africa-a-photo-essay

Obeng-Odoom, F. (2020). The African Continental Free Trade Area. *American Journal of Economics and Sociology, 79*(1), 167–197.

Ochami, D. (2016, November 8). *The unspoken scourge of racism in Kenyan tourist hotels.* Retrieved July 2022, from The Standard: https://www.standardmedia.co.ke/counties/article/2000222596/the-unspoken-scourge-of-racism-in-kenyan-tourist-hotels

Ochuko, R. (2020, March 8). *What is Africa's original name.* Retrieved July 2022, from Guardian Nigeria: https://guardian.ng/life/what-is-africas-ori ginal-name/

Okafor, J., & Aniche, E. (2017). Deconstructing neo-functionalism in the quest for a paradigm shift in African integration: Post-neo-functionalism and the prognostication of the proposed Continental Free Trade Area in Africa. *IOSR Journal of Humanities and Social Sciences, 22*(2), 60–72.

Oloko, A. (2022, July 5). *Massacre at the Morocco-Spain border.* Retrieved 11 2022, from Nigerian Tribune: https://tribuneonlineng.com/massacre-at-the-morocco-spain-border/

Oloruntoba, S. (2018). The state, regional integration and economic develop-ment in Africa: Rethinking the neoliberal paradigm. In C. Landsberg (Ed.), *Africa rise up! Perspectives on African renewal.* Real African Publishers.

Ombuor, R. (2018, March 26). *Kenya to import 100 Doctors from Cuba.* Retrieved July 2022, from VOA-Africa: https://www.voanews.com/a/kenya-to-import-100-doctors-from-cuba/4316601.html

240   E. ZWANBIN

Oni, E. O., & Okunade, S. K. (2018). The context of xenophobia in Africa: Nigeria and South Africa in comparison. In A. O. Akinola (Ed.), *The political economy of xenophobia in Africa* (pp. 37–51). Springer.

Orjuela, L. J. (2007). Ideologías, Tecnocracia y Sociedad: Implicaciones Para América Latina. In H. V. G., *Filosofía y Teorías Políticas Entre la Crítica y la Utopia* (pp. 219–234). CLACSO.

Ozel, M., Popova, N., Lee, J., & Cholewinski, R. (2017). Chapter 4: Work. *Global migration group: Handbook for improving the production and use of migration data for development* (pp. 33–40). Global Knowledge Partnership for Migration and Development.

Palmié, S. (2007). Introduction: Out of Africa? *Journal of Religion in Africa, 37*(2), 159–173.

Pasara, M. T. (2020). An overview of the obstacles to the African economic integration process in view of the African Continental Free Trade Area. *Africa Review, 12*(1), 1–17.

Quarshie, N. O. (2021). Mass expulsion as internal exclusion: Police raids and the imprisonment of West African immigrants in Ghana, 1969–1974. In M. Morelle (Ed.), *Confinement, punishment and prisons in Africa* (pp. 40–54). Routledge.

Saleh, M. (2022, April 14). *Total population of Africa from 2000 to 2022.* Retrieved August 2022, from Statistica: https://www.statista.com/statistics/1224168/total-population-of-africa/

Samah, W. (2021). Xenophobia and regional integration in Central Africa. In S. O. Abidde & E. K. Matambo (Eds.), *Xenophobia, nativism and pan-Africanism in 21st century Africa* (pp. 197–218). Springer.

Sansone, L. (2003). *Blackness without ethnicity.* Palgrave.

Signé, L. (2022, May 17). *Brookings.* Retrieved August 2022, from Understanding The African Continental Free Trade Area and how the US can promote its success: https://www.brookings.edu/testimonies/understanding-the-african-continental-free-trade-area-and-how-the-us-can-promote-its-su

Spel, C. O. (2020). African Continental Free Trade Agreement (AfCFTA) and migrants' social and economic rights. *Africa Insight, 50*(1), 107–121.

UN News. (2022, July 15). *South Africa 'on the precipice of explosive xenophobic violence', UN experts warn.* Retrieved from United Nations: https://news.un.org/en/story/2022/07/1122612

United Nations General Assembly. (1994, November 23). United Nations General Assembly 49th Session Report on Contemporary Forms of Racism, Racial Discrimination, Xenophobia and related Intolerance. In *Accordance with Commission on Human Rights, resolution 1993/20 and 1994/64 and Economic and Social Council decision 1994/307.* The Special Rapporteur of the Commission on Human Rights. Annex, note by the Secretary General UN Doc A/49/677.

AFCTA AND AFRICAN INTEGRATION: PROSPECTS ... 241

Vickers, B. (2017). *A handbook on regional integration in Africa: Towards agenda 2063*. The Commonwealth.

Viner, J. (1950). *The customs union issue*. Carnegie Endowment for International Peace.

Wapmuk, S., & Ali, J. M. (2022). The African Continental Free Trade Area (AFCFTA) and regional economic integration: Prospects and challenges. *Zamfara Journal of Politics and Development, 3*(1), 1–15.

Wroughton, L. (2022, June 5). *Vigilantes and violence have migrants in South Africa scared for their lives*. Retrieved July 2022, from The Washington Post: https://www.washingtonpost.com/world/2022/06/05/south-africa-operation-dudula-immigration/

Yeboah, K. A. (2019, December 19). *We need to talk about Ghana's year of return and its politics of exclusion*. Retrieved July 2022, from African Arguments: https://africanarguments.org/2019/12/ghana-year-of-return-politics-of-exclusion/

Transnationalism Revisited: Interrogating Structural Factors Impacting Prospective Migrants' Decision-Making Process in Nigeria

Olufemi Mayowa Adetutu, Oluwaseun Joseph Onaolapo, Abayomi Folorunso AWOLEYE, and Fumnanya Ofili

1 BACKGROUND

Nigeria is Africa's most populous country with an estimated 186 million inhabitants, which comprises more than 250 ethnic groups (World Bank, 2016). In the pre-colonial era, Nigerian migration was mainly linked to the slave trade, warfare and inter-ethnic conflicts, while the post-colonial era was tilted towards Europe and North America in pursuance of educational opportunities and colonial ties (Isiugo-Abanihe & International Organisation for Migration [IOM] Nigeria, 2014). Until recently, the flows of emigration were mainly accessible to highly skilled professionals for the pursuance of education and employment opportunities (de Haas, 2006b; Mberu & Pongou, 2010). Mass exodus of emigration from the

O. M. Adetutu (✉) · O. J. Onaolapo · A. F. AWOLEYE · F. Ofili
Obafemi Awolowo University, Ile-Ife, Nigeria
e-mail: oadetutu@cartafrica.org

© The Author(s), under exclusive license to Springer Nature Switzerland AG 2023
A. I. Adeniran (ed.), *African Development and Global Engagements*,
https://doi.org/10.1007/978-3-031-21283-3_12

243

country spurred profound brain-drain and made a number of professionals move to the developed countries due to the dwindling economy characterized by a decrease in oil prices in the 1980s (de Haas & Flahaux, 2016). The dismal economic situation also lured younger, able-bodied and unskilled labour migrants to seek greener pastures in the informal sectors of the Gulf States and Europe (Mberu & Pongou, 2010).

Another key driver of migration in Nigeria is recurring ethnic conflict and insurgency characterized by fatal clashes, terror attacks on innocent citizens orchestrated by dissenting rebel groups which most often lead to fatal clashes between the government security agencies and non-state citizen militias (Mberu & Pongou, 2010). As a result, a large number of people are displaced and uprooted from their place of abode and their means of livelihood in dire strait. Incessant violent conflicts carried out by the dreaded Boko Haram have resulted in close to two million internally displaced persons in Nigeria (IOM-DTM Nigeria, 2017). There is also a surge in the population of refugees due to insurgency, which has made Nigerians to seek refuge in neighbouring countries such as Niger, Cameroon and Chad (UNHCR, 2017). Of the entire Nigerian emigration stock in 2015, 30% were in Europe, another 30% within the African continent and the remaining one-third in North America (UN DESA, 2015; UNHCR, 2015). Meanwhile, available evidence from IOM (2014) Nigeria's reports revealed that more than 60% of internal migration within Nigeria is oriented towards urban areas (de Haas & Flahaux, 2016).

Socio-economic and development indices in Nigeria are currently deplorable as a result of ravaging insecurity, poor political leadership, pervasive corruption, humongous cost of governance, mismanagement of public funds and inordinate greed on the part of the political class (Idio et al., 2015; International Monetary Funds, 2015). The ripple effects have resulted into frustration and a life of privation which spur aspiration for the emigration of a large number of Nigerians who find life unbearable. However, there are stringent challenges to be surmounted by would-be emigrants who are lured to pursue a better quality of life in the developed countries. Currently, there exists a dilemma of making migration decision amidst unceasing insecurity, generalized poverty and the ambivalent disposition of aspiring migrants towards migration decisions and how to navigate migration hurdles en-route countries of destination. This has generated a serious concern as to whether aspiring migrants should decide to get to the Eldorado of the developed countries and seek greener pastures based on the notion that misery with hope abroad is better than a life of misery without hope in Nigeria. There is a research lacuna as to whether the ravaging insecurity and other constraints abroad outweigh the potential gains in the decision of aspiring migrants because economic reasons are the fulcrum of most research studies that have investigated the decision of people to migrate (de Haas, 2011; Moyo et al., 2020). Clearly, there is a systematic absence of studies that tease out the nuanced socio-demographic, economic and migration-related factors that spur migration decision amidst the potential risks and gains at countries of origin and destination.

One of such non-economic reasons described to influence migration decision which has been largely overlooked in Nigerian studies is the connection and contact that would-be migrants have with people such as, families, friends, neighbours and social groups through which support on migration is received (Tabor et al., 2015). While studies have investigated the influence of social supports network on health-related needs, factors accountable for migration decisions are yet to be explored. Contrasting information from unsuccessful return migrants and views of diaspora on the risks and gains of emigration make decision of aspiring migrants uncertain, while desire to emigrate remains unabated in the context of dismal economic and security situation in Nigeria. As result, most able-bodied, skilled and unskilled aspiring migrants prefer misery with hope than misery without hope in sub-Saharan Africa countries, including Nigeria (Römer & Tjaden, 2020; Smith, 2019). Thus, aspiring migrants are desperate to seek informal support to emigrate from the Global South because formal channels of migration are believed to be infused with restrictive migration control policies and stern visa application in the Global North (Auer et al., 2020; Smith, 2019).

Furthermore, it is difficult for aspiring migrants to make rational migration decisions with uncertainty that has beclouded conditions in the countries of destination and the general perception of the developed countries regarding sub-Saharan Africa migration as massive, even invasion-like outflow of desperately poor people and that the flow is predominantly directed towards the developed countries (de Haas, 2006b). Published evidence, however, by different scholars from the developing countries echoed a prominent voice in the debates that are steeply dominated most by the developed countries, critiqued their viewpoints and put it into different perspectives. The main points of departure have been that migration must be seen as a profound and normal element of African social life, and that migration, in general, is not an undesirable phenomenon, but an inherent component of the development processes (Adepoju et al., 2008a, b; Awumbila et al., 2008). However, the dismal economic situation and lopsided political system have diminished the well-being of the people and negated the stance of the Afrocentric views in Nigeria.

We argue that the issues in currency in Nigeria are counterfactual to the stance of African critics of European restrictive migration agendas and policies. What is more, aspiring migrants prefer any negative eventuality in the course of their migratory sojourn, and most of the times, they plan to migrate through illegal means working with syndicates in transit countries devising diverse ways of emigrating from Nigeria. Meanwhile, migration policy from the developed world has been transformed within the recent significant policy shift from migration control to management using an integrated approach (Adepoju et al., 2009). Yet, scholars have pointed out that the integrated management of migration is control-biased, including polarization of migrants into wanted and unwanted, development assistant in favour of developing countries with more migration volume and undue emphasis devoted to migration control from the Global South (Schapendonk, 2010; VandeBrug et al., 2015).

Available evidence has shown that migration desire must be differentiated from the capability to do so (Carling & Schewel, 2018; de Haas, 2021). In this sense, social factors have broadened our understanding on the deficit of migration despite the substantial wage differentials between the countries of destination and origin (Collier, 2013). There is some sense in giving premium to socio-economic and migration-related factors which depict connections with the diaspora on the rationality of migration decisions (Kahneman, 2011). The uncertainty of getting migration information from the legal channels lends credence to the need to tap from informal sources of migration information, including unsuccessful return migrants, social groups, friends, co-community residents and neighbours, among others.

Access to information varies according to social and personality characteristics, which may include previous migration experience and social networks (Baláž et al., 2016). In the literature, the influence of migration-related factors couched in social networks on migration decision is sorely missing, and the main thrust of studies is on wealth and income differences at the macro level, and human capital at the individual level. The main assumption is that individuals and families diversify their income and hone their skills and this informed the current notion of migration as a win–win situation (Constant & Zimmermann, 2013). While this assumption has contributed to the knowledge base on rationality and economic reasons for migration decisions, studies that examined a range of structural factors that have an element of connections with people in diaspora namely financial support, and migration information have been largely overlooked. Migration studies are mostly based on the economic rationality of individual and national economies, however (de Haas, 2011; Moyo et al., 2020). This study, therefore, brings to the fore contextual issues which are composed of socio-economic and migration-related determinants, and its influence on migration decision.

2 THEORETICAL FRAMEWORK

This study was anchored on social network of migration and planned behaviour theories. The social network of migration theory argues that migration decision is not only influenced by economic motives but also migration network which enhances access to information and other resources, within the web of contacts between sending and receiving countries. This connection reduces the cost and increases the expected net returns to migration (Arango et al., 2020; Massey et al., 1993). Aspiring migrants from the country of origin inquire about opportunities and are provided with transportation, initial accommodation and an arranged employment (MacDonald & MacDonald, 1964). Migration networks are sets of interpersonal ties that connect migrants, former migrants and non-migrants to one another through relations of kinship, friendship and shared community origin. The network theory of migration can be connected with the neo-classical, new economics of labour migration and cumulative causation (Garip, 2007; Massey et al., 1993).

Research on social networks was intended to mitigate a lack of concern with the social element of migration process in theories which prioritized economic reasons for migration. Yet, the network theory of migration is related to the cost–benefit equation of rational migrants in deciding whether to migrate or not (Epstein, 2008). Similarly, the social network theory migration is also connected with the new economic labour of migration, in that, members of household chosen to migrate may be the ones having the most connections with prior migrants. In the context of this study, aspiration to emigrate finds meaning in reliance on remittances, ever lived outside the shores of Nigeria, ease of moving across the borders of the country and membership of a social group which are all connected to sharing information and other resources with relevant others within the circle of people with migration experience.

To be sure, the influence of social network of migration has a profound influence on the aspiration to emigrate. The dismal economic situation spurs people to rely on people within their networks to get necessary information about getting resources and taking proactive steps towards emigration. As such, the social network variables are more crucial in understanding migration decision-making within the lens of migration-related information and sharing other resources which motivate emigration.

This research was also inspired by the theory of planned behaviour. The theory of planned behaviour emphasizes the primacy of cost–benefit analysis in relation to intention and actual behaviour. The theory of planned behaviour is couched in social psychology, with the underlying thesis that the intention of individuals informs their tendency to behave in a particular way (Ajzen, 1991). The intention to perform a particular action depends on motivating and non-motivating factors, including time, money, skills and cooperation of others (Ajzen, 1991). Published evidence has differentiated migration intention from behaviour (De Jong, 2000). There is mixed evidence in the literature on the two-phased model as migration intention is not mostly fulfilled as migration behaviour (Creighton & Riosmena, 2013; van Dalen & Henkens, 2013; De Jong, 2000). The key issue in this discourse is that migration is made when a rational decision taken is informed by the expectation of realizing a certain benefit in the country of destination (De Jong, 2000). Building on De Jong (2000) stance on migration decision, Kley (2011) proposed a three-phase model which includes pre-decisional, pre-actional and actional stages. The position of this perspective is that individuals make decisions to emigrate based on weighing the socio-economic situation at the country of origin in comparison to the destination. The aspiration and actual behaviour to emigrate is tied to the socio-economic status of aspiring migrants at the country of origin, the likely challenges being face in the course of movement to the country of destination. However, in this study, we argue that aspiration to emigrate depends not only on the current socio-economic characteristics of aspiring migrants but also the migration-related variables which speak to intention to emigrate and actual attempt to take migration decision. This intention-actual migration behaviour depends on the socio-economic situation at country of origin and availability of information, other resources and connections within the circle of aspiring migrants.

3 Data and Methods

Afrobarometer, a nonprofit organization with headquarters in Accra, Ghana, is a pan-African, non-partisan research network consisting of about 35 National Partners. Regional coordination is provided by the Ghana Center for Democratic Development (CDD-Ghana), the Institute for Justice and Reconciliation (IJR) in South Africa and the Institute for Development Studies (IDS) at the University of Nairobi in Kenya. Michigan State University (MSU) and the University of Cape Town (UCT) provide technical support to the network.

Afrobarometer collected a nationally representative secondary data for African countries. A face-to-face interview was conducted from a randomly selected sample between 1200 and 2400 people in each country. This study extracted data for Nigeria with a sample of 1600. Information on sample size determination and sampling procedures are available elsewhere (www.afrobarometer.org). For good quality data, national partners were worked within each of our survey countries. National partners are responsible for training interviewers before collecting data for Afrobarometer. National partners made sure the interviewers have the right skills and qualifications to perform an Afrobarometer survey. Although a number of research methods were used during the project design, Afrobarometer relies predominantly on personal interviews to obtain information from individual respondents. A standard questionnaire, which contains identical or functionally equivalent items, is applied to every respondent in each country. Because questions are standardized, responses can be compared across countries and over time. In the personal interview, the interviewer goes to a randomly selected household and interviews a randomly selected adult individual—defined as citizens aged 18 and above from that household. The interviewer asks this respondent a series of questions in a face-to-face situation and in a language of the respondent's choice.

The interviewer records the responses (i.e., the answers) provided by the respondent. Advantages of this approach are that the survey response rate is usually high; refusal rates are very low; the respondents have the opportunity to clarify their answers and, by aggregating responses, we are able to make inferences about public opinion. On this last point, it should be noted that Afrobarometer surveys are based on national probability samples. As a consequence, the aggregated results are representative of larger groups. Afrobarometer sample sizes range from 1200 to 2400.

250   O. M. ADETUTU ET AL.

Both the 1200 and 2400 sample sizes are large enough to make inferences about all voting age citizens with an average margin of sampling error of no more than plus or minus 2.8% at a 95% confidence level (with a sample size of 1200) or plus or minus 2% for sample sizes of 2400.

3.1   Measurement of Variables and Data Analysis

The dependent variable of the study was migration decision coded 1, aspiring and 0, not aspiring to suit a binary logistic regression at the multivariable level. The main independent variables were membership of a social group, discussion of migration issues in a group and reliance on remittances, ease of moving across borders and ever lived outside Nigeria before. Other control variables were socio-economic and demographic characteristics and these were measured at individual, household, community and national levels. All the relevant variables were either re-coded using composite indices or re-categorized to suit analysis. Data were analysed at a univariable level using frequencies and percentages. At the bivariate level, Chi-squared statistics of independence were used to examine the relationship between variables in categorical forms. At the multivariable level, binary logistic regression was used because the outcome variable was dichotomous and the independent variables were categorical. All the relevant variables at the bivariate level were considered in the multivariate analysis.

3.2   Results

Table 1 shows the percentage distribution of socio-demographic and migration-related factors. In this sub-section, we present a discussion of the descriptive evidence on social factors that influence migration decisions to provide a solid foundation for other levels of analysis. The results revealed a substantial proportion of the respondents were between the age grouping 21–34 (88.0%). Half of the respondents were males, 55.4% were Christians, and more than one-third (36.9%). Further results showed that 50.9% had secondary education, 56.5% reside in the rural areas. As regards household index, the results revealed that 58% were worse-off, and 46.6% of women participated in household decision-making. More than four-fifth (78%) of the respondents reported they were not discriminated by ethnic origin, while 17.1% reported ethnic discrimination.

TRANSNATIONALISM REVISITED: INTERROGATING ...   251

Table 1   Percentage distribution of respondents by related factors associated with migration decision

Characteristics	Frequency (%) (n = 1600)
Age group (in years)	
21–34	1408 (88.0)
35–45	192 (12.0)
Sex	
Male	802 (50.1)
Female	798 (49.9)
Level of education	
Never	232 (14.5)
Primary	330 (20.6)
Secondary	591 (36.9)
Higher	447 (27.9)
Religion	
Christian	886 (55.4)
Islam	676 (42.3)
Others	38 (2.4)
Employment status	
Unemployed	815 (50.9)
Employed	785 (49.1)
Access to media	
Good	892 (55.6)
Fair	588 (36.8)
Worse	120 (7.4)
Household deprivation index	
Poor	935 (58.4)
Fair	630 (39.4)
Good	35 (2.2)
Women's decision autonomy	
Wife alone	743 (46.4)
Husband alone	195 (12.2)
Jointly	579 (36.2)
Others	83 (5.2)
Ethnic discrimination	
Never	1249 (78.1)
Ever	351 (21.9)
Experience discrimination based on gender	
Never	1315 (82.2)
Ever	285 (21.9)

(continued)

Table 1 (continued)

Characteristics	Frequency (%) (n = 1600)
Community factors	
Environmental vulnerability	
Severe	983 (61.4)
Moderate	617 (38.6)
Freedom to exercise human rights	
Poor	595 (37.2)
Fair	968 (60.5)
Good	37 (2.3)
Neighbourhood safety	
Unsafe	1341 (88.8)
Fair	233 (14.6)
Safe	26 (1.6)
Quality of life index	
Poor	951 (59.4)
Fair	564 (32.3)
Good	85 (5.3)
Living conditions versus others	
Worse	374 (23.4)
Same	473 (29.6)
Better	753 (47.0)
Current economic situation compared to a year ago	
Worse	1466 (91.6)
Better	134 (8.4)
Mode of Governance	
Poor	1023 (63.9)
Good	577 (36.1)
Membership of social group	
Non-member	799 (49.9)
Member	801 (50.1)
Corruption index	
High	1143 (71.4)
Medium	434 (27.1)
Low	23 (1.5)
Level of corruption	
Increased	687 (42.9)
Same	224 (14.0)
Decreased	689 (43.1)

(continued)

TRANSNATIONALISM REVISITED: INTERROGATING ... 253

Table 1 (continued)

Characteristics	Frequency (%) (n = 1600)
Mode of handling challenges by government	
Poor	755 (47.1)
Fair	748 (46.8)
Good	97 (6.1)
Management of fear during crisis	
Worse	1568 (98.0)
Fair	26 (1.6)
Good	6 (0.4)
Difficulty of emigrating	
Tense	917 (57.3)
Easy	683 (42.7)
Lived outside Nigeria	
No	1254 (78.4)
Yes	346 (21.6)
Migration decision	
Aspiring	560 (35.0)
Not aspiring	1040 (65.0)
Reason for emigration	
Job search	200 (12.5)
Better condition in country of destination	117 (7.3)
Family reunion	38 (2.4)
Economic hardship	1051 (65.7)
Poor infrastructure at home country	194 (12.1)
Environmental vulnerability	
Severe	983 (61.4)
Moderate	617 (38.6)
Reliance on remittances	
Never	1112 (69.5)
Sometimes	431 (26.9)
Ever reliant	57 (3.6)
Planning emigration through discussions within social groups	
Not planning	290 (18.1)
Planning	262 (16.4)
Indifferent	1048 (65.5)

The results revealed 61.4% experienced severe environmental hazard, 37.2% adjudged ability to express their human rights poorly, 88.8% opined their neighbourhood was unsafe. While two-thirds reported worst quality of life, almost one-third claimed their living condition remains

254   O. M. ADETUTU ET AL.

invariable relative to others. Furthermore, a huge proportion (91.6%) opined that their lives were worse-off currently compared to it used to be a year ago. More than two-thirds (71.4%) rated corruption of government officials high, 43% claimed corruption has increased and 47% blamed government in the way they handle violent crimes. As expected, 57.3% expressed tense situation of migrating from Nigeria, 78.4% had never left the shores of the country while 35% were aspiring to migrate. In addition, economic hardship was mentioned as the predominant reason for considering migration decision (65%), followed by a desire to secure a better job (12.5%). The results showed further that 16.4% were planning to leave Nigeria and sourcing migration information from their social networks and relevant others and 69% claimed they never really on remittances from people overseas.

In Table 2, we presented the Chi-squared test of independence to show relationship between related social factors and migration decisions. The results showed age was significantly associated with migration decision ($p < 0.05$). As would be expected, the older age group, 21–34 years, aspired migration (43%) compared with those aged 35–45 years. Regarding gender, more females aspired migrating relative to males and this was statistically significant ($p < 0.05$). The results further revealed a significant relationship between educational status and migration decision. Across all levels of education, aspiration for migration increased steeply, with those who had tertiary education aspiring most (43%). Similarly, employment status was a key predictor of migration decision. As would be expected, the unemployed had higher proportion of aspiration to migrate. Religion was also a significant predictor of migration decision, with Christian faithful aspiring to migrate most. The analysis showed that access to mass media was associated with migration decision. However, the result is counterfactual as the respondents least exposed to mass media aspire migration most (50.8%). Furthermore, self-rated quality of life index was significantly related to migration decision as those who had the best rating aspired emigrating from Nigeria most (40.0%).

Moreover, household deprivation index was also an influential predictor of migration decision and respondents who had the best rating aspire emigrating from Nigeria most (48.6%). In addition, women's household decision-making autonomy was associated with migration decision, with respondents that adjudged the husband as the sole decision-maker aspired migrating most (38.9%). Besides household-level factors,

Table 2 Bivariate analysis of migration decision by social factors

Variable	Migration decision		χ^2	p-value
	Aspiring (%)	Non-aspiring (%)		
Age				
21–34	33.74	66.26	8.24	
35–45	44.3	55.7		
Gender				
Male	32.0	68.0	5.58	0.001
Female	37.6	62.4		
Religion				
Christianity	38.3	61.7	9.47	0.000
Islam	30.8	69.2		
Others	34.2	65.8		
Employment Status				
Unemployed	38.3	61.7		0.000
Employed	31.6	68.4	7.86	
Education				
No formal education	22.4	77.6	37.29	0.000
Primary	28.8	71.2		
Secondary	36.9	63.1		

(continued)

Table 2   (continued)

Variable	Migration decision		χ^2	p-value
	Aspiring (%)	Non-aspiring (%)		
Tertiary	43.6	56.4		
Access to mass media				
Good	29.1	70.9	34.89	0.000
Fair	40.7	59.3		
Poor	50.8	49.2		
Quality of life				
Worse	32.4	67.6	79.09	0.02
Fair	38.6	61.4		
Good	40.0	60.0		
Household index				
Worse	27.8	72.2	51.34	0.00
Fair	44.9	55.1		
Good	48.6	51.4		
Women's autonomy				
Husband alone makes decision	38.9	61.1		
Wife decided alone	28.2	71.8	10.55	0.00
Joint decision	32.6	67.4		
Others	32.5	67.5		
Discriminated based on gender				
Never	32.2	67.8	24.65	0.00
Ever	47.7	52.3		
Level of corruption				

Variable	Migration decision		χ^2	p-value
	Aspiring (%)	Non-aspiring (%)		
Increased	35.9	62.6	7.23	0.02
Same	38.8	61.2		
Decreased	31.3	68.7		
Membership of a group				
Non-member	30.1	69.9	16.41	0.000
Member	39.8	60.2		
Aspiration for migration based on information sought from groups				
Not planning	100.0	0.0	1.60	0.000
Planning	100.0	0.0		
Indifferent	0.86	99.2		
Reasons for aspiring migration				
Job search abroad	100.0	0.0		
Poor infrastructure at home	100.0	0.0		
Better standard of living at destination country	100.0	0.0		
Family reunion	100.0	0.0		
Economic hardship at home	1.05	98.9	1.60	0.000
Lived outside Nigeria before				
No	26.6	73.4	181.78	0.000
Yes	65.6	34.4		
Difficulty to cross Nigeria's border				
Difficult	37.8	62.2	7.62	0.000
Easy	31.2	68.8		
Dependence on remittances				
Never	28.5	71.5	70.31	0.000
Somewhat reliant	48.5	51.5		
Ever reliant	59.7	40.3		

258   O. M. ADETUTU ET AL.

some community, national and other migration-related correlates influenced migration decision. For instance, the results showed that being discriminated by gender influenced migration decision and those who had been discriminated against had more percentage of aspiration to migrate (47.7%). Additionally, level of corruption among government officials was related to migration decision of aspiring migrants. Respondents whose rating was high and invariable on corruption index aspired emigrating from Nigeria most (38.8%).

Also, membership of social groups influenced migration decision, with respondents who engaged in social group activities aspiring to emigrate from Nigeria most (39.8%). The results further revealed that respondents who sought migration information from their social networks had similar migration aspirations and capabilities for migration. Across the range of reasons for considering migration, the results showed invariant proportions in all variables. The result found that unsuccessful return migrants had higher aspiration for migration (65.6%), and the respondents that adjudged it was difficult to move across borders in Nigeria had higher proportion of emigrating from Nigeria (37.8%). Finally, respondents who were ever reliant on remittances had higher proportion of aspiring migration (59.7%) (Table 3).

These multivariate results were based on the odds of migration decision in relation to some structural socio-demographics, at individual, household, community and meso-level relationships. The results revealed that age was significantly related to migration decision, as respondents between the ages of 35 and 45 had higher odds (43%) of aspiring to migrate relative to those aged 21–34 years (OR = 1.43; CI: 1.04–1.97) in Model 1. The result also revealed that female respondents were 24% more likely to emigrate from Nigeria compared to their male counterparts (OR = 1.24; CI: 1.00–1.54). As would be expected, the odds of aspiring migration increase across higher educational ladder. Respondents who had tertiary education are almost 3 times more likely to consider emigrating from Nigeria relative to those uneducated (OR = 2.44; CI: 1.60–3.72). Employment status was also significantly related to migration decision, with the employed 33% less likely to aspire to migrate compared with the unemployed (OR = 0.67; CI: 0.54–0.83). In addition, access to mass media was found to be associated with migration decision. The result indicated that respondents who reported the worst access to mass media had higher odds (87%) of aspiring to migrate compared with those who had access (OR = 1.87; CI: 1.23–2.86). The rating of quality of

Table 3 Multivariate analysis of social factors and migration decision

Variables Individual	Model I OR (95% CI)	Household	Model II OR (95% CI)	Community	Model III OR (95% CI)
Age		**Household index**		**Member of a group**	
21–34	1.00	Poor	1.00	Non-member	1.00
35–45	1.43 (1.04–1.97)*	Fair	2.06 (1.66–2.55)***	Member	1.34 (1.07–1.67)**
		Good	2.35 (1.18–4.64)**		
Gender		**Women's autonomy**		**Ever lived outside Nigeria**	
Male	1.00	Husband only	1.00	No	1.00
Female	1.24 (1.00–1.54)*	Wife only	0.69 (0.48–0.98)*	Yes	4.49 (3.45–5.83)***
		Jointly	0.81 (0.64–1.02)		
		Others	0.76 (0.47–1.25)		
Education				**Ease of moving across borders**	
No formal	1.00			Difficult	1.00
Primary	1.46 (0.97–2.19)			Easy	0.79 (0.63–0.99)*
Secondary	1.95 (1.32–2.89)***				
Tertiary	2.44 (1.60–3.72)***				
Employment status				**Reliance on Remittances**	
Unemployed	1.00			Never	1.00
Employed	0.67 (0.54–0.83)***			Somewhat	1.80 (1.41–2.31)***
				Ever reliant	2.54 (1.40–4.58)***
Religion					
Christianity	1.00				

(continued)

Table 3 (continued)

Variables Individual	Model I OR (95% CI)	Household	Model II OR (95% CI)	Community	Model III OR (95% CI)
Islam	0.97 (0.77–1.24)				
Others	1.15 (0.57–2.32)				
Access to media					
Better	1.00				
Fair	1.28 (0.99–1.66)*				
Worse	1.87 (1.23–2.33)*				
Self-rated QoL					
Poor	1.00				
Fair	1.35 (1.07–1.69)*				
Good	1.46 (0.92–2.33)				

* is p<0.05, ** is p<0.01 and *** is p<0.001

life was associated with migration decision of respondents who rated their quality of life as fair, with 35% higher odds of aspiring migration relative to those who rated it poor (OR = 1.35; CI: 1.07–1.69).

In Model 2, household deprivation index was found to be related to migration decision, as respondents whose indices were good had higher likelihood of aspiring to migrate relative to those whose ratings were poor (OR = 2.35; CI: 1.18–4.64). Regarding women's household decision-making autonomy, the results showed respondents who reported wife made decision alone were 29% less likely to aspire to migrate relative to those who reported husbands alone make household decision (OR = 0.69; CI: 0.48–0.98). In Model 3, community and national level-related variables namely membership of a social group, ever lived outside Nigeria, ease of moving across Nigerian border and reliance on remittances were significantly related to migration decisions. The results revealed that respondents with social groups were 34% more likely to aspire to migrate relative to those without social groups (OR = 1.34; CI: 1.07–1.67). Also, the results showed return migrants were almost 5 times more likely to aspire to migrate compared with those who had never left the shores of Nigeria (OR = 4.49; CI: 3.45–5.83). As regards the ease of moving across the borders of Nigeria, the results showed that those who found it easy to navigate had 21% lower odds of aspiring to migrate relative to those who found it a herculean task (OR = 0.79; CI: 0.63–0.99). The results further revealed that reliance on remittances was statistically significant and related to migration decision, as respondents who reported to be ever reliant on remittances are almost 3 times more likely to aspire to migrate compared with those who had never relied (OR = 1.80; CI: 1.41–2.31).

4 Discussion

This study investigates structural factors to provide insightful contributions to knowledge base on migration decision in Nigeria. The study made some salient findings and recommendations for policy, research and practice. First, it assessed the influence of migration-related factors on migration decisions. Second, it examined the influence of structural factors at individual, household, community and national level on migration decisions. Third, it explored the association between migration-related factors and migration decisions among people aged 21–45 years in Nigeria. Addressing the relationship between membership of social groups and migration decisions, the study found that migration information and discussions influenced decisions to emigrate from Nigeria. A plausible explanation for this is that social groups could provide the requisite migration supports and information that will trigger the aspiration to move. This position corroborates the findings of previous studies that argued that improved information from diverse sources influence aspirations and capabilities to drive future migration (Flahaux & de Haas, 2016; Tabor et al., 2015). Scholarly literature has established that every out-of-mouth discussion in social groups facilitates information on migration (Case, 2012; Sin & Kim, 2013). As a corollary, published evidence showed Nigerian do not only make their migration decision on their own but also often consult relevant others, such as family and friends, who vastly supported their decision to migrate (IOM, 2018). Yet, some migrants often made migration decision independently. Some also take advantage of information technology, using different social media platforms. The policy implication of this is that policymakers should design and focus migration policies which make emigration a win–win situation and target social groups, especially the youthful population.

Moreover, this study found that having lived outside Nigeria before influenced aspiration to migrate. This could be because return migrants are spurred to continue trying to emigrate until success is achieved and given their hitherto migration experience having tried to move in collaboration with commercial syndicates in transit countries. Countless number of studies have established that return migrants have an unquenchable thirst for emigrating from their home countries given the pull and push factors that influenced their emigration ab initio (Koomson-Halley, 2021; Reading, 2021). Policymakers should target return and unsuccessful migrants for empowerment, informative and transformative discussions which would change their golden flee and unbridled orientation of greener pastures abroad during the integration of return migrants. The study further found that reliance on remittances influenced that aspiration to migrate. Previous studies have echoed this stance (de Haas, 2011; Moyo et al., 2020). The main points of arguments are that remittances alleviate poverty of many households in Nigeria and as such a number of individuals and households are determined to follow through the same path of financial success. This position also contributes to the theory of social networks such that in social relationship and dissemination of migrations ideas, the gains, be it financial, emotional and psychosocial are discussed and not glossed over. There is an urgent need to encourage would-be migrants with access to remittances to use the financial and material support for productive investment but not consumptive purposes.

Our results affirmed that poor socio-economic status at the household level motivated migration decisions. This finding lends credence to existing studies regarding how poor socio-economic status spurs migration aspiration and confirms the hypothesis that migration is poverty-driven in contexts where development is stagnant (de Haas, 2011). This result is imperative and requires an urgent need to empower poor people so as to relieve the obsessive desire to emigrate from the country at every available opportunity, and surprisingly through illegal and deadly channels. Our study also confirmed a contemporary issue that patriarchal values influenced migration decisions in Nigeria. Similar studies indicated that women are more likely to embark on migration when there is development failure and poor standard of living of household (Adepoju, 2010; Oucho, 2011) A possible explanation for this is that traditionally male-dominated migration pattern is becoming increasingly feminized. This shows that migration aspiration among women is attributable to increased poverty. Our results also showed that females are more likely to migrate than their male counterparts and this further lends credence to the argument that autonomous female migration is now in ascendancy.

The study has made insightful contributions to the literature and knowledge base on migration studies considering relatively neglected areas, such as the influence of meso-level factors, that is, social support networks, considered social determinants and shifted the debates on migration decisions from wealth and socio-economic differences between the developed and developing countries but that both economic and social disparities and social relationships, including friends, families, neighbours and social groups influence migration decisions. Migration policies and bilateral agreements should focus on social relationships and other structurally disadvantaged socio-economic statuses. Nigerian government must design migration policies that enhance social inclusion, alleviate poverty and support diaspora organization in managing migration-related issues.

Underdevelopment is a symptom and a cause of migration not only in Nigeria but also in many developing countries across the globe. In a bid to reduce or discourage people from emigrating from the country, there is an urgent need to address issues that make people migrate. This could be done by improving economic growth and massive developmental projects, such as providing infrastructural facilities, ensuring security of lives and property, providing better jobs and equal chances to the youths, promoting gender equality and reducing high population growth rates through family planning or other birth control measures. If these problems are solved, Nigerians will not continue to migrate in droves for better living conditions and opportunities. This study has some limitations. One is that it used a cross-sectional data that may not address the issue of causality adequately and respondents may want to answer questions to portray social desirability. There could also be recall bias, although the questioning pattern in the data was based on the last 12 months prior to the survey. Yet, the study contributed substantially to the knowledge base and used a nationally representative data on very important migration issues that might be difficult to collect by individuals through primary data collection methods.

Acknowledgements The data for this research was provided by AfroBarometer.

Conflict of Interest The authors declare no conflict of interests.

REFERENCES

Adepoju, A. (2008a). Issues and recent trends in international migration in sub-Saharan Africa. *International Social Science Journal, 52*(165), 383–394.

Adepoju, A. (2008b). Migration in sub-Saharan Africa. Retrieved from Nordiska Afrikainstitutet website: http://urn.kb.se/resolve?urn=urn:nbn:se:nai:diva-144

Adepoju, A. (Ed.). (2010). *International Migration within, to and from Africa in a Globalised World*. Accra: SubSaharan Publishers.

Ajzen, I. (1991). The theory of planned behavior. *Organizational Behavior and Human Decision Processes, 50*(2), 179–211.

Akesson, L., & Alpes, J. (2019). What is a legitimate mobility manager? Juxtaposing migration brokers with the EU. *Journal of Ethnic & Migration Studies, 45*(14), 2689–2705.

Arango, M. S., Singelmann, J., Sáenz, R. (2020). Cognitive Decline Among the Elderly: A Comparative Analysis of Mexicans in Mexico and in the United States. In Singelmann, J., Poston, Jr, D. (Eds.), *Developments in Demography in the 21st Century*. The Springer Series on Demographic Methods and Population Analysis, vol 48. Springer, Cham. https://doi.org/10.1007/978-3-030-26492-5_12

Auer, D., Römer, F., & Tjaden, J. (2020). Corruption and the desire to leave quasi-experimental evidence on corruption as a driver of emigration intentions. *IZA Journal of Development and Migration, 11*(1). https://doi.org/10.2478/izajodm-2020-0007

Awumbila, M., & Manuh, T (2008). Migration country paper (Ghana). Centre for Migration Studies, University of Ghana, Legon.

Awumbila, M., Manuh, T., Quartey, P., Tagoe, C. A., & Bosiakoh, T. A. (2008). *Migration country paper* (Ghana). Legon: Centre.

Baláž, V., Williams, A. M., & Fifeková, E. (2016). Migration decision making as complex choice: Eliciting decision weights under conditions of imperfect and complex information through experimental methods. *Population, Space and Place, 22*(1), 36–53.

Batista, C., & McKenzie, D. (2020). *Testing classic theories of migration in the lab.* Paper presented at the Annual Migration Meeting, UCD Geary Institute for Public Policy, Ireland. Retrieved from https://research.unl.pt/ws/portal files/portal/26626231/batista_c2249.pdf

Belloni, M. (2016). Refugees as gamblers: Eritreans seeking to migrate through Italy. *Journal of Immigrant & Refugee Studies, 14*(1), 104–119.

Bob-Milliar, G. M., & Bob-Milliar, G. K. (2013). The politics of trans-Saharan transit migration in the Magreb: Ghanaian migrants in Libya, c.1980–2012. *African Review of Economics & Finance, 5*(1), 60–73.

Bolay, M. (2014). When miners become "foreigners": Competing categorizations within a gold mining spaces in Guinea. *Resources Policy, 40*, 117–127.

van der Brug, W., D'Amato, G., Berkhout, J., & Ruedin, D. (Eds.). (2015). *The politicisation of migration.* Routledge.

Carling, J., & Schewel, K. (2018). Revisiting aspiration and ability in international migration. *Journal of Ethnic and Migration Studies, 44*(6), 945–963.

Case, D. (2012). *Looking for information: A survey of research on information seeking, needs and behavior* (3rd ed.). Academic Press.

Castles, S., de Haas, H., & Miller, M. (2014). The *age of migration: International population movement in the modern world.* Palgrave Macmillan Higher Education.

Collier, P. (2013). *Exodus: How migration is changing our world.* Allen Lane.

Constant, A. F., & Zimmermann, K. F. (2013). *International handbook on the economics of migration.* Edward Elgar Publishing.

Creighton, M. J. (2013). The role of aspirations in domestic and international migration. *The Social Science Journal, 50*(1), 79–88.

Creighton, M. J., & Riosmena, F. (2013). Migration and the gendered origin of migrant networks among couples in Mexico. *Social Science Quarterly, 94*(1), 79–99.

Cresswell, T. (2010). Towards a politics of mobility. *Environment and Planning D: Society & Space, 28*(1), 17–31.

266   O. M. ADETUTU ET AL.

Czaika, M., & Vothknecht, M. (2014). Migration and aspirations–Are migrants trapped on a hedonic treadmill? *IZA Journal of Migration, 3*(1), 1–21.

Dalen, H. P., Groenewold, G., & Schoorl, J. (2005). Out of Africa: What drives the pressure to emigrate? *Journal of Population Economics, 18*(4), 741–778.

van Dalen, H. P., & Henkens, K. (2013). Explaining emigration intentions and behaviour in the Netherlands, 2005–10. *Population Studies, 67*(2), 225–241.

De Jong, G. F. (2000). Expectations, gender, and norms in migration decision-making. *Population Studies, 54*(3), 307–319.

Denzin, N. K., & Lincoln, Y. S. (Eds.). (2005). Introduction: The discipline and practice of qualitative research. In N. K. Denzin & Y. S. Lincoln (Eds.), *The Sage handbook of qualitative research* (3rd ed., pp. 1–19). Sage Publications.

Epstein, G. S. (2008). Herd and network effects in migration decision-making. *Journal of Ethnic and Migration Studies, 34*(4), 567–583.

Faist, T. (1997). The crucial meso-level. In T. Hammar, G. Brochmann, K. Tamas, & T. Faist (Eds.), *International migration, immobility and development. Multidisciplinary perspectives* (pp. 187–217). Berg Publishers.

Ferro, A. (2006). Desired mobility or satisfied immobility? Migratory aspirations among knowledge workers. *Journal of Education and Work, 19*(2), 171–200. https://doi.org/10.1080/13639080600668028

Findlay, A. M., King, F. R. M., Smith, A. G., & Skeldon, R. (2012). World class? An investigation of globalisation, difference and international student mobility. *Transactions of the Institute of British Geographers, 37*(1), 118–131.

Fischer, P. A., Reiner, M., & Straubhaar, T. (1997). Should I stay or should I go? In T. Hammar, G. Brochmann, T. Hammar, & K. Tamas (Eds.), *International migration, immobility and development* (pp. 49–90). Berg Press.

Flahaux, M. L., & de Haas, H. (2016). African migration: Trends, patterns, drivers. *Comparative Migration Studies, 4*(1), 1–25.

Franck, A. K., Brandström, A. E., & Anderson, J. T. (2018). Navigating migrant trajectories through private actors: Burmese labor migration to Malaysia. *European Journal of Southeast Asia Studies, 17*(1), 55–82.

Garip, F. (2007). Discovering diverse mechanisms of migration: The Mexico–US stream 1970–2000. *Population and Development Review, 38*(3), 393–433.

Global Displacement Tracking Matrix (DTM) Support Team. (2017). *Maps on routes from Ethiopia, Nigeria, and Somalia to Europe.* Geneva.

de Haas, H. (2006a). *International migration and national development: Viewpoints and policy initiatives in countries of origin—The case of Nigeria.* Nijmegen: Working papers Migration and Development series.

de Haas, H. (2006b). Migration, remittances and regional development in Southern Morocco. *Geoforum, 37*(4), 565–580.

de Haas, H. (2007). Turning the tide? Why development will not stop migration. *Development & Change, 38*(5), 819–841.

de Haas, H. (2009). International migration and regional development in Morocco: A critical review of the literature. *Journal of Ethnic & Migration Studies, 35*(10), 1571–1503.

de Haas, H. (2010). *Migration transitions: A theoretical and empirical inquiry into the developmental drivers.* International Migration Institute.

de Haas, H. (2011). *The determinants of international migration: Conceptualizing policy, origin and destination effects.* IMI Working Papers, 32, 1–35.

de Haas, H. (2021). A theory of migration: The aspirations-capabilities framework. *CMS, 9*(8). https://doi.org/10.1186/s40878-020-00210-4

de Haas, H., & Flahaux, M. (2016). African migration: Trends, patterns, drivers. *Comparative Migration Studies, 4*(1), n.p.

Hewstone, M. (2018). Ethnic diversity, ethnic threat, and social cohesion: (Re)-evaluating the role of perceived out-group threat and prejudice in the relationship between community ethnic diversity and intra-community cohesion. *Journal of Ethnic and Migration Studies, 45*(3). https://doi.org/10.1080/1369183X.2018.1490638

Hiller, H. H., & Franz, T. M. (2004). New ties, old ties, and lost ties: The use of the internet in diaspora. *New Media & Society, 6*(6), 731–752.

Hoppe, A., & Fujishiro, K. (2015). Anticipated job benefits, career aspiration, and generalized self-efficacy as predictors for migration decision-making. *International Journal of Intercultural Relations, 47*, 13–27.

Idio, E. E., Rogers, W., & Akadi, A. P. (2015). The impact of International Migration on socio-economic development of Nigeria. *GOJAMSS,* (8)32–35. Retrieved from http://www.gojamss.net/journal/index.php/gojamss/article/view/41/39

International Monetary Funds (IMF). (2015). *International migration: Recent trends, economic impacts and policy.*

International Organization for Migration (IOM). (2014). Dimensions of crisis on migration in Somalia: Working paper February 2014. Retrieved from https://www.iom.int/files/live/sites/iom/files/Country/docs/Dimensions-of-Crisis-on-Migrationin-Somalia.pdf

International Organization for Migration (IOM). (2016). *Migration in Nigeria: A country profile 2014.* Retrieved from https://publications.iom.int/system/files/pdf/mp_nigeria.pdf

International Organization for Migration (IOM). (2017a). *Enabling a better understanding of migration flows and (its root-causes) from Ethiopia towards Europe* (Desk-Review Report). Displacement Tracking Matrix (DTM). International Organization for Migration.

International Organization for Migration (IOM). (2017b). *Enabling a better understanding of migration flows and (its root-causes) from Nigeria towards*

268   O. M. ADETUTU ET AL.

Europe (Desk-Review Report). Displacement Tracking Matrix (DTM). International Organization for Migration.

International Organization for Migration (IOM). (2017c). *Enabling a better understanding of migration flows (and its root causes) from Somalia towards Europe* (Desk Review Report). Displacement Tracking Matrix (DTM).

International Organization for Migration (IOM) DTM Nigeria. (2017). *Nigeria—Round XIV report.* Retrieved from https://drive.google.com/file/d/0B3CEVcVlpFxORmU4TDlLcEtBemM/view

International Organisation for Migration Displacement Tracking Matrix (DTM). (2018). *Enabling a better understanding of migration flows (and its root-causes) from Nigeria towards Europe Final Report.*

Isiugo-Abanihe, U., & International Organisation for Migration (IOM) Nigeria. (2014). *Migration in Nigeria: A country profile.* Retrieved from https://publications.iom.int/system/files/pdf/mp_nigeria.pdf

Kahneman, D. (2011). *Thinking, fast and slow.* New York: Farrar, Straus and Giroux.

Khoir, S., Du, J. T., & Koronios, A. (2015). Linking everyday information behaviour and Asian immigrant settlement processes: Towards a conceptual framework. *Australian Academic & Research Libraries, 46*(2), 86–100.

Kleist, N. (2017). Disrupted migration projects: The moral economy of involuntary return of Ghana from Libya. *Africa, 87*(2), 322–342.

Kley, S. (2011). Explaining the stages of migration within a life-course framework. *European Sociological Review, 27*(4), 469–486.

Lutz, P. (2017). Two logics of policy intervention in immigration integration: An institutionalist framework based on capabilities and aspirations. *Comparative Migration Studies, 5*(19), 1–18.

MacDonald, J. S., & MacDonald, L. D. (January 1964). Chain migration ethnic neighborhood formation and social networks. *The Milbank Memorial Fund Quarterly, 42*(1), 82–97. Published By: Wiley.

Massey, D. S., Arango, J., Hugo, G., Kouaouci, A., Pellegrino, A., & Taylor, J. E. (1993). Theories of international migration: A review and appraisal. *Population and Development Review, 19*(3), 431–466.

Mberu, B., & Pongou, R. (2010). *Nigeria: Multiple forms of mobility in Africa's demographic giant.* Migration Policy Institute. Retrieved from http://www.migrationpolicy.org/article/nigeria-multiple-forms-mobility-africasdemographic-giant

Mengiste, T. A. (2019). Precarious mobility: Infrastructures of Eritrean migration through the Sudan and the Sahara Desert. *African Human Mobility Review, 5*(1), 1482–1509.

Moyo, I., Nshimbi, C. C., & Laine, J. (2020). *Migration conundrums, regional integration and development: Africa-Europe relations in a changing global order.* Palgrave Macmillan.

TRANSNATIONALISM REVISITED: INTERROGATING ... 269

Newell, B. C., Gomez, R., & Guajardo, V. E. (2016). Information seeking technology use and vulnerability among migrants at the United States-Mexico border. *The Information Society, 32*(3), 176–191.

Oucho, J. O. (2011). "Transforming migration from the stepchild of demography to the core of African development agenda: The Legacy of Aderanti Adepoju." In *Migration in the Service of African Development*. Ibadan: Safari Books Ltd.

Ruedin, D., & Nesturi, M. (2018). Choosing to migrate illegally: Evidence from return migrants. *International Migration, 56*(4), 235–249.

Schapendonk, J. (2010). Staying put in moving sands. The stepwise migration process of sub saharan African migrants heading north. In P. Nugent & U. Engel(Eds.), *Re-shaping Africa* (pp. 113–138). Leiden: Brill.

Sibal, H. T., & Foo, S. (2016). A study on the information seeking behaviour of Singapore-based Filipino domestic workers. *Information Development, 32*(5), 1570–1584.

Smith, S. (2019). *The scramble for Europe: Young Africa on its way to the old continent*. Wiley.

Tabor, A., Milfont, T., & Ward, C. (2015). International migration decision-making and destination selection among skilled migrants. *Journal of Pacific Rim Psychology, 9*(1), 28–41.

UNHCR. (2017). Nigeria situation UNHCR regional update. Retrieved from https://reliefweb.int/sites/reliefweb.int/files/resources/UNHCRRegi onalUpdate-NigeriaSituation-May2017.pdf

United Nations Department of Economic and Social Affairs (UN DESA). (2015). *International Migration Stock 2015*. Retrieved from http://www.un. org/en/development/desa/population/migration/data/estimates2/estima tes15.shtml

United Nations Department of Economic and Social Affairs (UN DESA). (2016). *International Migration Report 2015: Highlights*. Retrieved from http://www.un.org/en/development/desa/population/migration/publicati ons/migrationreport/docs/MigrationReport2015_Highlights.pdf

United Nations High Commissioner for Refugees (UNHCR). (2015). *Population statistics*. Retrieved from http://popstats.unhcr.org/en/persons_of_c oncern

United Nations High Commissioner for Refugees 53. World Bank. (2016). *Population, Nigeria*. Retrieved from https://data.worldbank.org/country/ Nigeria

China in Africa: Whose Interest?

Folasade Abiodun

1 Introduction

China and Africa's relationship is not a recent development. Nevertheless, in recent times it has become a topical issue, as the relationship continues to grow and stable. Despite the geographical distance between China and the Continent of Africa, the relationship/ties keep strengthening across several sectors, ranging from trade relations, health, education, etc.

The burgeoning relationship between Africa and China continues to generate divergent controversies. One school of thought thinks that the relationship will be beneficial for the development of both parties while another school of thought is of the view that China is the major beneficiary of the relationship in the long run such that the mineral resources of Africa will be transferred to China for its development leaving Africa empty with environmental and economic consequences.

The first diplomatic relationship between China and an African country was with Egypt in 1955, a fallout of the 1955 Bandung Conference (Large, 2008). China's presence at this time is after many countries

---

F. Abiodun (✉)
Migration and Development in Africa Monitors (MDAM), Ile-Ife, Nigeria
e-mail: jegedefolasade80@gmail.com

© The Author(s), under exclusive license to Springer Nature Switzerland AG 2023
A. I. Adeniran (ed.), *African Development and Global Engagements*,
https://doi.org/10.1007/978-3-031-21283-3_13

271

had established a presence in Africa. The Bandung Conference of 1955 signified the hallmark of an official/notable relationship between China and Africa. Few countries (6) that were independent of colonialists participated in the Conference. The countries are Egypt, Ethiopia, Liberia, Libya, Ghana, and Sudan. Among the principles emphasized at the Conference, Five Principles were dubbed to be essential to China's foreign policy. They include, Mutual Respect for Sovereignty and Territorial Integrity, Mutual Non-Aggression, Equality, Mutual Benefit, Peaceful Coexistence, and Non-Interference with Political Affairs of Host States unlike the Western colonial with remarkable political interference (Hanauer & Morris, 2014).

Initially, the alliance between Africa and China was politically inclined toward two objectives: The emancipation of colonized African countries from Western colonialists and the recognition of China as a member of the United Nations Security Council.[1]

Global development and a conspicuous deficit in infrastructure in many African countries created a gap for China to fill. Foreign Direct Investment in Africa covers several sectors with a greater focus on mineral resources. The achievements of China in providing infrastructures in several countries especially less developed countries are applaudable. Bilateral trade partnerships between China and African countries have improved the economy.

Albeit the benefits the relations between the parties have attained, this work has not lost direction on the adverse effect which may not necessarily be immediate the relations may generate in Africa such as environmental degradation (a current ravaging threat in Africa), an outcome/stemming from mining activities. The trade imbalance between the parties may lead to total self-reliance of Africa on importation discouraging local producers.

Aside from assessing the instant/short-term benefits of infrastructure, and the economic benefits of revenue from mineral resources, this work will carry out a holistic effect of the long-term impact of the consequential environmental degradation and overly reliant on importation. The

---

[1] Anastasia, China in Africa: the history of Sino-African relations, place of Africa in Chinese foreign policy, and the main spheres of cooperation. People's Friendship of Russia, August 2020. ResearchGate, p. 75. AnastasiaZabellaChinainAfricathehistoryofS ino-AfricanrelationsplaceofAfricainChineseForeignPolicyandthemainspheresofcooperation SokaUniversity.2020.Vol.13.P.74–89.pdf.

significance of engagement with foreign investors for the development of a country is considered. Also, this work creates an awareness of the imbalance of engagement between China and Africa, and the long-term effect on the environment and economy of African countries. It can be deduced from the outcome of this work that international aid, economic growth, and human development are not at par. International/foreign intervention and economic growth may provide immediate social stability, but it is not a guarantee for sustainable human development.

This paper starts with an explanation of its theoretical framework in which the study approaches are embedded, with its methodology which explains the study's research design. The vacuum that necessitated the engagement of China in Africa with historic and current factors will be discussed. The role of institutions such as the Forum on China–Africa Cooperation (FOCAC) and the African Union (AU) in enhancing China's presence in Africa will be discussed. The progressions and outcomes of China's engagement across Africa with empirical evidence to indicate the development of China in African countries will be considered.

Conclusively, the work ends with a discussion of findings and comments which put the outcome of this work in perspective.

2 THEORETICAL FRAMEWORK

This work focus is centered on the political-ecology approach which refers to a diversity of political, social, and economic interplay/interface and their effect on environmental dynamics and livelihood (Basset & Peimer, 2015). Human activities are expected to have an impact on the environment.

The engagement of China and Africa is bound to have consequences. The social and political needs of both parties initiated their relationship; however, it has traversed these initial reasons. The deficit in development especially infrastructure-wise and the lack of funds by its African counterpart further deepened the relation between China and Africa. The ability of China to make available resources for the development of many African countries initiated the economic relationship between the parties. Since many African countries are heavily endowed in natural/mineral resources, it has provided a leeway to compensate/pay for the infrastructure provided by China. The engagement between the parties appears to be lopsided/asymmetric which will become evident and more disastrous in the long run.

As observed by Simon in Political ecology, vulnerable communities are prone to environmental challenges calculable/fueled by social and political inequities (Batterbury, 2018).

China has also invested enormously in many projects in many African countries, providing physical and social infrastructures. FOCAC has further solidified the relations between African countries and strengthened AU participation in China activities in Africa, FOCAC platform has witnessed writing off debt, an increase in grants and aid, loan, and FDI into many African countries.

In recent times, China's FDI seems to flow to countries rich in raw materials and mineral resources. Bi-lateral trade relation between Africa and China has witnessed exporting of raw materials and mineral resources from African countries to satisfy the needs of the Chinese large population and at the same time improve China's economy. Mining and exploration of raw materials and mineral resources continue to leave environmental concerns in host countries. Importation from China into African countries is mostly manufactured goods.

Aside from the global effect of climate change taking a general heavy toll generally. The constant exploration and mining of raw materials and mineral resources from African countries could adversely affect the Continent, of Africa. This imbalance between Africa and China's trade relations and the downside effect of environmental degradation is inevitable as it promotes the social and economic crisis plaguing Africa especially the Sub-Saharan region of Africa which is termed the poorest part of the world.

The importation into African countries has posed a big threat to manufacturing industries, especially local industries leading to the loss of jobs in this sector and causing African countries to be overly dependent on importation.

Going by this assumption/observation, political ecology runs into inherent political economies as "any change in environmental conditions must affect the political and economic status quo" (Adeniran, 2017).

3   Methodology

This study employs a qualitative methodology approach, and also considers existing works similar to this study, i.e., on China and Africa relationship. This work uses secondary data derived from Government and international institutions this is due to the scarcity of reliable data on China–African relations especially loan agreements (Courage, 2022).

Some African countries especially Sub-Saharan countries that have the largest number of ongoing projects and investments funded by China are considered. Countries such as Nigeria, the Democratic Republic of Congo, Sudan, South Africa, etc. also, countries with a historical background like Egypt are briefly considered. This study also relies on news especially press releases from representatives of government and institutions.

4 ENGAGEMENT OF CHINA IN AFRICA, BALANCE OF ENGAGEMENTS, AND THE ROLES OF INSTITUTION(S)

4.1 Engagement of China in Africa

As stated earlier in the introduction, a diplomatic tie between African countries and China was established in 1955 and since spread to other African countries. This marked a significant era of engagement between China and African countries. China's financial aid to Africa in 1956–1976 is estimated at US$2.4 billion, even though during this period China was struggling economically but it still was providing aid to African countries. Egypt, Somalia, Zaire (now the Democratic Republic of Congo), and Algeria were beneficiaries of financial aid from China.

One of the significant infrastructures in this era by China in Africa is the construction of a railway from Tanzania port to the Cooper field of Zambia (Shinn, 2016). Another successful non-financial aid which is instructive in Africa between 1956 and 1976 is sending medical teams to Africa from China. The first medical team was sent from Hubei Province to Algeria in 1963, a practice maintained and expanded to other African countries. The Sino-Africa relationship has expanded since then, China has shifted from its initial objective of providing aid toward the liberation of African countries from colonization.

As stated earlier, China has become Africa's largest trade partner displacing Europe. The crux of engagement of China in Africa was initially political but has traversed over the years to diverse areas such as health, military, academics, etc., but among these areas, trade ranks prior in the relationship (Hanauer & Morris, 2014).

China's interest in Africa revolves around the following: Access to natural oil and gas, markets for China exports, and political legitimacy in international fora (Hanauer & Morris, 2014). Africa has and continues to provide support for China on the international scene. In 1971 African countries voted in favor of China as a member of the United Nations Security Council and have on occasion obstructed resolutions against China for human rights violations. An AU official has said the relationship between China and Africa is reciprocal looking at the significant historical roles each played; China helped in the decolonization of Africa and Africa's role in securing a seat for China in the UN security council (Asegbe, 2017).

As stated earlier, there is a robust existing trade partnership between China and Africa with remarkable import and export activities between the parties. Nevertheless, there seems to be disparity in the trade partnership. Reports have shown concern about the trade imbalance between China and the host country's economy, especially in Chinese-related investment (Wang & Zadek, 2016).

It is of general knowledge that Africa is naturally endowed with natural resources such as hydrocarbons, minerals, timbers, etc., which have remained untapped. Nigeria, Algeria, Libya, and Angola are large producers of a sizeable amount of fuel globally, other non-fuel minerals are platinum, manganese, cobalt, copper, gold, iron ore, etc., with quite a large number present in Africa.

These resources form the major source of many African countries' income and the major driver of their economy. There continues to be a high demand for these natural resources by China to cater to its large population, fuel, and promote China's economy. On the part of Africa, China represents a major trading partner and investor that buys its mineral resources, provides a market for cheap/affordable goods, and helps to build its infrastructure (Gamache & Hammer, 2013).

China's large population explains its enormous need for its insatiable mineral resources for sustenance from Africa. This has been linked to China's resource security for its population hence its social stability (Alves, 2009). Even though China produces oil, it is not enough to meet up with its domestic needs/demands. According to the Organization of the Petroleum Exporting Countries (OPEC), over the years

China's consumption of oil has doubled making it the second-highest oil consumer in the world, which is expected to double by 2030.[2] The oil and gas industry is not the only industry China is deeply engaged in Africa, there are other sectors of extractive industry that China is engaged in Africa. There has been a steady increase in the export of minerals from Africa to China since early 2000. Chinese imports of non-fuel mining products from Africa increased from $286 million in 2000 to $2.6 billion in 2006. In 2006 diamonds imports occupied the largest share (27%), followed by platinum (17%), copper (15%), cobalt, and manganese (11% each). Here as well, an evolving reliance is starting to show. Over 80% of China's cobalt and 40% of manganese imports originate in Africa, with the Democratic Republic of Congo (DRC) and Gabon, respectively, the main suppliers (Alden & Alves, 2009).

According to World Bank, China surpassed other countries on the chart of trade partners with Sub-Saharan Africa in 2019.[3] Between 2015 and 2019, the Sub-Saharan Africa Export to China stands at USD 45,548 million. Top of the list of goods exported to China from Sub-Saharan Africa is raw materials, fuels, and minerals, while China's imports to Sub-Saharan Africa stand at USD 25,987 million. Top of the list of the imported goods from China to African countries are capital goods, machines and electronics, consumer goods, and intermediate goods while ranking least are fuels, vegetables, minerals, and animals. Sub-Saharan countries form most countries in the African continent, 48 out of the 54 countries in Africa are Sub-Saharan countries.

China is known for its big market to produce consumer goods, Africa being an abode of less developed countries with its large population provides a large market for China's 'affordable' consumer goods in Africa. The affordability of the large teaming population of the less developed countries dominant in Africa may readily explain its dominance in African countries (Hanauer & Morris, 2014).

Albeit, Activities of China in Africa have not been entirely smooth, there have been some diplomatic rows that have cost China some form of a setback in their relations with some African countries as a result of cultural revolution, communal crisis, conflict of locals, etc. (China

---

[2] OPEC (Organisation of Petroleum Exporting Countries), World Oil Outlook 2008, p. 46. http://www.opec.org/library/world%20oil%20outlook/WorldOilOutlook08.htm.

[3] World integrated Solutions. https://wits.worldbank.org/CountrySnapshot/en/SSF.

2019, p. 66). The outbreak of Coronavirus pandemic also challenged the China–Africa relations, albeit, this has not been strong enough to deter the continuous and burgeoning presence of China in Africa.

5 Forum on China–African Cooperation (FOCAC)

FOCAC is a forum for solidarity and cooperation between China and Africa toward the development of both parties. It was established in the year 2000. The objectives of the Forum are equal consultation, enhancing understanding, expanding consensus, strengthening friendship, and promoting cooperation. The birth of FOCAC is to further strengthen the ties between China and Africa. True to its goal, several initiatives and mechanisms were put in place that facilitated relations between the parties. Between 1999 and 2008, trade soared between China and Africa from US$2 billion to US$108 billion.[4] Through FOCAC China pledged a huge amount of money to Africa for its development, the most recent is the pledge of a 60 billion USD loan by the President of China to Africa during the 2018 FOCAC Summit. Incentives such as debt relief, unprecedented financial assistance by China in favor of Africa, increase in loans and grants from China, construction of infrastructure facilities, tariff exempted goods between Africa and China are on the rise. The exchange program and cultural interaction are all geared to strengthen the Africa–China relationship.

6 Role of the African Union (AU) in China–Africa Relations

African Union was established in 2002 it consists of African Countries. AU is a successor of the Organization of African Union (OAU) which was initially established in 1963. One of its objectives is to rid the continent of any form of colonization and apartheid, promote unity and solidarity, safeguard sovereignty, play a vital role in the global economy, etc. Part of these objectives aligns with the principles adopted at the Bandung conference and FOCAC's Objectives. Generally, AU continues to provide

---

[4] Institute of Developing Economies Japan External Trade Organization. https://www.ide.go.jp/English/Data/Africa_file/Manualreport/cia_04.html.

support, and collaborate with China toward its expansion in Africa in different areas.

Apart from bilateral pacts with individual states, China also partners with regional and sub-regional bodies. Although there are early dealings between AU and China, AU was officially admitted as a full member of FOCAC in 2011 lifting it from the position of an observer, with rights to attend meetings.[5] China's partnership with AU has recorded tremendous progress and has further reinforced the China–African relationship. The AU complex was built and donated by the Chinese government free of charge in 2012 a year after its admission into FOCAC. Among other activities, China is involved in peacekeeping missions in Africa.[6]

AU and China interactions continue to deepen and expand China's tentacles in Africa. The recently concluded FOCAC summit held in Dakar Senegal in 2021 emphasized this. The Summit agreed and reiterated cooperation in the following areas;

The two sides recognize the significant role of the AU in safeguarding peace and stability and promoting the integration of Africa. China commends the new progress made by Africa in seeking strength through unity and notes the important results achieved in the institutional reform of the African Union. The African side appreciates China's efforts and contributions to promoting peace, stability, and development in Africa.

The two sides agree to consolidate and strengthen China's cooperation with the AU and its affiliated institutions, Africa's sub-regional organizations, to continue holding the China–African Union Strategic Dialogue, and to strengthen communication and coordination between China and Africa's sub-regional organizations so that China–Africa transnational and trans-regional cooperation will deliver more outcomes.

The African side commends China for supporting the AU and Africa's sub-regional organizations in upgrading public service facilities, improving office conditions, and enhancing public service capacity. China

---

[5] African Union, Africa-China, China–Africa Cooperation (FOCAC). https://au.int/en/partnerships/africa_china.

[6] Asegbe Debelo (2017), African Peacebuilding Network, The African Union's Peace and Security Partnership, Social Science Researvh Council. https://s3.amazonaws.com/ssrc-cdn1/crmuploads/new_publication_3/the-african-union-s-peace-and-security-partnership-with-china.pdf.

pledged to continue to support the capacity building of the AU and Africa's regional organizations.

China notes with appreciation that the African Continental Free Trade Area (AfCFTA) has entered the implementation stage and will set up an expert group on economic cooperation with the secretariat of the AfCFTA, and continue to support the development of the free trade area and the secretariat of the AfCFTA.

7 Impact/Effect of Coronavirus Pandemic (COVID-19) on China–African Relations

COVID-19 pandemic took the entire world by surprise, consequently, countries and regions had to make decisions they deem reasonable/necessary to tackle the pandemic. Several countries were placed on lockdown restricting movement within and out of many countries for a while in the year 2020. China and African countries were not left out of the lockdown, consequently affecting the relations especially trade activities.

Howbeit, the pandemic period reinforced the China–African relationship despite the challenges posed by it. According to a press release by Mr. Gao Feng the Spokesperson of China's Ministry of Commerce (MOFCOM) in January 2021, he stated that both parties provided medical support to each other during the pandemic such as medical supplies and personnel were made available, and the Africa headquarters of CDC was constructed by China.

There was a bit of a setback in trade and project completion in Africa but the same gathered momentum and stabilized shortly afterward. This ease of comeback is attributed to the resilience of the China–African relation. China's investment in Agriculture in Africa also witnessed a considerable change during this period. The use of technology was useful in minimizing the effects of the pandemic on trade between China and Africa. Digital online activities such as big data, cloud computing, mobile payment, live streaming of trade fairs, etc. were deployed by both parties.[7]

The pandemic surprisingly fostered a stronger and better relationship between Africa and China.

[7] Regular Conference of MOFCOM. http://english.mofcom.gov.cn/article/newsrelease/press/202101/20210103032253.shtml.

8 EXTENT OF BALANCE OF ENGAGEMENTS

There are diverse opinions on the relations between China and African countries, there are speculations that its asymmetric. President Xi Jinping, during the 2018 FOCAC noted that it is a mutual benefit between China and African countries and a win–win situation leading to growth in both Africa and China, especially since things such as food, security, etc. that form the basis of human rights and development are the core being promoted in Africa (Taylor, 2008).

However, Western countries are of a divergent view, they hold the opinion that China is not genuinely interested in the development of Africa rather its 'voracious' and 'insatiable' appetite for the continent's mineral resources will further perpetuate underdevelopment in countries in Africa (Hanauer & Morris, 2014).

On the part of Africa, there have been mixed reactions to the asymmetric or otherwise nature of the parties, while governments in Africa view China's presence in Africa as helpful and pivotal to the growth of the continent, especially in the area of infrastructure. Institutions, Civil societies, and individual persons have raised alarm and expressed concern about China's engagements in some of the countries, especially in terms of loan agreements and other financial aid between some African countries and China institutions. Between 2000 and 2019 Chinese financiers have signed 153 billion worth of USD with different African governments.[8] Other concerns are environmental degradation from mining activities, unfair labor practices, violation of human rights, etc. All these concerns are feared to be gradually towing the path of colonialism of Africa by China.

Between 2013 and 2020, the bulk of outward projects into Africa from China are majorly mining activities and the construction of infrastructure. Some of these projects are equity investment projects which mean China owns shares in the project while some are joint ventures i.e., public–private cooperation between the host country and China.

Some of these projects are geared toward the improvement of the livelihood and condition of the citizens of the host country while some of the infrastructure projects are designed to boost international and regional

---

[8] China Africa Research Initiative, John Hopkins, School of Advanced International Studies. http://www.sais-cari.org/data.

trade for example the construction of the BUBA regional port/rail in Guinea Bissau.

Some of the terms of some projects may not be to the advantage of some African countries in terms of development and self-reliance, for example, construction according to part of the terms of the contract, shows that a large number of real estate construction in Nigeria is handled by Chinese owned companies, thereby placing real estate contractors at disadvantage in Nigeria. Profits made from these projects are taken back to China.

9 IMPACT OF CHINA'S ENGAGEMENT IN AFRICA—WHOSE INTEREST?

At the macroeconomic level, the economic relationship between China and African countries has recorded remarkable economic growth (Wang & Zadek, 2016). For example, in 1956 shortly after the Bandung conference of 1955, China opened a trade office in Cairo, Egypt. China became the largest exporter of Egypt's cotton helping to stabilize the economy of Egypt in times of crisis, China's trade activities with Egypt played a significant role back then (David Shinn, 2016).

Infrastructure development orchestrated by China in Africa cannot be underestimated. Infrastructural projects that facilitate transportation, and communication has been widespread on the continent. Even though infrastructural development has been linked to economic development, this has become debatable in Africa, some of these infrastructures are said to be at the advantage of China's ease of access and movement of Africa's mineral resources, for example, the railway built in Tanzania, from Tanzania port to the Cooper field of Zambia.

Again, the impact of economic growth facilitated by infrastructure has become questionable in Africa and the infrastructure has done little to the diversification of Africa's economy which is majorly centered around natural resources and it is yet to promote industrialization (Alves, 2013). There are other contrary views considering the GDP and per capita, for example, there are clear indications that Ethiopia and Kenya's production capacity has increased due to the construction of infrastructure by China in these countries (Cooper, 2019).

Chinese investments in Africa are widespread across different countries and sectors. It is worthy of note that China's investments are no longer solely funded by states, there has been a shift to private enterprises as part of investors in projects in African countries (Kragelund & Van Dijk, 2009). It is observed that in recent times, Chinese investment has been more concentrated in oil-producing states such as Nigeria, Angola, and Sudan. Between 2003 and 2008, China's investment concentration shifted from North Africa to other parts of the Continent. The reason behind the shift has alluded to the economic diversification of investment by China but a further look at the beneficiaries of these investment consists of countries rich in raw materials (Claassen et al., 2012). This is not to say that other countries without resources are not beneficiaries of investment from China but not as enormous as their counterparts.

To buttress the findings above, twenty (20) African countries were beneficiaries of FDI from China between 2003 and 2008. South Africa, Nigeria, Zambia, Algeria, and Sudan top the list of the FDI recipient, respectively, as they account for 86.5% of the total Chinese investment in Africa. South Africa tops with an average of USD 896 m. Countries that are large recipients of the FDI are Countries that are the drivers of Africa's economy responsible for 97% of Africa's GDP growth between 2000 and 2008. "As stated earlier, there is a massive demand for energy in China with a matching resource from Africa, about 37.9% of China's FDI in Africa is directed toward the energy sector.[9] These countries were classified as either diversified, oil-exporting, pre-transition, or transition economies, according to their exports per capita and economic diversification" (Claassen et al., 2012).

From 2005 to 2019, the total FDI flow from China into Africa amounted to $95.7 billion, within this period, only 6.5% of China's FDI went to North Africa compared to what was formerly obtainable. About one-third of the investment was directed to West African countries. Over 40.3% of China's FDI flows in Africa are concentrated in just three countries: Nigeria, South Africa, and the Democratic Republic of Congo.

While China's presence in Africa is significant especially in the extractive industry, China has played a significant role in the construction of infrastructures in Africa. China has signed about 544 construction

---

[9] Chinapower unpacking the complexity of China's rise, Does China dominate global investment? https://chinapower.csis.org/china-foreign-direct-investment/. See also United Nations Conference on Trade and Development (UNCTAD), World Investment Project. https://unctad.org/en/Pages/DIAE/FDI%20Statistics/FDI-Statistics.aspx, see also https://project.mofcom.gov.cn/.

contracts in Africa from 2005–2019 worth $267.7 billion. Nigeria, Algeria, Ethiopia, Egypt, and Angola record the highest destination for construction contracts. Most of the Chinese contracts in this region are in the Transportation and Energy sector. The highest contract was a contract for the construction of a major railway in Nigeria connecting Lagos state the highest populated and the commercial hub of Nigeria located in the Western part of the Country to Kano State in the Northern part of the Country; the contract is worth USD 6.7 billion executed by China Civil Engineering Construction Company (CCECC). Within the energy sector, the largest contract was a $4.4 billion deal signed in 2018 between two Chinese companies—Dongfang Electric and Shanghai Electric—and the Egyptian government to build multiple coal-fired power plants in Egypt.

10   Long-Term Projections of China and Africa Relations

FOCAC continues to be a significant forum for Sino-Africa relations, at the recent FOCAC summit a long-term plan, and vision 2035 between Africa and China was declared. In the execution of this long-term projection, China and Africa considered the following, the Long-Range Goals for 2035 of China, the 2030 Agenda for Sustainable Development of the United Nations, and the Agenda 2063 of the African Union, thus drawing a long-term blueprint for China–Africa practical cooperation.

Beyond the laid-out projections by the parties, the impact of the activities of the parties needs to be considered especially the trade and mining activities that form the fulcrum of the present relations between the parties and the indebtedness of African countries to China.

10.1   Environmental Impact

The recent/continuous China–Africa relations are premised on the meeting of China's burgeoning need and energy demand to meet up with their needs and on the flipside a supply from African countries to keep servicing the energy needs of China, a population of 1.3 billion people making it the one of largest energy consumer globally. The environmental impact of the continuous supply of energy may pose a challenge that is more than the immediate economic benefit to the host country, some of the environmental effects are irreversible. This is besides the fact that natural resources from Africa are taken away to build up the economy and improve the economy of China.

The African continent does not have uniform climates and ecological zones, hence determining or generalizing the environment may be impossible. Africa host about 1.1 billion people and the population keeps expanding by the day. Already, the Continent has the largest number of poorest people in the world and is vulnerable to side effects of global climate change (Shinn, 2016). Several African countries are battling environmental degradation caused by deforestation, desertification, mining, reduced soil productivity, pollution, etc. (Shinn, 2016). Mining activities especially oil exploration, gold mining, etc. are common in Africa, being the major source of the economy of many African countries. Undoubtedly, this has led to an increase in revenue for the countries, but it carries adverse effects alongside.

For example, in Nigeria, oil exploration in the Niger Delta region of the country has led to disastrous unquantifiable environmental degradation such as land and water pollution which has led to the destruction of aquatic resources, destruction of farmland, among others (Elum et al., 2016). Aside from oil pollution, there is the menace of air pollution caused by gas flaring by oil-producing companies, which in turn reduces the quality of air. This environmental degradation has led to loss of lives, means of livelihood especially farming and fishing are the major occupation of residents in oil-producing communities. The exploration activities have also led to communal conflict and crises in the regions. These have undermined the benefits of oil richness and exploration in the immediate community and the country at large. Some of these oil-rich communities are yet to record any improvement in their livelihood but rather have fueled poverty partly due to the environmental effect (Elum et al., 2016).

China itself as a country is threatened with environmental pollution from industrialization. In time past, Chinese companies have been observed not to follow the best practices in ameliorating environmental impact in their dealings/activities. Also, Chinese companies operating overseas may ignore social and environmental impacts due to competitiveness and profitability (Wang & Zadek, 2016). In recent times there are arguments on whether China has been active in curbing/ameliorating the environmental challenges posed by its activities. There is suggestive participation by China in environmental assessment policies, law-making, etc. that tend to address environmental issues, all geared toward enhancing the environment by China and Chinese-owned companies. For example, the Export–Import Bank of China has urged Chinese companies to observe and comply with laws on the environment in the host countries in which they are investing (Shinn, 2016). In 2013, the MOFCOM and Ministry of Environment issued a 'voluntary' guideline urging Chinese companies investing abroad to follow the guidelines to also carry out environmental impact assessments further, make effort to mitigate environmental risks and respond in case of emergency. Also, FOCAC Summits, 2006 Beijing Summit, and 2021 Dakar Senegal Summit have highlighted sustainable environmentally friendly practices as one of FOCAC's objectives.

These endeavors alongside other activities such as active participation with the United Nations on environmental enhancement send a signal of China's genuine commitment toward environmental alertness by China.

However, the implementation and sincerity in the enforcement of these laws and steps have been in doubt. Compliance by Chinese companies with the ethics of environmental protection compared to Western countries differs, the former, not in total observance of environmental guidelines. There are arguments that the penalty on offenders is mild, not strong enough to encourage compliance. Correspondingly there are no incentives for those that comply with environmentally friendly guidelines. Another study shows that Chinese companies have made tremendous efforts in implementing pollution control practices and are increasingly promoting the use of clean energy and environmentally friendly practices. It is concluded that Chinese businesses still observe minimal adherence to local environmental standards, rather than complete adherence to the best environmental management practices.[10]

As China keeps facing environmental challenges/threats due to its industrial activities, there are indications that China may ameliorate the threat by moving some industries with a high environmental threat to other parts of the world including Africa (Shinn, 2016). African Countries continue to press China to open industries in their countries for development purposes and to provide for its burgeoning population. For example, Hebei Iron and Steel signed a deal to start the construction of the largest overseas steel in South Africa in 2017 although South Africa is not the only country in China that is making plans to establish steel companies (Yap, 2014). What stands this construction out is the fact

---

[10] See Institute for global ethics, sustainable business relations between China and Africa: Report on the dialogue in South Africa 25–27 (Ignace Haaz ed., 2015).

CHINA IN AFRICA: WHOSE INTEREST? 287

that Hebei Province which hosts the largest iron and steel company may close its industries in China. It is worthy of note that this steel and iron company emits so much sulfur, nitrogen dioxide, and dust that adversely pollutes the air in Beijing (Shinn, 2016).

Chinese state-owned and private-owned companies are engaged in several mining activities in Africa. In Sudan, activities of oil exploration by The China National Petroleum Corporation (CNPC) (the leading oil company in China) have led to the destruction of farmlands, deforestation, pollution of water leading to loss of water resources, diseases in the immediate community, loss of livestock. etc. Although Chinese companies tried to mitigate the effect by providing infrastructural and social facilities, it has been opined that the activities of CNPC leading to environmental degradation overseas are not a surprise because "the company has a deplorable track record in environmental management at home."[11]

Aside from the above concern, there have been a series of complaints of environmental pollution by Chinese-owned companies in some African countries. For example, in Ethiopia, a Chinese company was forced to shut down for a while due to complaints of pollution shortly after it kick-started operation (Shinn, 2016). In Somaliland, residents have made complaints against a Chinese subsidiary firm, Jeronimo Group Industries and Trading PLC for water pollution by dumping waste into the water causing danger to livestock. Somaliland's government has been reluctant to intervene for fear of discouraging foreign investors (Williams, 2013). In Nigeria, the Government of Rivers State sealed off a Chinese company for aggravated air pollution, and breach of environmental laws in the State, following complaints by residents in the area (Ukpong, 2017). There are also accusations of Chinese companies fueling deforestation in some parts of West Africa by engaging in illegal timber felling in conspiracy with some of the government officials (Akana, 2016).

This is not to say that environmental degradation is peculiar to Chinese companies as investors in Africa, however as indicated earlier, China is presently the largest African trade partner, therefore their activities in Africa are enormous with a potential for a long-term presence.

---

[11] Qian Zhen, Chinese Oil Companies in South Sudan's Conflict Environment, in Oil, Security, and Community Engagement, 31, 32–33 (Saferworld ed., 2013) (discussing the efforts undertaken by Chinese corporations to offset negative environmental impacts in Africa).

288   F. ABIODUN

African leaders have been accused of being docile in taking active steps to combat investors' activities prone to environmental degradation activities for fear of losing investors, desperation to create jobs, corruption of officials responsible to enforce the laws, and non-fulfilling existing obligations to foreign investors.

11   CHINA'S LOAN TO AFRICA COUNTRIES

There is no gainsaying that the infrastructure deficit explains the enormous presence of China in Africa in contemporary times. Despite extant orthodox financiers such as International Monetary Fund, World Bank, etc., not only China has become Africa's largest trade partner, it has become its largest creditor (Mlambo, 2022). Many African Governments still prefer to lend from China, this preference has been attributed to fewer strict terms such as low-interest rates, long maturity period, grace period, etc. With all of these advantages, there are worries that some of the loan agreements are not transparent (Courage, 2022). The growing indebtedness of Africa to China has raised several potential consequences such as control and dominance of the continent tilting the continent back to neo-colonialism and debt trap diplomacy among others. Even though some of these infrastructures have been implemented it doesn't pay off the debt owed by African countries. The motives behind the loans to Africa have been questioned especially the inability of some African countries to pay off the loan.

11.1   Local Producers—Trade Imbalance

As observed earlier, African countries export more natural resources to China while most importation of China into African countries are intermediate goods. The data from the World Bank on trade between China and Sub-Saharan countries which consists of 48 out of 54 African countries indicates that many Saharan countries are large importers of commodities from China due to its low cost irrespective of the quality. The importation of goods into many African countries has reduced local production within the continent and therefore increase dependent on importation. This has threatened local producers and local markets in Africa. Zambia has had to put measures in place to protect its local market (Wang & Zadek, 2016, p. 17).

The former President of South Africa Jacob Zuma at the Beijing FOCAC Summit stated that there is an unequal trade relationship between China and South Africa, which may not be sustainable. This imbalance relationship has raised concerns about deindustrialization in South Africa. Importation from China has been at the expense of local production (Edward & Jenkins, 2015). This continues to drift African countries away from self-reliance and total dependence on importation for survival.

In Kenya, an interview of the local producers shows that the massive importation of Chinese goods into Kenya has become a threat to local producers, the local artisans have complained that they are losing their market to Chinese trade.[12]

12 Discussion of Findings

In this work, I have explored the relationship between China and African countries; the relations between the parties and the impact on the economy of both countries and ultimately on the environment of the African countries. In so doing, I looked briefly at the impact of the various investment project especially the environmental effect of some of these investment projects on the host countries and the long-term role/effect of the trade relationship between the parties. Alongside I looked at the economic impact on the local producers.

I, therefore, made some recommendations, it is suggested that one of the several ways to improve an economy is opening up such an economy by encouraging investors just like the existing relations between China and African countries. If the relationship is done appropriately and there is a balance between Africa and China, there is likely to be a sustainable relationship between the two parties that will be beneficial to the development of both China and African countries. There has been improvement in the economy of some African countries since the relationship between Africa and China, there must be an assurance of sustainability. It is observed that there is an imbalance between China and many African countries. This disparity is reflected in the type of commodities that form trade relations, the immediate and long-term effect is a point of concern that constitute social, physical, and political. It is suggested/hoped that

---

[12] Victoria Amunga, Chinese Import Edging Out Kenya's Local Product. https://www.voanews.com/a/chinese-imports-edging-out-kenya-s-local-products-/6480276.html.

for a sustainable relationship, measures should be taken to ameliorate the effect of environmental impact in the host countries by deploying measures and technologies that will aid the minimal impact/effect of mining activities. An effective monitoring and evaluation (M&E) mechanism must be in place to ensure compliance with the safest and best practices of mining activities. The goal of this study is to show that there is an imbalance/disparity in the relations between China and African countries.

In some instances where the environmental effect cannot be escaped, there should be plans/technical know-how to cushion the effect of impact/consequences of mining activities and or return to the original state as close as possible. There should be a collaboration between local producers/manufacturers for the production of commodities to ensure balance in imported and exported commodities.

The second goal of this work is to create awareness among the policymakers on the imbalance of the existing relationship in relation to the host country who will suffer the effect/impact on the host countries.

13 Conclusion

There is no doubt that Chinese relations in African countries have improved the economy and engineered development, especially the infrastructure. However, the existing obstacle/barriers such as institutional corruption, trade imbalance, and environmental degradation must be addressed.

To ensure sustainable healthy and balanced relations between the parties, there should be a transformation from reliance on majorly Chinese goods to self-reliance and sustainable growth of the economy. Also, the continuous indebtedness of many African countries to China may propagate the inability of many African countries from being self-reliant. There should be a transfer of technical know-how from Chinese companies to African countries, to reduce the importation of human power from China.

There is no doubt that investment loans can lead to development by looking at their immediate and long-term benefits, however, it should be borne in mind that excessive loans can be detrimental to the economy in the long run thereby undermining the aim of infrastructure. Debt obligation may limit the chances for African countries of self-reliance and independence.

References

Adeniran, A. I. (2017). Repository Africa in the evolving "Chinese Century": The Uneven Sino-Nigerian water conservation partnership. *Journal of Current Chinese Affairs, 46*(3), 33–52.

Akana, D. (2016, January 18). *How China fuels deforestation in Nigeria, West Africa*. https://infocongo.org/fr/how-china-fuels-deforestation-in-nigeria-west-africa/

Alden, C., & Alves, A. (2009). *China and Africa's natural resources: The challenges and implications for development and governance*. South African Institute of International Affairs, https://www.africaportal.org/documents/771/SAIIA_Occasional_Paper_41.pdf

Alves, A. C. (2009). *China and Africa's natural resources: The challenges and implications for development and governance*. South African Institute of International Affairs. https://www.africaportal.org/publications/china-and-africas-natural-resources-the-challenges-and-implications-for-development-and-governance/

Alves, A. C. (2013). China's 'win-win' cooperation: Unpacking the impact of infrastructure-for resources deals in Africa. *South African Journal of International Affairs, 20*(2), 207–226. https://doi.org/10.1080/10220461.2013.811337

Asegbe, D. (2017). African peacebuilding network. *The African Union's Peace and Security Partnership, Social Science Researvh Council*. https://s3.amazonaws.com/ssrc-cdn1/crmuploads/new_publication_3/the-african-union-s-peace-and-security-partnership-with-china.pdf

Batterbury, S. (2018). *The companion of environmental studies* (p. 4). University of Melbourne, Routlege. https://www.researchgate.net/publication/325943652_Political_ecology

Claassen, C., Loots, E., & Bezuidenhout, H. (2012). Chinese foreign direct investment in Africa: Making sense of a new economic reality. *African Journal of Business Management, 6*(47), 11583–11597. http://www.academicjournals.org/AJBM

Cooper, R. (2019). *The development impact of Chinese development investments in Africa* (K4D Emerging Issues Report). Institute of Development Studies. https://www.usitc.gov/publications/332/2013-04_China-Africa%28GamacheHammerJones%29.pdf

Courage, M. (2022). China in Africa: An examination of the impact of China's loans on growth in selected African States. *Economies, 10*(7), 154. https://doi.org/10.3390/economies10070154

Edward, L., & Jenkins, R. (2015). The impact of Chinese import penetration on the South African manufacturing sector. *The Journal of Development Studies, 51*(4), 447–463. https://doi.org/10.1080/00220388.2014.983912

Elum, Z. A., Mopipi, K., & Henri-Ukoha, A. (2016). Oil exploitation and its socioeconomic effects on the Niger Delta region of Nigeria. *Environmental Science and Pollution Research, 23,* 12880–12889. https://doi.org/10.1007/s11356-016-6864-1

Gamache, L., & Hammer, A. (2013). *China's trade and investment relationship with Africa.* USITC Executive Briefings on Trade. https://assets.publishing.service.gov.uk/media/5e9d791386650c031f757047/EIR26_The_development_impact_of_Chinese_development__nvestment__in_Africa.pdf

Hanauer, L., & Morris, L. J. (2014). *Chinese engagement in Africa, drivers, reactions and implications for U.S policy.* RAND National Security Research Division. https://books.google.com.ng/books?hl=en&lr=&id=6YZFAwAAQBAJ&oi=fnd&pg=PP1&dq=China+engagement+in+Africa+&ots=hJ0lmCpk8J&sig=odAW7OmZgNMDXkEA9Rkw_oe-RlQ&redir_esc=y#v=onepage&q=China%20engagement%20in%20Africa&f=false

Kragelund, P., & Van Dijk, M. (2009). China's investment in Africa. *The New Presence of China in Africa.*

Large, D. (2008). Beyond 'Dragon in the Bush': The study of China–African relations. *African Affairs, 107*(426), 45–61.

Shinn, D. H. (2016). "The environmental impact of China's investment in Africa. *Cornell International Law Journal, 49*(1), Article 2. https://ww3.lawschool.cornell.edu/research/ILJ/upload/Shinn-final.pdf https://scholarship.law.cornell.edu/cilj/vol49/iss1/2

Taylor, I. (2008). Sino-Africa relations and the problems of human rights. *African Affairs, 107*(426), 67.

Thomas, J. B., & Peimer, A. W. (2015). Political ecological perspective and socioecological relations. *Dans Natures Sciences Societes, 23*(2), 157–165.

Ukpong, C. (2017, February 11). *Rivers Toxic Emission: Govt. seals off Chinese company, two others.* https://www.premiumtimesng.com/news/top-news/223235-rivers-toxic-emission-govt-seals-off-chinese-company-two-others.html

Wang, Y., & Zadek, S. (2016, January). *Sustainability impacts of Chinese outward direct investment: A review of the literature* (p. 13). International Institute for Sustainable Development (IISD) Winnipeg Canada. https://www.iisd.org/system/files/publications/sustainability-impacts-chinese-outward-direct-investment-literature-review.pdf

Williams, S. (2013). Chinese factory accused of poisoning Somaliland water supplies. *The Guardian,* July 2. http://www.theguardian.com/environment/2013/jul/02/chinese-factory-somaliland-water

Yap, C.-W. (2014). China's Hebei iron and steel to build plant in South-Africa. *Wall Street Journal.* https://www.wsj.com/articles/chinas-hebei-iron-steel-to-build-plant-in-south-africa-1410497371

Strategic Framework of African Union on the Management of Migration in Africa

Serifat Bolanle Asiyanbi and Omolara Victoria Akinyemi

1 INTRODUCTION

Migration in Africa is as old as human existence (Adepoju, 2008) and has become part and parcel of African culture and tradition. The age-long history of migration in Africa turned migration into a thing of inevitable, particularly in response to natural disasters, political instabilities, and socio-economic impediments. As some households intend to relocate in search of a greener pasture to exit poverty, some are forcefully evicted from their comfortable abode due to persistent internal hostilities. The inflow of migration with severe implications on the economies and social activities of choosing states, aside from reshaping the population

S. B. Asiyanbi (✉) · O. V. Akinyemi
Department of History and International Studies, Federal University, Oye-Ekiti, Nigeria
e-mail: serifat.asiyanbi@fuoye.edu.ng

O. V. Akinyemi
e-mail: akinyemiv@oauife.edu.ng

O. V. Akinyemi
Department of International Relations, Obafemi Awolowo University, Ile-Ife, Nigeria

© The Author(s), under exclusive license to Springer Nature Switzerland AG 2023
A. I. Adeniran (ed.), *African Development and Global Engagements*,
https://doi.org/10.1007/978-3-031-21283-3_14

293

density of such states, makes some member states tighten their borders against further infiltration. Aside from this, the economic war between the migrants and the citizens of host countries over limited resources coupled with the security imbroglio makes the governments of the concerned countries view migration from the lens of burden rather than a propeller of economic growth. Several policies have been put in place to uproot the causes of internal hostilities with the mindset of changing the perception of African leaders towards migration positivism to a sustainable economy in Africa. How do the policies unlock the benefit of migration towards economic equity and development? To what extent have the policies uprooted the roots of internal hostilities and bestowed to the citizens of member states the commitment of African leaders towards the implementation of African policies on migration? These are some of the significant issues addressed in this paper.

2   Conceptual Clarification and Theoretical Underpinning of Migration

Migration is a situational concept without a uniform definition. The complexity of the concept makes different scholars conceptualize it based on their perceptions. Tanja and Ronald (2019) defined migration and situated it within the context of change, and such change remains beneficial to the households at large. This is because it is a unanimous decision within the family households on the need to attract socio-economic fortune in the new environment. Azam and Gubert (2006) view migration as a household decision to get rid of poverty, while Ratha et al. (2011) see migration from the economic point of view and define it as a critical stakeholder in maintaining the principle of reciprocity.

On the one hand, migrants bring innovation and ideas, increase the population density of the host countries, and increase the gross domestic products and their per capita income. In return, migrants contribute to the economy by sending states through their remittances. This remittance is expected to boost the education and health sectors of the sending states viz-a-viz alleviate the family and community from extreme poverty by creating small-scale businesses. This is why Fatemeh and Abdolahi (2014) call migration a coping and reviving strategy for someone's ailment. *The ailment* in this context is the ability to resuscitate someone's life in a new environment after battling socio-economic depression, internal strife, and natural and artificial disasters.

Further, the study used the functionalist theory of migration to buttress the point made above and explains that migration is a propeller behind the wheel of socio-economic development and per capita incomes through the free flow of human and capital resources across the member states. Castle et al. (2014) explain functionalism theory from an economic equality perspective. They argue that the principle of reciprocity displayed by migrants brings equity and equality to the level of socio-economic development among the member states. The functionalism theory of migration concludes that migration is a phenomenon that pulls societies together towards a singular aim: equality and sustainable socio-economic development across the member states.

3 Methodology

The methodological approach for this chapter is unassuming. The chapter explored the Kampala Conventions and Strategic Framework on Migration to illuminate their effectiveness on migrant movement in Africa towards the region's development. The study based its primary tool on the snowballing method to elucidate the significance of the Kampala Convention and the attractiveness of migration towards achieving developmental goals in Africa. The study also used the desk review method as secondary data to unfold scholarly works on migration.

4 Migration Trends and Patterns in Africa

Africa, being a frequent continent on the move, has been subjected to various reasons; first, the presence of European merchants in Africa brought a new dynamic into the migration system as millions of young African vibrant were lured into forced labour in their various plantations (Asiwaju, 1976; Cooper, 1996; Cross, 2013; Lucas, 2015) to work as cheap labourers with their natural resources exploited. Second, the arbitrary boundaries drawn by the colonial masters during the Berlin Conference of 1884/1885 fenced out more than 190 ethnic groups from their ancestral homes (Asiwaju, 1976). Third, the doldrums economy in Africa after the exit of colonial masters make Africa the centrepiece of migration, particularly intra-regional mobility in the post-1960s.

The post-1960s saw migration in Africa on the high side, from nine (9) million in 1960 to 14 million in the 1970s (Hania, 2004). Between the 1970s and 1980s, Africa recorded the highest number of international migrants due to the oil boom experienced, with large amounts of migrants concentrated in major economic regions. For example, out of the eight (8) regional economic communities in Africa, the Western African sub-region has the most significant number of migrants as it grew from 2.5 million in the 1960s to 6.8 million, with 42% of international migrants residing in various member states. In comparison, Eastern Africa recorded 28%, Northern Africa, 12%, and 9% each in Middle and Southern Africa (Flahaux & De Haas, 2016; Hania, 2004).

The end of oil booms in Africa gave a new face to African economies, where most member states' governments could not provide basic needs for their citizens, let alone the migrants. The issue degenerated into economic and ethnoreligious crises in Africa, making millions of people trace their steps by reviewing their coping measure strategy (from a prone area) to another region. This generated an increased number of international migrants between 2000 and 2017, from 15 to 25 million, an increase of 67% at an average of 2.8% per year (UNCTAD, 2017). This further increased the percentage harboured by the West African sub-region to more than 80% of migrants due to the free entry and exited economic policy in operating, 65% in Southern Africa, 50% in Central Africa, and 47% in Eastern Africa to harness the economic prospect (Awumbila, 2017). This shows that more than 79% of sub-Saharan African migrants live within the region, and less than 22% emigrate outside the continent (Abebe, 2018). At the same time, the UNDESA (2017) estimated that more than 53% of African migrants live in Africa, 26% in Europe, 12% in Asia, and 7% in North America.

Contemporarily, the inactivity of the region's economy and security impediments across the member states has made paradigm shifts in the contemporary movement beyond the socio-economic and financial implosion that crippled the labour markets across the major economic destination in Africa viz-a-viz security imbroglio, which paved the way for extremist poverty, unemployment or underemployment, and natural disasters. It is instead driven by the new social transformation that could not be achieved on the surface of Africa remains the tempo and aspiration of migrants (that is, easy access to quality education and good life) (Balawell & Bonfiglio, 2013). It is estimated that out of 34 million of African descent, more than 55% of the migrants live outside the continent, which amounts to 14% of world migrants (Akinyi & Gregory, 2019).

For instance, in 2019, the percentage of African citizens in Europe is 82 million, in Northern America, 59 million, while the African population in Northern Africa and Western Asia is 49 million (Akinyi & Gregory, 2019). It should be noted that most of the 55% of African migrants living outside the continent are professionals and skilled labour, while less than 45% of international migrants in Africa are of no or low skilled labours. The torpidity of the African economy will continue to be responsible for the upsurge of people's migration beyond the African continent, which may lead to a brain drain in the various African sectors.

5 Internally Displaced Persons and Refugees' Management in Africa

The post-independence period in Africa witnessed a series of protracted wars, such as the war of liberation, attrition, and secession, coupled with struggles against apartheid in South Africa (Moses, 2014). The repercussions of these protracted wars generated a high number of refugees who fled from war-torn colonial towns and sought refuge outside their borders for the safety of their lives. Though the total number of refugees could not be ascertained, the study shows an estimated number of refugees generated in some African member states in the 1960s and 1970s. For example, during the eight (8) years of the Algerian war of independence, 200,000 Algerian refugees fled to the neighbouring countries of Morocco and Tunisia; Angola's war of independence from Portugal witnessed 1,048,800 refugees; Guinea-Bissau, 148,000; and Mozambique, 47,000; Ethiopia, 460,000; and Uganda, 200,000 refugees (Harmrell, 1967; Nindi, 1984), among others.

The statistical numbers of refugees in the African region are disheartening as the continent generated more than one-quarter of the world's refugees. In addition to this, Somalia alone hosted more than 700,000 refugees from Ogaden and Tigre in Ethiopia (Hodge, 1984, cited in Nindi, 1984), while 5000 refugees from Zaire settled in Equatorial Guinea, 54,500 Rwanda refugees settled in Burundi, and 48,000 in Uganda in 1972 (Brooks, 1976; Harmrell, 1967; Hodge, 1984). The emergence of high numbers of refugees in their chosen destinations resulted in a severe crisis in the management of the political and economic structures of the destination countries due to population explosion and structural deterioration, which remains a difficult task for the governments of the concerned countries. Aside from this, most refugees could not exercise their basic fundamental rights, such as the right to primary education, employment, public service, housing, and freedom of movement, among others, without stigmatization.

A bid to uproot the wars of attrition that generated a high number of refugees through the African remedy led to the adoption of the OAU Convention Governing the Specific Aspects of Refugee Problems in Africa in 1969, and came to force in 1974. The OAU convention was not the first international instrument on refugees in Africa. Africa has been a signatory to the 1951 United Nations Convention relating to the Status of Refugees and the 1967 Protocol relating to the Status of Refugees. The two legal instruments were comprehensive instruments detailing the fundamental rights of refugees without being stigmatized in the countries of destination. However, the instruments were designed to address European refugees in the aftermath of the Second World War and could not address African differences in refugee management. After due consultation, the African Union (AU) policymakers drafted a new Convention on African peculiarities, which was not part of the 1951 Convention and 1967 Protocol on the Status of Refugees in 1968 and adopted in 1969. The ratification and implementation of the 1969 OAU convention are based on the recognition and adoption of the first two legal instruments, from 1951 and 1967, so that people can get most out of their rights to gainful employment, freedom of movement, and labour laws, among other things.

The OAU Convention yielded positive results as member states inculcated the promulgated Conventions and Protocol on refugees into their national laws, while some member states adjusted and amended their immigration laws to incorporate the management of refugees (Medard, 1983). Senegal, Zambia, Botswana, and Uganda, among others, adapted international refugee instruments to their national laws, while Lesotho and Kenya amended their immigration laws (Medard, 1983). Aside from this, several countries signed bilateral and multilateral agreements among themselves. For example, Sudan and Uganda signed a bilateral agreement through a six-man committee set up by both states to facilitate the refugees to their original homes in 1964. Also, in 1967, the tripartite agreement between the Zaire, Rwanda, and Burundi governments on rendering helping hands to repatriate refugees is another reference point.

Member states adhere strictly to the principles of the legal framework by maintaining an open-door policy with all the refugees in their various countries and catering to their needs without discrimination. Most African governments were generous to refugees, allowing them to freely move to neighbouring countries in exchange for fundamental rights like participation in the formal economy, access to primary education, and other social activities. Despite the several instruments on refugees, the region continues to experience the influx of refugees; Sudan, for example, has 490,000 refugees; Tanzania, 140,000; Cameroon, 270,000; Burundi, 234,594; Somalia, 1.5 million refugees; and Tanzania, 140,000 (Medard, 1983).

Several arguments have been raised on the infiltration of refugees in Africa, with the inclination that the European world is the originator of refugees. This is because the artificial and arbitrary boundaries arrived at during the Berlin Conference of 1884/1885 solidified the boundary disputes in Africa immediately after independence and generated thousands of million refugees. For example, the boundary disputes between Sudan and Kenya over the Ilemi Triangle, Kenya, and South Sudan over Nadapal; Eritrea and Ethiopia; Algeria and Morocco (Medard, 1983), etc., to mention a few, continue to generate tension among the member states. Secondly, the pertinacity of colonial masters to vacate some of their colonies in Africa, especially in Mozambique, Angola, Guinea-Bissau, Namibia, and Madagascar in the 1960s, led to ethnic conflicts and rivalries that increased the numbers of refugees in Africa. Thirdly, most African countries are classified as low-income economies, where 70% of the citizens are in penury, except the likes of Nigeria and Cameroun. The presence of refugees in these countries collapsed their economies and generated an economic warship between the refugees and citizens. The inadequate screening facilities at the African borders to differentiate between the refugees and criminally minded people further threatened the national security of some member states, which further degenerated into internal strife; and to cap it all, the failure of the Conventions to cater to the internally displaced persons (IDPs) in Africa. All these factors rendered the 1969 Convention and its companion on refugees fruitless and caused political and internal uprisings with the culpability of the economic downturn in each member state.

The implication of internal hostilities and environmental disasters on the national security and economy of the member states in the 1970s and 1980s served as a turning point for Africa. Most African countries changed from open-door policy to the policy of securitization by deporting and closing their land borders against further refugees.

The securitization of borders made the African leaders, particularly the most affected areas (Sudan, Uganda, the Democratic Republic of Congo [DRC], and Burundi, among others), think inwardly during the Great Lakes international conference in the 2000s and the pact was unanimously signed in December 2006. The pact came up with two significant protocols; the Protocol on the Protection and Assistance to internally displaced persons (IDPs) and the Protocol on the Property Rights of Returning Persons. The pact also set up a regional instrument for the compliance and implementation of the protocols to their national and regional policies.

Unfortunately, restoring peace and orderliness degenerated into another internal crisis beyond the Great Lakes countries to the rest of the African countries. This makes the Great Lakes region seek a comprehensive framework for restoring peace in the region. By 2006, an African Union (AU) group of experts met in Addis Ababa and proposed the Convention for the prevention, protection, and assistance of IDPs and refugees in Africa. The Convention was signed at the end of the AU special summit in Kampala, Uganda, in 2008 and tagged the "Kampala Convention" and became effective in 2009 when the nine (9) African countries (Liberia, Malawi, Niger, Nigeria, South Sudan, Somalia, and Zambia, etc.) adopted and ratified it (Romola et al., 2019). Presently, more than 35% of African countries have ratified the Convention, but only the Niger Republic has domesticated the Convention into its national law (Romola et al., 2019). Nigeria drew its national policy on IDPs from the Kampala Convention on the government's commitment to the obligations of state parties under international treaties and upholding the respect for international humanitarian law and human rights protection of IDPs, particularly in the case of emergency. In contrast, Liberia and Malawi drew the definition of IDPs from the Convention (Romola et al., 2019).

Unlike its OAU Convention counterparts, the Kampala Convention is a holistic and comprehensive legal framework that takes cognizance of African peculiarities in addressing IDPs and refugees. The Convention calls on the African Union leaders to support the states in protecting and assisting the IDPs across the member states with an emphasis on the principle of responsibility to protect (R2P) in the case of an international crime committed against the IDPs (Flavia, 2011). Article II also calls on states to guide and protect the fundamental rights of the IDPs and prevent them from stigmatization while enjoying their fundamental rights. Article III forbids any political, social, cultural, or economic marginalization that may further destabilize the vulnerable (Kampala Convention, 2008). Article 8 of the Convention invites International Organizations (IOs) and Civil Society Organizations (CSOs) to assist and collaborate with states in protecting and coordinating refugees and internally displaced persons (IDPs) across member states (Kampala Convention, 2008). The Kampala Convention also shows that Africa is pragmatic in finding a legal framework that would uproot the causes of forcibly fleeing people, protect the vulnerable ones, and restore the past glory of the war-torn areas of the continent (Article II, Kampala Convention, 2008).

It is quite disheartening that the ratification of the Kampala Convention in Africa has not restored the glory of African peace, stability, and orderliness, as African countries continue to languish in high numbers of IDPs daily. As of 2011, for example, Sudan had 2.2 million IDPs and 387,300 refugees; the Democratic Republic of the Congo (DRC) had 1.7 million IDPs and 476,700 refugees. In addition, Somalia had 1.5 million IDPs and 770,150 refugees due to a series of conflicts, while more than 500,000 people were evicted from their homes due to natural environmental problems (Elizabeth, 2012). At the end of 2013, there were more than 12.5 million IDPs in 21 sub-Saharan African states, according to the analysis of the internally displaced monitoring team, with Nigeria, the DRC, and Sudan topping the table of IDPs (Adepoju, n.d.). The tables turned in 2014 when Nigeria alone accounted for more than 10% of the global IDPs due to Boko Haram activities.

The persistent rise of internal conflicts across the member state, which doubled the number of IDPs, made the member states adopt the Harare Plan of Action in 2017 through the conference and workshop organized by AU related to the Kampala Convention in Harare, Zimbabwe, in 2016. The Harare Plan of Action is a guiding document and model law on the Convention to guide the member states in drafting and formalizing domestic legislation and policies related to the Kampala Convention. Despite this, the Kampala Convention and its model law are still far from reducing the causes of IDPs and refugees in Africa. For instance, as of 2021, Nigeria accounted for 3.4 million IDPs, South Sudan generated 4 million IDPs, Burkina Faso 1.5 million, Mali 700,000, and DRC 6 million, among others (Christophe et al., 2021). This shows that the number of IDPs is in arithmetic progression as the number increased from 29 million in 2020 to 32 million in 2021, while the effort remains in geometric progression (Christophe et al., 2021). At least ten African countries accounted for 88% of IDPs on the continent.

Several criticisms have been levelled against the incompetency of the Kampala Convention in addressing the impediment of internal crisis in Africa and providing maximum protection for the IDPs and refugees without jeopardizing their fundamental rights. The facts remain that the effort put in place by the AU in addressing the challenges confronting the region is only cutting the tree from the narrow hedge without uprooting it. It would be difficult for such a tree to die naturally on such occasions. It will be tough for Africa to have a workable instrument for its internal crisis for the following reasons:

1. The original creator of African problems is the western world, mainly European countries, due to arbitrary boundaries drawn during the 1884/1885 Berlin conference, which have no African countries in attendance.
2. Africa remains a ready market for the western world, keeping them destabilized would not give them a sense of liberating themselves from the post-colonial circuit.
3. As the original creator of the African problems, they give European prototype solutions to the African issues with financial backing; since the African economy is nothing to write about, such practice continues to keep the African states to the dictate of the western world.

These factors will continue to suffer the African countries at the hands of the western world.

6 Management of Labour Movement in Africa and Beyond

It is of no news that migration is the bedrock of African development, particularly in the trade and economic realm. Some policymakers believe labour migration is a driving force behind extremist poverty and advocacy of monetary wars, which can only be cured through border securitization. However, the contemporary economic reality and the interference of international agencies changed African policymakers' perception and people's generality on the significance of labour migration in developing the countries' origin and host (Minh, 2021). The study shows that labour migrants, whether skilled or unskilled, serve as a demographic booster in terms of population density and reshape the existing pyramid of the receiving states. They contribute a new set of ideas and innovations to the host countries, viz-a-viz benefitting from the host countries' health and education sector, making migration inevitable for the country's sustainable development. It also contributes substantially to the labour productivity of the destination countries as the rise in the stock of immigration paved the way to an increase in the growth rate of productivity sectors. For example, labour migrants contribute between 1 and 90% of the Gross Domestic Product (GDPs) to the economies of host states (Minh, 2021). At the same time, migrants also spend more than 85% of their income on developing the economies of the host countries through tax deductions and daily consumption (Minh, 2021).

In addition, labour migrants contribute to developing the countries of origin through remittance inflow. *Remittance* is the money sent home by the migrants, irrespective of their status in the foreign lands, to maintain socio-economic ties with their families, relatives, and communities. Although the accurate data on the amount generated through remittance could not be ascertained, the study has it that the remittance inflow to African countries is more than private capital inflow to the continent (Minh, 2021). For example, the estimated $38.4 and $64.9 billion were recorded between 2005–2007 and 2014–2016, respectively, as remittances generated by the countries of origin (Minh, 2021). The remittance (formal and informal) directly and indirectly increases per capita income and stimulates socio-economic growth, production, and asset accumulation in various destination countries (Gagnon, 2014). The remittance is used to uplift people from the circle of poverty through self-employment and sometimes serves as a coping strategy for the rest of the family members. The remittance is also significant for the stability of domestic savings as it serves as additional financial resources for the region's sustainability (UNDP, 2014) if appropriately managed after the Foreign Direct Investment (FDI). It constitutes more than 10% of the development of most African countries, such as Senegal, Haiti, Liberia, and Nigeria (WB, 2009). However, what is this benefit's survivability in the border securitization phase in Africa?

The survivability of labour migration benefits in African countries made the Organization of African Unity (OAU) take a bold step in 1991 in managing and coordinating the movement of people across the member states and tagging it as 'Abuja Treaty'. The Abuja Treaty birthed the adopted African Economic Communities (AEC) in 1991. It came to force in 1994 to foster socio-economic development by promoting the Free Movement Protocol (Ottilia, 2017). The OAU acknowledged ECOWAS' commitment as the first sub-region to promote free movement of people, right to residence, and establishment and implored the rest of the regional economic communities to emulate the ECOWAS region and implement the Abuja Treaty on their national policy. Article 71(e) emphasizes the need to engage skilled people from other member states in the shortage area to encourage regional cooperation and integration.

Moreover, African Union adopted the Migration Policy Framework in Africa (MPFA) and the African Common Position on Migration and Development (the Common Position) in 2006, which was reviewed in 2016 to incorporate new labour governance and the social protection of migrants for the betterment of the region as agreed upon during the reviewed and extension of MPFA framework (2018–2030). It also adopted the Plan of Action on Employment Promotion and Poverty Reduction in 2004 and the Plan of Action on Boosting Intra-African Trade in 2012. Also, in conjunction with international agencies such as International Labour Organization (ILO), International Organization for Migration (IOM), and the United Nations Economic Commission for Africa (UNECA), AU adopted the Joint Labour Migration Programme (JLMP) through the heads of states and government at the 24th session of AU assembly in Addis Ababa, Ethiopia, in 2015 (Africa Migration Report, 2020). All these instruments were rolled out to effectively discharge good governance on the management of labour mobility, including the protection of migrant workers' rights and the portability of social security across the member states.

The increasing number of labour migrants to the rest of the world beyond the African continent makes the AU solidify the cooperation and interrelationship of other western and Gulf countries for the benefit of African migrants abroad through bilateral and multilateral agreements on labour management. Aside from this, several bilateral and multilateral agreements on economic trade relations have been signed between and among region member states on the monitoring and coordinating labour mobility. In 2005, for example, the three (3) sub-regions (COMESA, the EAC, and SADC) proposed a tripartite economic agreement on trade harmonization, infrastructure relationship, and border management which was launched in 2015, while the policy related to free movement was slated for phase II of the negotiation.

Despite this, the implementation and domestication of labour law is still a far cry, particularly labour law coverage of workers' rights in the informal sectors such as the agricultural, mining, and construction sectors. Most workers in these sectors work under unprotected and unregulated labour laws with inadequate social protection and low-income wages; for example, 66% of labour in the informal sector in sub-Saharan Africa and 52% in North Africa are working outside the labour social right protection (Africa Migration Report, 2020). This lacuna remains a significant challenge bedevilling the region in managing and promoting labour right in Africa.

7 INTERROGATING THE EXISTING MIGRATION POLICIES IN AFRICA

Africa and migration are inseparable as trade remains the backbone of African economic development; therefore, proper management for the protection of fundamental migrants' rights becomes sacrosanct for the concerned stakeholders across the region. The Organisation of African Unity (OAU) Council of Ministers championed the decision to formulate a strategic framework for Migration in Africa in 2001 during the 74th Council of Minister Ordinary Session Meeting in Lusaka, Zambia. The OAU Council of Ministers proposed and recommended nine (9) major thematic areas of migration, such as border management, irregular migration, labour migration, internal migration, sharing migration data, fundamental rights of migrants, migration and development, interstate cooperation, and partnership (African Union Executive Council, 2006). The draft of the framework also covered the migrants' social right protection, such as migrants' health, environment, gender, and conflict, among others. The essence of the migration framework is to promote interrelationship and cooperation between and among member states for socio-economic development and strengthening of the continent's regional security and stability agenda.

The policy framework is a comprehensive and non-binding document on managing Migration in Africa. The framework was proposed in 2001 and adopted five years later (2006), during the African Union (AU) meeting of heads of states and governments in Banjul Gambia and tagged 'Migration Policy Framework in Africa (MPFA).' The AU policy-makers aim to encourage the member states and the regional economic communities (RECs) to implement the framework as a guide to the government of the member states and the RECs in drafting and formulating their individual national and regional policies on the management of migration based on states and regional peculiarities. The AU calls on member states and RECs to prioritize their needs and seek financial obligations and technical support from international organizations, non-governmental organizations, civil society organizations, and other United Nations Agencies for resource mobilization and implementation of the MPFA framework policy. The policy was also entrusted to the RECs for proper monitoring and evaluation of the policy across the member states based on each state's competency and economic capacity.

In 2016, the MPFA framework was re-assessed to incorporate the dynamism process of Migration in Africa by the AU policymakers. By 2018, the AU policymakers recommend the extension of the MPFA framework for another twelve years (12 years) (2018–2030) due to new emerging issues and trends of Migration in Africa with the adoption of the Plan of Action for easy implementation across the member states (MPFA, 2018–2030). The extension of the framework covered the central new thematic area such as migration governance, labour migration, education, diaspora engagement, border governance, irregular Migration, forced displacement, internal Migration, and other cross-cutting issues (The RMPFA, 2018–2030). The review of the MPFA framework is to capture the new trend of challenges facing Migrants in Africa and beyond for the betterment of Africa at large. The African political leaders acknowledge the similitude of Migration towards African development and encourage the concerned and critical stakeholders to inculcate all the identified thematic areas into their national and regional policies across the board. It is necessary to address the challenges confronting the migrants both within and beyond to improve the safety of the migrants for remittance facilitation, harmonize national policies to incorporate the migration framework, and strengthen cross-border cooperation against external invasion (Action Plan, 2018–2030).

The MPFA, though it is still an ongoing process, has tremendously recorded great success at national and regional levels, particularly in implementing appropriate policies on migration, an improvement on various border security, migrants' youth employment, education, and quality of good services. However, the survivability of the framework has been in doubt for some reasons;

1. The migration framework is a mere instrument with no enforcing capacity; this may render and trivialize the MPFA as a toothless bulldog that makes Migration in Africa as a matter of choice rather than a necessity.
2. The economic condition of African countries has also raised an eyebrow which further probes the effectiveness of migration policy in Africa. It is of no news that most African countries' economies are meagre, which are not sufficient to cater to the needs of their citizens, let alone migrants; then, how would they manage without resulting in economic wars between the citizens of host countries and the migrants?
3. The AU policymakers ask the states to seek financial cooperation and technical assistance from the international communities for the implementation and monitoring of the compliance of the MPFA across the member states; the framework may therefore promote the donour agenda at the expense of Africa's development. Though the policymakers and regional leaders entrusted the implementation and monitoring of the MPFA to the RECs, since more than 80% of the migration is either intra-regional or inter-regional, a lack of commitment and cooperation between and among the regional leaders may jeopardize the original plan of the migration framework (Christophe et al., 2021).
4. Securitization of African borders is another major obstacle for MPFA policy. Most African states put their borders under heavy locked or heavily manned against further infiltration without being mindful of migrants' rights. This also calls the survivability of the migration framework into question. This is because some states see migration and refugees from the lens of national security problems by attributing the refugees and migrants as a potential threat to their national survival.

By and large, migration policy and the Plan of Action is still ongoing as the pattern and trends are still unfolding. It is believed that it will take cognizance of African peculiarities and promote the African agenda in managing the migration towards sustainable development in Africa.

8 The Interconnectedness Between Migration Policies and Development Planning in Africa

According to the analysis of the Economic Development report in Africa, 2018, titled "Migration and Structural Transformation," Africa remains a significant beneficiary of migration. It explains the benefit of adequate protection of migrants, including the diaspora people, to the structural transformation of African economic states. According to the Economic Development report, the UNCTAD recommended proper protection of all migrants (former and informer) to African governments, RECs, and AU policymakers. Such protection would adversely affect socio-economic development viz-a-viz reduction in security challenges across the member states (UNCTAD Report, 2018).

In its further reports, the free flow of immigrants has substantially increased the African continent's gross domestic product (GDP) and per capita income. For example, in 2016 alone, the average value of GDP per capita income in Africa was $2008 in 2016 (UNCTAD Report, 2018), with a projected increase of $3249 per capita income for 2030. This would grow at a compound annual rate of 3.5% since 2016 (UNCTAD Report, 2018). In addition, the remittance flow into the African purse has risen from $38.4 billion on average in 2005–2007 to $64.9 billion in 2014–2016. In 2019 alone, the remittance to the African purse was $48 billion, while 35% of South Sudan GDP, 21% of Lesotho's GDP, and 15% of the Gambia's GDP were through remittance (Philip, 2021). The new normal situation made the remittance of 2020 drop by 8.8% to $44 billion and by 5.8% to $41 billion in 2021 (Philip, 2021), respectively. This means that migration is giving Africa economic leverage with the hope of working towards economic equity and equality across the member states.

The tremendous achievement has been attributed to the African regional leaders' cooperation and commitment to implementing existing migration policies across the member states. The inclusion of migrants' social protection to the extended families in RMPFA, 2018–2030 has given the African economies a new outlook reaching their projection of 4.3% in 2018 compared to 2.1% in 2016 (ILO, 2018 WESO Report; AEO, 2022). According to the African Union report on labour migration statistics of 2015, the continent seems to witness high participation of international migrants in the economic development of the member states due to the cooperation of African leaders, with a high rate of

93.3% for Mauritius to the lowest of 71.7% for Ghana (ILO, 2018 WESO Report). The analysis of the African Union regional report also explained the significant increase in the registration of international migrants: EAC with 2.2%, ECOWAS with 2.1%; CENSAD with 1.6%; and IGAD with 1.2% (UNCTAD Report, 2018). The data analysis shows that the existing migration policies in Africa have generated a rapid response to socio-economic development as African leaders continue to play a critical role in labour migration governance. This is why the AU policymakers and key stakeholders on migration call on member states, RECs, and governments on the continuity of the existing cooperation to fully implement migration policies for the massive development of Africa's economy.

Good migration governance policies can transform the continent's economy into a world economy as the free flow of migrants continues to increase the GDP per capita income of the region. It is, therefore, apparent to strengthen the implementation of the RMPFA (2018–2030) framework and Abuja Treaty and its Plan of Action on the free movement of people, right to residence, and establishment signed by all African leaders in 1991 for the potential benefit of migration in Africa. Though the African economy predicaments (unemployment, underemployment, inadequate job creation), economic wars between the host citizens and migrants, political instabilities, inequalities, and border securitization, among others, remain obstacles affecting economic growth and equality, the truth remains that the policymakers, RECs, and government of individual member states should see migration and all the migration policies as a blessing to economic development rather than be a curse, just like the former Secretary General of United Nations noted and I quote;

> We cannot ignore the real policy difficulties posed by the migration, but neither should we lose sight of its immense potential to benefit migrants, the countries they leave, and those to which they migrate.
>
> Kofi Annan, former UN secretary General

9   Concluding Remarks

Migration is inevitable in Africa as it remains a coping strategy for unforeseen African circumstances such as economic imbroglio, environmental and human-made disasters viz-a-viz economic builder of member states.

Therefore, it is pertinent for all African leaders and policymakers to indoctrinate African peculiarities into the existing migration policies for the betterment of the region.

References

Abebe, T. (2018). *A new dawn for African migrants.* Institute for Security Studies. Accessed online at https://issafrica.Org on 15 August 2022.

Adepoju, A. (2008). *Migration in sub-Saharan Africa.* Current African issues no. 37. Nordic Africa Institute, Uppsala, Sweden.

Africa Migration Report. (2020). *Challenging the Narrative.* Published by IOM.

African Union. (1969). Convention governing the specific aspects of refugee problems in Africa. Addis Ababa, Ethiopia.

African Union. (2018). *Protocol to the treaty establishing the African Economic Community Relating to Free Movement of Persons, Right of Residence and Right of Establishment.* Accessed online at https://au.int/en/treaties on 10 August 2022.

Africa Union Executive Council. (2006). *The Migration Policy Framework for Africa.* Accessed online at http://www.unhcr.org on 25 August 2022.

African Union Migration Policy Framework for Africa and Plan of Action (2018–2030). African Union Department for Social Affairs.

Asiwaju, A. (1976). Migrations as revolt: The example of the Ivory Coast and the Upper Volta before 1945. *Journal of African History, 17.*

Awumbila, M. (2017). *Drivers of migration and urbanization in Africa: Key trends and issues, United Nations Expert Group Meeting on Sustainable Cities, Human Mobility and International Migration.* Population Division, Department of Economic and Social Affairs, United Nations Secretariat.

Azam, J., & Gubert, F. (2006). Migrants' remittances and the household in Africa: A review of the evidence. *Journal of African Economies, 15*(suppl. 2), AERC.

Christophe, B., Amal, E., & Mattieu, T. (2021). *The African Union's migration agenda: An alternative to European priorities in Africa?* Centre for Migration and Citizenship. Notes del'ifri.

Cooper, F. (1996). *Decolonization and African Society: The labor question in French and British Africa.* Cambridge University Press.

Cross, H. (2013). *Migrants, borders and global capitalism: West African Labour Mobility and EU Borders.* Routledge.

Fatemeh, P., & Abdolahi, U. (2014). Migration literature: A theoretical perspective. *The Down Journal, 3*(1).

Flahaux, M., & De Hass, H. (2016). African migration: Trends, patterns and drivers. *Comparative Migration Studies (CMS), 4*(1). Springer.

STRATEGIC FRAMEWORK OF AFRICAN UNION ... 311

Flavia, Z. (2011). New hopes and challenges for the protection of IDPs in Africa: The Kampala convention for the protection and assistance of internally displaced persons in Africa. *Denver Journal of International Law & Policy* (2). Spring.

Gagnon, J. (2014). *Demographic change and the future of the labour force in the EU27, in other OECD countries and selected large emerging economies.* OECD Publishing.

Harmrell, S. (Ed.). (1967). *Refuge problem in Africa.* Uppsala Scandinavian Institute of African Studies. Holmes and Meier.

Kampala Convention. (2009). *African Union convention for the protection and assistance of internally displaced persons in Africa.* African Union. Accessed online at https://www.unhcr.org/afr on 16 September 2022.

Lucas, R. (2015). African migration. In Barry R. Chiswick & Paul W. Miller (Eds.), *The Handbook on the Economics of International Migration.* Elsevier.

Medard, R. (1983). Some reflections on the OAU convention on refugees: Some pending issues. *The Comparative and International Law Journal of Southern Africa, 16*(2).

Minh, D. (2021). The impact of migration on economic growth and human development: The case of the Philippines. *Journal of International Business and Management (JIBM), 4*(18).

Nindi, B. (1984). Africa's refugee crisis in a historical perspective. *Trans-African Journal of History, 15.*

Ottilia, A. (2017). *Policy brief: Freedom of movement unlocking Africa's development potential.* International Organization for Migration.

Romola, A., Lutz, O., Olivia, L., & Frans, V. (2019). Introduction: Refugees, returnees and internally displaced persons in Africa. *Journal of African Law, 65,* S1.

Tanja, B., & Ronald, S. (2019). *Conceptual classification and theoretical underlying of migration and development.* Routledge Handbook of Migration and Development: Taylor and Francis.

Historicising Urhobo Migration, Settlement and Identity in Jos, 1940–1970

Meshach Ofuafor

1 Introduction

Communities are formed on the basis of their centrality to nature's existence and survival. The nature and character of these communities is shaped by waves of migrations. That is, taken against the backdrop of humanity's quest for survival, leisure and experiment, people move on a permanent or semi-permanent level. Ultimately, in their various natures, shape and character, communities play vital roles of shelter, protector and provider for its population. They also in their complexities provide the social space where each individual is given room to play various roles within each segment of our social life. By implication, playing roles within each of these segments of our social lives brings us into union with others; we become a community.[1] The composition of its population is predicated on the nature of its emergence. However, there is also

---

[1] Masolo, D.A. 2002. Community, identity and the cultural space. *Rue Descartes.* 36: 22.

M. Ofuafor (✉)
Obafemi Awolowo University, Ile-Ife, Nigeria
e-mail: mofuafor@oauife.edu.ng

© The Author(s), under exclusive license to Springer Nature Switzerland AG 2023
A. I. Adeniran (ed.), *African Development and Global Engagements*,
https://doi.org/10.1007/978-3-031-21283-3_15

314   M. OFUAFOR

the complex sense of community which is 'based on the premise[2] that the identities of persons are shaped by the social worlds in which they play various roles, and are susceptible to change as such social worlds mutate through time and space'. The social construction of communities notwithstanding, cities such as Cambridge, Frankfurt, London, Pisa, Genoa, Ibadan, Zungeru, Lagos, Kaduna and Jos, emerged either as ruins of war, or were named after monuments or edifices that surround or near their locations, or they were trade posts before, during and after colonisation.

The colonisation process in Nigeria opened a new set of opportunities and challenges that were mostly available in the urban cities. These opportunities and challenges acted as catalyst that stimulated the push–pull factors[3] that began to manifest in urban cities such as Lagos, Kaduna, Kano, Port Harcourt, Lokoja, Warri and Jos. The totality of the manifestation of the theoretical push–pull factors led to the migration of various groups from the rural areas to the urban centres. The determinants which are adjudged as the motivating factors for individuals' participation in migration activities can be explained thus: 'push factors' include demographic growth, low living standards, lack of economic opportunities and political repression, while 'pull factors' are demand for labour, availability of land, good economic opportunities and political freedoms.[4]

Meanwhile, in the case of the Urhobo migrants, their tradition of migration can be traced and situated within their traditions of origin. Urhobo traditions of origin are connected to about four sources; which, unlike some other traditions of origin make specific reference to a symbolic ancestral heritage. Rather, what obtains as Urhobo traditions are

---

[2] This premise is based on Patel's appeal for recognition of a new and more complex sense of community. Masolo, D.A. 2002. Community, identity and cultural space. 36: 22.

[3] The push–pull factors increasingly manifested and stimulated a massive rural–urban migratory movement that had a rippling effect on the economic and social conditions of the urban cities. As with some other African cities, the migratory flow into Nigerian cities began to witness the influx of foreign nationals from India, Cameroon, Ghana, Syria, Lebanon and Great Britain. The approach perceives the causes of migration to lie in a combination of 'push factors', impelling people to leave the areas of origin, and 'pull factors', attracting them to certain receiving countries. See Castles, S. and Miller, M.J. 1998. *The age of migration: international population movements in the modern world*, London: Macmillan. 20.

[4] Castles, S. and Miller, M.J. 1998. *The age of migration: international migration*. 20.

derived from, first as an autochthonous people in their present location.[5] Secondly, is the theory of Urhobo origin linked to the Benin territories. Thirdly, is the tradition that traces Urhobo origin to an Ife territory. Fourthly, is the controversial tradition of origin which draws similarity with some other Nigerian groups such as the Yoruba and Edo-speaking peoples. This traces Urhobo traditions of origin to the Sudan and Egypt. Ikime identified five Urhobo traditions which link them with the Ijo. He went further to corroborate submissions of Hubbard, Alagoa and Otite in examining another tradition which link Urhobo origin to Bini.[6] This tradition arguably fits Urhobo description in terms of geography and people. This has, however, suffered the problem of accurate dating.

Linked with the problem of accurate dating is the issue around the identity of the people they met when they came to the Urhobo territories. This goes to show ultimately the strength in the argument of the autochthonous version which states that before all forms of migrations in and out of the Urhobo territories, there had always existed an Urhobo people in the area where they are found today. One point that was clear, however, was that, these various strands of migration accounts have imposed on the Urhobo people a linguistic variation. The linguistic variation perhaps gives credence to the strands of tradition of origins of Urhobo people. While the question of linguistic variation could be seen in the various traditions of origin of Urhobo people, it also manifested in their various trades. For instance, some clans are known to be more dexterous than others in particular trades. Specific mention can be made of trades or preoccupation such as farming, fishing and local gin (*ogogoro*) distillery which were arguably the mainstay of Urhobo economy in the pre-colonial and colonial periods.

The origin of migration and settlement of Urhobo people in Jos metropolis and its environs can be traced using the push–pull theoretical framework for analysis. The principles of this framework are generated from the various factors that led individuals to relocate from their homelands to seek greener pastures or recreation in another land. The push–pull factors are so referred to because, they perceive the causes of migration to lie in a combination of 'push factors'; impelling people

---

[5] Otite, O. 1993. A profile of Urhobo in Andah, B.W., Okpoko, A.I. and Folorunsho, C.A. Eds. *Some Nigerian peoples.* Ibadan: Rex Charles. 197–198.

[6] Ikime, O. 1980. The Peoples and Kingdoms of the Delta Province. Ikime, O. Ed. *Groundwork of Nigerian history.* Ibadan: Heinemann. 92–93.

316   M. OFUAFOR

to leave the place of origin, and 'pull factors'; attracting people to a new destination. The 'push factors' as emphasised include demographic growth, low living standards, lack of economic opportunities and political repression. The 'pull factors' on the other hand include demand for labour, availability of land, good economic opportunities and political freedoms. Thus, the paper found out that the origin of migration of Urhobo people to Jos metropolis and its environs had started at about 1910 when some itinerant farmers, fishermen and artisans moved northwards from the Yoruba areas where they had earlier settled, towards the Niger area along the Niger River. Meanwhile, there were traces of some Urhobo migrants who had served the Europeans working on the rail tracks as stewards, cooks and labourers.[7] As they journeyed on along the waterways some of them pitched their tents along the river bank to form settlements, while others continued; along tortuous foot paths to journey to neighbouring villages and towns in the hinterland. With the formal introduction of colonial fiscal policies that entailed the colonised people to pay rates and fines with the use of currency, came the need to take up paid employment or revert to commercial farming in cash crop production instead of the subsistence farming which they were used to.

Jos, the present capital of Plateau State was established as a colonial entity in 1915. It owes its creation chiefly to the activities of tin miners. Jos is located almost in the geographical centre of Nigeria; about 1000 km north-east of Lagos, 400 km south of Kano, 900 km north of Port Harcourt, 600 km south-west of Maiduguri, 1000 km south-east of Sokoto. As Bingel puts it, in 1915 Jos was officially founded as a town by an order from the Governor General of Northern Nigeria.[8] This is corroborated by Gonyok thus, between 1911 and 1920, Jos continued to grow. The most important development was the extension of the Zaria railway into Jos in 1915, with it came both traders, craftsmen, miners and the labourers, seeking wage employment in the mines. It was also in that year 1915 that Jos was said to have been officially founded or rather confirmed as a town by an order from the Lt. Governor of the

[7] Interview held with Hon. (Chief) J.K. Akporido, 90, Retired Tin Miner and former Member Plateau State House of Assembly, Warri. 28-05-2018.

[8] Bingel, A.D. 1978. *Jos: Origins and Growth of the Town, 1900–1972.* Jos: Department of Geography, University of Jos. p. 6.

then Northern Nigeria.[9] The City's allure and accommodating people has made it a cosmopolitan town. On the average, Jos metropolis and its environs play host to people from various Nigerian backgrounds and even foreigners. Moreover, the economic potentials offered by the tin mines have made Jos a migrants' destination from the early twentieth century. Thus, by the 1930s, when the price of tin had risen in the world market, and the tin industry was able to pick up once more, the City of Jos witnessed renewed economic and demographic growth. The flurry of migrants that left in the wake of the decline in price of tin, all came back by the mid-1930s.

The paper, therefore, seeks to historicise Urhobo migrations and settlement patterns in Jos metropolis and its environs, with emphasis on issues of identity; which dovetails into their cultural expressions in Jos. The start and end dates of 1940 and 1970 have been chosen by this study because those were the most active and lucrative years of Urhobo involvement in the tin mines industry in Jos, which translates to their years of utmost popularity and relevance in Jos metropolis and its environs. The paper will also establish the back–forth linkages foisted between the homeland and the hostland. By this, the paper will examine the phenomenon of culture retention as it is applied to Urhobo migrant groups in Jos metropolis and its environs.

2   CONCEPTUAL CLARIFICATIONS

2.1   Migration

The concept of migration has its roots in the existential realities of humankind. The history of the human race is that of migration. Therefore, the various uses the concept has been put, suggest that in all ramification, migration, the movement of people from one geographical location to another, has remained at the centre of West African history for several centuries.[10] Labo goes further to describe a migrant 'as a person who uproots himself from his original home and moves to a new place

---

[9] Gonyok, C.K. The City of Jos In: Cities of the Savannah (A History of some Towns and Cities of the Nigerian Savannah) *Nigeria Magazine*. p. 85.

[10] Labo, A. 2000. "The motivation and integration of immigrants in the Nigeria-Niger Border Area: A Study of Magama-Jibia" IFRA-Ibadan, Occasional Publication no. 13. p. 1.

318   M. OFUAFOR

where he settles and establishes new links.'[11] Thus, in the context in which the concept is used in the paper, Urhobo migration is the wave of migrations undertaken by Urhobo people from their homeland to the host community of Jos metropolis and its environs.

2.2   Settlement Pattern

Conservatively described, settlements refer to designated areas/places occupied and lived by a group of people. Most important is the fact that these settlements are reflections of the culture and history of the people. Moreover, the functions attributed to these settlements make them unique. That is, these settlements exist in functional correlation to surrounding settlements. Thus, in the context in which the paper uses the concept, settlement is used to describe the way Urhobo migrants to Jos responded to their housing needs. That is, they were clustered in particular areas of the City in response to the need for communal living with their kindred. However, this need began to witness a change due to the diverse economic needs of the people.

2.3   Identity

The concept of identity has been defined as 'a sense of self that develops as the child differentiates from parents and family and takes a place in society'.[12] It has also been defined as 'a subjective sense of coherence, consistency, and continuity of self, rooted in both personal and group history'.[13] Identity, therefore, carries with it features which makes for similarities and differences to be established within the human race. Identity is often engaged in related social science discourses to depict an individual's conception and expression of his or her 'individuality' or

[11] Labo, A. 2000. p. 5.

[12] Jary and Jary, 1991 as quoted in Haralambos and Holborn, *Sociology: Themes and Perspectives*, London: HarperCollins. p. 665.

[13] Henry, F. and Tator, C. 2006. The Colour of Democracy: Racism in Canadian Society, Toronto, Ontario: Nelson. p. 250.

group affiliations (such as national identity, cultural identity and 'existential' or 'workplace' identity).[14] However, in the context it will be used in this paper, identity is shown to exhibit certain characteristics that are uniquely common to individuals and societies.

3 Waves of Urhobo Migrations to Jos: A Historical Survey

There is no precise and definite date as to when Urhobo migrants started leaving their homelands to seek greener pastures in other places. Rather, what can be gleaned from extant literature refers to their traditions of origin which have been linked to their traditions of migration. Suffice to say, therefore, that by the late nineteenth century, a wave of Urhobo migrant group had begun the movement from Urhoboland to other neighbouring towns and villages in the old Ondo District.[15] Specifically the groups that lived along the Ethiope River and its estuaries were arguably the first that noticeably began the movement along the riverside and charted the course that took them to the areas of Atijere, Igbekebo, Igbobini and Mahin; before migrating to the Ikale and Ilaje hinterland first, as fishermen, and then as farmers. Subsequently, there was the emergence of dotted market settlements along the routes created by these itinerant fishermen and farmers. Also, there was the emergence of artisans that specialised in fabrications of hoes, hooks, cutlasses and other farm implements. Thus, we had Urhobo migrants that interacted with these Ondo towns and villages before the advent of colonialism. This, however, climaxed in the 1920s when colonial interests in cash crop production, imposition of taxes and other fiscal policies were initiated by the colonial government. The consequences of this imposition of taxes necessitated the waves of migration from Urhobo land to other areas outside Ondo Division.

They ventured out first as fishermen, seasonal migrant farmers and later as migrant farmers. As the name implied, the seasonal farmer was

[14] Adeniran, A.I. 2012. Social Networking and Identity Integration within ECOWAS Framework by Ejigbo-Yoruba in Cote d'Ivoire. Unpublished Ph.D Thesis submitted to the Department of Sociology, University of Ibadan. 31.

[15] Obinta, R.F. 2007. Cash Crop Cultivation and Labour Migration in Ondo District, 1890–1970 (Being an Unpublished M.Phil Thesis, Department of History, Obafemi Awolowo University, Ile-Ife, Nigeria). pp. 28–42.

engaged during the farming season while the migrant farmer was more of a permanent resident in the hostland. The fisherman on the other hand was frequently at sea and had the sea and the sea shore as temporary homes. Therefore, while some travelled along the Ethiope River and its estuaries, others can be said to have trekked along the tortuous land routes that were highly risky and dangerous. An important point to note is that, as these groups migrated, they took with them ideas and cultures, which literally impacted on their host communities. These waves of migration of Urhobo groups could be attributed to what Falola[16] has described as a wider and larger emergent global market, which has been created as a consequence of the interactions between Europeans and Africans. While it is not possible to evade the issue of incorporation of the periphery markets with those of the metropolis, the paper is more concerned with the socio-economic and political realities created as a result of the incorporation. Movements within Urhoboland and between Urhobo groups and the rest of Nigeria have created national connections. The connections created have helped in the process of social cohesion, which has been achieved by the Urhobo migrant groups in their various destinations since the late nineteenth century.

The narratives around Urhobo migrations to the Jos metropolis and its environs are weaved around the personality of a certain Mr. K.D. Menta.[17] He it was, who had worked in the gold mines in and around the Ilesa axis in present-day Osun State; that initiated the move for some Urhobo people to emigrate to Jos. He was able to influence the first wave

---

[16] In the introduction to his seminal work on the subjects of Diaspora, Slavery, Modernity, and Globalisation, Toyin Falola examines the waves of migration that have taken pace from the African continent and concludes that the spates of migration that have taken place overtime, have helped to shape a global market facilitated by the forces of the Diaspora communities and the hostlands. This also applies to the local migrant groups in Nigeria. See Falola, T. 2013. *The African Diaspora: Slavery, Modernity, and Globalisation.* Rochester: University of Rochester Press. p. 23.

[17] Mr. K.D. Menta was born c.1870 (according to some family records which were made available to the researcher by his son). According to his son, his father had gathered some workmen from his Agbon clan and travelled to 'Urhie ri Yoruba' (a Yoruba suburb or town) to prospect for gold. The town referred to here was in the Ile-Ife/Ilesa axis. It was from here that he learnt about the tin mines on the Jos Plateau and was fortunate to have travelled with the white men that were in charge of the construction of the railway. Interview held with Mr. Churchill Menta, 77, Musician/Business man, Warri, Delta state. 03-06-2019.

HISTORICISING URHOBO MIGRATION, SETTLEMENT ...   321

of migrants to Jos in the mid-1930s because, first, he had a foreknowledge of the tin mines having read about it. This knowledge was gained as a result of his frequent travels within and around the old western region in search of mining sites and 'gainful employment.'[18] Also, officials of the colonial government introduced new policies of tax administration and farm settlement which were alien to Urhobo people. This arguably fuelled the fear that pervaded most Urhobo land in the early period of colonial rule.[19] This fear is further echoed thus: "in Africa, colonialism and white settlement led to the establishment of migrant labour systems for plantations and mines".[20] Thirdly was the expertise and mining experience most of them had acquired in the areas of foundry and blacksmithing which made them highly competitive for engagement in the tin mines in Jos metropolis and its environs.

This expertise and experience it must be explained is the manifestation of their engagement in farming, fishing and rubber tapping, which most Urhobo clans are involved in as a major preoccupation. The scythe knives and cutlasses used for these preoccupations are fabricated by Urhobo artisans who are well skilled in the trade. Moreover, these Urhobo artisans gradually evolved into itinerant craftsmen that began to move from one location to another in order to practice their trade. Oral evidence[21] suggests that some of these artisans went back home to give report about

[18] Evidence suggests that Mr. K.D. Menta constantly travelled out of his Kokori base in search of economic opportunities. He inherited acres of rubber plantations from his father, but he was not satisfied with staying back home. Thus, he forayed into other lands in search of the greener pastures. Interview held with Mr. Churchill Menta, 77, Musician/Business man, Warri, Delta state. 03-06-2019.

[19] The fear factor is attributed to the manner with which the colonial masters attempted to force the policy of taxation and farm settlement in Urhobo land. These were alien policies that were generally not acceptable to the people. Thus, there were revolts against their introduction in Urhobo land. These revolts were led by Eda and Oshue. For details see, Falola, T. 2009. *Colonialism and violence in Nigeria*. Bloomington, Indiana: Indiana UP. 93–97.

[20] Castles, S. and Miller, M.J. 1998. *The age of migration: international population movements in the modern world*. 6.

[21] Interview held with Hon (Chief) J.K. Akporido, 85, Retired Miner and former Law maker, Warri, Delta state, 28-04-2018. The respondent alluded to this point while discussing the primordial motive for migration by Urhobo people to other parts of Nigeria. He specifically referred to the waves of migration to the Northern part of the country; with reference to the Jos Plateau. He also mentioned the presence of Urhobo migrants in Ikale and its environs. These migrants according to him have successfully integrated themselves into their host communities to the extent that they control some of the

322   M. OFUAFOR

the opportunities and potentials of the areas they visited. This acted as a pull factor for others to move. Linked with this development is the factor of trading. This arguably is one preoccupation that most Urhobo people are involved in. Since most of the clans are involved in farming activities, there was the need for exchange. The driving force behind this exchange metamorphosed into a line of trade activities involving the sale of farm produce such as cassava, pepper, fish, okra, potatoes and palm oil.

By the 1910s when transportation was enhanced with the introduction of the railways, the trading activity as carried out by these Urhobo clans was also enhanced. The availability of transportation system made it possible for far-flung journeys to be undertaken to the North (urhie r'avwosa). They took along with them non-perishable goods such as dried fish, palm oil, cassava flakes (garri), edible starch, local gin (*ogogoro*) and smoked pig meat. In turn, the Urhobo groups began to return from their journeys to the Jos Plateau with Irish potatoes, hides and skin, and onions.[22] The consummation of the relationship from this exchange continued to expand with the inclusion of other ethnic groups in the trade-mix. Consequently, Urhobo people began to make settlements in the Jos Plateau. By virtue of their involvement in the tin mines, some of them first settled along the Naraguta axis, Mister Ali and Bukuru. There was also evidence to suggest that they also settled in Akpata/Jenta areas. Thus, their settlement pattern in Jos metropolis and its environs in the 1910s was characterised by job description, vocation and choice of place. By about 1915 when Jos was officially founded, however, their settlement pattern began to take a new dimension.

The new dimension referred to was due to the colonial policy of trying to keep culturally dissimilar ethnic groups separate.[23] By this measure, the colonial administration began the process of segregation which ultimately led to the 'Sabongari' phenomenon in Jos. This policy, which was tailored

---

vital economic resources of the land. See also, Otite, O. 1979. Rural Migrants as Catalysts in Rural Development: The Urhobo in Ondo State, Nigeria. *Africa: Journal of the International African Institute*. 49. 3: 227–228.

[22] Interview held with Mrs. Rhoda Emuvakpor, 68, Business woman, Warri, Delta state, 28-05-2018. The respondent's maternal grandmother was one of the earliest traders to have forayed into Northern Nigeria by the 1920s. She was well-known in the Agbassa area of Warri as a "tinko" merchant.

[23] Plotnicov, L. 1967. *Strangers to the city: urban man in Jos*, Nigeria. Pittsburg: UP. 41.

HISTORICISING URHOBO MIGRATION, SETTLEMENT ...   323

after the Lugardian model of colonial administration, was considered as elastic, expedient and flexible. Plotnicov, however, suggests that as applied to Jos, the policy was also paternalistic, preferential and inconsistent, which were the factors that eventually led to deep grievances among the immigrant Nigerian residents.[24] As a consequence of the workings of this policy, urban centre of Jos was divided into two separate administrative units: a Native Town, which was subordinate to the Jos Divisional Native Authority, located in Naraguta; and the Township, which was a separate entity of its own within Jos Division. The Township was where Asians and Europeans were settled exclusively in special "reservation"[25] apart from most of the Africans. Subsequently, segregation and discrimination led to the question of identity and history and the related challenges of division, pessimism, despondency and bigotry. These challenges and opportunities as enumerated operated within political structures, economic system and social milieu of the Jos metropolis and its environs.

Thus, increased activities in the tin mines resulted in an increase in labour requirement. This precipitated the migratory trend that characterised and was witnessed in Jos between the late nineteenth century and early twentieth century. The waves of migrations of Urhobo people to Jos metropolis and its environs caused a connection to be established between generations of Urhobo migrants who in so doing connected the histories of different generations of Urhobo migrants who maintained a connection with the homeland. Thus, the socio-economic opportunities created by the first and second waves of Urhobo migrants in Jos served as push factors, which caused Urhobo migrations to Jos metropolis and its environs.

[24] Plotnicov, L. 1967. *Strangers to the city.* 40.

[25] This measure was used to displace most Africans and Nigerians that had earlier settled in these so-called reserved areas. The discriminatory disposition of the colonial administrators promoted segregation, bitterness, and the promotion of class stratification between and among Africans, Asians, and Europeans. This example is seen in most Nigerian Cities such as Lagos, Port Harcourt, Kano, Kaduna, and Enugu. See Plotinicov, L. 1967. *Strangers to the city.* 40–41.

324   M. OFUAFOR

4   URHOBO CULTURAL EXPRESSIONS IN JOS, 1940–1970

In apparent response to what was perceived as 'the awakening of a racial, and not a territorial consciousness', which was a description of external influences during the interwar period,[26] was the emergence and proliferation of associations and movements. These associations were basic instruments established not only to engage in the political and economic space, but also in the social milieu. Thus:

> ..., in the late 1920s, and to an increasing extent throughout the 1930s and 1940s, those Nigerians who would have been most predisposed toward nationalist ideas- the so-called "detribalised," Western-educated, and urbanised elements- were preoccupied in organising tribal unions for the purpose of establishing or maintaining an identity with their lineage, clan, or tribe of origin. This, of course, is a phenomenon characteristics of individuals only recently removed from their close-knit home communities.[27]

Consequently, as a result of their activities:

> kingship and tribal unions sprang up in the main urban centres of Nigeria. These associations were known by various names: for example, Naze Family Meeting, Ngwa Clan Union, Owerri Divisional Union, Calabar Improvement League, Igbirra Progressive Union, and Urhobo Renascent

---

[26] The interwar period which spanned the end of the First World War in 1918 to the beginning of the Second World War in 1938–1945 (about 20 years) witnessed series of development in science and technology, culture, fashion, politics, the economy and military and strategic tactics. Consequently, the period brought upon the global community the unconscious division of the world into a haves and haves-not category. The intensification of the struggle between and among the different blocs in the international system for domination and supremacy led to territorial conquests which were covertly or overtly supported by allies. At this period, however, the developments witnessed in the areas enumerated above, had made for issues of race and racial equality to come to play in the determination of racial superiority. The effect of this external influence on the colonial state in Nigeria became manifested in the emergence of associations and movements that became identity symbols overtime. For more see, Coleman, J.S. 1986. *Nigeria: background to nationalism*. 210.

[27] Coleman, J.S. 1986. *Nigeria: background to nationalism*. 210.

HISTORICISING URHOBO MIGRATION, SETTLEMENT ... 325

Convention. They gave organisational expression to the persistent feeling of loyalty and obligation to the kinship group and the town or village where the lineage was localised.[28]

Although they were mainly localised, they extended their spread to other urban centres outside Lagos and along the Atlantic Coast to places such as Ghana, Togo, Cote d'Ivoire, Senegal and the Gambia. They were organised and mostly led by Western-educated Nigerians. These Western-educated Nigerians gave the impetus for the formation of these associations; but the membership of these organisations was drawn from all sectors of the economy from the illiterate peasant or labourer to the wealthy trader, titled native ruler, or Lagos barrister. As noted by Coleman, however, there have been several exceptions where the tribal union was the exclusive preserve for young schoolboys.[29] The educated elements became deeply involved in the formation and organisation of these associations because of their exclusion from government. Thus, these associations served as platforms for the ventilation of their political ambitions.

As indicative of the paper's objective of examining identity and connection history between the homeland and the host community in Jos, Coleman's postulation on the organisational development of these home associations is examined. According to him:

> The organisational development of tribal associations took two main forms; diffusion and integration. The association idea spread rapidly from the urban centres in three directions: (a) to the rural communities of expatriate groups where "home branches" were formed; (b) to previously inarticulate ethnic groups among whom there had been no associational development (for example, Idoma, Tiv, Birom, and Bakweri); and (c) to special interest groups within the kinship system (for example, women's, students', and farmers' associations). While this process of diffusion was going on, a programme of conscious integration and federation was being pursued. This integrative effort had three phases: (a) the federation of all branches abroad; (b) the integration of federated groups abroad with the home

[28] Coleman, J.S. 1986. *Nigeria: background to nationalism.* 213.

[29] Coleman, J.S. 1986. *Nigeria: background to nationalism.* 213.

326   M. OFUAFOR

branch; and (c) the formation of all-tribal federation in a pyramidal, beginning with the primary association (the extended family among the Ibo and the large urban towns among the Yoruba) and extending upward through the various social levels of the tribe.[30]

Based on the process of diffusion, home associations functioned primarily as platforms for the dissemination of association values to the homelands. By this measure, home branches were established; and these branches helped in the facilitation of the connection of histories of different generations of Urhobo migrants to Jos. This helped as well in maintaining a connection with the homeland. The connection stimulated socio-economic development of the homelands as a result of the encounters of the migrants in the hostland. For instance, the first of Urhobo scholars that travelled abroad for studies was sponsored by the Urhobo Progress Union (UPU) through the support of one Chief Joseph Akpolo Ikutegbe.[31] With this came the primary formation of special interest groups such as the Ufuoma Women's League of Okpe, Eguono Women's Club of Olomu, Kokori Social Club and the rest.

Subsequently, the organisational development took the integrative dimension which encompassed the federation of all branches abroad, and the integration of home branches with those abroad. It concludes with the formation of all-tribal federations in a pyramidal structure. At the base of the pyramid is found the smallest unit in the society; that is, the family. This is followed by the lineage groups and other social levels of the tribe.

---

[30] Coleman, J.S. 1986. *Nigeria: background to nationalism*. 214–215.

[31] Mr. Joseph Akpolo Ikutegbe was the first Financial Secretary, later becoming the Vice-President for many years of Lagos Branch. He was the first Urhobo citizen to sponsor an Urhobo student abroad (United Kingdom) for a professional study. The student was Thomas Michael Ighotite Borke. He left Nigeria for legal studies early in 1937 and died in England in 1955. For more, see Salubi, T.E.A. 1964. The Miracle of an Original Thought: The Origins of Urhobo College, Effurun, on Saturday, 1st August, 1964. Being the text of a speech he delivered on the occasion of the second "Speech Day" of Urhobo College, Effurun on 1st August, 1964.

5 THE URHOBO PROGRESS UNION (UPU), IDENTITY CONSTRUCTION AND CULTURE RETENTION IN JOS

The Urhobo Progress Union (UPU), like most of its counterparts from other parts of Nigeria, is basically an ethnic-based organisation involved in the protection of economic, political and social interests of Urhobo people anywhere they found themselves; especially in the emergent urban cities and towns. Historically, hometown associations functioned as a rallying point for people who came from the same cultural background who found themselves in the emergent urban centres of commerce, industry and politics in Nigeria.[32] As stated earlier and as well corroborated by Alao:

> The formation of such unions began in the second decade of the twentieth century with the formation of the Egba society in 1918. Later, there emerged the Ijebu Young Men (1923), the Yoruba Union (1924), the Egbado Union, the Ekiti National Union, Ibadan Progressive Union (1931). Others included the Ife Union, Ijaiye National Society, Offa Descendants' Union, Ogbomosho Progressive Union, Owo Progressive Union and the Oyo Progressive Union.[33]

The Urhobo Progress Union was established in 1930[34] in Warri with the following as pioneer members; Chief Arebe Uyo, Chief F.A.O. Susu, Chief T.E.A. Salubi, Chief A.S. Wowo, Mr. J.R. Noquapoh, Mr.

---

[32] The author had used "Ibadan" which was his own study area, but for emphasis, this study used "Nigeria". It must be stressed that this has not in any way corroded the import of his work. See, Alao, A. 2001. Associational Life in a Depressed Economy and Hometown Associations among the Yoruba in Ibadan, *Odu: a journal of West African studies*, No. 41, January/July 2001. 29–30.

[33] Like most of these unions, the Urhobo Progress Union (UPU) assumed political, economic and social significance between 1928 and 1948. This period was significant because it coincided with the Great Depression of the 1930s and the Second World War. See, Alao, A. 2001. Associational Life in a Depressed Economy and Hometown Associations among the Yoruba in Ibadan. 30.

[34] While this date remains a subject of controversy among some members of the Union, some were of the opinion that the union had been in existence before 1930; but inaccurate record keeping prompted the First General Council to be held in 1935. It was from this Council meeting that the date of its establishment was put at 1930. Interview held with Mr. David Egwabofo Ideh, 75, Retired Surveyor, Trikania, Kaduna state, 22-04-2018. This was further corroborated by the President-General of the Jos Branch, Mr. Johnson Iroroefe Usieta, 67, School Proprietor, Zaria road, Jos. 28-04-2018.

U.O. Johnson, Dr. F.O. Esiri, Chief J. Gordon Ako and Mr. David Unurhoro.[35] It was established with the initial narrow objective of a mere 'brotherly society.' It was the Lagos Branch, founded by Chief J. Arebe Uyo on 4th November, 1934, that carried the Union by broadening the basis of its constitution, from a mere brotherly society to the wide fertile region of a sturdy, progressive organisation. The actual date of the establishment of the Jos branch of the UPU is not well known. However, according to the President-General, the branch must have been established sometime in the late 1950s or early 1960s.[36]

From the broadening of its objectives, the Union began to emphasise on other core objectives such as provision of socio-economic and psychological security within the context of fierce competition, where the extended family ties were no longer strong. The Urhobo Union also began to function as financial institution which provided much needed funds for ceremonies like marriages and burials as well as capital for economic activities.[37] By extension, the Urhobo union also functioned in the capacity of offering assistance to new immigrants by way of helping them to get situated and settled in their new environment thereby involving them in local and regional politics. Secondly, these unions established linkages between the urban and rural areas. This translated to the organisation of resources to aid community development in the homelands.[38] This was mostly felt in the area of educational development.[39] In spite of these objectives, the Urhobo union, like most others, deviated from its set goals and veered into politics. This is succinctly expressed thus:

[35] The following made modest contributions to the growth and expansion of the Union which resulted in its expansion to other cities and towns in Nigeria. Text of Chief Salubi's speech on the occasion of the speech day of Urhobo College, 1st August, 1964.

[36] Interview held with Mr. Andrew Okiemute Bamwa, 62, Business man, Ferin Gada, Jos. 01-06-2022.

[37] Alao, A. 2001. Associational Life in a Depressed Economy and Hometown Associations among the Yoruba in Ibadan. 30.

[38] Falola, T. and Heaton, M.M. 2008. *A history of Nigeria*. 139.

[39] The consciousness for educational development began to take firm roots in most Urhobo communities as a consequence of their inability to meet up with the employment quota allocated to the group by the colonial administration. This perhaps explains Chief Joseph Akpolo Ikutegbe's gesture for the award of scholarship to an Urhobo citizen as early as 1937. For more see text of Chief Salubi's speech on the occasion of the Speech Day of Urhobo College, 1st August, 1964.

The emergence of parties along ethnic lines, forced many associations into politics with a view to securing political appointments for their members. This politicization became counter productive with disruptive consequences for many hometown associations. The intra party politics of the NCNC and the Action Group in the Western Region between 1951 and 1966 destroyed the cohesion of some of the associations that soon became champions of particularistic interests of members.[40]

As a consequence, hometown associations became enmeshed in bickering as a result of the shift of emphasis from their conventional role as providers of social welfare, economic needs and security for members. Since they could no longer meet with the socio-economic aspirations of their non-political members, it led to 'a shift in the operational emphasis of the associations and secondly to a proliferation of unions.'[41] The UPU was not left out of this political machination to the extent that it also used the platform of the union to sponsor candidates for elective positions in both Regional and Federal elections. For instance, Mr. Mukoro Mowoe was elected a member of the House of Representatives in the 1957 elections with the help of the UPU.

Secondly, the shift in emphasis led to the proliferation of unions. Since those of their members who were not politically inclined had nowhere else to go, they reverted to establishing new clans or town unions. Although this was not common within the ranks of the UPU, it must be stressed that some aggrieved members sometimes withheld their loyalty from the UPU and steadfastly paid loyalty to their clan unions.[42] When they did not withdraw their loyalty, they instead chose to sabotage the interest of the union through subversive activities in the form of deliberate causing of disaffection among members. Some of the younger members, who often

---

[40] Alao, A. 2001. Associational Life in a Depressed Economy and Hometown Associations among the Yoruba in Ibadan. 30.

[41] Alao, A. 2001. Associational Life in a Depressed Economy and Hometown Associations among the Yoruba in Ibadan. 30.

[42] The idea of associational life in Nigeria's urban centres helped in bridge-building among the various ethnic groups. Within each of these ethnic groups there is the tendency for a multiplicity of diverse groups; these are however not splinter groups but they tend to owe allegiance to other 'centres' outside the core union. Examples abound in what Alao has described as dissident groups within the Yoruba groups in Ibadan town. See Alao, A. 2001. Associational Life in a Depressed Economy and Hometown Associations among the Yoruba in Ibadan. 30.

were expected to form the youth wing of the union, reverted to other means of congregating and mobilising their interest which sometimes was inimical to Urhobo interest in Jos. The proliferation of these town and clan Unions engendered a deluge of political interests as witnessed in most urban cities and towns in Nigeria. Jos was not left out of this because of its cosmopolitan nature. On the Plateau were a number of ethnic nationalities from all over the world. The representation of these ethnic groups made Jos a potpourri of political, economic and social mix. Since military governments craved legitimacy, they reverted to the grassroots in order to become relevant. The relevance and legitimacy they sought was given by the elite members of the home associations. As Alao posits, the elite who had wanted to use the platform of the home associations to take part in regional and national politics soon introduced divisions and schisms into the associations.[43]

As earlier alluded to, the socio-economic and political opportunities created by Urhobo group in shaping identity and culture retention abounded in their various endeavours which highlighted and promoted their culture in the hostland. For instance, the mode of dressing for the men; that is, the wrapper, shirt complemented with either a fedora cap or a bowler hat with a walking stick. The women are attired in George or Holland wrapper with matching blouses made of lace materials. From the results of the paper's findings on the popularity of the mode of dressing among the Urhobo group in Jos metropolis and its environs, it is evident that to a large extent Urhobo people have deliberately retained and maintained their identity in Jos. Excerpts of the interviews conducted are presented below:

> I am an Urhobo man with a lot of dignity. I don't joke with my culture. This applies to some other Urhobo men you will meet in the course of your field work. When we have any occasion(burial, marriage or introduction, house-warming and celebrating the graduation of any of our children, we appear there in our Urhobo outfit. This stands us out as a peculiar people. For the Urhobo woman (whether of Urhobo descent or married to an Urhobo man), the wrapper must be worn in two-piece; that is, she cannot

[43] Alao, A. 2001. Associational Life in a Depressed Economy and Hometown Associations among the Yoruba in Ibadan. 30–31.

HISTORICISING URHOBO MIGRATION, SETTLEMENT ... 331

tie one wrapper as applicable to some other ethnic groups. It is not only a means of identity, but also a cultural requisite of her womanhood. It portrays her as a chaste woman.[44]

Our mode of dressing is significant in that it is an expression of our Urhobo identity and culture. Whenever we gather for any occasion as Urhobo people, it becomes pertinent for us to appear in our Urhobo dress. The man appears in his well tied wrapper, a shirt, a bowler hat and a walking stick to complement it. He should be accessorised in beads (which sometimes is used to identify a person with a chieftaincy title, or a man of means; that is, a rich man. This is so because, the beads can sometimes be very expensive).[45]

My Urhobo cultural dressing is impeccable. I was born and raised in Jos notwithstanding, my father and my uncles have always emphasised the need not to 'forget' the culture of my people. We were brought up to uphold the culture, even though there was the preponderance influence of the local culture that we were born into. For instance, my grand mother was a Fulani woman; it would have been expected, therefore, that we would be heavily influenced by the Fulani culture, but my father was able to inculcate the Urhobo tradition into us. To this end, whenever he wanted to host important dignitaries from within or outside Jos, he usually dresses in the traditional Urhobo wrapper, a shirt made of lace material, a bowler hat and his walking stick; which he always goes around with anyway! He has helped me to retain the culture. I am also doing all within my power to inculcate to my sons![46]

These interview excerpts show that all the respondents culturally identified with and promoted their ethnic dress culture in the hostland. They see their mode of dressing as the symbol of their identity that must not be allowed to die.

Alongside their dress culture, the Urhobo group also showcased and promoted their delicacies such as starch, *ukodo* (yam porridge), *banga* soup, *owho* (oil soup), *yellow garri* (cassava flakes embellished with palm

---

[44] Interview held with Mr. Solomon Ugege, 65, Miner/Businessman, Zaria road, Jos. 29-05-2018.

[45] Interview held with Mr. Prisetly Akpomien, 60, Businessman, Akpata area, Jos. 29-05-2018.

[46] Interview held with Mr. Andre Oruma Menta, 65, Miner/Businessman, Zebra road, Jos. 30-05-2018.

oil), dried fish, smoked pork meat and tapioca (sun-dried cassava flakes). Since most of these delicacies were mostly harnessed and processed in the homeland, it gave the opportunity to connect to the homeland.

6 CONCLUSION

The paper has shown that there exist an Urhobo migrant community in Jos metropolis and its environs between 1940 and 1970. The convergence of this community in Jos has been traced to its migration history which has been documented to have begun in the late nineteenth century, but climaxed in the second decade of the twentieth century. As in particular with the period covered by this paper, Urhobo migrant community in Jos metropolis and its environs was known to have contributed and recorded some successes in the tin mine industry. As a result of this, they are reputed to have been involved in the socio-economic and political development of Jos metropolis and its environs. In spite of their modest contributions and successes, they were able to use their cultural expressions as the most significant factor in the construction and negotiation of their identity in Jos metropolis and its environs through the platform of the Urhobo Progress Union (UPU). Urhobo migrants ethnic identity construction served to show the extent of attachment to their home culture despite the years spent in the hostland.

Climate Change, Conflicts and Environment

Repowering Local Governance for Sustainability: Climate Change Mitigation of Healthcare Delivery in Nigeria

Bolanle Waliu Shiyanbade, Wasiu Abiodun Makinde, and Gbeminiyi Kazeem Ogunbela

1 INTRODUCTION

In recent decades, global warming and sea level rise and other issues due to greenhouse effects causing climate change have been a subject of scientific and social research, discussion and public debates, policy direction and general governance concern. Amuka et al. (2018) argued that natural and human activities generate greenhouse effect causing the rise in the average atmospheric temperature of the earth resulting in global warming. They further argued that global warming changes the average weather conditions of the earth and hence, climate change.

B. W. Shiyanbade (✉) · W. A. Makinde · G. K. Ogunbela
Obafemi Awolowo University, Ile-Ife, Nigeria
e-mail: bwshiyanbade@oauife.edu.ng

W. A. Makinde
e-mail: wasiu.makinde@federalpolyilaro.edu.ng

G. K. Ogunbela
e-mail: gbeminiyi.ogunbela@federalpolyilaro.edu.ng

© The Author(s), under exclusive license to Springer Nature Switzerland AG 2023
A. I. Adeniran (ed.), *African Development and Global Engagements*,
https://doi.org/10.1007/978-3-031-21283-3_16

335

However, climate change, argued Shehu et al. (2018), is one of the greatest challenges currently facing humans and the environment. Many researches and reports projected a worsening impact if effective measures are not taken immediately for mitigation and adaptation (Brink & Wamster, 2018; Mees & Driessen, 2019; Mees et al., 2019; Williams et al., 2020). Haider (2019) stated that Nigeria has not been exempted from the impact of climate change, though not the same, but across the entire country. He stated further that it has caused the spread of infectious diseases, food- and water-borne illnesses, increases air pollution and surge cases of meningitis. Corroborating, Shehu et al. (2018) revealed that flood and erosion, spread of health risk diseases and food scarcity due to shortage in agricultural output have become an issue of concern among levels of government in Nigeria. Adedotun and Adedotun (2020) supported that it is difficult to compare the health risk associated with climate change impact, as are many and vary. Olaleye et al. (2021) contributed to the above argument that in Nigeria, humans become increasingly susceptible to climate-related diseases and death, due to adverse climate conditions on millions of people in the country.

The entire world including Nigeria, at national and subnational levels, has made concerted efforts in tackling the challenges of climate on agricultural food production, migration, environmental degradation and health risk, among others. Potentially influential, but less appreciated in climate change mitigation initiatives are local governance structure. Harker et al. (2016) and Quayle et al. (2020) stated that local government has been among the most active jurisdiction on the climate change font, in creating a transactional network to share knowledge and take action. Moreover, the challenges of autonomy, finance and democratisation facing the local government system in Nigeria (Odu, 2014; Vambe & Adekeye, 2013) necessitate the focus on local governance ability for governing climate change mitigation with particular to healthcare in Nigeria. Local communities in their groups or individually, argued Dale et al. (2019), play significant roles in climate adaptation and mitigation due to their direct control over some critical sources of emission and operate on a scale that is most accessible and responsive to citizen through advisory session, town hall meeting, civic engagement, among others.

The focus on local governance efforts on climate change mitigation is recipes on the National Adaptation Plans (NAPs) adopted under the United Nations Framework Convention on Climate Change (UNFCCC) that gave greater consideration to local actors for implementing climate change adaptation or mitigation policy (UNFCCC, 2017; Williams et al., 2020b). This chapter intends to examine local governance effectiveness on climate change mitigation due to the proximity of climate change to local populace and businesses, which require all stakeholder's attention, especially at a local level. Therefore, this chapter seeks to examine the effectiveness of local governance in governing climate change mitigation on healthcare in Nigeria as well as the challenges facing local governance in governing climate change mitigation on healthcare in Nigeria, to provide a policy recommendation for improvement or repowering local governance for better performance.

1.1 The Discourse Multidimensionality of Climate Change

Climate change as a development issue has been widely captured in the literature. Different perspectives about the notion have been copiously documented in the literature. An argument in support of multidisciplinary ontology is deeply offered in Esbjorn-Hargens (2010). The writer deployed narrative research to establish overlapping and diverse contexts through which climate change can be studied. Deploying who, how and what questions, 18 professions were identified with the extent to which their professional activities contributed to climate change. Esbjorn-Hargens (2010) emphasised multidimensional project. This position is strengthened in Nerini et al. (2019) and Karlsson et al. (2020).

For Nerini et al. efforts were made to understand how climate change action is interconnected to other Sustainable Development Goals (SDGs). Using a structural review method, they discovered that climate change interventional activities are intersecting with 16 goals of the SDGs. Multidisciplinary interventional partnership between climate change action and naming of governance policies was highlighted as positive drivers of the climatic change projects. Karlsson et al. (2020) documented areas of SDGs that bear implementation gradient with climatic change action.

It was argued that implementing climate action produces beneficial results desired in health (relating to SDG 3), air cleanness (relating to SDG 11, 15) and energy management (relating to SDG 7). The bottom line is that achieving the agenda of climate action will be limited without framing climate change projects and a multidimensional problem which requires stakeholder collaboration. Therefore, investigating how local governance is contributing to climate change project as a stakeholder in the implementation chain requires brief documentation of previous research effort. Caetano et al. (2020) assessed integration of policies on climate change focussing on the impact on energy accessibility. It was observed that the collaboration and coordination required to manage multiple actors involved in the implementation of climate action policies and strategies was grossly inadequate. The authors analysed the importance of framing social peculiarities while implementing and integrating climate action policies among multiple levels of governance institutions.

1.2 Climate Change: Perception and Consequences

OYERO et al. (2018) conducted a descriptive mixed study to understand how communication strategy has translated into climate-friendly behaviour among local residents. The result revealed the continuation of unfriendly climate practices in terms of waste-burning activities, inordinate waste disposal culture and deforestation for unclean energy. They argued for cross-sectional communication and advocacy plan to scale up climate change awareness among the people. Hence, this provided explanation on the deployment of Multi-sectoral Communication Strategy (MCS) to reverse the dwindling climatic action awareness among the people.

Urama and Ozor (2010) documented one of the dire consequences of public neglect of climate change narratives. They provided text on the extent to which global warming and unfavourable climatic conditions undermined access to water in Africa especially in Sub-Saharan Africa. This is evident in dangerous dimension of water supply in the continent. The imbalance in flow of water has been linked to prolong flooding, drought, irregular rainfall, drying water bodies, lands and mountains eruptions (Urama & Ozor, 2010). The documentation of these authors suggested deleterious effects of unfriendly climate change threatening both humans and animals. Urama and Ozor identified internationalisation of climate actions, investment in scientific innovations, institutionalisation of policy instrument, multi-disciplinary climate action approach, and scaling up of disaster response management as adaptation cultures needed to fight back at climate change.

A decade after Urama and Ozor's publication, Coates et al. (2020) published a study on how climate change is driving public health concerns. This shows that previous antidotes applied to limit the navigational force of climate change have not yielded the desired outcome. Coates et al. did a mind-weakening documentary evidence suggesting brutal occupation of humanity by climate change. These infiltrations have been reportedly linked to life-threatening temperatures, ultraviolet radiation, poor air quality and skin attack as direct consequences of climate change. Apart from direct effects, food shortage, malnutrition, environmental-induced conflict, climatically induced migration and a host of infectious diseases have been traced to climate change order (Coates et al., 2020).

Similarly, Bishop-William et al. (2018) investigated the extent to which weather pattern and hospitalisations patterns can be linked to climate change. The aim of the authors was to suggest adaptation measures in Uganda. The study relied on descriptive and inferential statistics to draw positions. In the two selected hospitals, a total of 41,216 hospitalisations were recorded with acute respiratory infections being the highest diagnosis. This was followed by malaria, strong gastrointestinal sickness and trauma. This was explained to represent the impact of changes in daily temperature which has grown from 18.6 °C to above 30 °C within the period under review. The study also established a causal relationship between hospitalisations and meteorological variables in the community. The findings indicated that there was a significant association between seasonal variations and hospitalisations. The discomposed results revealed dry seasons which are synonymous with higher temperatures saw more hospital admissions. There was statistical assurance that across all form of diagnoses, hospital admissions were significantly higher on days of extremely hot temperatures. This shows climate change is raging havoc more than before. The study suggested that the application of climate adaptation strategies in the health sector of Uganda is still fragmented.

A related work documented a fair share of livestock in the ongoing climatic variations (Bett et al., 2017). Bett et al. investigated the trend of infectious diseases among livestock other than arthropod vectors and tsetse flies. The study found a positive causal association between drought and southern oscillation on one hand, and the association between increasing fever outbreaks and weather patterns in the rift valley of East Africa. Belt et al. further enlisted mitigation and adaptation necessary to adapt to new challenges posed by ongoing climatic change. It was observed that previous mitigation plans of pastoralist often result in the loss of livestock while practicing avoidance migration (Bett et al., 2017). Among the suggested adoption order are building capacity of livestock owners, transactional coordination of interventional policies, data knowledging, breeding to control exposure to infectious and more research for new development in livestock sector.

Other related climate-related studies revealed mixed factors that undermine the potency of climate adaptation policies. For instance, Hisali et al. (2011) mentioned weak capacity to adapt, which is dictated by age and sex of the head of the family, non-farm employment, agro-ecological peculiarities, education and others. Cheshmehzangi and Dawodu (2019) used De ceuval project in Amsterdam to construct how urban development approaches adaptation policies of climate action into a working narrative. They argued least-top hierarchy approach in handling climate action intervention draining basis from transition theory. The authors stressed the significance of mainstreaming local actors and agents into mobilisation for climate action.

Another adaptation study conducted by Forino et al. (2017) assessed the influence climate change adaptation has on reducing disaster risk using three local administrations in Australia. The study indicated some level of partnership and a common understanding of the need to confront rapidly deteriorating climate conditions. It also pointed to the need for adaptation strategies for built industry and public participation. This investigation further established the significant role local governance can play in meterialising actionable climatic policies and strategies.

1.3   Local Governance Narratives of Climate Action

Slack (2015) offered an enhanced argument in making the case for involvement are local government in planning and implementing climate change action. She articulated that almost all SDGs goals are incidentally jurisdictions of local government. For instance, when local governance is mentioned, we talk of water, sanitation, gender equality, sustainable use of resources, food security and social protection and a host of others. It is therefore incumbent to make available to local government adequate implementation resources needed to contribute to the fight against climate change.

Similarly, Perry et al. (2021) provided reasons to scale up local government drive for climatic change action. They documented challenges faced by the local government in contributing to climate change in Britain. Over-dependence on national direction, weak local engagement, unfinanced local responsibilities, concentration of limited SDGs, complexities

REPOWERING LOCAL GOVERNANCE FOR SUSTAINABILITY ...   341

of translating and adapting SDGs into the local context and limited coverage of SDGs knowledge in governance and practice. These findings are in a similar direction to that of Dale et al. (2019) where funding difficulties, deficit of human capital required to drive the transition of local governance into mainstream climate action, underutilisation of emissions tracking system, complicated and complex inter-local partnerships, discontinuity in climate action mandate as a result of regime change and risk of policy inconsistency and incongruity.

Caetano et al. (2020) argued for the need to bring local institutions into administration of climate action policies, this campaign was also raised in Perry et al. (2021) and Slack (2015). But this call is limited by institutional constraints local institutions faced in contributing their quota to the war against climate change

Cheshmehzangi and Dawodu (2019), Forino et al. (2017) and Slack (2015) undoubtedly located their argument in support of localisation of climatic action within local governance arrangement, yet, this critical mass is challenged by a high incidence of climatic changes especially healthwise. In line with this, Chersich and Wright (2019) employed a systematic review to assess how climate change action is producing targeted results in the health industry. It was revealed that despite the formation of climate action plan at natural and sub-natural levels, sharp neglecting is noticed in the area of health risk of climatic change implication on vulnerable communities. The study raised doubt about preparedness for future emergency of climate change events and stamina of the stressed health institutions to cope with climatic change response in times of emergency. Although this study was conducted in South Africa, it is important to document how prepared are local governance system in Nigeria for climate change shock. Focusing on local governance contribution to mitigation measures against health-related climate change is necessitated by weak local health infrastructure in most of the developing countries.

Research by Handayani (2021) assessed how local governments are responding to climate change in Indonesia, Pekalongan to be precised. The results revealed documentation of greenhouse gas history is still fragmented. The system only provided information on agriculture sector while other sectors' profile on gas emission are mostly inadequate. The study also pinpoints importance of local government in climate action response as policies are designed for local implementation. The study established the existence of several locality-induced strategies such as the creation of climate village, the development of coastal duke, spreading the presence of green open space and a host of other programmes.

It is obvious that a good number of research resources have been invested in probing climate action narratives, but few considered nexus between local governance and health-related climate change action. Empirical literature on the outcome of local governance institutions on climate change induced health challenges is still limited. Bringing local governance and climate action on local health challenges is significant because the first victim of climate change is always the vulnerable communities dwelling within the jurisdiction of local governments. Although, previous works studied health-related risk imposed by climate change but not from the perspective of local governance.

For instance, Opoku et al. (2021) assessed preparedness of healthcare professions for possible climate change emergencies. They used cross-sectional research to provide empirical insight on how health practitioners from six African countries (South Africa, Nigeria, Ghana, Namibia, Ethiopia and Kenya) perceived climate change as a serious health issue and how their respective countries prepared for climate change attacks. The study provided general results that health practitioners are aware of the danger posed by climate change but available resources undermine the potency of their preparedness. The author identified inadequate medical utilities and equipment, weak technical network, lack of proper coordination of emergency response system and deficit of other related resources for climate action implementation. Perhaps, one wonders if the level of national preparedness among notable countries in Africa appears insufficient, then, what is the faith of sub-national institutions in combating climate change? This empirical reality propelled the urgency to interrogate productivity and drawbacks of local governance in championing climate action at the critical mass level in Nigeria using selected local jurisdictions.

2 Methodology

The study adopted a mixed approach of qualitative and quantitative methods of descriptive survey research design through the administration of questionnaires, conduct of in-depth interviews and content analysis of secondary data. The population of the study comprised local government staff, members of traditional institutions and community development associations in Lagos State, Nigeria. The choice of Lagos State for data collection is a result of concentration of industries and headquarters of most registered companies in Nigeria including the headquarter of the Security and Exchange Commission (SEC). Also, it is the most populous city in Nigeria and Africa with more than 23 million people, but a very low geographical space of 3577 km^2 in which nearly a quarter is occupied by lagoons, creeks and rivers, exposing it to sea-level rise, intensity of tropical storms, warming air and sea surface temperature and increased variability in rainfall patterns. The study adopted a convenient sampling technique due to the larger size of the population with no accurate number, especially for that of community development associations. Therefore, 50 questionnaires were administered to two selected local government areas, each from three senatorial districts of Lagos State, totalling 300 questionnaires for six local government areas in the state. Those questionnaires were administered to the staff of local government, members of traditional institutions and community development associations. Data collected from questionnaire administration were complemented with information extracted from focus group discussions and in-depth interviews with selected respondents from sampled local government areas of Lagos State. Data collected from the questionnaire were analysed using descriptive and inferential statistics, and content analysis was used for data collected through in-depth interview. Out of 300 questionnaires administered, 273 questionnaires were recovered and useful for the research, representing 91% of the total questionnaires distributed. This methodology is connected to the postulations of the Gaia theory of metabolism traced to James Lovelock that emerged towards the end of the 1960s, which postulates that living organisms interact with their environment each time, and the interaction helps the living organism to adjust to any changes in the natural state of the environment. The theory hypothesised that the ability of an organism to live normal life depends on the relative ease of adjustment to the environmental changes. The Gaia theory assumes that whenever these natural compositions are altered, the life of an organism is threatened and its survival depends on how far and how fast it can adjust itself to the environmental changes. This proves that human activities such as excess greenhouse gas emission alters the composition of the atmosphere air with consequences on human health. The ability to mitigate this through local governance structure will reduce the threat to human life and helps their survival.

3 Analysis of Results and Interpretation

Respondents' Demographics

Local Government Staff	104
Member of Community Development Associations	67
Member of Community Development Associations	102
Total	**273**
Respondents from Local Government Sampled	
Kosofe Local Government	48
Ikorodu Local Government	49
Agege Local Government	45
Alimosho Local Government	51
Ibeju Lekki Local Government	42
Lagos Mainland Local Government	38
Total	**273**

4 Results of Data Collected

4.1 *Effectiveness of Local Governance in Governing Climate Change Mitigation on Healthcare in Nigeria*

The analysis of data collected on the effectiveness of local governance in governing climate change mitigation on healthcare in Nigeria was through descriptive and inferential statistics. Variables used to test this objective were rated in a 4-Likert rating of Highly Effective, Moderately Effective, Fairly Effective and Not Effective. The result shows that 91 respondents which equal 33.3% of the total sampled respondents agree that local governance is not effective, 104 respondents which equal 38.1% of the total sampled respondents stated that local governance is fairly effective, 39 respondents which equal 14.3% of the sampled respondents stated that local governance is moderately effective and 39 respondents which equal 14.3% of the total sampled respondents stated that local governance is highly effective in bringing changes to waste management recycling system to reduce global warming in the sampled local government area of Lagos State, Nigeria. This result shows that local governance needs to be empowered in the area of waste management to support the activities of other levels of government as well as international agencies in climate change mitigation.

Also, the result shows that 78 respondents which equal 28.6% of the total sampled respondents stated that local governance is not effective, 143 respondents which equal 52.4% of the total sampled respondents stated that local governance is fairly effective, 39 respondents which equal 14.3% of the total sampled respondents stated that local governance is moderately effective and 13 respondents which equal 4.8% of the total sampled respondents stated that local governance is highly effective in improving the planting of trees to reduce greenhouse gasses causing global warming leading to climate change in Nigeria. In the same vein, the result shows that 130 respondents which equal 47.6% of the total sampled respondents stated that local governance is not effective, 78 respondents which equal 28.6% of the total sampled respondents stated that local governance is fairly effective, 39 respondents which equal 14.3% of the total sampled respondents stated that local governance is moderately effective and 26 respondents which equal 9.5% of the total sampled respondents stated that local governance is highly effective in influencing citizen's use of energy saving bulb to reduce global warming causing climate change. This result shows that local governance needs to be empowered to govern climate change mitigation on healthcare in Nigeria.

However, the result of the data shows that 52 respondents which equal 19.0% of the total sampled respondents stated that local governance is not effective, 65 respondents which equal 23.8% of the total sampled respondents stated that local governance is fairly effective, 52 respondents which equal 19.0% of the total sampled respondents stated that local governance is moderately effective and 104 respondents which equal 38.1% of the total sampled respondents stated that local governance is highly effective in educating people against open-defecation to reduce greenhouse effect causing global warming and climate change in Nigeria. Also, 156 respondents which equal 57.1% of the total sampled respondents stated that local governance is not effective, 65 respondents which equal 23.8% of the total sampled respondents stated that local governance is fairly effective, 26 respondents which equal 9.5% of the total sampled respondents stated that local governance is moderately effective and 26 respondents which equal 9.5% of the total sampled respondents stated that local governance is highly effective in educating citizen on the moderate use of F-gases equipment such as fire extinguisher, air conditioner and power generating set to reduce global warming causing climate change in Nigeria.

Also, 26 respondents which equal 9.5% of the total sampled respondents stated that local governance is not effective, 26 respondents which

346   B. W. SHIYANBADE ET AL.

equal 9.5% of the total sampled respondents stated that local governance is fairly effective, 91 respondents which equal 33.3% of the total sampled respondents stated that local governance is moderately effective and 130 respondents which equal 47.6% of the total sampled respondents stated that local governance is highly effective in reducing deforestation to reduce global warming causing climate change in Nigeria. In the same vein, the result shows that 26 respondents which equal 9.5% of the total sampled respondents stated that local governance is not effective, 104 respondents which equal 38.1% of the total sampled respondents stated that local governance is fairly effective, 104 respondents which equal 38.1% of the total sampled respondents stated that local governance is moderately effective and 39 respondents which equal 14.3% of the total sampled respondents stated that local governance is highly effective in educating citizen on human activities causing global warming in Nigeria. This shows that local governance needed to be empowered to govern climate change mitigation on healthcare in Nigeria.

However, a linear regression test was adopted for inferential statistics. The model summary table (Table 1) tests the strength of the relationship between the variables considered for the hypothesis. It shows that R-value is 0.344, R Square is 0.118 and Adjusted R Square is 0.115. This means that there is a weak relationship between the variables tested. This indicates a weak relationship between local governance activities in governing climate change mitigation on healthcare in Nigeria. Also, the ANOVA table (Table 2) is used to accept the null or alternate hypothesis. The significance value of the F Statistics is 0.000 and F Value is 36.365. Since the significance value of F Statistics is less than 0.05, we accept the alternate hypothesis and reject the null hypothesis. Therefore, there is a significant relationship between local governance activities and governing climate change mitigation on healthcare in Nigeria. The study concluded that there is a weak significant relationship between local governance and governing climate change mitigation on healthcare in Nigeria.

4.2   Challenges Facing Local Governance in Governing Climate Change Mitigation on Healthcare in Nigeria

The analysis of data collected on the challenge facing local governance in governing climate change mitigation on healthcare in Nigeria was through descriptive and inferential statistics. Variables used to test this objective were rated in a 4-Likert rating of Highly Challenging, Fairly

REPOWERING LOCAL GOVERNANCE FOR SUSTAINABILITY ...   347

Table 1   Model summary[a]

Model	R	R Square	Adjusted R Square	Std. Error of the Estimate	Durbin-Watson
1	0.344[b]	0.118	0.115	0.96043	1.099

[a]Dependent Variable: Local Governance support the planting of trees and flowers in residential and industrial building in their domain
[b]Predictors: (Constant), Local Governance educates people against open defecation to reduce greenhouse gases causing global warming

Table 2   ANOVA[a]

Model		Sum of Squares	Df	Mean Square	F	Sig
1	Regression	33.545	1	33.545	36.365	0.000[b]
	Residual	249.979	271	0.922		
	Total	283.524	272			

[a]Dependent variable: Local governance support planting of trees and flowers in residential and industrial building in their domain
[b]Predictors: (Constant), Local governance educates people against open defecation to reduce greenhouse gases causing global warming

Challenging, Moderately Challenging and Not Challenging. The result shows that 39 respondents which equal 14.3% of the total sampled respondents stated that inadequate fund for local governance activities on climate change mitigation is not challenging, 39 respondents which equal 14.3% of the total sampled respondents stated that inadequate fund for local governance activities is a fairly challenging, 65 respondents which equal 23.8% of the total sampled respondents stated that inadequate fund for local governance activities is moderately challenging and 130 respondents which equal 47.6% of the total sampled respondents stated that inadequate fund for local governance activities is highly challenging to local governance activities on climate change mitigation on healthcare in Nigeria. This variable has a mean score of 3.05 which ranked it as the third most severe challenge facing local governance in governing climate change mitigation on healthcare in Nigeria. Also, the result shows that 26 respondents which equal 9.5% of the total sampled respondents stated that lack of constitutional power is not challenging local governance, 26 respondents which equal 9.5% of the total sampled respondents stated that lack of constitutional power is a fairly challenge to local governance, 104 respondents which equal 38.1% of the total sampled respondents stated that lack of constitutional power is a moderate challenge to local governance and 117 respondents which equal 42.9% of the total sampled respondents stated that lack of constitutional power is highly challenging local governance to partake in local issues concerning climate change mitigation in Nigeria. The mean score of this variable is 3.14 which ranked it as the second most severe challenge facing local governance in governing climate change mitigation on healthcare in Nigeria. This shows that to empower local governance on climate change mitigation, these problems need to be tackled.

However, the result shows that 104 respondents which equal 38.1% of the total sampled respondents stated that the absence of mutual cooperation with other levels of governance is not a challenge to local governance, 78 respondents which equal 28.6% of the total sampled respondents stated that absence of mutual cooperation with other levels of governance is a fairy challenge to local governance, 65 respondents which equal 23.8% of the total sampled respondents stated that absence of mutual cooperation with other levels of governance is a moderate challenge to local governance and 26 respondents which equals 9.5% of the total sampled respondents stated that absence of mutual cooperation with other levels of governance is a high challenge to local governance in governing climate change mitigation on healthcare in Nigeria. This variable is with a mean score of 2.05 which ranked it sixth among challenges facing local governance in governing climate change mitigation on healthcare in Nigeria. Also, the result shows that 52 respondents which equal 19.0% of the total sampled respondents stated that high level of illiteracy on climate change among local populace is not a challenge to local governance, 13 respondents which equal 4.8% of the total sampled respondents stated that high level of illiteracy on climate change among local populace is a fairly challenge to local governance, 117 respondents which equal 42.9% of the total sampled respondents stated that high level of illiteracy on climate change among local populace is a moderate challenge to local governance and 91 respondents which equal 33.3% of the total sampled respondents stated that high level of illiteracy on climate change among local populace is a high challenge to local governance in governing climate change mitigation on healthcare in Nigeria. This variable is with a mean score of 2.91 which ranked it fourth among challenges used to test factors affecting local governance in governing climate change mitigation on healthcare in Nigeria.

Also, the result shows that 91 respondents which equal 33.3% of the total sampled respondents stated that poor leadership capacity at local level is not a challenge to local governance, 91 respondents which equal 33.3% of the total sampled respondents stated that poor leadership capacity at local level is a fairly challenge to local governance, 52 respondents which equal 19.0% of the total sampled respondents stated that poor leadership capacity at local level is a moderate challenge to local governance and 39 respondents which equal 14.3% of the total sampled respondents stated that poor leadership capacity at local level is a high challenge to local governance in governing climate change mitigation on healthcare in Nigeria. This variable has a mean score of 2.14 which ranked fifth among challenges facing local governance in governing climate change mitigation on healthcare in Nigeria. In the same vein, the result shows that 26 respondents which equal 9.5% of the total sampled respondents stated that religious belief over science by local populace is not a challenge to local governance, 26 respondents which equal 9.5% of the total sampled respondents stated that religious belief over science by local populace is a fairly challenge to local governance, 65 respondents which equal 23.8% of the total sampled respondents stated that religious belief over science by local populace is a moderate challenge to local governance and 156 respondents which equal 57.1% of the total sampled respondents stated that religious belief over science by local populace is a high challenge to local governance in governing climate change mitigation on healthcare in Nigeria. This variable has a mean score of 3.29 which ranked it first among challenges facing local governance in governing climate change on healthcare in Nigeria.

4.3   Discussion of Findings

The study has shown that local governance has a role in governing climate change mitigation on healthcare in Nigeria. the study revealed from primary data collected that 38.1% of the total sampled respondents stated that local governance is fairly effective, 14.3% of the sampled respondents stated that local governance is moderately effective and 14.3% of the total sampled respondents stated that local governance is highly effective in bringing changes to waste management recycling system to reduce global warming in the sampled local government area of Lagos State Nigeria.

The study also revealed that 38.1% of the total sampled respondents stated that local governance is fairly effective, 38.1% of the total sampled respondents also state that local governance is moderately effective and 14.3% of the sampled respondents stated that local governance is highly effective in educating citizen on human activities causing global warming in Nigeria. The inferential statistics shows that there is a weak significant relationship between local governance and governing of climate change mitigation on healthcare in Nigeria. Williams et al. (2020a, 2020b) corroborate the above findings that lack of capacity for climate change adaptation and mitigation at the subnational levels, especially at local governance level, has been a subject of concern for implementing National Adaptation Plan on climate change.

Away from narratives of effectiveness of local governance on climate mitigation strategies, results on challenges confronting workability of local governance in making mitigation strategies actionable were situated within the body of empirical evidence. The study identified difficulty in raising funds necessary to scale up climate action at the local jurisdictions. The implication is that irrespective of stakeholder roles allotted to local institutions in combating climate change, the outcome will always remain minimal if not zero. Issues of funding have been repeatedly identified as key drivers of poor performance of local governance when it comes to climate action. Opoku et al. (2021) raised the issue of resource allocation, which they regarded as undermining the potency of preparedness of health sector against climate change in Africa. Funding also appeared in the positions of Perry et al. (2021) and Dale et al. (2019). For Perry et al., jurisdictionally empowering agents of local governance to contribute to anti-climate change policies' planning and implementation without adequately providing budgetary allocation contradicts the whole essence of the climate agenda.

Problem of constitutionality of local institutions' climate action was observed in the descriptive analysis. Local governance impact on climate change mitigation strategies has remained infinitesimal due to lording-over tendency of higher governance authorities. For instance, the Nigerian local government system is constitutionally enslaved to the operations of state governments, which in turn, are manned by governors with dictatorial ideologies. This constraint was articulated by Perry et al. (2021) with the Britain example. The authors nursed fear as to the ability of local institutions to lead climate action in their respective communities.

The doubt was linked to over-dependence on national direction when making climate action decisions, and this might drag any locally proposed innovation on mitigation of climate change. Local government might not be able to proactively engage in climate change emergency if the institutional substance it relieved is sourced outside constitutional coverage. This is more important than ever given the need to manage a multi-level governance network in the fight against climate change (Caetano et al., 2020).

Mutual cooperation was considered. The study discovered the absence of mutual cooperation limiting the productivity of climate change mitigation intervention of local institutions. This particular factor featured in the works of Caetano et al. (2020), Dale et al. (2019) and Forino et al. (2017). These previous works emphasised the need to orientate all stakeholders to institutionally embrace horizontal and vertical harmonisation all climate change response action. Dale et al. argued for inter-locals partnerships among local governance institutions that are vulnerable to climate change events. Caetano et al. focussed on how integration culture can be enhanced among all levels of governance to achieve optimal output as far as climate agenda is concerned. Hypothetically, managing a disaster which requires huge financial commitment in a locality call for involvement of higher level governance authorities (Federal Government or State Government), as such the local authorities must be adequately equipped to provide necessary information for a chain of action to be taken. The spirit of inter-locals partnership serves as a lift for local authorities suffering from human capital deficit necessary to drive climate action regime. Leadership capacity also threatened the efficacy of local institutions in mitigating climate change. The leadership context can be seen from diverse perspectives. For instance, challenges of political leadership were nursed by Caetano et al. while Dale et al. considered the leadership problem from transformational angle, they argued that constant mandate variations occasioned by election, and possible policy inconsistency and incongruity can be linked to poor performance of municipal authorities in climate action. Leadership configuration at the level of local institutions seems critical for effective local governance especially when leading the climate action agenda.

5 Conclusion

Local governance is a unique system whereby various actors can come together, discuss local issues and explore local options for a solution. Effective local governance systems are an imperative part of well-governing system as they are the closest units to the people. The prevailing environmental challenges as a result of climate change, mostly caused by human activities necessitate a wake-up call on local governance system to govern the mitigation or adaptation of it on human life, especially local citizens and their businesses. This study discovered a weak but significant relationship between local governance and climate change mitigation on healthcare in Nigeria. It was concluded that the ineffectiveness of local governance in governing climate change mitigation on healthcare was a result of challenges facing the local governance system, identified in this study, that require all stakeholder's (national and subnational government inclusive) attention to resolve. The key reason for weak climate change mitigation and adaptation in Nigeria is as a result of ineffective local governance activities in governing climate change mitigation in Nigeria.

Policy Recommendations The study recommends that:

(a) There should be a policy that will strengthen the power of local governance system in Nigeria to perform better in governing climate change mitigation and other environmental challenges.
(b) National and sub-national governments should collaborate with local governance system in formulating policy for climate change mitigation and adaptation.
(c) National and sub-national governments should improve funding of local governance system as well as reduce encroachment on their local sources of fund.
(d) More constitutional power is required to strengthen local governance system for improved governing of climate change mitigation on healthcare in Nigeria.

Acknowledgements We would like to thank and appreciate all the staff in local government area selected, Traditional Rulers and CDAs for this study.

Funding The authors received no financial support for the research, authorship and/or publication of the article.

Disclosure Statement No potential conflict of interest was reported by the authors.

Declarations

Informed consent and ethical approval The participants selected in the study gave informed consent and voluntarily participated in the study. There was no harm to the participants and also the staff of local government areas selected in Nigeria; Traditional Rulers and CDAs were given fictional names in order to ensure confidentiality and anonymity of the participants in the study.

Conflict of Interest The paper is co-authorship, the authors state that there is no conflict of interest in any form, the participants selected within the study areas participated voluntarily, and there is data availability for this study.

REFERENCES

Adedotun, D. O., & Adedotun, S. B. (2020). Resident's perception of the effect of citizen change on the incidence of diseases in Osogbo, Osun State Nigeria. *Osun Geographical Review, 3,* 1–9.

Amuka, J. I., Asogwu, F. O., Ugwuayi, R. O., Omeje, A. N., & Onyechi, T. (2018). Climate change and life expectancy in a developing country: Evidence from greenhouse gas (CO_2) emission in Nigeria. *International Journal of Economics and Financial Issues, 8*(4), 113–119.

Bett, B., Kiunga, P., Gachohi, J., Sindato, C., Mbotha, D., Robinson, T., & Grace, D. (2017). Effects of climate change on the occurrence and distribution of livestock diseases. *Preventive Veterinary Medicine, 137,* 119–129.

Bishop-Williams, K. E., Berrang-Ford, L., Sargeant, J. M., Pearl, D. L., Lwasa, S., Namanya, D. B., ... Harper, S. L. (2018). Understanding weather and hospital admissions patterns to inform climate change adaptation strategies in the healthcare sector in Uganda. *International Journal of Environmental Research and Public Health, 15*(11), 2402.

Brink, E., & Wamster, C. (2018). Collaborative governance for climate change adaptation: Mapping citizen–municipality interactions. *Environmental Policy and Governance, 28,* 82–97.

Caetano, T., Winker, H., & Depledge, J. (2020). Towards zero carbon and zero poverty: Integrating national climate change mitigation and sustainable development goals. *Climate Policy, 20*(7), 773–778. https://doi.org/10.1080/14693062.2020.1791404

Chersich, M. F., & Wright, C. Y. (2019). Climate change adaptation in South Africa: A case study on the role of the health sector. *Globalization and Health*, *15*(1), 1–16.

Cheshmehzangi, A., & Dawodu, A. (2019). Sustainable urban development in the age of climate change. In *Sustainable urban development in the age of climate change* (pp. 157–182). Palgrave Macmillan.

Coates, S. J., Enbiale, W., Davis, M. D., & Andersen, L. K. (2020). The effects of climate change on human health in Africa, a dermatologic perspective: A report from the International Society of Dermatology Climate Change Committee. *International Journal of Dermatology*, *59*(3), 265–278.

Dale, A., Robinson, J., King, L., Burch, S., Newell, R., Shaw, R., & Jost, F. (2019). Meeting the climate change challenge: Local government climate action in British Columbia. *Climate Policy*. https://doi.org/10.1080/146 93062.2019.1651244

Esbjörn-Hargens, S. (2010). An ontology of climate change. *Journal of Integral Theory and Practice*, *5*(1), 143–174.

Forino, G., Meding, V.J., & Brewer, G. (2017). Climate Change Adaptation and Disaster Risk Reduction Integration in Australia: Challenges and Opportunities. In C. N. Madu & C. Kuei (Eds.), *Handbook of Disaster Risk Reduction and Management*. World Scientific Press & Imperial College Press.

Haider, H. (2019). Climate change in Nigeria: Impacts and responses. *Knowledge, Evidence and Learning for Development*.

Handayani, A. (2021). Local government response to the impacts of climate change: a review of climate change strategies in Pekalongan, Central Java. In *IOP conference series: Earth and environmental science* (Vol. 724, No. 1, p. 012088). IOP Publishing.

Harker, J., Taylor, P., & Knight-Lenihan, S. (2016). Multi-level governance and climate change mitigation in New Zealand: Lost opportunities. *Climate Policy*. https://doi.org/10.1080/14693062.2015.1122567

Hisali, E., Birungi, P., & Buyinza, F. (2011). Adaptation to climate change in Uganda: Evidence from micro level data. *Global Environmental Change*, *21*(4), 1245–1261.

Karlsson, M., Alfredsson, E., & Westling, N. (2020). Climate policy co-benefits: A review. *Climate Policy*, *20*(3), 292–316. https://doi.org/10.1080/146 93062.2020.1724070

Mees, H., & Driessen, P. (2019). A framework for assessing the accountability of local governance arrangements for adaptation to climate change. *Journal of Environmental Planning and Management*, *62*(4), 671–691. https://doi. org/10.1080/09640568.2018.1428184

Mees, H. L. P., Uittenbroek, C. J., Hegger, D. L. T., & Driessen, P. P. J. (2019). From citizen participation to government participation: An exploration of the roles of local governments in community initiatives for climate change adaptation in the Netherlands. *Environmental, Policy and Governance, 29*, 198–208. https://doi.org/10.1002/eet.1847

Nerini, F. F., Sovacool, B., Hughes, N., Cozzi, L., Cosgrave, E., Howells, M., Tavoni, M., Tomei, J., Zerriffi, H., & Milligan, B. (2019). Connecting climate action with other sustainable development goals. *Nature Sustainability, 2*(8), 674–680. https://doi.org/10.1038/s41893-019-0334-y

Odu, L. U. (2014). Local government and the challenges of grassroots development in Nigeria. *Review of Public Administration and Management, 3*(6), 204–213.

Olaleye, Y. L., Ayodele, K. O., & Ariyo, E. A. (2021). Effect of climate change on social development programmes in Kosofe local government area, Lagos State Nigeria. *African Journal of Social Work, 11*(6), 354–361.

Opoku, S. K., Hubert, F., & Adejumo, O. (2021). Climate change and health preparedness in Africa: Analysing trends in six African countries. *International Journal of Environmental Research and Public Health, 18*(9), 4672.

Oyero, O., Oyesomi, K., Abioye, T., Ajiboye, E., & Kayode-Adedeji, T. (2018). Strategic communication for climate change awareness and behavioural change in Ota local government of Ogun State. *African Population Studies, 32*(1).

Perry, B., Diprose, K., Taylor Buck, N., & Simon, D. (2021). Localizing the SDGs in England: Challenges and value propositions for local government. *Frontiers in Sustainable Cities, 3*.

Quayle, B., Sciulli, N., & Wilson-Evered, E. (2020). Accountable to who, to whom, for what and how? Unpacking accountability in local government response to climate change. *Australasian Accounting, Business and Finance Journal, 14*(3), 56–74. ISSN 1834-2000.

Shehu, K., Auwal, I. N., & Dahuwa, A. A. (2018). A review of climate change: Its impacts and governance for enhancing Nigeria's environmental resources. *Dutse Journal of Pure and Applied Sciences, 4*(2), 77–86.

Slack, L. (2015). CLGF news: The post-2015 global agenda-a role for local government. *Commonwealth Journal of Local Governance*, (16/17), 3–11.

United Nations Framework Convention on Climate Change. (2017). National adaptation plans. Retrieved December 15, 2018, from https://unfccc.int/topics/adaptation-and-resilience/workstreams/national-adaptation-plans

Urama, K. C., & Ozor, N. (2010). Impacts of climate change on water resources in Africa: The role of adaptation. *African Technology Policy Studies Network, 29*, 1–29.

Vembe, J. T., & Adekeye, A. J. (2013). Financing local government for enhanced rural development in Nigeria. *International Journal of Social Sciences and Humanities Review, 4*(2), 79–89.

Williams, D. S., Celliers, L., Unverzagt, K., Videira, N., Máñez Costa, M., & Giordano, R. (2020a). A method for enhancing capacity of local governance for climate change adaptation. *Earth's Future, 8*, e2020aEF001506. https://doi.org/10.1029/2020EF001506

Williams, D. S., Rosendo, S., Sadasing, O., & Celliers, L. (2020b). Identifying local governance capacity needs for implementing climate change adaptation in Mauritius. *Climate Policy, 20*(5), 548–562. https://doi.org/10.1080/14693062.2020.1745743

Strategies for Mitigating Conflicts, Insecurity and Insurgency in Africa

Olasehinde Seun, Issah Moshood, and Noah Yusuf

1 INTRODUCTION

Western scholars have long downgraded the possibility of social uprisings in sub-Saharan Africa and Africa in general (Aidi, 2018). This was because they saw African countries, especially sub-Saharan Africa as being extremely rural and ethnically based with little or no class distinction and consciousness. The oft-cited and discussed African uprisings were the anti-apartheid struggle and labour movement in South Africa. Also, scholars have silenced or seem to be uninterested in how social uprisings within and outside the African continent affect each other (Eckert, 2017; Ford, 2012; Sharp, 2005). In other words, how social uprising in one country or continent inspires similar or related uprising in another country or continent. Many African scholars have been raising questions about the possibility and plausibility of similar uprising in sub-Saharan African region (Aidi, 2018; Mamdani, 2013). For instance, one of the Kenyan newspapers—The Daily Nation—posted a question in September 2011 on the possible spread of the Arab Uprising to Sub-Saharan Africa

---

O. Seun (✉) · I. Moshood · N. Yusuf
University of Ilorin, Ilorin, Nigeria
e-mail: seunlash@yahoo.com

© The Author(s), under exclusive license to Springer Nature Switzerland AG 2023
A. I. Adeniran (ed.), *African Development and Global Engagements*,
https://doi.org/10.1007/978-3-031-21283-3_17

(The Daily Nation, 2011). The spread of the Arab uprising southward must have surprised many Western scholars who doubted social uprisings and movements in sub-Saharan African region (Aidi, 2018; Schock, 2003).

Contemporary Africa has witnessed a series of social uprisings following the development in North Africa (Beinin & Vairel, 2013; Stephan & Mundy, 2006). The Arab spring, particularly the removal of Ben Ali—Tunisia President—inspired social uprisings in Gabon where some angry protesters converged at the United Nations Office in Libreville, Gabon demanding that the opposition figure should be recognized as president. In Malawi, a student uprising occurred at the University of Malawi, Lilongwe triggered by the intimidation of a Professor by the Malawian government who used Arab Spring as an illustration in his lecture. These protests could metamorphose into violence if Gabonese and Malawian government had clampdown on the protesters as we have repeatedly witnessed in some African countries. The situation was depicted in Zimbabwe where student activists and trade unionists, who publicly discussed the uprisings in North Africa, were arrested and charged with treasonable offenses. Any Zimbabweans who displayed images of the North African movements on social media were traced and arrested. In addition, the Arab Spring instigated the 'Walk to Work' movement in Uganda where protesters demonstrated against the incessant increase in fuel and basic foods. Also, in Uganda, the opposition attempted to organize what it referred to as 'victory parade' to show their support for the Libyan rebels. The Ugandan government quickly reacted and banned such a demonstration because of its likely socio-political implications. Moreover, inspired by Mohammed Bouazizi,[1] two Ethiopians attempted to self-immolate themselves in November 2011 (Aidi, 2018; Mamdani, 2013).

Emerging African scholars were not surprised by the contagiousness of the revolutionary protests in Tunisia and Egypt (Boothe & Smithey, 2007; De Goede, 2017; Fanon, 2007). As noted by Mamdani (2013), the memory of Tahrir Square might encourage intense social movements by the opposition groups culminating into heightened fears in many incumbent African political leaders. The development in the North African region has raised pan-African consciousness in the sub-Saharan region as

---

[1] The Tunisian street vendor who set himself on fire in protest against the then Tunisian government's harsh policies leading to worsening standard of living.

opposition groups and other activists in the region are 'playing catch-up'. Nonetheless, Scholars such as Branch and Mampilly (2015) argued that contemporary social uprisings in sub-Saharan Africa preceded the development in the North African region. In other words, sub-Saharan Africa had witnessed a series of social uprisings a decade before the Arab Spring. Therefore, Branch and Mampilly (2015) were surprised that existing scholarship and discourse on the Arab Uprisings did not make reference to how social uprisings in sub-Saharan Africa that occurred before the Arab Uprising connected or linked to it. This argument raises some fundamental and thought-provoking questions: did earlier uprisings in sub-Saharan Africa inspired Arab Spring or contemporary social uprisings in sub-Saharan Africa were consequences of the Arab Spring (Branch & Mampily, 2015; Gabay, 2012).

This chapter approaches the question of social uprisings from both analytical angles to understand the nature, dynamics and causes of social uprisings in sub-Saharan African region. Unravelling the nature and causes of social uprisings before, during and after Arab Spring would give a better understanding of the complexity and dynamism of socio-economic and political drivers of conflicts, insecurity and insurgency in Africa. This understanding is necessary to suggest feasible and effective policy frameworks to address the complicated challenges of conflicts, insecurity and insurgency in Africa. For the purpose of clarity, this chapter is divided into six sections. The first section introduces the chapter where an overview of social uprisings in Africa is presented. The second section clarifies some major concepts used and how they are used. The third section discusses the theoretical framework for this study where the social justice model is discussed in terms of its relevance to this chapter. The fourth section discusses the complex nature and causes of social uprisings in contemporary African society. The third section discusses the key findings or discourses of the chapter such as how social justice could be used as a veritable mitigating strategy, how driving and achieving economic prosperity could help in addressing social uprisings in Africa and how participatory approach could be used as a preventive mechanism. Lastly, the sixth section is a concluding remark where policy relevance of this chapter is shown.

2 Clarification of Concepts

Conflicts: Conflict is a disagreement between two or more parties which develops when they are holding different values, opinions, needs, interests and ideas (De Goede, 2017). Conflicts may result in different outcomes such as severe arguments, physical abuses and loss of peace and harmony (Aidi, 2018). However, in the context of this study, conflict is viewed from the angle of social uprisings. As used in this chapter, social uprising is an expression of displeasure by certain groups or sections of a state against the government. Sometimes, the displeasure may be violently or non-violently expressed. Also, the response of the target government determines the nature of social uprisings. Government may violently clampdown on the participants leading to serious conflicts, or it may peacefully address them and take care of their demands.

Insecurity: The term 'insecurity' has different connotations such as danger, hazard, uncertainty, lack of protection and safety. As noted by Béland (2005), insecurity implies a state of fear or anxiety which is the outcome or consequence of lack of protection. In other words, it indicates lack of or inadequate freedom from danger. To Ewetan and Urhie (2014), insecurity is the state of being exposed to threat and danger. In this chapter, insecurity is viewed as the lack of or inadequacy of peace, order and security due to persistent and sustained social uprisings. The African continent is categorized as one of the most insecure places in the world due to a series of social uprisings ranging from mild to severe. The unending social uprisings in the continent have made it insecure.

Demonetization of political system: This is defined as the outlaw or ban on sourcing funds for electioneering through unauthorized or illegal sources such as donations from corporates and rich donors. Also, it could imply banning spraying money during campaigns, distributing money at the polling units or selling nomination forms at higher prices among others. In the context of this chapter, demonetization is viewed as discouraging or forcing people to desist from vote-buying and vote-selling. Holding political offices or leadership positions should be seen as a call to services, not opportunities to invest and reap returns through siphoning of state funds from the national treasure.

Social justice: While there are divergent views of social justice, the chapter sees social justice from the utilitarian perspectives. Utilitarianists such as J. Benthem (1748–1832), James Mill (1773–1836), John Austin (1790–1859) and J.S. Mill (1806–1873) looked at social justice from the angle of its utility—like how many members of a particular community derive pleasure or benefit from social justice. Based on this, the basis of social justice is 'the maximum good of the greatest number of individuals'. Social uprising could be minimal or even non-existent in the presence of social justice. In other words, a just society would have a large number of people that are satisfied, which implies that social uprisings will be reduced.

3 Theoretical Framework: Social Justice Model

This chapter is anchored on social justice theory because some scholars have suggested social justice as a veritable mitigating strategy for preventing or addressing the challenges of social uprisings in Africa. As a point of reference, it is essential to conceptualize what justice and social justice imply in order to understand how relevant it is in addressing the complex problem of social uprisings in contemporary African societies. The term 'justice' has been largely used since the time immemorial (Hantal, 2022). Generally, it is defined as the fair and just distribution of benefits and burdens. Outhwaite and Bottomore (1993) viewed it as a situation where each individual in a society gets what is due to him or her. As noted by Aristotle, injustice could be said to have occurred when equals are treated as unequally and when unequals are treated equally. He also further used the idea of proportionality to conceptualize justice. According to him, collective resources should be distributed among individuals in proportion—not equally—using certain criteria or parameters. Different societies have different criteria or parameters upon which collective resources are allocated.

Having defined 'justice', what is social justice? Miller (1991) defined social justice as conscious and determined efforts to align the general pattern of distribution in a society with the general principles of society. To Jatava (1998), social justice entails the prescription of certain ideals or morals that are perceived to be functional and essential to human society; the presence and observance of these ideals bring about the sustenance of the individual, family, society and the nation. Also, the enforcement of these ideals protects the rights and interests of the poorer or weaker members of a society as well as helping in removing all the obstacles on the path of achieving a just and fair society. Utilitarianists such as J. Benthem (1748–1832), James Mill (1773–1836), John Austin (1790–1859) and J.S. Mill (1806–1873) looked at social justice from the angle of its utility—like how many members of a particular community derive pleasure or benefit from social justice. Based on this, the basis of social justice is 'the maximum good of the greatest number of individuals'. In this line, Bentham argued that the interests, needs, rights and welfare of the poor, oppressed and needy members of a society must be acknowledged and safeguarded through effective and fair policies. While supporting this claim, Jatava (1998) noted that anything that brings or that would bring pain, injustice and unfairness should be transformed, reformed or changed to serve the interest of the greatest number of individuals. To Rawls (1972) cited in Chapman (2013), inequalities in the distribution of resources or goods might be allowed provided that they are directed towards the poorest segment of society. In other words, social and economic inequalities must be geared towards providing the greatest benefits to the poorest or lease-advantaged members of society.

From the above definition, it is evident that social justice is a fundamental mitigating strategy for addressing social uprisings. This is because the idea of social justice implies removing and redistributing resources to address the problems of widening socio-economic inequalities and pervasive poverty. As shown earlier, the middle-class population is persistently shrinking because of worsening socio-economic conditions. To address the problem of social uprisings, it is fundamental for every government to embark on reforms that would help in removing obstacles that could hinder the achievement of just, fair and equitable society. Also, the underclass should be empowered through either informal or formal employment to address the complex problem of poverty. Based on the UN report, to reduce poverty and inequality—which are some of the key drivers of social uprisings, transition to formal employment is a critical condition (Sarkodie & Adams, 2020). Every government should develop its citizens by creating more jobs to absorb young citizens, mostly graduates.

4   Methodology

This study used secondary sources such as grey literature, published articles, official documents and reports. The sources were limited to Africa. The content analytic technique was adopted to analyse the sources.

STRATEGIES FOR MITIGATING CONFLICTS, INSECURITY ... 363

4.1   Nature and Causes of Social Uprisings in Africa

As a matter of emphasis, social uprisings in European, American and even Latin America might be different in terms of nature, analytical categories and designations from that of sub-Saharan African's experiences (Juma, 2011). In sub-Saharan African context, it might be difficult to differentiate demonstrators from rioters, political protest from economic protest as well as violent from non-violent protests. In addition, labour, civil society and the middle-class's inspired uprisings that characterized industrialized or advanced European countries may not be helpful as yardsticks for gauging, evaluating and analyzing the nature and causes of social uprisings in Africa (The Christian Science Monitor, 2011). In other words, the 'civil society approach to protestation' where protests are staged by (an) organized civil society group(s) to put pressure on any political regimes to embark or implement certain socio-economic and/or political reforms. These often take non-violent forms since the level of organization is high, messages are clear and appropriate strategies are employed. This is largely uncommon in African context perhaps due to the persistent shrinking 'civil space'.[2] This results in a situation where protests are organized and led by the underclass people which are mostly characterized by lack of organization and violence. It is important to state upfront that this section discusses contemporary social uprisings in Africa as there is a large body of knowledge on social uprisings before 2000s.[3]

Aside colonial and post-colonial social uprisings, Africa witnessed a new wave of social uprisings in the mid-2000s driven, largely by severe austerity emanating from harsh government policies. Excluding labour strikes and local labour strikes, 40 African countries witnessed more than 90 social uprisings between 2005 and 2014 (Branch & Mampilly, 2015). However, Western scholars and media started paying attention to African social uprisings when violent social movements broke out in North Africa (Branch & Mampilly, 2015). The uprisings may be connected to underclass ties or lack of ties to the state or political parties rather than civil

---

[2] In spite of repeated clampdown on the participants of social movements by the many regimes in Africa, the public spheres are intact, reclaim and significantly change in some regimes.

[3] The anti-colonial social uprisings were inspired by the need for self-determination, while the post-colonial (between 1950 and 2000s) was inspired by the need for democratization.

society politics or political crises. For instance, some Nigerian underclass youths led 'Occupy Nigeria' and also some Ugandan youths were at the vanguard of 'Walk to Work'. In these two examples, the participants were not members or tied to any political parties nor were they part or linked to any civil society groups. While politically motivated uprisings—often linked to political parties—always focussed on elections, civil society groups always concern with issues such as good governance and anti-corruption which are critical to Western donors. Rather than relying on civil society groups, urban poor mostly youths are now taking to the streets demanding for total change (Branch & Mampilly, 2015; Cooper, 1983a, 1983b).

Unarguably, the development in North Africa contributed to social uprisings in sub-Saharan Africa from 2012 onwards. One cited example was the development of Ethiopian People's Revolutionary Democratic Front (EPRDF) (Nega, 2011). Some scholars reported its effects in countries such as Malawi, Uganda, Ethiopia and Burkina Faso. For instance, the social uprising that evolved against the regime of Bingu wa Mutharika of Malawi resulted in the arrest of many Malawians who participated in the uprising and left about 18 people dead (Aidi, 2018, Branch & Mampilly, 2015). Mutharika condemned the opposition groups for the uprising as he stated that the participants were influenced and 'led by Satan'. Despite his dispositions towards the uprisings, some gains were recorded such as reshuffling of the cabinet in August 2011 and freezing of financial assistance from the UK (Aidi, 2018). In addition, the head of the country's army was changed. Nevertheless, the resulting Presidential Elections in May 2014 saw his brother—Peter Mutharika of the Democratic Progressive Party (DPP)—taking over from him (Aidi, 2018). See Table 1 for specific cases of social uprisings in Africa:

Having discussed the nature and dynamics of social uprisings in post-2000s Africa, let now look at the key causal factors driving or motivating the uprisings. Scholars have not really come to terms with the major drivers of social uprisings in the post-2000s era in Africa because of their intense complexity and dynamism (Fukuyama, 2013; Rueschemeyer et al., 1992). Western scholars have focussed on class structure based on their belief that the driving forces behind every social uprising are either organized labour groups or middle class populations (Rueschemeyer et al., 1992). According to Fukuyama (2013), the developments in North Africa, the Middle East and other parts could be described as a 'middle class revolution' against insensitive and ineffective government

STRATEGIES FOR MITIGATING CONFLICTS, INSECURITY ... 365

Table 1 For specific cases of social uprisings in Africa

The 2009–2010 revolt in Niger was largely influenced by what Mueller described as 'economic grievances'. The data obtained from the Nigerian citizens clearly showed that economic deprivations and pauperization motivated many poor Nigerians to participate and take to the streets (Mueller, 2018). Western journalists and protest leaders had false notions as to the drivers of the revolts. To them, the revolt was driven by the intention to pressure the Nigerian government to adopt constitutional democracy

Also, the M23 opposition movement developed in Dakar, Senegal in August 2012 as a result of the attempt of the then-president Abdoulaye Wade to change the constitution to remain in power. The M23 started the opposition via mobilization of people with the slogan 'Don't touch my constitution'. Soon, youths started burning tyres, thereby stalling vendors in Dakar. Consequently, the poorest members of M23 were chanting a new slogan 'Don't touch my table' (Aidi, 2018)

Morocco has witnessed different social uprisings such as Hirak protests of 2017, the economic boycotts of 2018 and the ongoing feminist #masaktach campaigns. Hirak protests of 2017 were staged in the Rif region of the country to protest against poor socio-economic conditions and corrupt government officials. Weekly demonstrations were held in this region until the government launched a coordinated and violent crackdown on the protestors in June 2017 leading to the arrest of about 400 activists and protestors (Abrougui & Sayadi, 2019; Masbah, 2017)

The 'Walk to Work' protest of 2011 and 2018 is one of the cases of social uprising in Uganda. Some of the key demands of the protestors include the freedom of musician and a member of parliament—Robert Kyagulanyi (aka Bobi Wine). The member of the underclass held his song—Freedom—to a high esteem who they regarded as the 'Ghetto President'. His song was taken off the air in 2017 because the then-Ugandan president perceived his song as capable of instigating social uprisings in the country. Despite the imposition of social media tax by the Ugandan government to discourage online social activism, many unemployed youths took to the streets demonstrating and demanding his immediate release (Aidi, 2018)

In Nigeria, the introduction of new taxes triggered protests against the government. This culminated in clashes between the protestors/demonstrators and security forces, leading to the arrests of many protestors. On 3 January 2012, hundreds of demonstrators to the streets of Lagos, Nigeria, protesting against the removal of fuel subsidy which was announced by the government on the 1st January 2012. Many petrol stations were shut-down and human barriers were formed along motorways. Over 1000 people were singing, chanting and waving placards reading: 'no to fuel hikes' and 'we demand living wages'. Some demonstrators set up a roadblock of burning tyres on a major highway (Ohuocha, 2012). Also, tens of thousands of young Nigerians took to the streets to protest against police brutality following a linked video where a man was allegedly killed by the so-called notorious Special Anti-Robbery Squad (Sars). This movement was known as #EndSars demonstrations. The demonstrations took about two weeks forcing the government to disband Sars and then established judicial panels of inquiry to investigate the allegations levelled against Sars's officers (Jones, 2021)

In Malawi, anti-corruption protests have been staged in different cities. The organizer of the protests was the Human Rights Defenders Coalition (HRDC). Despite the fact that the Malawian government used severe military actions against the protestors, the protests continue unabatedly. In 2021, thousands of Malawians took to the street to protest against the rising cost of living and the government's indifference to the plight of Malawians. They argued that the country is one of the poorest countries in the world with only 11 per cent of its population connected to electricity. In response, the Malawi police fired tear gas at the demonstrators in the capital Lilongwe (Redaction Africanews, 2021)

occasioned by large-scale corruption and poor management of collective resources. The author argued that social uprisings were masterminded and executed by young people with above-average education and income level in Turkey, Brazil, Tunisia and Egypt rather than the poor (Fukuyama, 2013). Similarly, the African Development Bank (2011) reported the rising number of middle class in Africa in 2011. According to the bank, the middle class in Africa had increased to about 350 million. Their significant growth might contribute to social uprisings in the continent because they are more likely to be dissatisfied with the existing political structure which incubates corruption and mismanagement of public funds.

However, some scholars countered the argument that the middle-class population is widening on the ground of 'false' or 'unconvincing' parameters (Blanchard & Willmann, 2016; Visagie & Posel, 2013). They noted that the population of the middle class is over-blown perhaps they 'mistakenly' included low-class population. Evidently, the reality in sub-Saharan African countries is that the population of middle class is shrinking due to complicated economic problems. In other words, the low-class people are expanding as more middle-class people are slipping into lower-class rung. As reported by the UNDP, more than 50 per cent of Africans are living in extreme poverty. In addition, it reported that the level of inequality is increasing and the population of middle class is reducing (United Nations, 2014). Based on this reality, the middle-class population has significantly reduced and they are largely dependent on state patronage to avoid being retrogressed into lower-class rung. As reported by Statista (2022a), about 460 million people in Africa were living in extreme poverty indicating that the number of poor people increased compared to the previous years— 454.3 million people in 2020 and 459.8 in 2021. Specifically, about 12 per cent of the world population in extreme poverty (with the poverty threshold at 1.9 US dollars per day) lived in Nigeria, followed by the Democratic Republic of Congo with about 10 per cent of the global population in extreme poverty (Statista, 2022b). Table 2 shows African countries with the highest share of global population living below the extreme poverty line in 2022.

Based on the above, it is evident that Nigeria and Democratic Republic of Congo (DRC) have the highest share of global population in extreme poverty in Africa. Consequently, some scholars have linked this to high level of social uprisings in Nigeria and DRC driven by the poor youths (underclass) (Aidi, 2018; Mamdani, 2013). Even in Tahrir Square, the uprising was dominated by the working class youths rather than

Table 2 African countries with the highest share of global population living below the extreme poverty line in 2022

Country	Share of global population in extreme poverty (%)
Nigeria	12.20
Democratic Republic of Congo	9.9
Tanzania	4.5
Madagascar	3.2
Mozambique	2.9

Source Statista (2022b)

the middle class who were just ratting on social media (Abul-Magd, 2012). What this argument denotes is that contemporary social uprisings in Africa are driven by a 'new proletariat'. Based on Marxism, the exploited or poor class is challenging the neo-liberal top-down development projects of national government and/or international financial institutions. This point of argument seems plausible due to the fact that most of the Western-imposed policy measures—such as austerity measures—have further pauperized many Africans (Beinin, 2014). Most Africans are suffering from severe economic hardship brought about harsh economic policies imposed and championed by Western donors or lenders. However, what is not clear is: why economic hardship caused by the imposition of obnoxious economic policies is inspiring and triggering social uprisings now? Another unresolved question is that those social uprisings did not articulate any clear agendas such as anti-privatization or anti-capitalism. The protesters have not really come up with any clear economic and/or political programmes.[4] Scholars argued that the participants were not making any economic or political demands.[5]

---

[4] Boko-Haram insurgency is one of the major social uprisings in Nigeria, Chad, Niger and northern Cameroon. It was founded by Mohammed Yusuf in 2002. Over tens of thousands people have been killed. Over 300,000 children have been killed and about 2.3 million people have been displaced (Chiroma, 2016). One of the causes of the insurgency is the concentration of wealth among members of a small political elite. About 60 per cent of Nigerians are living on less than $1 a day (Oriola, 2009). Other reasons as reported in the literature is the opposition of the westernization of Nigerian society which, according to the group, is the cause of corruption and bad governance in Nigeria.

[5] According to Mueller (2018), there are two driving forces of social uprisings in contemporary Africa. These are: (i) 'political grievances' which are driving the middle class to stage demonstrations and (ii) 'material grievances' which are propelling the poor

5   Discussion of Key Discourses

Discussion of the key arguments and discourses are presented in themes as follows:

5.1   Theme 1: Social Justice as a Veritable Mitigating Strategy

The previous section shows the increasing nature and complexity of social uprisings in Africa. As a way of mitigating it, some scholars have suggested social justice as a veritable mitigating strategy for preventing or addressing the challenges of social uprisings in Africa. As a point of departure, while social justice could be a veritable mitigating strategy for social uprisings in Africa, social uprisings could also affect its successful implementation. For instance, the implementation of programmes aimed at achieving or ensuring social justice have hit the bricks in several countries in the Lake Chad Basin and the Sahel zone due to Boko-Haram and related insurgency. The rights of the citizens have been undermined due to the frequency and intensity of the conflicts (Bonny, 2022). Observers of the development in the Sahel region have argued that the government interventions have not adequately addressed the people's needs. Specifically, about 10.6 million people need humanitarian assistance in the Lake Chad Basin of Cameroon, Chad, Niger and Nigeria. About 3.3 million people are food insecure and about 400,000 children are suffering from severe malnutrition. Also, due to the volatile nature of the region, about 1050 schools have not shut down or are non-functioning leading to the deprivation of thousands of children of schooling. About 2.8 million people are internally displaced where 2 million are Nigerians (Bonny, 2022).

Also, in Mali, citizens have been increasingly pauperized because of the stiffer sanctions imposed by the African and International organizations as a result of the failure of the military government to embrace democratic ideals. These sanctions have severely impacted many humanitarian projects and jobs in the country. Also, in Cameroon, a separatist

---

to organize and participate in social uprisings. Based on the data collected from Malawi, Senegal, Burkina Faso and Nigeria, Mueller (2018) concluded that 'political grievances' determine when social uprisings will occur; while 'material grievances' determine who are likely to participate in the demonstrations. The author added that while the middle class serves as the think-tankers or organisers of social movements, the poor are often used as the 'foot soldiers' (Mueller, 2018). Also, it is possible that people or groups with different interests and motivations may come together to organize and stage social movements.

conflict emanating from protests by the Anglophone minority against marginalization is bringing severe socio-economic hardships to Anglophone Cameroonians. Developmental projects have been put on hold in this region because of the persistent climate of insecurity. Bonny (2022) argued that development projects cannot be successful in the context of insecurity. For instance, about 700,000 students have been out of school since 2017. In Burkina Faso, more than 43 per cent of the country's population is living below the poverty line. In Niger, extreme poverty has reached 42.9 per cent implying that more than 10 million people out of a population of about 24 million (Bonny, 2022).

From the above discussion, it is evident that social justice has not been achieved as the level of economic inequalities continues to increase. Poverty rate is rising and unemployment level is worsening. It is against this backdrop that some thinkers think that the root causes of social uprisings in Africa can be uprooted or addressed through developing and implementing policies aimed at achieving economic prosperity. Therefore, the next section addresses the issue of achieving economic prosperity for mitigating social uprisings in the African continent.

5.2   *Theme 2: Economic Prosperity as an Essentiality*

It has been argued that achieving economic prosperity might be essential to mitigate social uprisings in Africa even though the economic factor is not the sole driver of social uprisings in Africa. As argued in the previous section, the underclass or the poor class people are easily mobilized for social movements because they are numerous and suffer the most. To mitigate social uprisings, their needs can be addressed if proper policies aimed at addressing their socio-economic problems are designed and implemented. Importantly, this section commences with the general overview of the economic climate of the continent and then suggests how economic prosperity can be achieved. While about 17 per cent of the global population resides in the African continent, it contributes around 3 per cent to global GDP (Coleman, 2020). This indicates that the continent is underutilizing its developmental potentials. Failure to explore and utilize its potentials, insurgency, instability and extremism would not elude the continent. In other words, if the continent utilizes its numerous human and material resources, economic prosperity is likely—an essentiality of addressing persistent social uprisings in Africa (Coleman, 2020).

Some scholars linked Africa's high poverty rate to historical relationships with other countries characterized by slavery, colonial plundering, exposure to negative externalities during the Cold War era as well as post-colonial conflicts[6] (Ayodele, 2020; Mekoa, 2019).

However, it is argued that the continent has some potential to achieve economic prosperity. For instance, Africa is the youngest and fastest-urbanizing continent in the world. It is projected that the continent would have 24 million more people living in its cities each year between 2015 and 2045 (Coleman, 2020). This would be greater than what India and China combined have (McKinsety & Company, 2016). The economic relevance of this development is significant increase in consumption which is one of the major requirements for economic prosperity. Currently, the total spending by both consumers and businesses in Africa is around $4 trillion (Coleman, 2020). Specifically, household consumption is projected to increase by 3.8 per cent every year until 2025—reaching like $2.1 trillion. Also, business expenditure is likely to increase from $2.6 trillion in 2015 to $3.5 trillion in 2025 (Coleman, 2020). Based on these figures, the McKinsey report predicted $5.6 trillion in African business opportunities by 2025. For instance, Africa has about 60 per cent of the world's uncultivated arable land (Coleman, 2020). Therefore, to achieve economic prosperity, African governments should intensify their agricultural productivity to generate more jobs for its growing unemployed youths. With good agricultural policies, the continent could produce about 2 to 3 times more cereals and grains (Coleman, 2020).

In addition, Africa has numerous natural resources required to achieve economic prosperity. Breakdowns reveal that it has 10 per cent of the world's oil reserves, 40 per cent of the world's gold and 80 per cent of the world's platinum. These resources have the potential of driving Africa's economic prosperity. Also, the continent needs to improve its infrastructure to expand its economic base. As of 2010, the continent needed to spend about $46 billion additional spending every year to develop its energy, water and transport networks (Coleman, 2020). The African Development Bank has created the African Investment Forum and billions

---

[6] For instance, the plundering and looting of Democratic Republic of Congo (DRC) of its ivory and rubber by King Leopold II of Belgium in the late 1890s was regarded as the major root cause of extreme poverty in the country. This was complemented by two major wars that the country experienced—1996–1997 and 1998–2002 followed by brutal genocide in Rwanda.

of dollars have been mobilized to fund infrastructural development on the continent. Also, the African Union Development Agencies such as New Partnership for Africa's Development and the Program for Infrastructural Development in Africa (PIDA) have been initiating and making significant efforts to unlock infrastructure potential. Scholars argued that the current infrastructure gap in the continent must be bridged (Ayodele, 2020; Mekoa, 2019). To unlock the economic potential of the continent, it is essential to have high-quality infrastructure. Furthermore, Africa needs to improve its digital development and technological innovation. Rwanda has been making giant strides in terms of technological innovations. It is also suggested that regional integration such as the African Continental Free Trade Area (AfCFTA) should be taken seriously because the role of trade liberation is critical in achieving sustainable economic prosperity in the continent (Coleman, 2020).

Some observers suggest that to achieve Africa's economic prosperity, African political leaders should show readiness by strengthening institutions, ensuring political stability, promoting democratization, enhancing policy coordination, improving ease of doing business, facilitating technology transfers, nurturing and developing human capital through education and healthcare, attracting foreign direct investment and encouraging technology transfers (Ogan, 2018; Otekunrin et al., 2019). Through effective economic reforms, Africa could reach the level of economic development that China is currently experiencing. Many smaller countries in East Africa have been embarking on major reforms to address the problems of poverty, unemployment and inequalities through the achievement of economic prosperity. Also, analysts pointed out the role of the continent's largest economies—Egypt, Nigeria and South Africa— in developing the African Continental Free Trade Area. Studies indicate the success of the continent has the potential of lifting millions of Africans out of poverty which has been linked to rising social uprisings in Africa (Ayodele, 2020; Ogan, 2018). However, some observers doubted this because of the existing institutional lethargy and corruption which have characterized African socio-political landscape. Some researchers viewed that one of the critical conditions for achieving significant and sustainable economic prosperity is that corruption and other political problems should be addressed (Babatunde, 2012; Drewes & Van Aswegen, 2013). They argued that some of the formidable African economic problems

372   O. SEUN ET AL.

are political, and they need political solutions. This leads this chapter to the exploration of demonetization of the political system as a basic intervention.

5.3   Theme 3: Demonetization of the Political System as a Basic Intervention

Political system and elections have been intensely monetized in Africa (Adetula, 2015). This development has been linked to growing cases of election conflicts in the African continent. Bad governance, corruption and large-scale insecurity have been pitched with incessant monetization of political systems. One critical shade of demonetization of the political system is the increasing phenomenon of vote-buying in African contemporary electoral systems. Vote-buying or pre-electoral distribution of private goods in exchange for support at the ballot has characterized African elections (Asante & Kunnath, 2018). This development has been blamed for high poverty rate in the region, culminating in increasing social uprisings. Vote-buying or monetization of political systems has undermined accountability as well as the implementation of effective and appropriate development policies. The implication of vote-buying is that the electorates are voted for candidates against their wish (Bagbin & Ahenkan, 2017). Many voters found the offer irresistible because of the deepened level of poverty in the region. According to Charles P. Sohner, 'money has been made to become the mother's milk of politics, which the political gladiators must drink to remain in business' (cited in Ochieng, 2022). In most African countries, monetization occurs at two major levels: (i) intra-party level during primary elections where delegates are paid and a huge amount of money is used to purchase tickets and (ii) inter-party level during general elections. While monetization of electoral politics and governance has become a worldwide phenomenon (Onah & Nwali, 2018), its intensity and frequency are phenomenal in African countries (Bryan & Baer, 2005).

In recent elections in Nigeria, billions of naira have been deployed to induce voters (Adetula, 2015). Also, Kenya has witnessed bizarre cases of vote-buying. Based on the Afrobarometer data between 2003 and 2014, more than a quarter of the Kenyan population admitted that they had engaged in vote-buying. The electoral process has been compromised in Kenya leading to a lack of free and fair elections in the country (Ochieng, 2022). Giving cash handouts has characterized political campaigns and electioneering in Kenya. Also, in Ghana, a 2017 survey of Parliamentarians indicated that it costs about $87,000 to get elected to Ghanaian Parliament (Asante & Kunnath, 2018). The costs are found to be equivalent to their, approximately, 2 years' salary. In addition, during the primary elections, some candidates alleged that they paid about GHC 3000 to each delegate (Corruption Watch, 2020).

Monetization of political systems has also been connected or resulted in corruptions among political office-holders in Africa. Politicians and African leaders see leadership position as a veritable investment or huge sources of income for them (Bedi, 2017). They are ready to spend and even get loans from financial institutions to fund their electioneering. After they win, they are likely to engage in corrupt practices—amassing public funds—to payback what the funds they borrowed during their electioneering. Also, scholars have established a relationship between monetization (money politics) and political corruption (looting) (Casal Bertoa & Sanches, 2019; Ichino & Nathan, 2016). Many potential voters attend political rallies because of the expectation that money is likely to be distributed. As noted by Chirinos as cited in Muñoz and Chirinos (2019), donors (or political investors) are likely to be encouraged to invest financially in a candidate that is able to attract large crowds during political rallies. To get donors that would bankroll or fund their electioneering, candidates often buy potential voters at campaign events. Political aspirants or leaders are left with no option than to siphon public funds to get enough funds to distribute to voters. Some studies revealed that some citizens are aware that vote-buying or monetization of political systems violates democratic norms and it is an electoral fraud. But, pervasive poverty in the continent makes many voters found it highly irresistible (Bedi, 2017).

To address the problem of insecurity arising from election conflicts, scholars have suggested that the demonetization of political positions as this is necessary for ensuring probity within the African political systems (Egwu, 2009; Fogg, 2003). Contemporary African leaders, just like those before them, are focussed on, motivated or driven by what they would benefit from their positions rather than serving their people. In other words, they are only interested in personal enrichment by amassing public wealth rather than using public wealth to transform both the state and citizens. Continued monetization of political systems in the continent has made development to be elusive or far-fetched. Similarly, scholars noted that African leaders weigh what they stand to gain personally before

374 O. SEUN ET AL.

assuming leadership positions rather than what they are expected to offer (Kramon, 2009; Strauss, 1994). They viewed that the continent's political systems have been enormously monetized as people are vying for political positions at all cost. Value-based leadership cannot be achieved without addressing or reducing the growing level of monetization. The monetization of political system could decrease the quality of services provided by the government (Casal Bertoa & Sanches, 2019).

To demonetize the political systems, excessive of money should be stripped off. While money is fundamental in politics (the mother's milk of politics according to Stanbury (1986: 795) and the fuel for engine of party politics (Haughton, 2012), it is essential to control or tame its negative or adverse influences on politics and governance in the continent (Ohman, 2013). It is suggested that democratizing party ownership, public funding for political parties, enforcement of existing electoral laws and general laws, establishment of multiparty democracy commission, strengthening of the developmental orientation of parties, engaging in internal party reforms and strengthening of the regulatory framework would help in achieving the goal of demonetization of political systems (Casal Bertoa & Sanches, 2019; Kramon, 2009; Strauss, 1994). It is argued that once the goal of demonetization has been achieved, as shown in the above discussion, poverty and corruption are likely to reduce which are some of the key drivers of social uprisings in contemporary Africa.

5.4 Theme 4: Participatory Approach as a Preventive Mechanism

Scholars have suggested participatory development approaches as alternative development approaches to address the root causes of social uprisings in the continent (Nyam et al., 2020; Pocock et al., 2019). This entails including and involving people more directly in development processes. Development programmes and projects' initiation, development and implementation should follow bottom-up development alternative. In other words, development programmes and projects should be made more participatory because it is one of the major essentials for achieving expected development outcomes. There are a number of empirical evidences indicating a more 'participatory' style of development intervention. Scholars argued that the notion of participatory development denotes involving the perceived or potential beneficiaries in the planning and implementation of programmes and projects. It is anchored on the argument that all development initiatives and interventions must be sensitive to the needs and responses of the people they are supposed beneficiaries (Larsson et al., 2018).

Similarly, local participation at the different stages of the development programmes and interventions has the potential of fast-tracking African development. Development projects that are integrated into local ideas, skills and resources are likely to be successful. Also, community-driven development projects or programmes are likely to have wider coverage and more impactful if local people are allowed to assume more responsibilities and provide resources for its spread. Also, the capacity and abilities of local people are likely to develop by being active players in development activities. Many experts have argued that participatory development is a veritable technique or techniques for implementing development policy. Some scholars viewed participatory approach to development as a process of collaborating, consulting and co-opting beneficiaries in the design and implementation of development projects, interventions or programmes (Larsson et al., 2018; Nyam et al., 2020). However, some critics have argued that some political elites use participatory approach to development to shift the burden of national development to the poor or the underclass (Lwoga & Sangeda, 2019; Robinson & Gottlieb, 2021). They added that may be good and effective for the designers or makers of development programmes, projects and interventions, it may help in adequately addressing the structural cause of poverty among citizens.

For instance, participatory development approach was adopted to address poverty among peasant organizations in the cocoa zone of Cameroon (Weimann et al., 2022). The economic problems of the country have been linked to the underutilization of natural and human resources. Thus, the peasants were involved in the design and implementation of development interventions to address the country's economic challenges. Particularly, the involvement of poor peasants in designing and implementing development programmes led to significant improvements in the cocoa production and peasant income. This development approach led to reduction in poverty level. Also, the Zimbabwean government has adopted participatory development to address increasing rate of poverty in urban areas. It was found that the introduction of the Economic Structural Adjustment Programme (ESAP) worsened the poverty level in the country. Thus, the government resorted to engaging the poor in order to find appropriate alternatives to addressing the problem. Through involving people, the government was able to understand major issues accounting for increasing cases of urban poverty in the country (Cleaver, 1999). In addition, in South Africa, participatory approach has been implemented in various development phases to address the country's problem of poverty and inequality (Job et al., 2020). South Africa is ranked second after Brazil as the unequal societies in the world. While it is categorized as the middle-income country in terms of its GDP and one of the major economic powerhouses in the African continent, many of its social indicators are similar to the poor sub-Saharan Africa. Scholars have linked the economic challenges of the country to its apartheid's experiences (Job et al., 2020; Nyam et al., 2020). Successive governments have seen participatory model of development as a mechanism for solving pervasive socio-economic inequality in the country as evident in the inclusion of decentralizing power and responsibility to the provincial and local levels. The development has led to the introduction of the Rural Development Programme (RDP) as a policy framework to solving poverty, unemployment and inequalities at the grassroots levels.

6   Conclusion and Recommendations

From the foregoing, it is evident that social uprisings are increasing unabatedly in Africa. These uprisings have been major threats to the fundamental existence of African countries as they have been worsening security issues in the continent. This chapter has established structural challenges being faced by the continent which have culminated into high level of poverty and social exclusion have led to persistent conflicts, insecurity and insurgency in Africa. The perceived failure of African leaders to resolve these highlighted structural challenges have made the continent to be known for its notorious social uprisings as evident evolution and development of terrorist groups—such as Boko-Haram in the Chad Basin—in the continent. This chapter, therefore, suggested some panaceas to address the emphasized structural challenges that are stimulating social uprisings in the continent. Specifically, the chapter recommends that achieving economic prosperity through sound policies, adopting participatory development approaches, demonetization of political system and ensuring social justice are veritable and effective strategies for mitigating conflicts, insecurity and insurgency in the African continent.

REFERENCES

Abrougui, A., & Sayadi, E. (2019). *Morocco's Hirak movement has gone quiet, but the crackdown on independent media continues*. https://www.accessnow.org/moroccos-hirak-movement-has-gone-quiet-but-the-crackdown-on-independent-media-continues/

Abul-Magd, Z. (2012). Occupying Tahrir square: The myths and the realities of the Egyptian revolution. *South Atlantic Quarterly, 111*(3), 565–572.

Adetula, V. (2015). *Godfathers, money politics, and electoral violence in Nigeria: Focus on the 2015 elections*. In A two-day national conference.

African Development Bank. (2011, April). The Middle of the pyramid: Dynamics of the middle class in Africa. *Market Brief, 20*.

Aidi, H. (2018). *Africa's new social movements: A continental approach*. https://www.policycenter.ma/sites/default/files/2021-01/OCPPC-PB1836.pdf

Asante, K., & Kunnath, G. (2018). *The cost of politics in Ghana*. Westminster Foundation for Democracy.

Avis, E., Ferraz, C., Finan, F., & Varjão, C. (2017). Money and politics: The effects of campaign spending limits on political competition and incumbency advantage (No. w23508). *National Bureau of Economic Research*.

Ayodele, J. O. (2020). Colonialism and victimization narratives in the context of Africa's development. In *Global Perspectives on Victimization Analysis and Prevention* (pp. 54–74). IGI Global.

Babatunde, M. A. (2012). Africa's growth and development strategies: A critical review. *Africa Development, 37*(4), 141–178.

Bagbin, A. S., & Ahenkan, A. (2017). Political party financing and reporting in Ghana: Practitioner perspectives. In *Political marketing and management in Ghana* (pp. 111–131). Palgrave Macmillan, Cham.

Bedi, I. (2017). Political financing and fund-raising in Ghana. In *Political marketing and management in Ghana* (pp. 97–109). Palgrave Macmillan, Cham.

Beinin, J. (2014). Civil society, NGOs, and Egypt's 2011 popular uprising. *South Atlantic Quarterly, 113*(2), 396–406.

Beinin, J., & Vairel, F. (Eds.). (2013). *Social movements, mobilization, and contestation in the Middle East and North Africa*. Stanford University Press.

Béland, D. (2005). *The political construction of collective insecurity: From moral panic to blame avoidance and organized irresponsibility*. Harvard University.

Blanchard, E., & Willmann, G. (2016). Trade, education, and the shrinking middle class. *Journal of International Economics, 99*, 263–278.

Bonny, A. (2022). *Crises affect social justice in Africa: Social activists*. https://www.aa.com.tr/en/africa/crises-affect-social-justice-in-africa-social-activists/2507047

Boothe, I., & Smithey, L. A. (2007). Privilege, empowerment, and nonviolent intervention. *Peace & Change, 32*(1), 39–61.

Branch, A., & Mampilly, Z. (2015). *Africa uprising: Popular protest and political change*. Bloomsbury Publishing.

Bryan, S., & Baer, D. (Eds.). (2005). *Money in politics: A study of party financing practices in 22 countries*. National Democratic Institute for International Affairs (NDI).

Casal Bertoa, F., & Sanches, E. (2019). *Political party finance regulation in 13 African countries*.

Chapman, T. K. (2013). Origins of and connections to social justice in critical race theory in education. In *Handbook of critical race theory in education* (pp. 121–132). Routledge.

Chiroma, N. H. (2016). Providing mentoring for orphans and vulnerable children in internally displaced person camps: The case of northern Nigeria. *HTS: Theological Studies, 72*(1), 1–7.

Cleaver, F. (1999). Paradoxes of participation: Questioning participatory approaches to development. *Journal of International Development: The Journal of the Development Studies Association, 11*(4), 597–612.

Coleman, C. (2020). *Africa is the last frontier for global growth*. https://www.project-syndicate.org/commentary/africa-growth-potential-reforms-by-colin-coleman-2020-02?a_la=english&a_d=5e3983edc751ba1f881ef509&a_m=&a_a=click&a_s=&a_p=%2Fsection%2Feconomics&a_li=africa-growth-potential-reforms-by-colin-coleman-2020-02&a_pa=section-commentaries&a_ps=

Cooper, F. (1983a). Urban space, industrial time, and wage labor in Africa. *Struggle for the city: Migrant labor, capital, and the state in urban Africa* (pp. 7–50).

Cooper, F. (1983b). *Struggle for the City: migrant labor, capital, and the state in urban Africa* (Vol. 8). SAGE Publications, Incorporated.

Corruption Watch. (2020). *Exposed: How candidates bought votes in NPP primaries*. https://corruptionwatchghana.org/2020/07/09/exposed-how-candidates-bought-votes-in-npp2020primaries/

De Goede, M. (2017). *An analysis of Mahmood Mamdani's citizen and subject: Contemporary Africa and the legacy of late colonialism*. Macat Library.

Drewes, J. E., & Van Aswegen, M. (2013). National planning in South Africa: A critical review. *WIT Transactions on Ecology and the Environment, 173*, 193–204.

Eckert, A. (2017). Social movements in Africa. In *The history of social movements in global perspective* (pp. 211–224). Palgrave Macmillan.

Egwu, S. (2009). Monitoring of the administration and finances of political parties in Nigeria—Legal and institutional limitations. *The Nigerian Electoral Journal, 3*(1), 33–41.

Ewetan, O. O., & Urhie, E. (2014). Insecurity and socio-economic development in Nigeria. *Journal of Sustainable Development Studies, 5*(1).

Fanon, F. (2007). *The wretched of the earth*. Grove/Atlantic, Inc.

Fogg, K. (2003). 'Preface' to International IDEA: Funding of political parties and election campaigns in Africa (P.V.). *Handbook Series*. Trydells Trpekeri AB.

Ford, J. (2012). Democracy and Change: What are the prospects for an "African Spring?" *African Futures*, *14*.

Fukuyama, F. (2013). The middle-class revolution. *The Wall Street Journal*, *28*, 06–13.

Gabay, C. (2012). Who's heard of the 'African Spring'? *Open Democracy*, *25*.

Hantal, B. (2022). A review of the perspectives of social justice with special reference to the Ambedkarism. *Contemporary Voice of Dalit*, 2455328X221076623.

Haughton, T. (2012). A law unto themselves: Money, regulation and the development of party politics in the Czech Republic. *The Legal Regulation of Political Parties Working Paper Series* (No. 20).

Ichino, N., & Nathan, N. L. (2016). *Democratizing the party: The effects of primary election reforms in Ghana*.

Jatava, D. R. (1998). *Social justice in India*. INA Shree Publishers.

Job, N., Roux, D. J., Bezuidenhout, H., & Cole, N. S. (2020). A multi-scale, participatory approach to developing a protected area wetland inventory in South Africa. *Frontiers in Environmental Science*, *8*, 49.

Jones, M. (2021). *Nigeria's #Endsars protests: What happened next?* https://www.bbc.com/news/world-africa-58817690

Juma, C. (2011). The African summer. *Foreign Policy*, *28*.

Kramon, E. (2009). *Vote-buying and political behavior: Estimating and explaining vote-buying's effect on turnout in Kenya*. Institute for Democracy in South Africa.

Larsson, I., Staland-Nyman, C., Svedberg, P., Nygren, J. M., & Carlsson, I. M. (2018). Children and young people's participation in developing interventions in health and well-being: A scoping review. *BMC Health Services Research*, *18*(1), 1–20.

Lwoga, E. T., & Sangeda, R. Z. (2019). ICTs and development in developing countries: A systematic review of reviews. *The Electronic Journal of Information Systems in Developing Countries*, *85*(1), e12060.

Mamdani, M. (2013). An African reflection on Tahrir square. In *Arab revolutions and world transformations* (pp. 21–28). Routledge.

Masbah, M. (2017). *A new generation of protests in Morocco? How Hirak Al-Rif endures*. Arab Reform Initiative.

Mekoa, I. (2019). How Africa got into a mess: Colonial legacy, underdevelopment, corruption and human rights violations in Africa. *Journal of Reviews on Global Economics*, *8*, 43–52.

Miller, D. (1991). Recent theories of social justice. *British Journal of Political Science*, *21*(3), 371–391.

Mueller, L. (2018). *Political protest in contemporary Africa.* Cambridge University Press.

Muñoz, P., & Chirinos, P. M. (2019). *Buying audiences.* Cambridge University Press.

Nega, E. (2011, February 25). Libya's Gadhafi and Ethiopia's EPRDF. *The Ethiopian Times.*

Nyam, Y. S., Kotir, J. H., Jordaan, A. J., Ogundeji, A. A., & Turton, A. R. (2020). Drivers of change in sustainable water management and agricultural development in South Africa: A participatory approach. *Sustainable Water Resources Management, 6*(4), 1–20.

Ochieng, O. (2022). *Vote buying the bane of genuine poll outcomes.* https://nation.africa/kenya/blogs-opinion/blogs/vote-buying-bane-of-genuine-poll-outcomes-3796818

Ogan, T. V. (2018). Achieving economic development amidst post-modern cross roads. *African Research Review, 12*(3), 58–63.

Ogunriola, F. (2021). *Industrialisation Africa as ticket to economic prosperity.* https://businessday.ng/opinion/article/industrialisation-africas-ticket-to-economic-prosperity/

Ohman, M. (2013). Controlling money in politics: An introduction. *International Foundation for Electoral Systems.*

Ohuocha, C. (2012). *Subsidy protesters block Nigerian petrol stations.* https://www.reuters.com/article/nigeria-protest-idafl6e8c318m20120103

Onah, E. I., & Nwali, U. (2018). Monetisation of electoral politics and the challenge of political exclusion in Nigeria. *Commonwealth & Comparative Politics, 56*(3), 318–339.

Oriola, E. O. (2009). A framework for food security and poverty reduction in Nigeria. *European Journal of Social Sciences, 8*(1), 132–139.

Otekunrin, O. A., Momoh, S., & Ayinde, I. A. (2019). How far has Africa gone in achieving the zero hunger target? Evidence from Nigeria. *Global Food Security, 22*, 1–12.

Outhwaite, W., & Bottomore, T. (1993). Twentieth-century social thought. *Twentieth-Century Social Thought.*

Pocock, M. J., Roy, H. E., August, T., Kuria, A., Barasa, F., Bett, J., ... & Trevelyan, R. (2019). Developing the global potential of citizen science: Assessing opportunities that benefit people, society and the environment in East Africa. *Journal of Applied Ecology, 56*(2), 274–281.

Redaction Africanews. (2021). *Malawi: Police break protests against rising cost of living.* https://www.africanews.com/2021/11/26/malawi-police-break-protests-against-rising-cost-of-living/

Robinson, A. L., & Gottlieb, J. (2021). How to close the gender gap in political participation: Lessons from matrilineal societies in Africa. *British Journal of Political Science, 51*(1), 68–92.

Rueschemeyer, D., Stephens, E. H., & Stephens, J. D. (1992). *Capitalist development and democracy* (Vol. 22). Polity.

Sarkodie, S. A., & Adams, S. (2020). Electricity access, human development index, governance and income inequality in Sub-Saharan Africa. *Energy Reports, 6,* 455–466.

Schock, K. (2003). Nonviolent action and its misconceptions: Insights for social scientists. *PS: Political Science & Politics, 36*(4), 705–712.

Sharp, G. (2005). *Waging nonviolent struggle* (p. 40). Porter Sargent.

Signe, L., & Dollar, D. (2020). *Africa's roadmap for long-term economic growth.* https://www.brookings.edu/podcast-episode/africas-roadmap-for-long-term-economic-growth/

Stanbury, W. T. (1986). The mother's milk of politics: Political contributions to federal parties in Canada, 1974–1984. *Canadian Journal of Political Science, 19*(4), 795–821.

Statista. (2022a). *Number of people living below the extreme poverty line in Africa from 2016 to 2027.* https://www.statista.com/statistics/1228533/number-of-people-living-below-the-extreme-poverty-line-in-africa/#:~:text=In%202022a%2C%20around%20460%20million,compared%20to%20the%20previous%20years

Statista. (2022b). *African countries with the highest share of global population living below the extreme poverty line in 2022.* https://www.statista.com/statistics/1228553/extreme-poverty-as-share-of-global-population-in-africa-by-country/

Stephan, M., & Mundy, J. (2006). A battlefield transformed: From guerilla resistance to mass nonviolent struggle in the Western Sahara. *Journal of Military and Strategic Studies, 8*(3).

Strauss, D. A. (1994). Corruption, equality, and campaign finance reform. *Columbia Law Review, 94*(4), 1369–1389.

The Christian Science Monitor. (2011, February 12). Now that Egypt's Mubarak is out, could Gabon's Bongo be next? *The Christian Science Monitor.*

The Daily Nation. (2011, September 8). Will the Arab uprising spread to Sub-Saharan Africa? *The Daily Nation.*

United Nations. (2014). *The millennium development goals report 2014.* UN 2014.

Visagie, J., & Posel, D. (2013). A reconsideration of what and who is middle class in South Africa. *Development Southern Africa, 30*(2), 149–167.

Weimann, A., Nguendo-Yongsi, B., Foka, C., Waffo, U., Carbajal, P., Sietchiping, R., & Oni, T. (2022). Developing a participatory approach to building a coalition of transdisciplinary actors for healthy urban planning in African cities- a case study of Douala, Cameroon. *Cities and Health, 6*(1), 87–97.

Air, Land, and Water Pollution in Africa

Ayobami Oluwaseun Aluko

1 INTRODUCTION

Africa with a population estimated to be the second largest in the world is immensely blessed with mineral resources making most African countries rely on the extraction of these resources for economic development. The extraction of these resources has largely contributed to the high level of environmental pollution in the continent. The rapid population growth, industrialisation, and urbanisation of the African continent are not without their negative consequences on the environment. It places a huge demand for essential resources and impacts the quality of air, land, and water in the region.[1] The environment is invaluable and irreplaceable and needs to be protected because a healthy environment is key, not

[1] Abioye O. Fayiga, Mabel O. Ipinmoroti and Tait Chirenje, 'Environmental Pollution in Africa' (2018) Environ Dev Sustain 20, 41–73.

A. O. Aluko (✉)
Department of Jurisprudence and Private Law, Faculty of Law, Obafemi Awolowo University, Ile-Ife, Nigeria
e-mail: ayo.aluko@oauife.edu.ng

© The Author(s), under exclusive license to Springer Nature Switzerland AG 2023
A. I. Adeniran (ed.), *African Development and Global Engagements*,
https://doi.org/10.1007/978-3-031-21283-3_18

only to the survival but to be the development of the human species.[2] In the same vein, it is becoming more evident that a healthy environment is necessary for the full enjoyment of human rights and only possible through the exercise of rights, i.e., participatory rights like the rights to access relevant information, participation, and remedy on environmental matters.[3] On account of this, there has been a rise in the recognition of environmental rights around the globe and the use of human rights law and institutions to seek redress for environmental injustices,[4] i.e., environmental damage, harm, or pollution.

It is not a coincidence that instances of environmental injustice are often accompanied by or constitute human rights violations. It has long been recognised that environmental harm can amount to a violation of human rights when it affects an individual's or a community's ability to enjoy or exercise their fundamental rights, such as the right to health, to an adequate standard of living, or to self-determination.[5] Notably, the preamble to the Paris Agreement on Climate Change states: '...climate change is a common concern of humankind, Parties should, when taking action to address climate change, respect, promote and consider their respective obligations on human rights, the right to health, the rights of indigenous peoples, local communities, migrants, children, persons with disabilities and people in vulnerable situations and the right to development, as well as gender equality, empowerment of women and intergenerational equity'.[6]

The effects of environmental degradation are borne disproportionately by the most vulnerable, the rural and urban poor, ethnic minorities, women, and indigenous peoples. Sadly, the communities most burdened by poverty, ill health, political disempowerment, and social exclusion are

---

[2] Funmi Abioye, 'Advancing Human Rights Through Environmental Rule of Law in Africa' in M. Addaney, A. Oluborode Jegede (eds.), *Human Rights and the Environment under African Union Law*, (Palgrave Macmillan, 2020) 81.

[3] John H. knox and Ramin Pejan, 'Introduction' in John H. Knox and Ramin Pejan (eds.), *The Human Right to a Healthy Environment*, (Cambridge University Press, 2018).

[4] Sumudu Atapattu and Andrea Schapper, *'Human Rights and the Environment: Key issues* (Routledge 2019).

[5] Bridget Lewis, Human Rights and Environmental Wrongs: Achieving Environmental Justice through Human Rights Law (2012) IJCJ 1(1), 65–73, 66.

[6] Conference of Parties, Adoption of the Paris Agreement, December 12, 2015, in force November 4, 2016, UN Doc. FCCC/CP/2015/19.

the ones most exposed to pollution and other environmental concerns like climate change.[7] The realm of a rights-based approach to development as this research suggests provides a normative approach to environmental governance which can help minimise environmental injustice, promote interests, and provide a pathway for sustainable development.

The aim of this chapter is to examine environmental pollution in the African context and examine attempts both at the regional and national levels to enhance environmental protection in the continent. Following the present introduction, Sect. 2 gives an overview of the state of the African environment and the general issues of environmental pollution. Section 3 discusses the conceptual frameworks, theory and methodology adopted. Section 4 examines the potential of employing a rights-based approach to addressing the imminent environmental concerns in Africa taking into consideration the regional legislative and judicial framework, and the domestic attempts by some African states. Section 5 draws a conclusion and makes appropriate recommendations.

2   ENVIRONMENTAL POLLUTION IN AFRICA

Africa is plagued with different environmental challenges including loss of biodiversity, climate change and its effects, deforestation, desertification, erosion, flooding, air, water, and land pollution, etc. These challenges have severe impacts on human health owing to limited coping capacities.[8] In general, African states face the environmental problems of poverty and in this context environmental degradation can have a negative effect on the observance of human rights.[9] Convincingly, some African Countries have been engaging in human rights violation and many have been unable to subject themselves to International Environmental Laws and its obligations.[10] Further, some states clamp down on participatory rights generally

---

[7] Carmen G. Gonzalez, 'Human rights, environmental justice, and the North–South divide' in Anna Grear and Louise J. Kotzé (eds.), *Research Handbook on Human Rights and the Environment*, (Edward Elgar Publishing, 2015).

[8] UNEP, *Africa Environment Outlook 3: Summary for Policy Makers* (2013).

[9] Werner Scholtz, 'Human rights and the Environment in the African Union Context' in Werner Scholtz and Jonathan Verschuuren (eds.), *Regional Environmental Law: Transregional Comparative Lessons in Pursuit of Sustainable Development*, (Edward Elgar, 2015).

[10] For example, Nigeria, Kenya, Sudan, Burundi, Rwanda, and Uganda.

386 A. O. ALUKO

in environmental matters thereby weakening environmental governance efforts which seek to hold governments responsible and accountable.[11]

While the primary responsibility for promoting and protecting human rights lies with the state, it has long been recognised that businesses and transnational corporations have contributed to or have been complicit in the violation of human rights in various ways.[12] Developing countries may lack the capacity to control foreign companies extracting minerals, oil, or other natural resources in a manner that harms both the local population and the environment. Classic examples are Shell's impact on the environment, natural resources, health, and living standards of the Ogoni people in Nigeria, or the health effects of toxic waste disposed of in Abidjan by a ship under Charter to Trafigura, an oil trading company based in the EU.[13]

In Africa, air pollution is caused by various factors which include industrial and traffic emissions, use of solid cooking fuel, use of insecticides, waste incineration, bush burning, etc. Pollution from industrial and agricultural activities, poor sanitation practices have resulted in the pollution of surface and groundwaters in Africa. Land pollution has increased with increased levels of mining activities, farming, and the disposal of domestic and industrial wastes.[14] Environmental degradation has the ability to, and the consequence of, constraining developmental goals. This is because the full effects or manifestation of developmental efforts are stymied by prevailing situations of environmental degradation.[15] This has been the case in Africa for many years, due to the cost of development being historically high on the environment due to lax laws, and non-existent enforcement in cases where laws do exist.[16] Environmental pollution

[11] Louis J. Kotzé, 'Africa', in Lavanya Rajamani and Jacqueline Peel (eds.), *The Oxford Handbook of International environmental Law*, (2nd edn, Oxford University Press, 2021) 1061.

[12] Alan Boyle, 'Human Rights and the Environment: Where Next?' in Ben Boer (ed), *Environmental Law Dimensions of Human Rights*, (Oxford University Press, 2015) 209–10.

[13] Ibid.

[14] Abioye O. Fayiga, Mabel O. Ipinmoroti and Tait Chirenje, n 1.

[15] Funmi Abioye, n 2, 81–2.

[16] Ibid. See also, United Nations 'New and Emerging Challenges in Africa Summary Report' available at: https://sustainabledevelopment.un.org/index.php?page=view&type=400&nr=502&menu=1515.

may affect the economic growth and development of a nation or region because the health effects may reduce productivity of the workforce.[17] With all the attempts to develop within the continent, economic development outside the social and environmental objectives will only result in pygmy development.

3 CONCEPTUAL FRAMEWORKS: ENVIRONMENTAL RULE OF LAW, ENVIRONMENTAL JUSTICE, AND SUSTAINABLE DEVELOPMENT

3.1   Environmental Rule of Law

Most countries have developed environmental laws and also put in place the needed environmental institutions at different levels for proper implementation. Effective implementation now remains the challenge facing both developed and developing countries alike. Environmental rule of law which describes when laws are widely understood, respected, and enforced and the benefits of environmental protection are enjoyed by people and the planet is key to addressing this implementation gap.[18] Advocates of the concept emphasise the need to legislate developmental efforts along with the protection of the environment as a key consideration.[19]

Environmental rule of law provides an essential platform which supports the pillars of sustainable development— economic, social, and environmental.[20] Hence, it is pivotal to the concept of sustainable development, i.e., development cannot be sustainable outside of environmental rule of law. It incorporates environmental needs with the essential elements of the rule of law and provides the basis for improving environmental governance.[21] It reflects universal moral values and ethical norms

---

[17] Abioye O. Fayiga, et al., n 1, 43.

[18] United Nations Environment Programme (UNEP), *Environmental Rule of Law: First Global Report* (2019). Available at: https://wedocs.unep.org/20.500.11822/27279, accessed 24 July 2022.

[19] Funmi Abioye, n 2, 87.

[20] Ibid.

[21] Environmental Rule of Law, available at: https://www.unep.org/explore-topics/environmental-rights-and-governance/what-we-do/promoting-environmental-rule-law-0, accessed 24 July 2022.

of behaviour, and it provides a foundation for environmental rights and obligations. Without environmental rule of law and the enforcement of legal rights and obligations, environmental governance may be arbitrary, that is, discretionary, subjective, and unpredictable.[22] In essence, legal provisions (and judicial mechanisms to enforce these provisions) help to govern our interaction with our environment in order to achieve the goal of protecting the environment for the benefit of the present and future generations.[23] The judiciary plays a key role in the fragile state of the environment. As a guardian of the Rule of Law, enforcement of laws in the field of environment and sustainable development is needed to alleviate poverty, sustain enduring civilisation and ensure intragenerational and intergenerational equities.[24]

3.2 Environmental Justice

Environmental justice is concerned with the fair and equal distribution of environmental burdens and benefits at local, national, and international levels. It also strives to secure the meaningful participation in decision-making processes of those who are most likely to be affected by environmental changes which implicate them and to ensure that those who are negatively affected have adequate recourse to compensation or other remedies.[25]

The four-part characterisation of environmental justice from a range of justice considerations are (a) distributive justice; (b) procedural justice; (c) corrective justice; and (d) social justice.[26] Distributive justice requires equal treatment and equal access to resources and lowering of environmental risk. Procedural justice requires the participation of all stakeholders in decisions that affect them. Corrective justice requires punishing wrongdoers and remedying harm inflicted on individuals and communities. Social justice overlaps with the social pillar of sustainable development

---

[22] Ibid.

[23] Funmi Abioye, n 2, 88.

[24] See 'The Johannesburg Principles on the Role of Law and Sustainable Development' (adopted at the Global Judges Symposium, 2002). https://www.eufje.org/images/Doc Divers/Johannesburg%20Principles.pdf, accessed 1 August 2021.

[25] Bridget Lewis, n 5.

[26] Robert R. Kuehn, 'A Taxonomy of Environmental Justice' (2000) *Environmental Law Reporter* 30: 10681–703.

AIR, LAND, AND WATER POLLUTION IN AFRICA 389

which agrees with the goal of achieving a more just society.[27] As further described, environmental justice is a 'marriage of the movement for social justice with environmentalism', integrating environmental concerns into a broader agenda that emphasises social, racial, and economic justice.[28]

In countries in transition, environmental justice often involves challenges to actions of those in power who increase their wealth or status at the expense of others. There, the environmental justice concept is most relevant when it is applied to situations where power elites govern in the absence of sufficient legal controls, taking advantage of gaps in legal processes and standards and the flux in the application of the rule of law to grant themselves privileges.[29] It shows not only the disproportionate burdens on certain marginalised groups entailed by hazardous activities and substances but also highlights the lack of real opportunities for participating in decision-making processes.[30]

Human rights provisions, particularly constitutional environmental rights, are essential to promote environmental justice. They provide the basis upon which citizens may challenge and thereby limit government's potential to abuse its powers to deny the citizenry's fundamental freedoms, which in the contemporary world we live in includes environmental rights.[31] While an increasing number of national constitutions now recognise the importance of integrating environmental concerns, many have not adopted a rights-based approach yet.[32]

---

[27] Sumudu Atapattu and Andrea Schapper, n 4.

[28] Robert R. Kuehn, n 26.

[29] Stephen Stec, 'Environmental justice through courts in countries in economic transition', in Jonas Ebbesson and Phoebe Okowa (eds.) *Environmental Law and Justice in Context*, (Cambridge University Press 2009), 173.

[30] Jonas Ebbesson, 'Introduction: dimensions of justice in environmental law', ibid, 2.

[31] Rhuks Ako, 'Mainstreaming Environmental Justice in Developing countries: Thinking Beyond Constitutional Environmental Rights' in Chile Eboe-Osuji and Engobo Emeseh (eds.), *Nigerian Yearbook of International Law*, (Springer International Publishing AG, 2018).

[32] For example, the recognition of environmental protection under the Constitution of the Federal Republic of Nigeria in Section 20 remains non-justiciable in any court of law till date as it is located under Part II which is titled '*Fundamental objectives and Directive principles of state policy*'. The provisions in Chapter 2 are meant to guide the arms of government in the task of nation building and in the daily performance of the duties of governance. See Olu Awolowo, 'Environmental Rights and Sustainable Development in Nigeria' (2017) 10(06) OIDA International Journal of Sustainable Development, 17.

3.3   Sustainable Development

Sustainable development has been defined as development that meets the needs of the present generation without compromising the ability of the future generations to meet their needs.[33] Fundamentally, in meeting the needs of the present generation and those of the future generations, the balancing of economic, social, and environmental objectives is key against prioritising any of these objectives. More than a concept, sustainable development has evolved into a norm of international law. This is made possible simply by observing its reference in legal practice, not only in policy instruments but also in treaties and judicial decisions.[34] Therefore, in plain terms, sustainable development implies the preservation of natural resources for the benefit of the present and future generations, the exploitation of natural resources without compromising the environmental rights of the people, the integration of environmental factors into economic and other development programs.[35]

Sustainable development contains both substantive and procedural elements.[36] The substantive elements include the integration of environmental protection and economic development, the right to development, the sustainable utilisation of natural resources, the equitable allocation of resources both within the present, and between the present and future generations, i.e., intra-generational and inter-generational equity.[37] The procedural aspects deal with access to information, public participation in decision-making, and environmental impact assessment.[38] Three 'interdependent and mutually reinforcing pillars of sustainable development'

---

[33] WCED: *Our Common Future*. Report of the World Commission for Environment and Development. (Oxford University Press, 1987).

[34] Jorge E. Viñuales, 'Sustainable Development' in Lavanya Rajamani and Jacqueline Peel (eds.), *The Oxford Handbook of International environmental Law*, (2nd edn, Oxford University Press, 2021) 289.

[35] Olu Awolowo, n 32, 21.

[36] Alan Boyle and Catherine Redgwell, *Birnie, Boyle and Redgwell's International Law and the Environment* (4th edn, Oxford University Press, 2021) 117.

[37] Principles 3–8 of the Rio Declaration on Environment and Development 1992.

[38] Principles 10–17 of the Rio Declaration on Environment and Development 1992.

were identified in the Johannesburg Declaration—economic, social, and environmental pillars.[39]

Essentially, sustainable development from a global perspective states that while recognising the right to pursue economic development is an attribute of a state's sovereignty over its own natural resources and territory, it cannot lawfully be exercised without regard for the detrimental impact on the environment or on human rights.[40] In effect, the process of decision-making and compliance with environmental and human rights obligations constitutes the key legal tests of sustainable development in current international law, rather than the nature of the development itself.[41]

Practically and in pursuance of sustainable development, a study carried out emphasised the importance of political consensus forged by a long-term implementation of strong environmental controls alongside economic development that resulted in a deep respect for courts and environmental institutions. This ultimately led to the emergence and maintenance of environmental rule of law.[42] Reference to the needs of both present and future generations categorically gives insight into the link to considerations of both intra-generational and inter-generational justice as seen under environmental justice.[43] The relationship between social justice and sustainable development was included in early stages of the sustainable development discourse. According to the Brundtland Report, relevant to environmental justice is the inference that social justice cannot be achieved without an equitable sharing of the costs and benefits of environmental protection.[44]

---

[39] *Report of the World Summit on Sustainable Development*, UN Doc. A/CONF.199/20 (26 August–4 September 2002), Resolution 1, para. 5.

[40] Alan Boyle, n 12, 223.

[41] Patricia Birnie, Alan Boyle, and Catherine Redgwell, *International Law and the Environment* (3rd edn, Oxford University Press, 2009) 125–7.

[42] UNEP, n 8, 2. Here, we find out that there is such a notable connection between sustainable development and environmental rule of law. Costa Rica, a nation intensely dependent on natural resources achieved notable feats. The country has increased life expectancy to more than 79 years, achieved 96 per cent adult literacy, and built per capita income to almost US$9000 while setting and meeting ambitious environmental goals, including already having doubled its forest cover to over 50 per cent, and is on track to be climate neutral.

[43] Sumudu Atapattu and Andrea Schapper, n 4, 18.

[44] Stephen Stec, n 29, 159.

4 THEORY AND METHODOLOGY

4.1 'Environmental Democracy' Theory

According to this theory, environmental procedural rights such as the rights to participation, remedies, and access to justice are necessary to empower citizens, communities, and civil society groups to challenge industrial projects and shape public environmental decisions and policies.[45] Concisely, 'environmental democracy' contends that reconciliation between the ideals could be achieved largely through reforming existing institutions of liberal democracy and capitalism to incorporate environmental values and expanding participatory governance.[46] Therefore, the theory introduces democratic governance into the fabric of environmental sustainability. It begins with not only gradual transformation of the form, style, and content of democracy but also of society's relationship with the rest of nature.[47]

Pivotal to this theory are procedural rights, also referred to as access rights which include access to information on environmental quality and concerns, participation in decision-making processes and access to justice in environmental matters. At the international level, there exists already the recognition of environmental procedural rights mainly drawing from recognised concepts under international human rights law. The recognition of the interdependence between human rights and the environment can be traced to the 1992 United Nations Conference on Environment and Development (UNCED). Principle 10 of the Rio declaration adopted at the UNCED is the result of the development and acceptance of environmental procedural rights.

From a human rights-based approach, the study employs a doctrinal legal research methodology. The desktop review is supported by a review of scholarly work and legal sources, including primary and secondary

[45] Linda Hajjar Leib, *Human Rights and the Environment: Philosophical, Theoretical, and legal Perspectives* (Martinus Nijhoff Publishers 2011) 81.

[46] Jonathan Pickering, Karin Bäckstrand and David Schlosberg, 'Between environmental and ecological democracy: theory and practice at the democracy-environment nexus' (2020) Journal of environmental policy and planning 22(1), 1.

[47] Giulia Parola, 'Environmental democracy: a Theoretical Construction' available online at: https://www.degruyter.com/document/doi/10.2478/9788376560144.ch1/pdf, accessed 22 August 2022.

sources. The review is carried out qualitatively to ascertain the legal formalism and realism of environmental matters in Africa for general discussion.

5   Potential of Human Rights-Based Approach to Environmental Protection in Africa

A high-quality environment is being regarded as a necessary prerequisite for the enjoyment of some of the most fundamental human rights especially the rights to life and health. The rights to adequate food, clean water, and even proper housing are also dependent on a quality environment.[48] As a significant public interest, a decent environment has become of relevance to environmental quality by focusing on rightly balancing economic and developmental priorities. The existing concept of human rights protection should be extended in order to include the right to a healthy and decent environment, to include freedom from pollution, and corresponding rights to pure air and water.[49] Three theoretical approaches to the relationship between human rights and the environment have been identified. The first sees the environment as a 'precondition to the enjoyment of human rights'. The second views human rights as 'tools to address environmental issues, both procedurally and substantively'. The third integrates human rights and the environment under the concept of sustainable development.[50]

A rights-based approach seems to directly address environmental impacts on the life, health, private life, and property of individuals rather than on other states or the environment general. It may also serve to secure higher standards of environmental quality, based on the obligation

---

[48] Ben Boer (ed), *Environmental Law Dimensions of Human Rights*, (Oxford University Press, 2015).

[49] R Cassin quoted by C Peter, Taking the environment seriously: The African Charter on Human and Peoples: Rights and the environment (1993) 3 Review of the African Commission on Human and Peoples Rights 39. See also Morné van der Linde and Lirette Louw, 'Considering the interpretation and implementation of Article 24 of the African Charter on Human and Peoples' Rights in light of the SERAC communication', (2003) 3 African Human Rights Law Journal 167, 175.

[50] UN HR Council, *Analytical Study on the Relationship between Human Rights and the Environment, Report of the United Nations High Commissioner for Human Rights*, UN Doc. A/HRC/19/34 (16 December 2011), para. 6–9.

394   A. O. ALUKO

of states to take measures to control pollution affecting health and private life. Ultimately, it helps to promote the rule of law, i.e., governments become directly accountable for their failure to regulate and control environmental nuisances, including those caused by corporations, and for facilitating access to justice and enforcing environmental laws and judicial decisions.[51] As the discussion progresses, it becomes clear that the approach simply refers to the 'greening' of existing human rights law rather than the addition of new rights to existing treaties as provided in human rights treaties.[52] It offers a platform for merging environmental protection, economic development, and the guarantees of human rights.[53]

The development of a rights' regime in Africa had to take into account the contexts and realities obtaining, and those realities were and still are a reality of 'abysmal poverty; with its largescale shortages of food, shelter, clothing, education and health; with its unsatisfactory planning of resource use; with its poverty of basic administrative structure; with its uncontrolled pace of population growth; with its numerous political upheavals, cases of turmoil, war and destruction'.[54] A critical issue is the place of development in the human rights discourse in light of the endemic poverty levels in the continent. The consequence was the inclusion of the obligation on states to 'individually and collectively ensure the exercise of the right to development'.[55]

---

[51] Alan Boyle, n 12, 202.

[52] Ibid., 203.

[53] D. Shelton, 'Communication 155/96 (Social and Economic Rights Action Center/Center for Economic and Social Rights v. Nigeria). Case No. ACHPR/COMM/A044/1', 96 AJIL (2002) 937, at 942.

[54] J.B. Ojwang, Laying a Basis for Rights: Towards a Jurisprudence of Development, Inaugural Lecture Delivered Before the University of Nairobi on 9th July 1992, (University of Nairobi Press, 1992) 20.

[55] Collins Odote, 'Human Rights-based Approach to Environmental Protection: Kenyan, South African and Nigerian Constitutional Architecture and Experience' in Michael Addaney and Ademola Oluborode Jegede (eds.), Human Rights and the Environment under African Union Law, (Palgrave Macmillan, 2020) 392. ACHPR, Article 22(2).

AIR, LAND, AND WATER POLLUTION IN AFRICA   395

5.1   Regional Level

Fundamentally and from the African Union perspective, the Constitutive Act of the Union while stating its objectives in Article 3 provides opportunities for the rights-based approach in consideration. Article 3(h) states:

> promote and protect human and peoples' rights in accordance with the African Charter on Human and Peoples' Rights and other relevant human rights instruments.

The promotion of sustainable development at the economic, social, and cultural levels promotes cooperation in all fields of human activity to raise the living standards of African peoples and the promotion of good health on the continent.[56] The principles to which the Union functions include democratic principles, human rights, the rule of law and good governance, and the promotion of social justice to ensure balanced economic development.[57]

The African Charter on Human and Peoples' Rights in Article 24 states:

> All peoples shall have the right to a general satisfactory environment favourable to their development.[58]

Prior to this provision, the recognition of the relationship between the environment and human rights was found only in soft laws.[59] Therefore, the Charter has been described as the first and only international binding treaty that includes significant solidarity rights, i.e., the right to a generally

---

[56] See Article 3(j, k, and n), Constitutive Act of the Africa Union (2000).

[57] Article 4(m and n).

[58] African Charter on Human and Peoples' Rights (Banjul Charter) Organization of African Unity (OAU) CAB/LEG/67/3 rev. 5, 21 I.L.M. 58 (1982).

[59] See the resolution passed by the United Nations General Assembly recognising the relationship between the quality of the environment and the enjoyment of human rights (UNGA Res 2398 XXII of 1968), the Declaration of the United Nations on the Human Environment (1972) which recognised the fundamental right to freedom, equality, and adequate conditions of life in an environment of a quality that permits of dignity and well-being.

satisfactory environment and the right to development.[60] This provision remains important because it is the most direct normative statement of an environmental right in any binding human rights instrument.[61] The provision on the right to environment reflects the recognition that a satisfactory environment is significant for economic, social, and cultural development as well as the realisation of other human rights in Africa.[62] It is thus of significance that, at the African regional level, environmental rights are recognised as explicit treaty norms, with normative accord with other rights and corresponding obligations.[63]

The right under Article 24 has been declared a collective right, a right to be claimed by 'peoples'.[64] The African Commission however developed an interpretation for the term 'people'. The Commission adopted a state-centred interpretation of the term by approximating 'state' membership with the meaning of the term 'peoples'.[65] In other words, to be recognised as 'peoples' in relation to the collective right, they should manifest 'a common historical tradition, racial or ethnic identity, cultural homogeneity, linguistic unity, religious and ideological affinities, territorial connection, and a common economic life or other bonds, identities and affinities they collectively enjoy'.[66] Notwithstanding the provision of the right to a satisfactory environment as a collective right in the African

[60] Articles 24 and 22 respectively. See Werner Scholtz, n 9, 104.

[61] Ibid., 107.

[62] Michael Addaney, Chantelle Gloria Moyo and Thabang Ramakhula, 'Human Rights, Regional Law, and Environment in Africa: Legal and Conceptual Foundations' in Michael Addaney and Ademola Oluborode Jegede (eds.), *Human Rights and the Environment under African Union Law,* (Palgrave Macmillan, 2020) 13.

[63] Lilian Chenwi, 'The Right to a Satisfactory, Healthy, and Sustainable Environment in the African Regional Human Rights System' in in John H. Knox and Ramin Pejan (eds.), *The Human Right to a Healthy Environment*, (Cambridge University Press, 2018) 59.

[64] Ibid.

[65] DRC v Burundi, Rwanda and Uganda Communication 227/99 (2004), paras 87 and 95. The Commission refers to the violation of the 'Congolese people's rights' and the deprivation of the right of the 'people of the Democratic Republic of the Congo'. Werner Scholtz, n 9, 110.

[66] Centre for Minority Rights Development (kenya) and Minority Rights Group International on behalf of Endorois Welfare Council v. Kenya, Communication 276/2003 (African Commission, 2009) para. 151. See Lilian Chenwi, n 13, 63.

Charter, its nature 'is relatively uncontested in that it is a right to which individuals, communities and the public at large can be beneficiaries of'.[67]

Questions relating to the scope of a 'general satisfactory environment' have to be addressed. Also, clarifications on whether the focus of environmental measures should only encourage development or rather focus on economic development in cases of conflict with environmental objectives.[68] The African Commission on Human and Peoples' Rights in the case of *Social and Economic Rights Action Centre, and the Centre for Economic and Social Rights v. Nigeria*[69] was able to make clear the content of this right. The communication alleges that the military government of Nigeria has been directly involved in oil production and that these operations have caused environmental degradation and health problems resulting from the contamination of the environment among the Ogoni People. Among other rights whose violations were complained of, the Commission ruled that due to the government's failure to prevent pollution and ecological degradation, there was a violation of Article 24. According to the Commission, the right to a satisfactory environment is important in improving the quality of life and safety of individuals and in promoting development.[70] Therefore, as a composite right, it refers to the protection of the environment as well as the promotion of development in Africa.[71]

As argued by Scholtz, the Commission failed to clarify the link between the right to a satisfactory environment and favourable development although the ecological element of sustainable development as a component of Article 24 was recognised. Scholtz further argued that in light of the inclusion of 'favourable development', it may have been intended to place sustainable development as the bridge between the right to a satisfactory environment in Article 24 and the right to development in Article 22.[72]

---

[67] Morné van der Linde and Lirette Louw, n 49, 174.

[68] Werner Scholtz, n 9, 108.

[69] Social and Economic Rights Action Center & the Center for Economic and Social Rights v. Nigeria (Communication No. 155/96).

[70] Ibid., para. 51.

[71] Lilian Chenwi, n 63, 66.

[72] Werner Scholtz, n 9, 110.

5.2 National Level

The international recognition and adoption of human rights to a healthy environment which includes environmentally related procedural rights and substantive political and socio-economic human rights bearing on environmental interests is a testimony of their increasing popularity.[73] In the opinion of Louis Kotzé, environmental human rights are predominantly sanctioned at the national level, suggesting that constitutions are almost always the legal avenue of choice to entrench environmental human rights.[74] This is succinctly referred to as environmental constitutionalism. There is indisputably something inherently constitutional about human rights law in that it functions to limit what governments can do to persons within their jurisdiction.[75]

Environmental constitutionalism is a transformative process that provides constitutional environmental protection, although while no nation has achieved the holy grail of ecological sustainability, constitutional protection of the environment can be a powerful and potentially transformative step towards this elusive goal.[76] The incorporation of provisions requiring environmental protection in national constitutions in Africa particularly following the Earth Summit in Rio saw 47 nations follow the trend. Out of these African nations, only 36 incorporated provisions recognising the right to a healthy environment in their constitution.[77] The others only recognised the provision as governmental environmental duties at best.

In Nigeria, the right to a healthy environment is not recognised under the 1999 constitution but the constitution placed a duty on the state to

---

[73] David Boyd, *The Environmental Rights Revolution: A Global Study of Constitutions, Human Rights, and the Environment* (UBC Press, 2012).

[74] Louis J. Kotzé, 'Human rights and the environment through an environmental constitutionalism lens' in Anna Grear and Louise J. Kotzé (eds.), *Research Handbook on Human Rights and the Environment*, (Edward Elgar Publishing, 2015) 146.

[75] S. Gardbaum, 'Human Rights and International Constitutionalism' in J. Dunoff and J. Trachtman (eds.), Ruling the World? Constitutionalism, International Law, and Global Government (Cambridge University Press 2009) UCLA School of Law Research Paper No. 08-01. http://ssrn.com/abstract=1088039.

[76] David Boyd, n 73.

[77] David R. Boyd, 'Constitutions, human rights, and the environment: national approaches' in in Anna Grear and Louise J. Kotzé (eds.), *Research Handbook on Human Rights and the Environment*, (Edward Elgar Publishing, 2015).

protect and improve the environment and safeguard the water, air, land, forest, and wildlife of Nigeria in the absence of a corresponding right.[78] This provision remains non-justiciable as it is contained in Chapter 2 titled 'Fundamental Objectives and Directive Principles of State Policy', whereas fundamental human rights are located in Chapter 4. However, the judiciary has been challenged to interpret the section proactively by imposing an enforceable duty on the State.[79] In *Jonah Gbemre v. SPDC and Others*,[80] a case of alleged uncontrolled gas flaring while exploring and producing oil. The plaintiff argued that his community's constitutional rights to life [Section 33(1)] and human dignity [Section 34(1)] reinforced by provisions of the African Charter, including the right to enjoy a healthy environment (Article 24), had been infringed. It was argued that oil exploration and production activities in the community contributed to air pollution and acid rain, adverse climate change, reduction in crop production, respiratory diseases, and premature deaths. The judge upheld the plaintiff's argument and decided in his favour on the basis that the right to life and human dignity might be interpreted broadly to include the right to enjoy a healthy environment. The judgment focused more on recognising the right to a clean, pollution-free environment which was aimed at putting an end to gas flaring by declaring the practice as inconsistent with the provisions of the 1999 constitution as amended.

Interestingly, the right to the environment as recognised under the African Charter in Article 24 has been made accessible in Nigeria through the process of re-enacting the Charter as part of the laws by an Act of the National Assembly. In *General Sani Abacha and Others v. Chief Gani Fawehinmi*,[81] it was decided that the African Charter had the force of law in Nigeria. Ejiwunmi JSC observed in the case that:

> The African charter on Human and People's Rights, having been passed into our municipal law, our domestic courts certainly have the jurisdiction to construe or apply the treaty. It follows then that anyone who felt that his rights as guaranteed or protected by the charter have been violated could well resort to its provisions to obtain redress in our domestic court.

[78] Section 20, 1999 Constitution of the Federal Republic of Nigeria.

[79] Rhuks Ako, n 31, 276.

[80] Federal High Court of Nigeria in the Benin Judicial Division, suit FHC/B/CS/53/05, 14 November 2005.

[81] (2000) 6 NWLR (Pt.660) 228.

Drawing from the above, the 1999 constitution as amended does not recognise the existence of the substantive right to a healthy environment but can be made available through the provision of the African Charter, and the attitude of broad interpretation of the right to life to include environmental protection is not yet an established legal principle in Nigeria.[82]

Remarkably, the case is different in South Africa where the right to environment is constitutionally recognised. The right to an environment that is not harmful to health or well-being and to have the environment protected for the benefit of both present and future generations through legislative and other measures is found in the 1996 Constitution.[83] This section provides a platform for contemporary environmental legislative and governance frameworks in South Africa. Found in Chapter 2 which lists the Bills of Rights and is described as the 'highest possible constitutional level'.[84] Section 24 is wide in ambit and comprises both fundamental and socioeconomic rights. While Section 24(a) has the flavour of a fundamental right, guaranteeing an enforceable right to enjoy a state of the environment that is not 'harmful to health or well-being', subsection (b) is couched in terms of government responsibility to 'promote the attainment' of certain environmental values.[85] While South Africa is a good example of a country that recognises the substantive right to environment and a system that proactively protects and promotes the right, the jurisprudence of the right has not fully developed to concretise the right. Section 32 provides for access to information as a procedural right which apply to issues including the environment. The Supreme Court of Appeal in the South Africa once invoked the

---

[82] Rhuks Ako, *Environmental Justice in Developing Countries: Perspectives from Africa and the Asia–Pacific* (Routledge, 2013).

[83] See Section 24 of the 1996 Constitution of the Republic of South Africa.

[84] Kotzé L and Du Plessis A, 'Some Observations on Fifteen Years of Environmental Rights Jurisprudence in South Africa' (2010) 3 (1) J Ct Innovation 157–176.

[85] Jan Glazewski, 'The Rule of Law: Opportunities for Environmental Justice in the New Democratic Order' in D. McDonald (eds.), *Environmental Justice in South Africa*, (OUP 2002) 171–198.

Brundtland Report's definition of sustainable development and further linked sustainable development with the right to a healthy environment.[86]

In Kenya, Article 42 of the constitution provides that:

> Every person has the right to a clean and healthy environment, which includes the right;
> (a) to have the environment protected for the benefit of present and future generations through legislative and other measures, particularly those contemplated in Article 69; and
> (b) to have obligations relating to the environment fulfilled under Article 70.[87]

The constitution went further to create a specialised court particularly for environmental cases according to article 162. The Environmental and Land Court of Kenya was created and has been described as the only specialised court in the English-speaking parts of Africa with an environmental mandate.[88] The Court through its decision was able to address more of the procedural aspect of environmental human rights. In *Joseph Leboo & 2 others v. Director Kenya Forest Services & another*,[89] the ELC had to decide on the granting of a permanent injunction to stop the logging of trees from the Lembus forest without an Environmental Impact Assessment (EIA) being carried out. The court held that before any kind of economic development (logging activities in this case) can be carried out on a parcel of land, a management plan and an Environmental Impact Assessment (EIA) are compulsory steps that must be taken before such.[90] The Court was concerned with the fact that irreparable damage would be meted out on the forest if the illegal activities were allowed to continue.[91] Though the Court in this case did not analyse the scope of article 42 of the constitution, it however used the right to locate

---

[86] See *Director: Mineral Development Gauteng Region v. Save the Vaal Environment* (1996) 1 All SA 2004 (T) 20. See Lavanya Rajamani and Jacqueline Peel (eds.), n 11, 1057–8.

[87] Constitution of Kenya, 2010.

[88] See Funmi Abioye, n 2, 100.

[89] eKLR (2013).

[90] Ibid., para. 46.

[91] Ibid., para. 50.

a legal basis for the claim.[92] Cases decided by the ELC in Kenya have contributed to the environmental rule of law in Kenya and thereby stand as persuasive foreign authority for other African countries. The Court in *Kamau* applied precaution and went against the trend that we see on the continent, where commercial goals tend to trump environmental concerns in both political and legal spheres. The jurisprudence of the court has further highlighted a 'higher mandate' for everyone to protect the environment and to ensure that sustainable development practices are in place.[93]

In Zimbabwe, the right to a healthy environment found its way into the constitution through 48.87% of support from the wards recognising the need for environmental protection through a rights-based approach.[94] According to the Constitution, the rights state:

1. Every person has the right—

(a) to an environment that is not harmful to their health or well-being; and

(b) to have the environment protected for the benefit of present and future generations, through reasonable legislative and other measures that—

(i) prevent pollution and ecological degradation;
(ii) promote conservation; and
(iii) secure ecologically sustainable development and use of natural resources while promoting economic and social development.[95]

---

[92] Funmi Abioye, n 2, 101.

[93] Ibid., 102.

[94] Brewsters Caiphas Soyapi, 'The Judiciary and Environmental Protection in Zimbabwe' in M. Addaney, A. Oluborode Jegede (eds.), *Human Rights and the Environment under African Union Law*, (Palgrave Macmillan, 2020) 358. See for more information, COPAC *National Statistical Report Version 1: Second All Stakeholders Conference*, October 2012 (COPAC, 2012) 189.

[95] Section 73 of the Zimbabwean Constitution 2013. Sub-Section 2 further mandates the state to take reasonable legislative and other measures, within the limits of the resources available to it, to achieve the progressive realisation of the rights set out in this section.

In the case of *Manyame Park Residents v. Chitungwiza Municipality* (*Manyame Park Residence*),[96] where ZELA[97] sought an order to compel the Chitungwiza Municipality to construct proper sewage systems. ZELA demonstrated that the municipality was negligently discharging raw sewage into a public stream and a residential area in contravention of the then recently enacted Environmental Management Act and its right to a healthy environment. The court granted the order, and the municipality admitted to the pollution but pleaded that it did not have the resources to either rehabilitate the contaminated land or build proper sewage structures. Places like Chitungwiza were subsequently hit hard by the 2008–2010 cholera outbreak, which clearly illustrates that the government has been unable to apply a precautionary approach and take preventive measures.[98]

The lack of human and financial resources for institutions tasked with enforcing and investigating issues relating to the right to a healthy environment render them inactive.[99] Notably from cases decided by the courts, for environmental protection to be effective, the courts rely on other organs of state to play their part. Clearly, the courts have not been hesitant to order government environmental agencies to take action, yet the government and its agencies have been found wanting.[100] What the Zimbabwean situation ultimately illustrates which is the case in many African nations is that a country could have provisions on the right to a healthy environment entrenched in its laws, and it could have a structured court system, but the efficacy of these systems is to a large part conditional on political will and respect for the (environmental) rule of law.[101]

In Ethiopia, Article 44 (1) of the Constitution provides 'All persons have the right to a clean and healthy environment'. Furthermore, in Article 92 (1), the Constitution provides the environmental objectives of

[96] HC 11,552, 2003.

[97] Most of the environment-related cases discussed below were instituted by the Zimbabwe Environmental Law Association (ZELA) in its capacity as an environmental NGO.

[98] Brewsters Caiphas Soyapi, n 94, 364.

[99] Ibid., 362.

[100] Ibid., 365.

[101] Ibid., 374.

the country where it obliges federal and regional governments to strive to ensure that Ethiopians live in a healthy and clean environment. The constitution also in article 43 (1) guarantees the right to sustainable development for its citizens.[102] Indeed, Ethiopia has a robust guarantee of environmental human rights but practically, there are hindrances to the realisation of these rights. Lack of timely legislative practices as well as poor institutional capacities are identified hindrances.[103]

6   CONCLUSION

The appeal of human rights to social movement energies and energetic global solidarities indicates their increasing popularity as legal constructs that supplement the traditional instrumentalist functions of law.[104] The environment is now regarded as a precondition for the enjoyment of certain rights like the rights to life, health, food, water, and an adequate standard of living. In the African context as discussed, as a collective right, the right to a satisfactory environment has been connected to and also considered auspicious to human development. In other words, development is a crucial part of the right because development depends on the state and quality of the environment. The statement 'favourable to their development' may serve as a means for defining and understanding this right. As well established, environmental harm or degradation following environmentally unsound activities can only bring about pygmy development. Where the loss of the natural environment leads to loss of livelihoods, increased exposure to health problems, reduction in food and water supplies resulting from pollution, the term 'general satisfactory environment' becomes inconceivable. Further, it means there is a specific threshold of harm done to the environment which cannot afford either individual or communal development.

African states in pursuit of development must be ready to embrace the balancing of economic, social, and environmental objectives as against

---

[102] The Constitution of the Federal Republic of Ethiopia 1995.

[103] Desalegn Amsalu, 'Implementing Human-Rights-Related Environmental Obligations in Ethiopia' in M. Addaney, A. Oluborode Jegede (eds.), *Human Rights and the Environment under African Union Law*, (Palgrave Macmillan, 2020) 282.

[104] Louis J. Kotzé, n 74, 145. See also, C. Gearty, 'Do Human Rights Help of Hinder Environmental Protection?' (2010) Journal of Human Rights and the Environment 1(1), 7–22.

prioritising particularly economic development. At a time as this, only through a rights-based approach will individuals, corporations, and even government be held accountable for environmental harm. The approach is not a disregard of environmental laws but the application of rights as a supportive agency for the elusive goal of ecological sustainability.

REFERENCES

Abioye, F. (2020). Advancing human rights through environmental rule of law in Africa. In M. Addaney & A. Oluborode Jegede (Eds.), *Human Rights and the Environment under African Union Law*. Palgrave Macmillan.

Addaney, M., Moyo, C. G., & Ramakhula, T. (2020). Human Rights, Regional Law, and Environment in Africa: Legal and Conceptual Foundations. In M. Addaney & A.O. Jegede (Eds.), *Human Rights and the Environment under African Union Law*. Palgrave Macmillan.

Ako, R. (2013). *Environmental Justice in Developing Countries: Perspectives from Africa and the Asia-Pacific*. Routledge.

Ako, R. (2018). Mainstreaming Environmental Justice in Developing countries: Thinking Beyond Constitutional Environmental Rights. In C. Eboe-Osuji & E. Emeseh (Eds.), *Nigerian Yearbook of International Law*. Springer International Publishing AG.

Amsalu, D. (2020). Implementing human-rights-related environmental obligations in Ethiopia. In M. Addaney, & A. Oluborode Jegede (Eds.), *Human Rights and the Environment under African Union Law*. Palgrave Macmillan.

Atapattu, S., & Schapper, A. (2019). *Human Rights and the Environment: Key issues*. Routledge.

Birnie, p., Boyle, A., & Redgwell, C. (2009). *International Law and the Environment* (3rd edn.). Oxford University Press.

Boer, B. (Ed.). (2015). *Environmental Law Dimensions of Human Rights*. Oxford University Press.

Boyd, D. (2012). *The Environmental Rights Revolution: A Global Study of Constitutions, Human Rights, and the Environment*. UBC Press.

Boyd, D. R. (2015). Constitutions, human rights, and the environment: National approaches. In A. Grear & L.J. Kotzé (Eds.), *Research Handbook on Human Rights and the Environment*. Edward Elgar Publishing.

Boyle, A. (2015). Human rights and the environment: Where next? In B. Boer (ed.), *Environmental Law Dimensions of Human Rights*. Oxford University Press.

Boyle, A., & Redgwell, C. (2021). *Birnie, Boyle and Redgwell's International Law and the Environment* (4th ed.). Oxford University Press.

Chenwi, L. (2018). The Right to a Satisfactory, Healthy, and Sustainable Environment in the African Regional Human Rights System. In J.H. Knox & R. Pejan (Eds.), *The Human Right to a Healthy Environment*. Cambridge University Press.

Ebbesson, J. (2009). Introduction: dimensions of justice in environmental law. In J. Ebbesson & P. Okowa (Eds.), *Environmental Law and Justice in Context*. Cambridge University Press.

Gardbaum, S. (2009). Human Rights and International Constitutionalism. In J. Dunoff & J. Trachtman (Eds.), *Ruling the World? Constitutionalism, International Law, and Global Government*. Cambridge University Press.

Glazewski, J. (2002). The rule of law: Opportunities for environmental justice in the new democratic order. In D. McDonald (Ed.), *Environmental Justice in South Africa*. OUP.

Gonzalez, C. G. (2015). Human rights, environmental justice, and the North-South divide. In A. Grear & L.J. Kotzé (Eds.), *Research Handbook on Human Rights and the Environment*. Edward Elgar Publishing.

Knox, J. H., & Pejan, R. (2018). Introduction. In J. H. Knox & R. Pejan (Eds.), *The Human Right to a Healthy Environment*. Cambridge University Press.

Kotzé, L. J. (2015). Human rights and the environment through an environmental constitutionalism lens. In A. Grear & L. J. Kotzé (Eds.), *Research Handbook on Human Rights and the Environment*. Edward Elgar Publishing.

Kotzé, L. J. (2021). Africa. In L. Rajamani & J. Peel (Eds.), *The Oxford Handbook of International environmental Law* (2nd edn). Oxford University Press.

Odote, C. (2020). Human rights-based approach to environmental protection: Kenyan, South African and Nigerian constitutional architecture and experience. In M. Addaney & A.O. Jegede (Eds.), *Human Rights and the Environment under African Union Law*. Palgrave Macmillan.

Kotze, L. J., & du Plessis, A. (2019). The African Charter on Human and Peoples' Rights and Environmental Rights Standards. In S. J. Turner (Ed.), *Environmental Rights the Development of Standards*. Cambridge University Press.

Ojwang, J. B. (1992). *Laying a Basis for Rights: Towards a Jurisprudence of Development*, Inaugural Lecture Delivered Before the University of Nairobi on 9th July 1992. University of Nairobi Press.

Scholtz, W. (2015). Human rights and the Environment in the African Union Context. In W. Scholtz & J. Verschuuren (Eds.), *Regional Environmental Law: Transregional Comparative Lessons in Pursuit of Sustainable Development*. Edward Elgar.

Soyapi, B. C. (2020). The judiciary and environmental protection in Zimbabwe. In M. Addaney & A. Oluborode Jegede (Eds.), *Human Rights and the Environment under African Union Law*. Palgrave Macmillan.

Stec, S. (2009). Environmental justice through courts in countries in economic transition. In J. Ebbesson & P. Okowa (Eds.), *Environmental Law and Justice in Context*. Cambridge University Press.

Viñuales, J. E. (2021). Sustainable Development. In L. Rajamani & J. Peel (Eds.), *The Oxford Handbook of International environmental Law* (2nd ed.). Oxford University Press.

Journal Articles

Awolowo, O. (2017). Environmental rights and sustainable development in Nigeria. *OIDA International Journal of Sustainable Development, 10*(6).

Fayiga, A. O., Ipinmoroti, M. O., & Chirenje, T. (2018). Environmental Pollution in Africa. *Environment, Development and Sustainability, 20*, 41–73.

Gearty, C. (2010). Do human rights help of hinder environmental protection? *Journal of Human Rights and the Environment, 1*(1), 7–22.

Kotzé, L., & Du Plessis, A. (2010). Some observations on fifteen years of environmental rights jurisprudence in South Africa. *Journal of Court Innovation, 3*(1), 157–176.

Kuehn, R. R. (2000). A taxonomy of environmental justice. *Environmental Law Reporter, 30*, 10681–10703.

Lewis, B. (2012). Human rights and environmental wrongs: Achieving environmental justice through human rights law. *International Journal for Crime, Justice and Social Democracy, 1*(1), 65–73.

Peter, C. (1993). Taking the environment seriously: The African charter on human and peoples: Rights and the environment. *Review of the African Commission on Human and Peoples Rights, 3*, 39.

Shelton, D. (2002). Communication 155/96. Social and Economic Rights Action Center/Center for Economic and Social Rights v. Nigeria. Case No. ACHPR/COMM/A044/1. *American Journal of International Law, 96*, 937.

van der Linde, M., & Louw, L. (2003). Considering the interpretation and implementation of Article 24 of the African Charter on Human and Peoples' Rights in light of the SERAC communication. *African Human Rights Law Journal, 3*, 167.

Internet Sources

Environmental Rule of Law, Available at: https://www.unep.org/explore-top ics/environmental-rights-and-governance/what-we-do/promoting-enviro nmental-rule-law-0

'The Johannesburg Principles on the Role of Law and Sustainable Development' (adopted at the Global Judges Symposium, 2002). https://www.eufje.org/ images/DocDivers/Johannesburg%20Principles.pdf

United Nations Environment Programme (UNEP), *Environmental Rule of Law: First Global Report* (2019). Available at: https://wedocs.unep.org/20.500.11822/27279

United Nations 'New and Emerging Challenges in Africa Summary Report' available at: https://sustainabledevelopment.un.org/index.php?page=view&type=400&nr=502&menu=1515

INDEX

A
Africa, 1, 271–289, 293–302, 305–309, 338, 357, 359, 361–366, 368–374, 376, 383, 385, 386, 393, 394, 396–398, 401
Africa Continental Free Trade Area (AfCFTA), 218, 221–223, 232–235
African education, 142
Africanness, 223–225, 235
African Studies, 163
Afrophobia, 218, 227–230, 232, 235
Air pollution, 385, 386, 399
Aspiring migrants, 244–248, 258
Asylum seekers, 199
Attitude, 173
Authority, 173

B
Begging continent, 2
Bilingual education, 145, 146, 157, 158

C
Caregivers, 94
Caregivers' perception, 85
Child mortality, 97
China, 271–290
China's engagement, 282
Climate change, 335–342, 344–352
College, 188
Communities, 350
COP-26, 2
COVID-19, 2, 67–70, 73, 76–79, 116–118, 124, 130, 132
Crime prevention, 10
Cross-border movement, 306

D
Decolonization of African Education, 142, 144, 157, 159
Decolonization of knowledge, 2
Deconstruction, 106
Demographic dividend, 36
Demonetization, 360, 372–374, 376
Deportees, 199
Descriptive, 108

© The Editor(s) (if applicable) and The Author(s), under exclusive license to Springer Nature Switzerland AG 2023
A. I. Adeniran (ed.), *African Development and Global Engagements*, https://doi.org/10.1007/978-3-031-21283-3

409

410 INDEX

Development, 271–273, 278–282, 286, 289, 290
Development partners, 78
Diaspora, 245–247, 263
Digital technologies, 118
Displaced persons, 78
Dwelling, 342

E
Economic diversification, 283
Economic nationalism, 233, 235
Economic prosperity, 359, 369–371, 376
Education, 2, 171
Employability, 116
Energy, 338
Environment, 3, 336, 343, 352, 383, 385–388, 391, 393, 395–404
Environmental degradation, 336, 384–386, 397
Environmental disasters, 198
Environmental governance, 385–388
Environmental pollution, 383, 385, 386
Environmental research, 107, 109
Environmental sustainability, 392
Ethnic conflict, 244

F
Failed State Index (FSI), 198
Fertility, 32
Flooding, 338
Forced return, 200
Forum on ChinaAfrica Cooperation (FOCAC), 278

G
Gender-based violence, 67
Globalisation, 103–105, 111, 220, 221

Global warming, 335
Governance, 335–338, 340–352
Government, 3, 340
Group history, 318

H
Healthcare, 336, 337, 342, 344–350, 352
Health facility, 76
Households, 68

I
Infrastructure, 272, 273, 276, 278, 281, 282, 288, 290
Innovation, 2
Insecurity, 359, 360, 369, 372, 373, 376
Instability, 198
Insurgency, 244, 359, 368, 369, 376
Interaction, 174

J
Japa syndrome, 1
Jos, 314–323, 325, 326, 328, 330–332

K
Kenya, 200
Knowledge creation, 140, 141, 143, 156, 157, 159, 161, 162, 164

L
Labour migrants, 303
Labour migration, 302, 303, 305, 306, 308, 309
Land pollution, 385, 386
Language of instruction, 139–141, 143, 144, 146, 152, 154–157, 160

Leader, 174
Leadership, 182
Linguistic imperialism, 141
Local governance, 336, 337, 340–352
Lugardian, 323

M

Masters students, 116, 118–121, 126, 132, 134
Middle East, 200
Migrant community, 332
Migrants, 197–200, 202, 203, 208, 210–213
Migration, 1, 293–295, 297, 302, 303, 305–310
Migration decisions, 263
Migration policies, 263
Misery with hope, 244, 245
Misery without hope, 245
Mixed approach, 110
Mortality, 32
Mother Tongue Education, 141, 150, 157, 159, 161–163
Municipal authorities, 351

N

National Development Plan (NDP), 7
Nigeria, 170
Non-prescription, 94

P

Participatory approach, 359, 374–376
Personality, 173
Policy, 337
Politics, 364, 372–374
Population, 31
Population density, 86
Post-Colonial Theory, 141, 154, 159
Post-return experience, 204, 210
Public health, 97, 338

Q
Qualification, 116

R
Refugees, 197
Regional integration, 217–221, 223, 232–235
Relations, 271, 272, 274, 275, 277, 278, 280, 281, 284, 289, 290
Religion, 86
Research, 2
Research degree, 119

S
Saudi Arabia, 200
Scientific environment, 104
Security, 360, 365, 376
Self-medication, 83–86, 89–91, 93–97
Social distancing, 84
Social integration, 220, 222, 225, 226, 230–232, 235
Social justice, 359–362, 368, 369, 376
Social network, 246–248, 254, 258, 262
Social uprisings, 357–369, 371, 372, 374, 376
Socio-philosophical, 3
South Africa, 9, 116, 117, 127–129, 134
South-North, 1
Specialization, 116
Strategic policies on migration, 305
Strategies, 16
Students, 187
Style, 185
Supervision, 119
Susceptible, 336
Sustainability, 18, 117, 171, 201, 289, 303, 392, 398, 405

412 INDEX

Sustainable Development Goals (SDGs), 337

T
Trait, 178

U
Uprising conflicts, 360

Urhobo migration, 317–320, 323

W
Water pollution, 385
Weather, 339

Y
Yemen, 200